A New Japan for the Twenty-First Century

Many people in the West portray Japan as being fixed in its ways and unable to change, and consequently risking national decline and international loss of prestige. However, Japan is, in fact, at present in a significant transition period, comparable to the Meiji Restoration of 1868 or the period immediately after the Second World War. This transition period comes with a mixture of events and situations which are difficult to interpret, for both foreign and domestic commentators and decision makers. In this book a range of senior experts from inside Japan outline the many considerable changes currently taking place in a wide range of fields, including the economy, business and technology, politics, governance and international relations, and a wide range of social issues – the media, the position of women, nationalism and national consciousness, and religion. Overall, the book provides a corrective to misplaced Western and Eastern views; it aims to redirect stereotyped thinking about contemporary Japan inside as well as outside the country. In addition, it gives a summary overview of contemporary Japan, its current changes and problems – in short, the inside story of the second strongest national economy in the world, which is in the process of fundamental re-engineering and which will continue to have a huge impact globally in the future.

Rien T. Segers is Director and Professor at the Center for Contemporary Japanese Studies, University of Groningen, the Netherlands. He was previously Visiting Professor at the International Research Centre for Japanese Studies, Kyoto (2006–2007).

Routledge Contemporary Japan series

A New Japan for the Twenty-First Century

An inside overview of current
fundamental changes and problems

Rien T. Segers
Editor

Routledge
Taylor & Francis Group

LONDON AND NEW YORK

First published 2008
by Routledge
2 Park Square, Milton Park, Abingdon, Oxon OX14 4RN

Simultaneously published in the USA and Canada
by Routledge
711 Third Avenue Avenue, New York, NY 10017

Routledge is an imprint of the Taylor & Francis Group, an informa business

First issued in paperback 2012

Typeset in Times New Roman by
Bookcraft Ltd, Stroud, Gloucestershire

British Library Cataloguing in Publication Data
A catalogue record for this book is available
from the British Library

Library of Congress Cataloging in Publication Data
A new Japan for the twenty-first century: an inside
overview of current fundamental changes, edited by Rien
T. Segers.
    p. cm. (Routledge contemporary Japan series: 21)
Includes bibliographical references and index.
1. Japan–Economic conditions–21st century. 2. Japan–Politics and
government–21st century. 3. Japan–Social conditions–21st century.
4. Social values–Japan. 5. Popular culture–Japan. I. Segers, Rien T.
HC462.95.N452 2008
952.05–dc22   2007044035

ISBN13: 978–0–415–45311–0 (hbk)
ISBN13: 978-0-415-54182-4 (pbk)

Contents

Illustrations

Tables

Contributors

Yumiko Hada is Associate Professor at the University of Osaka.

Yo Hamada was Research Fellow at the International Research Center for Japanese Studies, Kyoto, 2002–4. He is Associate Professor at Teikyo University, Tokyo.

Takashi Inoguchi is Professor Emeritus of the University of Tokyo and currently Professor of Political Science at Chuo University, Tokyo.

Koichi Iwabuchi is Professor at the School of International Liberal Studies of Waseda University, Tokyo.

Toshihisa Nagasaka was Director of the Japan External Trade Organization until 1999; currently he is Professor at the Faculty of International Studies of Takushoku University, Tokyo.

Narunto Nishigaki is Associate Professor of Economics at Okayama University.

Kazuo Ogoura was Ambassador of Japan to Vietnam, South Korea and France; he is now President of the Japan Foundation and an Invited Professor at Aoyama Gakuin University in Tokyo.

Hisashi Owada was Permanent Representative of Japan to the United Nations and President of the Japan Institute of International Affairs (JIIA); he has taught at the University of Tokyo and at Waseda University as a Professor of international law and organization. Currently he is Judge of the International Court of Justice and Professor at Leyden University, the Netherlands.

Junko Saeki is Professor at Doshisa University, Kyoto.

Rien T. Segers is Director and Professor at the Center for Contemporary Japanese Studies, University of Groningen, the Netherlands. He was previously Visiting Professor at the International Research Center for Japanese Studies, Kyoto (2006–7).

Kei Ushimura is Professor at the International Research Center for Japanese Studies, Kyoto.

Taizo Yakushiji was Vice-President for Academic and International Affairs of Keio University, Tokyo and since 2003 is a Member of the Council for Science and Technology Policy, Cabinet Office, Government of Japan.

Shoji Yamada is Associate Professor at the International Research Center for Japanese Studies, Kyoto.

Tetsuo Yamaori is Professor Emeritus and was Director-General at the International Research Center for Japanese Studies, Kyoto (2001–2005).

Nobuyoshi Yamori is Professor and Associate Dean of the Graduate School of Economics, Nagoya University.

Preface
The background to this book

Contemporary Japan is faced with a severe perception gap in which the distance between developments in Japan and how they are perceived abroad is rather wide. The distance can be said to be so large that the distorted perception is detrimental both for the foreign countries in which those perceptions are being constructed as well as for Japan itself. This consistent perception gap, which I saw in my daily life in Japan as well as in my reading and viewing of the Western media in this respect, was the initial drive to compile a book such as this.

While the idea of such a book dates back a long time, its direct cause lies in a company visit I conducted to the Toyota factories some years ago. It was an impressive visit, based on Toyota's information concerning their most recent technological results, planning and strategy: the Toyota Prius was in the making! That very week I found *The Economist* in my mailbox with an article about Japanese car makers. *The Economist* concluded in that article that Toyota was vulnerable 'to the fact that, although its cars delight and its factories astound, its management remains distinctly old fashioned and Japanese [!]'. My perception from the inside, from the Toyota plant and the stunning developments there, however, appeared to be completely the opposite to the outside, Anglo-American perception in *The Economist*. Later developments justified the superiority of the inside over the outside perception. For instance, the Toyota Prius became Car of the Year in 2005, based on its advanced hybrid technology and sophisticated design, and in the first quarter of 2007 Toyota took over from General Motors as the number one car maker in the world.

To this Toyota example many others could be added. Let me give here just one concerning 'change' as such. As far as change in itself is concerned, many opinion leaders in the West have as their basic perception that Japan is unable to change and is more or less 'on the road to ruin', as *The Economist* put it so nicely (7 September 2002). The sun has chosen to rise in a neighbouring country, China, but no longer in Japan itself, according to a continuing Western perception. But the reality in Japan is different. Not only will the chapters of this book testify to this, but currently at the Cabinet level, the so-called Innovation 25 Strategy Council, led by Minister of State Sanae Takaichi, is busy drafting a report in which 'change' and 'innovation' are considered the key strategies for a New Japan in the Twenty-First Century. This Council sees Japan in 2025 as a model nation for the world, with a society that allows lifelong health, safety, assurance and diversity, and which as a nation helps to address global issues and open its doors to the world. (See: www.kantei.go.jp/foreign/innovation/index_e.html.)

The initial idea for a book such as this was also based on the fact that there are enough interpretations concerning contemporary Japan available in Western languages (mainly, however, in English) constructed by Western observers (mainly, however, by Americans). Contemporary Japanese developments covered by Western journalists and academics are readily available, especially in English, to which also non-English speakers in the West have easy access. That means that the foreign perspective – contemporary Japan as seen through Western eyes – is relatively well covered, despite the diminished interest in Japan due to the rise of China, which is perceived as more easily accessible and faster to deal with than Japan. Moreover, the perception of China is associated with a market of an almost mythical size.

As a necessary contrast, I thought it would be interesting to put together a book concerning developments in contemporary Japan, seen primarily through Japanese eyes, but introduced, structured and summarized by a foreign research director. In 2003 I met Heita Kawakatsu, at that time Professor at the International Research Centre for Japanese Studies (Nichibunken) in Kyoto. We discussed the ins and outs of such a project and he wanted to help in realizing such a book.

In 2006–2007 I was appointed as a Visiting Research Professor at Nichibunken with compiling a book consisting of an overview of current fundamental changes in Japan being a main task. The idea was to select a number of fields that are crucial for Japan's attempts to escape the standstill of the 1990s, the so-called lost decade, by introducing fundamental changes. The chapters should be written by Japanese experts while the structure and philosophy of the book should be developed by the foreign research director, obviously in close consultation with the Japanese specialists. The following 13 fields were selected, in the order in which they appear in this book: economy, technology, politics, civil society and non governmental organizations, foreign policy, (cultural) globalization, television commercials, education, historical consciousness, position of women, religion, nationalism and national identity. An extensive introduction and a concluding chapter were added to give the 13 chapters the necessary background and to draw some major conclusions from them.

The collaborators in each field were asked to reflect on what they considered to be major changes in their field of expertise and then to write their reflections as a chapter for the book. Three discussion meetings were organized in the International Research Center for Japanese Studies in Kyoto and in addition the editor was in frequent contact with the contributors. It goes without saying that this book does not purport to give a *complete* overview of *all* current and major changes occurring in Japan.

The book has two important limitations. First of all the realization of the aim of completeness – if that could ever be attained – would involve the publication of a whole series of books. Apart from the fields represented here, areas such as the ageing of the population, arts and literature, business, defence and military operations, the environment, employment and unemployment issues, information technology, law, medical care, the service sector and many others should be added. That would make the picture more complete.

The second important limitation concerns the necessarily restricted scope of each particular chapter. Obviously, it is impossible in one chapter to outline all changes within a particular field; that would imply a book in itself. That means that each author has selected a particular aspect of his or her domain. For example, the chapter on education focuses on higher education; the changes occurring in the kindergarten, primary and secondary school systems are not dealt with. And even in the selected area of higher education choices had to be made about what to present and what not.

The major objective of the book is based on the hypothesis that a thorough analysis of a major aspect in each of the 13 fields can function as a test case. On that basis, by surveying all 13 analyses a reliable impression can be inferred concerning what changes, and especially what kind of changes, are taking place in contemporary Japan, and in addition what their implications are for the future of the country. It is the task of the concluding chapter (15) to give the reader this particular perspective.

The realization of the book's objective was not easy and has drawn heavily on the excellent collaboration of many people to whom I owe many thanks. There is first of all Professor Heita Kawakatsu, President of Shizuoka University of Art and Culture and a former Professor of the International Centre for Japanese Studies in Kyoto, who stimulated this project from its beginning stage. Then there are the 13 contributors who each generously took time off their busy schedules to write a chapter for the book. I am also very grateful for the editorial help I received from Mr Ian C. Stirk (Osaka University of Foreign Studies) and his investment of time and thought concerning the honing of the text.

The International Research Centre for Japanese Studies invited me for a Visiting Professorship during the academic year 2006–2007. It proved to be the ideal working environment for the realization of this project. I am very grateful for the Centre's hospitality and its provision of all necessary means to complete the project. I am especially indebted to the library staff for their professional assistance. I also would like to thank Ms Yukiko Okuno, Ms Yasuko Omura, Ms Ayako Sasaki and Ms Tomoko Shirai for helping me in various ways at various stages of this project. During my absence from my home institution, the Center for Japanese Studies at the University of Groningen in the Netherlands, my colleagues Ms Alette Arendshorst LLM, Dr Janny de Jong, Dieneke Niks MA and Dr Herman Voogsgeerd LLM took excellent care of the Center, its students and partners. Finally, while I was stationed in Kyoto, the nearby University of Osaka provided great hospitality from time to time; in this respect I am especially indebted to my colleagues Professors Shigeru Akita, Mamoru Fujiwara and Toru Takenaka.

Rien T. Segers
Kyoto

Part I

Introduction

1 A new Japan in the twenty-first century

Introduction to a changing nation

Rien T. Segers

Japan is reinventing itself on earth – this time as the coolest nation culture.
(*Washington Post*, 26 December 2003)

The gap between the identity and the image of contemporary Japan

Some time ago I visited Toyota Motor Company in Toyota City close to Nagoya, as briefly described in the Preface to this book. I was briefed on its corporate strategy, on the progress made on its hybrid vehicles and on its advanced initiatives taken in innovative electronic controls. It was impressive. In that very week *The Economist* carried an article about Japanese car makers in the US, ambiguously titled 'Twenty years down the road'.[1]

The article, which carries the names of the cities of Tokyo and Detroit as at its head, starts by praising the strategy and quality of Japanese car makers and poking fun at former Ford chairman Harold Poling, who thought, twenty years ago when Japanese cars were still only manufactured in Japan, that the secret of efficient Japanese car making was 'superhuman labourers working like crazy apes on the assembly lines back home'. The article in *The Economist* continues to talk about 'the most efficient car factory in the world', which is Nissan's plant in Smyrna in Tennessee. In addition, there is an analysis of the Japanese successes in the US in terms of such basics as product quality, inventory control and market research.

Then, there is a sudden, rather unexpected turn in the tone and colour of the article, unexpected at least for those not familiar with the type of discourse used by *The Economist* vis-à-vis Japan until about September 2005. The bridge from positive to negative discourse is constructed by a stereotype: 'But the Japanese cannot afford to be complacent'. This almost automatically invokes the reader's question: which business can afford to be complacent nowadays? Then there comes a quick, superficial listing of things that should support that stereotype of non-complacency, based on the failure of the Indiana factory in the US of Isuzu and Subaru, the initial flop of the Toyota T100 (later a great success as the Tundra) and the fact that Mercedes and Volkswagen are expanding on the American market.

The article concludes as follows:

> All this means that the Japanese have little room to make mistakes. Being
> bigger, Toyota can afford to run more risks than Honda. But it is vulnerable
> to the fact that, although its cars delight and its factories astound, its manage-
> ment remains distinctly old fashioned and *Japanese*.[2]

What is 'Japanese'? Based on *The Economist* discourse until recently, and its
subsequent subtexts in most articles on Japan, it means: 'on the road to ruin'.

This article in *The Economist* is not highlighted because of its content or because
Japan or the Japanese car need to be defended or even rescued, but I draw attention to it for two reasons. First of all, it was published in a serious, prestigious
and highly influential magazine, implying that it is one of the major agents in
constructing a contemporary global image of Japan. Second, because of the nature
of its discourse, which touches on the very heart of the aims of this book, namely
to show that the existing ways of looking at Japan and interpreting and evaluating
this country are outdated due to a number of significant developments, which will
be outlined in this chapter. These developments will detect a great discrepancy
between the identity and the image of contemporary Japan, between self-image
and outside image.

As mentioned, *The Economist* is a very influential magazine – for boardrooms
all over the world, for government officials, investors, journalists, and even for
some professors. In short, it is a magazine that is highly decisive for the image
construction of the socio-economic sector of a nation, both inside and outside that
nation. One negative article does not hurt, but if the subtext of articles concerning
a particular country appears to be systematically based on a somewhat ambivalent, not to say negative, discourse that does not correspond with the 'reality
representation' of that country, then there is something structurally wrong with the
perception of that reality, with the so-called reality itself, or with both factors.

Based on the above argumentation it will be evident that the representation of
Japanese reality by *The Economist* has resulted in the construction of an inadequate image. In this article *The Economist* demonstrates a discourse convention
vis-à-vis a leading industrial sector in Japan that is based on a misrepresentation
of the real developments in that sector. This misrepresentation is subtle, especially
for superficial readers and non-specialists. It can be detected only after a careful
analysis and if one has some knowledge concerning the actual situation. The
essential meaning of the misrepresentation is to be found in the subtext, which
makes its effect even more dangerous.

Many examples of that same discourse could be given. To mention just one
additional example: former prime minister Koizumi could not do much good in
the eyes of *The Economist*, at least not until his overwhelming victory in the snap
elections of September 2005. Even the things *The Economist* has already been
urging Japan to do for a long time – for instance to become more involved with
Asian affairs – are cited against him. A case in point is the visit of the prime minister
to North Korea in 2002. The magazine carried an article under the heading 'Roads

to Ruin', starting as follows: 'Which map is Junichiro Koizumi using? Having wandered a long way from his initial reform pledges, he is now trying to redirect himself by straying overseas, with a trip to North Korea ...'.[3] The word 'straying' is the key to the subtext: the construction is that Mr Koizumi *is* a failure: he lost his way and the new way he found for himself is leading to just to ruin.

If content analysis is applied to *The Economist* issues concerning Japan during the years 2001–2005, the general discourse construction is that of a country that really is on the road to ruin, headed by a prime minister who is 'a dashing disappointment'. It is high time 'to abandon any remaining hope in Junichiro Koizumi'.[4] Obviously, this statement concerns only the perception of *The Economist* for the period mentioned. No claim is made here that this is *the* American image or *the* British image. This is simply the construction of *Economist* journalists covering Japan in Tokyo, maybe in consultation with or influenced by what kind of articles and discourse the London-based headquarters would like to see. However, somewhat unfortunately for Japan, articles appearing in *The Economist* carry a lot of weight when it comes to making dominant image (and investment!) constructions.

Obviously, the above stories concerning Toyota, Koizumi and *The Economist* are more than just anecdotes; they provide two cases on the basis of which the perception gap between the identity and the image of contemporary Japan can be clearly demonstrated. They also form a justified point of departure for the claim that a reinterpretation of Japan is highly necessary. There is a major reason for this necessity, for the urgent need to bridge the gap between the identity and the image of contemporary Japan. That reason is based on the structural inadequacy of currently existing interpretive models.

The structural inadequacy of existing interpretive models concerning Japan

Since the Second World War a great number of Western journalists, observers, politicians, business people and scholars, as well their Japanese counterparts, have been active in describing, interpreting and evaluating Japanese society. Their texts are being circulated and reproduced, in the press and in academic work, as the dominant discourse on contemporary Japan. Two observations should be made concerning the status of the methodology on the basis of which many of these texts are written: the interpretive methodology itself and – more specifically – its Eurocentrism and Japanocentrism.

A first observation concerns the status of the interpretive methodology, where the question could be asked as to whether it is possible to distinguish some interpretive categories among the large volume of journalistic and (popular) academic articles, book publications and news items on radio and TV since the 1970s that have as their aim to explain what happens in Japan and how to look at Japan. The aim here is not to construct a categorization based on the contents or the themes of those publications. This would lead to the rather trivial conclusion that the interpretations of the 1970s and 1980s are mainly concerned with explaining Japan's economic success and underlining the specificity and uniqueness of its culture, whereas the publications since the 1990s are looking for arguments and evidence to interpret Japan's supposed fall from grace. In this way it would be possible to plot each of those hundreds of publications and news reports on a scale, running from the fawning *Japan as Number One* to the vilifying *Japan as – Anything but – Number One*.[5] The argumentation here is lined up based on a discourse which constructs Japan either as a success or as a failure.

Much more interesting and revealing than simply looking at the contents of media coverage of Japan, is focusing on the methodology and the implicit points of departure that constitute the basis of all those interpretations. In principle, there are three methodological positions that can be distinguished: a mainstream, a revisionist and a culturalist perspective.[6]

The *mainstream perspective* is based – implicitly or explicitly – on a comparative stance, where Japan is being contrasted and compared with another country, which means in most cases the USA. The reason for this comparison with the USA is not so much the striking similarities these two cultural systems share, but simply because most foreign specialists on Japan can be found in that country.

During the occupation (1945–1952), the American government seems to have tried to turn Japan into a kind of forty-ninth state (Alaska and Hawaii had not yet joined the union). Seen superficially, in the period directly after the war this seemed to work nicely. Thus Japan's constitution is indeed, for all its intents and purposes, a copy of the American. Mainstream specialists follow this lead: they view Japan as democratic, as a free-market economy and in fact as a Western nation, naturally with its own character variations, which, however, do not fundamentally deviate from its role model, the USA. Approached kindly, Japan is often interpreted as a nation deserving of emulation. It is not astonishing that the mainstreamers had their heyday in the late 1970s and 1980s when Japan was at the peak of its economic power and unchallenged in Asia. A number of them also took the position that Japan stood at the threshold of overtaking the USA's leading position in the world. Noteworthy representatives of the mainstream interpretation, whose publications have had a great deal of influence on Japan's image in the USA are, for example: Gerald Curtis, Edwin O. Reischauer and Ezra F. Vogel.[7]

Whereas the mainstream perspective focuses on Japan's similarities to the West and takes a (very) positive stance towards Japan, the *revisionist perspective*, on the other hand, is directed at constructing a fundamental difference between Japan and the West, and sometimes even between Japan and the Rest. This methodology leads to a rather negative view of Japan, in many cases based on the same data that the mainstreamers used to construct a positive image. As McCargo observed:

> [They] view Japan as operating according to distinctive principles of its own: typically, they regard it as undemocratic, and as characterized by a deeply flawed political system that features a considerable degree of structural corruption. They view Japan's economic system as far more state-led and far less open to outside competition than analysts typically acknowledge. Some revisionists go so far as to see Japan as a kind of 'soft authoritarian'

state, characterized by repressive elements of social and political conformity. Revisionists typically view Japan's relations with the rest of the world with a skeptical eye, arguing that Japan cynically manipulates its trade, aid and defence policies for its own advantage.

(McCargo 2000: 4)

The heyday of this kind of Japan-bashing was during the 1980s, when Japan and the USA were at odds over trade. The final decade of the last century was a particularly good period for revisionists. Japan's economic stagnation, the large-scale outsourcing of production, the inadequate assistance after the Kobe earthquake (1995) and its limited international role were grist for the revisionist mill. Not surprisingly, their conclusion was that the enormous economic prosperity of the 1970s and 1980s was more the product of good luck than of wisdom. Representative authors of this position include Chalmers Johnson, Gavan McCormack and Yoshi Sugimoto, Clyde Prestowitz, James Fallows, and Karel Van Wolferen.[8]

The third perspective, the *culturalist*, explains the Japanese socio-economic system on the basis of an inherent cultural distinctiveness. Originally the domain of American anthropologists such as Ruth Benedict, this perspective was received by Japanese academics and journalists with open arms. For centuries the Japanese have believed that the character of their land, its inhabitants, the climate and the language were so specific that Japan boasted a unique identity. Belief in the myth of Japanese uniqueness found fertile soil last century in Nihonjinron, the study and theory of Japan by Japanese scholars, which reached its height in the 1970s.

In the introduction to his highly critical book on Nihonjinron, Peter Dale (1988) observed that the pseudo-academic Nihonjinron scholars argue three points. First, that the Japanese people are culturally and socially a homogeneous race whose core has remained unchanged since prehistoric times. Second, it is supposed that the Japanese radically differ from all other peoples. Third, a conscious nationalism generates great hostility to any analysis of Japanese culture by foreigners.

Since the mid-1970s, when Japanese science was internationalized, a growing number of Japanese sociologists, psychologists and anthropologists have rejected much of what Nihonjinron publications have put forward as speculative humbug. This, however, has not purged years of intense education in their culture's uniqueness from the minds of most Japanese. Nihonjinron writings employ cultural constructions consisting of many artificial oppositions between Japanese culture on the one hand and other (principally Chinese and Western) cultures on the other. For example, well-known social oppositions are: society versus community; individualism versus groupism; equality versus hierarchy; private orientation versus public orientation; rights versus duties; independence versus dependence. The first element of those oppositions is ascribed to Western culture, whereas the second element applies to Japanese culture; it is implied that the positive term refers to Japanese and the negative to Western culture.

The explanations offered for these oppositions are striking. For example, as is well known, Tsunoda (1985) hypothesized that the Japanese brain structure is unique, as stimuli are processed in the left hemisphere, where thought processes are aimed toward producing harmony with nature. In the West, however, stimuli are processed in the right lobe, which is considered to be more rational and less harmonious.

A wide range of culturalist publications can be mentioned here; maybe the most influential ones were written by people from various backgrounds such as Chie Nakane, Takeo Doi and, as already mentioned, Tadanobu Tsunoda.[9]

The three categories into which interpretations of post-Second World War Japanese culture can be generally classified – mainstream, revisionist and culturalist – imply each a fundamentally different interpretive methodology on Japan. Of course, it is not always easy to clearly differentiate between them, and hybrid forms are also employed.

This short analysis of the three existing methodological perspectives is not designed to determine which perspective is 'the best', or which interpretation based on what perspective deserves first prize. Instead it is more interesting to look briefly at two important similarities that exist between the otherwise clearly different perspectives.

On the one hand, in all three perspectives there is a demonstration of a strong need not only to describe and interpret, but also to judge. Final judgement is, of course, provided by the interpreter and overwhelmingly based on his or her own value system. On the other hand, the interpretations themselves, in all three categories, are also based on the interpreter's own sublimated value system. For instance, the Japanese Nihonjinron interpreter bases his or her analysis on his or her own Japanese frame of reference. The interpreter looks west, but only in order to confirm his or her already existing Japanese views. In many cases Western sources are consequently not read or used seriously. By contrast, the Western mainstream specialists and revisionists actually often employ the same methodology in their interpretations of Japan. They also view Japan primarily from their own interpretive conventions. It often happens that most primary sources are ignored and hardly any attention is paid to Japanese perspectives. Consequently, this provides a dominantly Western perspective.

A second observation concerning the inadequacy of existing interpretive models is directed at the Eurocentrism and the Japanocentrism involved in the interpretive methodology. Irmela Hijiya-Kirschnereit (1988: 193) has called Eurocentrism an essential problem in research on Japan. In the first two categories (the mainstream and the revisionist) we may encounter a fair amount of Eurocentrism, the imposition of Western interpretive conventions on a foreign culture. An interpretation is deemed to be complete when a particular cultural element which is 'strange' is adapted and translated into the interpreter's own conventions. What holds for Eurocentrism is also true for Japanocentrism, which can be encountered in the third category (that of the culturalist perspective). If even scholarship cannot completely escape from Eurocentrism, it is not difficult to imagine what happens in the interpretive conventions of the opinion-leading institution, the media.

Eurocentrism can exaggerate the adaptation process so much that it presumes that certain important components of Japanese society are not Japanese, but

Western. As regards Japanese literature, Marleigh G. Ryan (1976) has proposed that it is necessary to counteract this Western prejudice: Western scholars should stop expecting Japanese literature to be non-Japanese. Obviously, this observation is also valid for other domains of Japanese society, such as the economy, business life, politics, religion, education and medical care.

On the other hand, in two periods of Japanese history we find an explicit form of auto-Eurocentrism, a phase in which Japan, at least within its most influential circles, accepted, adapted and promoted Western Eurocentrism. The first of these periods was the Meiji era (1868–1912), the second during the American occupation (1945–52). Harumi Befu describes Japan's auto-Eurocentrism (which he calls 'auto-Orientalism') in the post-war years as follows:

> In this situation, discourse on Japan's identity of the late 1940s and the 1950s became one of comparing Japan with the West as Japan's way of convincing itself how wrong it was – a way of providing a rationale for the lost status of the wartime ideology. The West was upheld as the model and the ideal, and whatever the West had and Japan did not have was the reason for Japan's defeat and for criticizing Japan, be it its cultural traits, social institutions, or personality. Legions of Western observers, including MacArthur (who claimed the Japanese mentality to be that of a twelve-year-old), saw and analysed Japan against the mirror of their own social values, and in their free, unabated, naive ethnocentrism denigrated everything Japanese. Japanese intellectuals, in the post-war skeptical mood, were delighted to have their newfound conviction confirmed by observers from countries that represented a superior civilization and the new model for Japan.
>
> (Befu 1997: 117)

The other side of Eurocentrism is relativism, which, as applied to Japan, is to say that Japanese cultural identity can only be interpreted and evaluated with Japanese criteria. Any Western specialist should first identify with Japan. He or she must analyse Japanese culture from the inside out and in this way learn to understand its specific conventions and institutions. 'Understanding' here means projecting oneself into the foreign culture. The greater the identification with Japan the more perfect the harmony with Japanese thought and behaviour patterns, and thus the closer one comes to the ideal interpretation.[10]

Relativism is the reverse of Eurocentrism, and consequently equally lopsided and objectionable. In addition to a methodological danger, Hijiya-Kirschnereit also points out that relativism supports the myth of Japan's uniqueness, as propagated by Nihonjinron.

Thus neither relativism nor Eurocentrism lead toward an adequate interpretation. The alternative, which Hijiya-Kirschnereit indicates with a quote from Helmut Plessner, denotes the correct theoretical direction, but fails to give precise information on how the theory can be put into research practice. Plessner writes: 'Comprehension does not mean identification with the other, in which the distance to the other vanishes, but familiarity with the distance so that the other can be seen as other and simultaneously as a strange thing' (Plessner 1982: 179; my translation from German). To repeat, it remains unclear, however, how exactly one is to operate in a research situation based on this accurate philosophical pronouncement.

The above three methodological perspectives, mainstream, revisionist and culturalist, imply that the process of interpreting Japan can be characterized to a great extent by partiality or unipolarity. In many cases the interpretive process is based on a single cultural perspective: the culture to which the interpreter belongs. In practice this means that the interpretation of Japan bears a heavily American, European or Japanese etc. imprint, which in many cases contains a high degree of one-sidedness, not necessarily a virtue in journalism or scholarship. This implies that the three existing interpretive perspectives can no longer fulfil the require-ments for the construction of an adequate interpretation of a rapidly changing Japan, caught between globalization and localization.

How does partiality or unipolarity work in practice and what are the conse-quences? In order to answer this question an article by James Fallows (1989) will be analysed from an interpretive-methodological point of view and may serve as a case in point. This article was published at the height of Japan's interna-tional economic power, 1989, a time when Japan's trade surplus was still gigantic, thanks to a series of measures and many promises on the part of the Japanese government; it should also be noted that at this time the US economy was not at its best.

Fallows' position throughout the article is very clear, stating that: 'Japan's one-sided trading will make the US–Japanese partnership impossible to sustain – unless we impose limits on its economy' (Fallows 1989: 1). His analysis employs power play with inherent rhetorical tools in order to support this position. Fallows proposes that a serious conflict has arisen between Japanese and American inter-ests. This conflict is entirely Japan's fault: the impossibility or its unwillingness to limit the one-sided and destructive expansion of its economic power. Fallows explains:

> The expansion is one-sided because Japanese business does to other countries what Japan will not permit to be done to itself. It is destructive because it will lead to exactly the international ostracism that Japan most fears, because it will wreck the post-war system of free trade that has made Japan and many other nations prosperous, and because it will ultimately make the US–Japa-nese partnership impossible to sustain.
>
> (Fallows 1989: 2)

Fallows supports this perspective by pointing to the gulf between Japan's export successes and the – in his eyes – artificially suppressed domestic consumption. He also provides a statistical argument: in 1989 the US trade deficit with Japan ran at about $1 billion per week. Another argument concerns Japan's refusal to import expensive products and Japan's deliberate attacks on noted Western corporations.

My analysis of Fallows' perspective is not so much concerned with the factual accuracy of his statistics, but rather with the discourse and the interpretive conventions that underlie his factuality. Statistics change and can be manipulated, but interpretive conventions are tougher, and involve the mental programming of members of a particular community.

Fallows' interpretation is based on the 'obvious' fact that the US is the gold standard against which everything and everyone on the planet can be measured. Fallows believes that history has clearly proven this standard valid, and thus for him it is an incontrovertible fact. Even the Marshall Plan is paraded in order to polish up the golden American standard. Look, Fallows argues, how, in contrast to Japan, the United States works for the betterment of all. At the end of the Second World War

> the United States could have completely swamped all competitors in an outright production contest. Instead, the United States rapidly and deliberately opened its markets to imports, and through the Marshall Plan it helped rebuild foreign factories so that they could produce something for Americans to buy.
>
> (Fallows 1989: 8–9)

An interpretation in which the US is viewed as the epitome of altruism bodes poorly for any subsequent analysis of its relations with Japan. Indeed, in many places Fallows consciously or unconsciously misinterprets Japan, which he continuously measures against the American gold standard, arguing for a change in Japan's 'internal behavior'.

Fallows sees this 'wrong' internal behaviour as an important source of Japan's undoing. In contrast to 'our' weak, universal values, such as charity, democracy and world brotherhood, the Japanese base their behaviour on personal loyalty to family, teacher and boss. Fallows' knock-out blow reads as follows: 'The members of a tight-knit Japanese work group or neighbourhood will spontaneously sacrifice more for one another than their counterparts in the United States – but they are a lot less likely to sacrifice for someone outside the group' (Fallows 1989: 14). This is supposed to serve as 'explanation' for the fact that Japan places less importance on trade imbalance, since trade is being conducted with people outside of their own group!

Finally, Fallows asks how frightened the United States should be of Japan. He assures his readers that they need not prepare for an invasion and can sleep well. After all Japan is finished:

> The population will soon have the world's highest proportion of retirees and will be using up some of the savings it is amassing now; Korea and Taiwan will exert unrelenting pressure; at some point the yen may rise so far that it actually does price Japanese exporters out of the world market.
>
> (Fallows 1989: 18)

Then, the final straw, this American analyst disqualifies himself ethically by writing: 'And let's not forget the next big earthquake' (p. 18).

Fallows' interpretation rests on two pillars. First and foremost, he is guilty of gross interpretive bias which is so America-centric that his analysis mirrors perfectly the Nihonjinron theorists who employ the same biased interpretive convention, only based on the Japanese gold standard. The publication of a particularly biased interpretation of a nation is regrettable for the author, for scholarship and the nation in question. If the foreign policy of the author's country is subsequently based on this and similar articles a dangerous situation could arise. At any rate it is not altogether clear whether Fallows' article actually influenced American policy toward Japan, although Tamotsu Aoki (1996: 117) thinks it 'likely'.

Second, Fallows focuses on the exceptionality of Japanese behaviour and values, which he presents as the basis for American–Japanese conflict and the reason for Japan's 'unreasonable' economic imperialism, two phenomena otherwise not easily understood by Westerners. Fallows is not alone in this interpretation; many other Western interpreters of Japan, particularly the revisionists, do the same. This sort of interpretation begins with the negative exceptionality of Japanese culture, which is constructed so that prevailing and essential elements of Western culture are, by definition, missing. Fallows is thus concerned with elements such as fairness in trade practices or concepts such as charity, democracy and world brotherhood. In Fallows' view all these elements are clearly present in Western, but not in Japanese, culture. Factual support for this is paltry and of a dubious nature, but these principles work well as a grid for his interpretation.

Hidehiro Sonoda (2000) has attacked this kind of biased thinking. He argues that many social scientific theories take Western culture as the norm and attune their research accordingly. As soon as the subject is Japanese – or any non-Western – culture, an immediate state of alert is declared, for these cultures cannot be explained with standard theories. The exceptional nature of Japanese culture is then put forward – Fallows is merely one example of this – because certain Western standards such as democracy and charity are not based on and practised according to similar principles to those existing in the West. Sonoda believes that such theories do not deserve to be called scientific, for scholarliness implies universality.

Sonoda therefore proposes a 'theory of reverse absences' to counter the Western 'theory of absences'. This theory interprets Western nations by researching those elements that are primarily determined by Japanese or non-Western cultures. He then asks whether and to what extent these elements are also present and how they function in Western cultures. In this way Sonoda seeks to avoid the label 'unique' with which Japanese culture has been branded by Western specialists (revisionists such as Fallows) and by the Nihonjinron theorists.

The localization–globalization paradox in contemporary Japan as a new interpretive model

The context of the three interpretive models (mainstream, revisionist and culturalist) mainly consisted of the question of the extent to which Japan could reasonably be compared with the West. The basic question in all three models was whether Japan could or could not be called a 'normal' Western country. This question and its subsequent answers have lost their validity due to significant changes in Japan itself and due to a new set of structural problems that partly have risen based on some of these changes. Those changes and problems are the topic of this book, which is based on the assumption that most fundamental changes and problems in Japan are based on the localization–globalization paradox. This paradox shows the necessity of undertaking a fundamental reinterpretation of contemporary Japan.

As is well known, Japan was hit by a great number of serious setbacks in the 1990s. To mention just the major ones: the collapse of the bubble economy, major currency fluctuations, a prolonged recession, the Great Hanshin (Kobe) Earthquake, scandals involving leading politicians, bureaucrats and corporations, the Aum Shinrikyo cult gas attacks, and increased violence and drug-related crime. All these developments have affected the very cohesion that helped Japan achieve its stunning economic success in the post-war period, eroding self-confidence and leading to reflection on the state of society. On the positive side, the shocks have also precipitated necessary changes and – on the negative side – have brought a new set of structural problems.[11]

These developments have led to a fundamental increase in the localization–globalization debate in Japan. What should be retained of the traditional way of doing things, and what should be adapted and adopted from the ways leading foreign cultures do things? Obviously, Japan is not the only country where this discussion is being pursued. But the quality and quantity of the representation of this paradox seem to be much more manifest in Japan than anywhere else. If we examine the interrelations between cultures now, at the beginning of a new millennium, we can perceive two strong but contradictory tendencies. On the one hand we acknowledge the search for cultural authenticity, the pride in particularisms, the admiration for cultural self-sufficiency and the maintenance of national traditions. On the other hand we find the spread of a uniform world culture, an ever-growing political and economic interdependence, the emergence of supranational myths and the adoption of similar lifestyles in widely different settings.[12]

At this particular moment Japan faces a great number of catalysts for fundamental change, due to the long and intensive search for a resolution to the dramatic events that happened in the 1990s. 'Catalyst' is a concept that is, in some cases, to be preferred to the concept of 'change'. Change is an institutionalized deviation from conventional practice, realized by the help of catalysts, stimuli or incitements for change. A set of really fundamental changes in a society may result in a restoration, such as, in Japan, the Meiji Restoration or the situation in the years following the Second World War. The current socio-economic situation in Japan is such that the phase of fundamental changes in some of the major domains of society has arrived or is about to arrive. 'Change' is being used here as a *vox media*, a concept with neutral – neither positive, nor negative – meaning. The dominant connotation – both in Japan and elsewhere – of 'change' is in many cases positive, something that should be realized as soon as possible. Here the neutral meaning of the concept is chosen, since not all changes to be undertaken in Japan (or elsewhere) are necessarily positive. One example: the dispatch of Self-Defence Forces to Iraq and Afghanistan may have the positive effect of deconstructing Japan's image of insisting on chequebook diplomacy; but it may also have the horrible effect of Japan's becoming a top priority on the target lists of international terrorists.

The catalysts for changes and the major structural problems are to be found in most domains of contemporary Japanese society. Obviously, in some domains they are stronger than in others. There are four domains in which the current changes seem to be the markers of a future 'new' Japan and which are dealt with in this book:

- Business and technology
- Politics, governance and foreign policy
- Social issues
- National identity.

Obviously, there are more domains in Japanese society in which changes, catalysts for change and problems are visible. For instance, the health care domain is not represented. Furthermore, in each of the four domains on which the essays in this book focus, it is clear that there are many more changes and problems than the ones dealt with. For instance, within the contemporary social structure of Japan demographic changes (e.g. declining birth rate and ageing) are not dealt with. Also the changes and problems concerning Japan's younger generation could not be addressed. One could think here of problems such as those of the so-called *freeters* (college graduates who work in temporary, low-paid jobs), of the *hikiko-mori* (youngsters who shut themselves up in a room for fear of people and society) and the *parasite singles* (young adults of thirty years and older preferring to live unmarried at home). An important change in the business domain, the privatization of the postal service, is also not covered.

It is not the intention of this book, however, to cover *all* changes and problems. The contemporary situation of Japan as a rapidly changing society makes such an all-encompassing intention a sheer impossibility. The book presents the domains and the changes and problems within each domain as cases that should show the specificity of a changing Japan. In the conclusion of this book this specificity will be outlined in more detail.

Business and technology

The Japanese business and technology domain provides first-rate changes, catalysts for change and important problems. As a background to the two chapters devoted to this topic in the book, six challenges will be explained here. They all clearly show that this domain is on the way to being completely restructured.

First of all, there are clear signs that foreign investors are becoming far more significant equity shareholders in Japanese companies. Porter *et al.* (2000: 184) give the example of Sony, where 45 per cent of the shares are held by foreigners, which was unthinkable 15 years ago! The percentage of foreign shareholders will grow in the future and lead to a greater emphasis on profitability.

Second, the number of foreign companies entering Japan is rapidly growing, and increasingly doing so by acquiring Japanese companies. This phenomenon started on a large scale in 1998, when foreign companies either acquired (in whole or in part) or merged with a record number of 85 Japanese companies. It is evident that these acquisitions and mergers will significantly change strategic thinking and ways of operating. The most famous example in this context is the 37 per cent acquisition of Nissan by Renault, which became its largest shareholder in May 1999. Carlos Ghosn was appointed as Nissan's new CEO and started to turn the elephant around: from the red into the black, mainly by streamlining the organization. In the mean time, he changed the initial scepticism and sometimes downright hostility towards him as a *gaijin* into being a brand personality. Nevertheless, it should be mentioned that foreign direct investment into Japan is still remarkably low relative to other industrialized countries.

The third catalyst consisted of the change of guard in many Japanese companies in the second half of the 1990s when

> a new generation of CEOs is assuming leadership in many Japanese companies. This generation is far less inhibited than its predecessors about changing long-standing practices. Leaders at Honda (President Hiroyuki Yoshino), Toyota (Chairman Hiroshi Okuda), Sony (President Nobuyuki Idei), Orix (President Yoshihiko Miyauchi), and Softbank (Masayoshi Son) all have significant overseas experience. In the past, overseas experience would have been a negative for corporate advancement. Because these new CEOs possess greater familiarity with international business practices and are taking leadership at a time of financial and competitive pressure, they are likely to do things differently [...]. They see change as inevitable.
>
> (Porter *et al.* 2000: 185–6)

The fourth catalyst is a highly interesting one. It concerns a new generation of entrepreneurial companies that is getting larger, some even joining the ranks of major corporations. Here companies could be mentioned such as Nidec Corp. (established in 1973; it controls 73 per cent of the world market for the spindle micromotors used in computer hard-disk drives), Rohm (established in 1954; it holds around 34 per cent of the world market in print heads for fax machines), Kyoden (established in 1983; it leads the market in Japan for prototype printed circuit boards (PCBs) with 50 per cent), Shimano (established in 1946; it controls more than 70 per cent of the world market for derailleurs, speed hubs, brakes and other components for racing bikes; 65 per cent of the teams participating in the *Tour de France* use Shimano components; in 1995 English was made the company's official language). Some other companies could be added as well; Porter *et al.* mention in this respect Softbank, Orix and Pasona as well as the Japanese dotcoms such as Rakuten and NetAge: 'Many of these companies are highly profit oriented, compete with clear strategies, and have developed distinctly un-Japanese organizational models. They will certainly influence the way other Japanese companies compete' (Porter *et al*. 2000: 186). In most cases these new companies have a limited product offering, with a sharp, customer-oriented focus.

The fifth catalyst for change within the business context is based on the attitudes of the young workers, who have a distinctly different orientation from their elders:

> Many joined the workforce during the prolonged recession of the 1990s, and they do not expect to be protected by lifetime employment. They are more comfortable with merit-based compensation, more literate in information technology, and more flexible in accepting change. They will become a driving force for changing their companies and government policy.
>
> (Porter *et al*. 2000: 186)

Also the *Keiretsu* system may be a catalyst for real changes. To mention a striking example in this respect:

> In October 1999, Sumitomo Bank announced it would merge with Sakura Bank, following a consolidation plan involving the International Bank of Japan, Fuji Bank, and Dai Ichi Kango Bank. The *keiretsu* system, where these banks each served as a main bank, is likely to decline. Cross-holdings among companies are also being sold off. This will trigger a chain reaction of new possibilities, including new financing approaches and more focused strategies.
>
> (Porter *et al*. 2000: 185)

This last category of changes brings us to the chapter about Japanese banks in this book, by Nobuyoshi Yamori and Narunto Nishigaki. They explain the enormous shift in perception and rating of major Japanese banks in a period of just ten years. In 1988 Japanese major banks were ranked as leading among world banks, obtaining at least Aa3 ratings. After the bubble burst, the changes could not have been more dramatic. Even Mitsubishi Bank, which achieved the top rating in 1993 among Japanese banks, dropped to the fourth rating, Aa3. Even thereafter, financial conditions continued to worsen, further propelling a drop in the ratings of many banks, with some not even able to obtain an investment grade rating of BBB-. The first table in that chapter gives a clear overview of the changes in rating concerning major Japanese banks in just ten years.

The spectacular drop in the global ratings of Japanese banks did not significantly disturb the Japanese public. But another fact did finally make the public aware that something had to be done to help get the economic train back on track. That was the bankruptcy of a number of financial institutions in the second half of the lost decade. No single financial institution had gone bankrupt in the post-Second World War period until the bubble collapsed. In 1995, however, a series of large-scale bankruptcies started, beginning with the Hyogo Bank. In 1997 the Hokkaido Takushoku Bank collapsed, causing extreme distrust among depositors in the management of financial institutions. Despite the promise of the government to protect all bank deposits at the time, there was a run on some major banks. In 1998 two further bankruptcies occurred: the LTCB and Nippon Credit Bank failed.

The complete reversal in ratings and the unheard-of bankruptcy of a number of banks were the incentives for a great number of fundamental changes that have occurred over the past ten years in Japan's financial system. Yamori and Nishigaki describe these changes and some of the problems resulting from them in great detail.

The business environment is heavily dependent on the successful handling of the various technological options that a particular country may or may not have at its disposal. Taizo Yakushiji clearly shows this in his chapter on 'Japan's current and future technological agendas'. After all the changes in the 1990s, he distinguishes four agendas for Japan's technology in the twenty-first century.

The first is that of enhancement of technological emulation; it implies that strongly competing countries, like China for instance, could sooner or later emulate the economy of a front-runner country (Japan) by the superb quality and low prices of emulated technological products. The second agenda consists of the pitfalls of technological parochialism. In a leading technological nation parochial pride leads to technological arrogance, blinding people to the very secret of technological pre-eminence: 'emulous power', the drastic improvement of advanced technologies. The third agenda contains the vulnerability and paradox of international technological cooperation. On the one hand technological cooperation can leak crucial high-tech knowledge and research; on the other hand strong protectionism could end existing cooperation. The fourth agenda is based on the paradox of mass production. Economically efficient mass production with a rather standardized technology is believed to add wealth to a nation, so that it often rejects new technological endeavours that would shut down the currently profitable production lines.

Which options should Japan take in the near future to adjust to the changes that these four agendas embody? Yakushiji states that Japan's problem is that it has neither an internationally acknowledged ideology nor a worldwide penetrating culture. However, Japan's strength is its technology, which should be used in the near future to enhance its soft power. Japan could find an excellent solution to most problems related to the four agendas above by concentrating on its unique technological position in the world. This position could be strengthened by a further focus on civilian (non-military) technology, global manufacturing and soft power enhancement of energy-saving and environmental technologies.

Politics, governance and foreign policy

In principle, governance and politics are different entities. The latter concept involves processes by which a group of people with, initially, in many cases, divergent opinions or interests reach collective decisions generally regarded as binding on the group, and enforced as common policy. Governance, on the other hand, conveys the administrative and process-oriented elements of governing rather than its antagonistic ones. But in practice these two areas overlap each other, as will become apparent in the three chapters devoted to these topics in this book.[13]

In a democracy all important changes in a society are dealt with sooner or later by its political system. In this respect the political system of a country can function as a mirror showing the major changes or catalysts for those changes. Therefore Takashi Inoguchi's chapter on 'Japanese contemporary politics: towards a new interpretation' may very well function as an introduction to many of the changes discussed in this book.

Inoguchi divides Japanese political development since the end of the Second World War into three periods: 1945–1960, the occupation and reconstruction period; 1960–1985, the strong economic growth period; 1985 onwards, the period of globalization. In his chapter Inoguchi explains the characteristics of the LDP-dominated political system during those three periods. He suggests that Japan's current governance system is not prepared to deal with the daunting changes and adjustments required due to accelerating globalization, from which 'even' Japan cannot escape.

Japan is a nation following a long-standing tradition of bureaucracy-driven development. This was particularly noticeable in the second period, of strong economic growth (1960–1985). In this developmental model, bureaucrats take the lead in directing the strong momentum behind economic development to most effectively manage the national economy. This bureaucracy-driven development is in reality led by a tri-partite structure formed by government agencies, business and the governing party (the LDP).

Inoguchi states that globalization demands deregulation and smaller government, but Japan's long tradition of bureaucracy-driven development has in fact slowed down progress in those two areas to a considerable extent. This slow development strongly contrasts with the many competitive, globally operating Japanese companies that have already shifted their energy and resources to successful international developments. However, the Koizumi and Abe administrations have demonstrated changes in this respect: the prime minister and the cabinet are taking increasingly prominent roles in driving government policy. They are now more directly in charge than bureaucrats in an increasing number of matters.

There are two crucial problems connected with a successful global role for Japan in the world, a role commensurate with its strong economic position. The first is: can the Japanese political system adjust to the strict requirements of globalization? The second: if so, to what extent? In the current political situation these questions need to be directed at the LDP. Is the LDP, as the major ruling party in Japan, able to implement the necessary changes?

Inoguchi voices some concern regarding this last problem. He acknowledges three limitations that may prevent the LDP from taking the necessary steps: a significant lack of leadership, a lack of competence and an unwillingness and/or an inability to end the situation in which civil servants instead of politicians carry too much responsibility. Kasumigaseki and Nagatacho (the places where many ministry buildings and the Diet are located) were and still are considered to be the

LDP brains trust. According to Inoguchi a government cannot afford this type of structure in a globalized world. The time is ripe for politicians to take the reins!

For politicians to take the reins is highly necessary, as a great number of reforms are under way. A process of governmental organizational reform has been in existence for some years, for instance. One of the reforms stipulated that on 1 January 2001, under the Central Government Law, the then existing 22 central government ministries and agencies were to be reduced to 13 and the cabinet reduced from 20 members to 17.

Another far more difficult problem to solve is the decentralization of the national government into a number of local governments – 'states', larger geographical units consisting of a certain number of prefectures. There is a proposal for a test run of this sort of revolutionary change by granting Hokkaido increased authority; that is to say, to treat Hokkaido as a sort of state. Under this proposed change, Japan's northernmost prefectural authority would be significantly enhanced.[14] Hokkaido would be granted the right to collect consumption, corporate and other taxes and it would also take over operations from the development bureau and the local offices of other national government ministries and agencies. The role of the central government would be restricted to defence, diplomacy and major public works programmes, such as building expressways and Shinkansen lines. But this revolutionary idea is still in the planning phase, and even the test case of a 'Hokkaido state' still has to pass all its legislative hurdles.

Toshihisa Nagasaka deals with a completely different governance aspect of Japan, which has undergone dramatic changes over the last ten years: the NPO (non-profit organizations) sector. With the enforcement of the Non-Profit Activities Promotion Law in December 1998, the number of NPO registrations went up from a few hundred in 1998 to more than 30,000 at the beginning of 2007! The NPO sector has created for itself a new and an important role in the contemporary socio-economic system in Japan.

Nagasaka describes the failure of the 'two-sector model' of a society divided into a governmental and a corporate sector, which led to an economic struggle for supremacy. After the 1980s the corporate sector swallowed up the governmental sector, leading, among other, things to a strong economic globalization. Corporate strength has created a 'dog-eat-dog' world. Strong countries and strong corporations become richer, while poor institutions become increasingly poorer. Social services, education, health care and the environment have deteriorated to a significant extent. In addition, a 'democratic deficit' has arisen, accounting for the gap between government and electorate. Therefore Nagasaka states that the three-sector consensus model (government, corporate and NPO sector) is urgently needed. Through dialogue between these three sectors, based on equal partnership, a more adequate socio-economic system can be constructed.

The problem in Japan is that the NPO sector does not have a long history, is still small scale and lacks expertise. This sector is still based on the goodwill of numerous individuals, since its staff are paid extremely low salaries. Currently, however, the perception of NPOs among the Japanese public is changing drastically. The Japanese public realizes that the governmental system has monopolized the public sphere and that it is high time for civil society to take it over from the government. This process is under way and will change Japanese society to a significant extent.

A third chapter in this section on politics and public policies is devoted to another domain in which many changes have occurred over the last decade. In an article in the *Japan Times* (8 February 2007) Kazuo Ogoura nicely summed up the power and status of Japan inside and outside Asia:

> Prior to World War II, Japan's position in the international community was dependent on its power in Asia. From the time of the Meiji Restoration in 1868, it was essential for Japan to have considerable stature within Asia so that the country could associate on equal terms with Western nations and assume a position of influence in the international community. This was a historical imperative rooted in Japan's determination to protect its independence against Western colonial rule in Asia.
>
> Japan's domestic modernization, however, which was implemented under the slogan 'Enrich the country and strengthen the military', was not always conducive to entrenching democratic institutions, and Japan undertook a colonialist expansion into Asia, creating a pattern in which it used Asia as a steppingstone to major-power status.
>
> Learning from these events, Japan has, since World War II, dealt with Asia from its position as a model student of modernization and Westernization, and as the only industrialized democracy in Asia. One could say, in fact, that the prewar situation has been turned on its head, with Japan's status in Asia now defined by its standing in the community of 'Western' nations.

But the last decade of the twentieth century arrived with globalization and remarkable changes in Asia: the rise of China and a growing tendency towards regionalization (first ASEAN, then ASEAN+3 and again later ASEAN+6). In his chapter in this section Kazuo Ogoura states that Japanese foreign policy since the mid-1990s has been determined by three major factors: (1) domestic economic and political trends; (2) conditions and changes in the international community; (3) Japan's own choices of strategy and policy based on the options existing within the framework of the first two factors.

Overall, the second category of grand changes seems to have had the major influence on the course Japanese diplomacy is currently taking. Ogoura here distinguishes six important developments. In brief, it first of all concerns the shift in US security policies and the strengthening of global antiterrorism measures since 9/11. The second major change has been the advance of globalization and its advantages and disadvantages regarding political and economic issues, which became a focus of frequent debate. The third change in the international community is the much-discussed emergence of China and India as economic and political powers. Especially, the rise of China is of crucial importance for the positioning of Japan, also in combination with China's overwhelming need for energy (Segers *et al.* 2007). Then, fourth, there are the developments on the

Korean peninsula, especially the growing threat posed by North Korea. A fifth important development is the expansion of NATO and the European Union, encouraging Japanese moves towards economic integration in Asia.

The sixth development consists of the 1997 Asian economic crisis, which cast doubts on the viability of the Asian model of economic development.

Based on these fundamental changes in the international arena, Ogoura analyses in detail the shifts in strategies and policies of Japanese diplomacy over the last years. He concludes by positing two major foreign policy problems to be addressed by Japan over the next five to ten years.

The first issue concerns finding an answer to the question of to what extent the Japan–US alliance can be strengthened and further globalized in tandem with efforts to enhance the function of the UN. The second issue deals with the biggest challenge for Japanese foreign policy: how to deal with China. Ogoura concludes by saying that, to cope with those two problems, Japan must develop a vision for the future of the international community and the country must increase its efforts to share this vision as much as possible with the USA, Europe and its Asian neighbours.

Social issues

There are many social issues that have acted as dramatic catalysts for change and also that have undergone actual changes over the last ten years. We have chosen the following five issues as test cases to show to what extent changes did take place and as a result what new problems did arise in Japanese society: cultural globalization, television commercials, the higher education system, historical consciousness and the position of women.

In his chapter on the Japanese contribution to cultural globalization Koichi Iwabuchi mentions that the increasing spread of Japan's media culture is perhaps one of the most significant changes to have taken place over the last ten years. On that basis Iwabuchi concludes that the outside perception of Japan as a faceless economic power has been displaced by an image of a cultural power that produces and disseminates 'cool' and 'cute' cultures to many parts of the world, such as animation, characters, comics, fashion, film, food and video games. This implies the relative demise of the Western, especially American, cultural hegemony and it induces a salutary corrective to a West-centric analysis of the media and cultural globalization.

The spread of Japanese media culture has three implications within the context of decentring trends in media globalization. First of all the cliché was that Japan is only supplying capital and markets to the global media system and little else. But in the mid-1990s Mario appeared to be a more well-known character among American children than Mickey Mouse. Second, the Japanese television industry started selling Japanese TV formats to Western markets in the late 1980s. Ten years later those formats became great successes in many countries, based on 'glocalization' tendencies, whereby the Japanese format was adapted by the foreign TV station. Third, it is East Asian countries that have provided the Japanese media culture with its largest export market and its most avid audiences. The success of Japanese media products in East Asian countries is such that it will undoubtedly improve the image of Japan.

Concerning most Japanese cultural exports to Western markets it is interesting to note that they are culturally neutral. That means that the positive image and association of a Japanese culture or way of life is not generally related to the consumption of the products. In other words, as Kawabuchi correctly notes, animation, computer games and characters may be recognized as originating in Japan and their consumption may well be associated with high technology or miniaturization; however, the appeal of such products is relatively independent of cultural images of the country of production, Japan. In contrast to their American counterparts, these products do not attempt to sell the Japanese way of life.

In generalizing this observation, one could say that what is valid for Japanese media products in this respect also holds for most other products from Japan, be they cars or cameras. The world brands from Japan (Sony, Panasonic, Toyota, etc.) do link to the country as a geographical entity but not as a cultural one. In other words, Japanese world brands do not brand Japanese culture. This is a great problem and a highly unfortunate development, given the prominence of Japanese products in an age when nationalism and nation branding has (again) become very important (see, e.g. Starrs 2001).

On the other hand it is interesting to look at the reverse side of the coin: how do Japanese people look at 'the world' now, and what changes and problems have occurred in their perception over the last decade or so? Shoji Yamada in his chapter 'Reidentified Japan' undertakes this very task by means of a unique instrument in this respect: Japanese TV commercials. He departs from the hypothesis that commercials reflect the perceptions of Japanese society concerning the West, Asia and Japanese culture itself. His conclusion is that the Japanese perceptions implicit in these clips can be divided into two stages: before and after the 1990s.

In TV commercials before the 1990s the Japanese were trying to reidentify themselves. In the 1970s and 1980s this was done by a strong focus on the West, for instance by showing commercials in which major Western cities (Paris, London, New York, etc.) constituted a background for the selling of a product. At the same time, especially in the 1970s, a returning-to-Japan trend was visible. This showed the emergence of a soft nationalistic discourse against the background of traditional Japanese scenery.

In the commercials of the 1980s the Japanese seemed to obtain a kind of self-confidence, not necessarily relying on Western discourse and background to sell a product. But this positive self-image eroded again in the mid-1990s, with the burst bubble being followed by a depression. Consequently, a new image of the West emerged in commercials, which Yamada calls 'Bondage to the West'. The essence of this new discourse is that the Japanese are culturally occupied by the West, especially the USA, from which they do want to escape, but cannot. The resulting problem from this cultural occupation is that many Japanese portrayed in these clips are suffering from an identity crisis.

The most recent trend, however, is the turn toward more 'Asianness' in Japanese TV commercials. Koreans especially are appearing in the commercials, for instance the famous Korean actor Bae Yong Joon. It will be interesting to see to what extent this Asian trend will further develop.

The Japanese educational system has been long praised as one of Japan's success factors, but nowadays it is under severe criticism, from kindergarten to postgraduate university studies. The standard perception of Western observers concerning the Japanese educational system runs more or less as follows:

> The system, by perpetuating loyalty to the status quo, focusing on rote learning and failing to foster inquisitive minds, is hindering attempts to revitalize the economy. Education tends to be highly structured and inflexible, disadvantaging students who attend schools that do not prepare them for entrance examinations in Japan. After exposure to Western schooling, Japanese parents often despair that their children are discouraged from even asking questions in class [...]. Improved education is essential to keep Japan internationally competitive, yet in some key areas (for example, foreign languages and computers) Japan has fallen behind other developed countries.
>
> (Department of Foreign Affairs and Trade 1997: 41)

But also from inside Japan the educational system is heavily criticized, based on various criteria. One of these is the educational attainment of Japanese students, until recently acclaimed to be ranked among the highest in the world but now said by some sources to be declining rapidly (Satō 2005: 30). In the OECD 2003 Programme for International Student Assessment (PISA), Japan was ranked fourteenth as far as reading literacy is concerned, sixth concerning mathematical literacy and second for scientific literacy. On the whole, this is a deterioration from the ranking in a study done by the OECD three years earlier. This leads Manabu Satō to the following conclusion:

> Overall, the results of the PISA study indicate clearly not only that the academic proficiency of Japanese schoolchildren is declining but also that their abilities are circumscribed by an outdated concept of academic attainment that is inadequate to prepare them for the demands of the complex and fluid 'knowledge society' of the twenty-first century.
>
> (Satō 2005: 30–1)

These recent problems give rise to all kinds of discussions, speculations and proposals for reform on a large scale running from right (restoring young people's pride in the country) to left (improvement of individuality). Articles are being published with such titles as 'The Sorry State of Japanese Education' and 'Japan's School Crisis: A Trail of Misguided Reform'.[15] Discussions on primary education take a similar path in many other post-industrial societies.

If one looks at the field of higher education the same turmoil seems to be taking place. The Ministry of Education, Science, Sports and Culture (MEXT) has been active over the last ten years in drawing up all kinds of changes, many of which were (severely) criticized by the educational field itself; from an international point of view also, not an unusual development.

In the field of education there have been not only catalysts for change, but also actual significant changes and, obviously, many problems do remain or new problems are being created. Most public attention on reform in the higher educational sector has been focused on the fact that, as from 1 April 2004, Japan's national universities were turned into independent agencies and their staff were no longer national civil servants with the automatic guarantee of a job for life. Some elements of this reform imply – at least in principle – a strengthening of the power of the University Board, greater emphasis on transparency and accountability, and funding by the Ministry increasingly based on competition (for projects, innovations, etc.). For somebody who knows something of the university situation in Great Britain, this all sounds familiar, since the Japanese 'Big Bang' of 1 April 2004 is mainly based on reforms undertaken in that country in the 1980s.[16]

Another implication of the 'Big Bang' is the idea of reducing the difficulty in obtaining external accreditation to open up new departments and schools. An example of this decision is the go-ahead of the Ministry to open professional graduate schools in Japan. The first was Hitotsubashi University's Graduate School of International Corporate Strategy, a business school offering an MBA and a financial engineering programme. The daytime MBA programme at Hitotsubashi will be taught entirely in English and will accommodate students from around the world.[17]

In her chapter in this book on the changes within the Japanese higher education system Yumiko Hada summarizes the background to all these rapid changes. She shows that it consists of three international factors, namely mass popularization, marketization and globalization, intertwined with the following three domestic factors.

First, dramatic demographic change: a significant decline in prospective entrants to university is becoming clearly visible. The 18-year-old population reached a peak of a little more than 2 million in 1995 and then steadily declined to 1.5 million in 2000. This decline still continues, and the figure will drop to around 1.2 million in 2010. This implies that in the late 1990s a number of universities and junior colleges failed to meet their admission targets. At present about 60 per cent of all private junior colleges and about 30 per cent of all private senior colleges are failing to reach their admission targets.

Second, there is the economic factor. After the collapse of the bubble economy in the early 1990s, collaboration projects were set up between the business sector and higher education institutions in order to make industry more competitive. This collaboration had a severe impact on the functioning of a large number of universities.

Policy change is the third domestic factor. Deregulation and structural reform became key concepts in the education field also. Responding to the demands of the business sector, MEXT initiated a process of deregulation concerning the university system. This resulted in a differentiation of research and education among the universities, in new establishments of specialist and professional graduate schools, as mentioned above, and in a decrease in the number of entrants to junior colleges to one-third of the peak. In addition, evaluation by third-party institutions was made obligatory.

Will the Japanese university system become completely globalized – which is to say Americanized – since most of the reforms are based on an American, or at least Anglo-Saxon model? Hada regards this as a serious problem. She states that a major difficulty is achieving harmony of the current and future reforms with the specificity of the national culture (in this case: Japanese), while simultaneously developing a system that is internationally competitive. Regarding this, Hada deals with the problem of global competition for the best international students. Japan, with its new system, has the clear intention of becoming the major international hub in higher education for North-East Asia. Will it be able to realize its intentions in this respect? Japan is likely to face increasing competition, even within its own region, from China, Korea, Singapore and Taiwan. On the other hand, as English proficiency becomes increasingly important, to enhance chances in the job market, more and more Japanese students will choose to study overseas in English-speaking countries (mainly the USA, the UK and Australia).

A final but not unimportant observation regarding educational reform: in order to make the Japanese university system more competitive the government should realize that what is good for politics and the economy is not necessarily also good for education and research.

In his chapter on the Class-A war criminal syndrome Kei Ushimura describes the changing historical consciousness of the Japanese (especially Japanese journalists) by looking at how the so-called Class-A war criminals have been regarded since the 1940s. During the International Military Tribunal for the Far East in Tokyo (1946–48) twenty-eight Japanese wartime leaders, high-ranking generals and admirals, were prosecuted on the assumption that they had committed crimes of category 'A', which were defined as 'crimes against peace'. During the Tokyo trial two suspects died and one was further excluded from the trial due to mental disorder.

Until about the end of the twentieth century, during more than fifty years, the remaining twenty-five criminals were almost invariably lumped together, concluding that all of them were the 'same villains'. Obviously, if one studies the court proceedings, one finds it quite difficult or even impossible to label them all with the same phrase. It could therefore be said that the usage of 'Class-A war criminal' is a product of the intellectual negligence of post-war Japan. In addition, Ushimura mentions that the concept of 'Class-A war criminal' was a Western invention. The Japanese were eager to stick to this label, using it over and over again to such an extent that it became a sort of a syndrome. Even in daily discourse somebody could be labelled as a 'Class-A' war criminal, indicating that he performed his job or task rather badly. This reflects a typical example of the Japanese attitude towards foreign ideas. It is a manifestation of *haigo shiso*, or respect for foreign, in particular Western, ideas dating back to the Meiji era.

The six visits of Prime Minister Koizumi to Yasukuni shrine in Tokyo, where also fourteen Class-A war criminals are enshrined, changed this collective view on 'the' criminals. These visits ignited the anti-Japanese movement abroad, forcing Japanese journalism to provide its readers with more detailed information on the Tokyo trial and the individuality of the suspects. This trend has become stronger over the last years. The change is to be found in the fact that now the differences of each of the war criminals are being discovered; a distinction is now being made between their characters and their different responsibility for the warfare.

In this sense the Tokyo Trial can be seen as a globalized form of war tribunal, modelled on the Nurnberg example. The initial Japanese adaptation was to regard the 28 (and later 25) criminals as a group. Since 2001, however, largely due to foreign pressure (*gaiatsu*) the criminals are seen as individuals with individually committed crimes.

In the last chapter in the section on social issues the position of women in Japanese society is discussed by Junko Saeki: 'Beyond the geisha-stereotype: changing images of "New Women" in Japanese popular culture'. By the mid-1990s single-member households comprised 25 per cent of all households; two-generation families comprised about 60 per cent, whereas three-generation households comprised 13 per cent, but now:

> The number of single-member households is rising, as affluence, education and increased adaptability enable more young and old people to lead independent, self-reliant lifestyles. When grandparents live in an extended family it is often at the request of their children who benefit from pooling family assets and having live-in housekeepers and baby-sitters. Increasingly, grandparents object to this role being thrust on them. Most newly wed couples are now living apart from their parents.
>
> (Department of Foreign Affairs and Trade 1997: 31)

In addition to these changes in family structure, it should also be noted that the divorce rate, traditionally very low in Japan, is on the rise. In 2001 the rate was 2.3 per 1000 people, which equals the German rate in 1997; the American rate stood at 4.2 in 1998 (Japan Almanac 2003 (2002)).

Partly responsible for this rising divorce rate has been the changing mental programming of Japanese women. Japanese women were once stereotyped as 'meek and patient'. While Japanese women had power within the home, their influence outside was very limited. However, this is changing, albeit slowly. Younger Japanese women are losing their fear of being thought 'unfeminine' if they speak their minds, and teenage girls increasingly adopt the curt 'male' speech patterns. Older women, too, are more assertive. For example, in March 1996, hundreds of housewives in Hiroshima Prefecture forced through a referendum that deposed the local mayor, because he would not build a new hospital for the aged, who are mainly taken care of by housewives.[18] So far this change in attitude has not resulted in a spectacular growth of higher managerial functions for women in the private and public sectors. Here we are dealing with a catalyst that will undoubtedly result in fundamental changes when the new generation of young women, among the best educated in the world, reach maturity.

Junko Saeki shows some aspects of the status of women that have dramatically changed since the 1970s. She distinguishes four phases in the development of women's status and attitude; additionally she points to the parallel development of the position of women in manga and in reality.

In the first phase, in the 1960s and 1970s, the main topic in shojo-manga (manga for young girls) was the heroine's love affair with a boyfriend, which ended in most cases happily in a marriage. The readers of those manga appreciated structure and style, since they knew it was necessary to follow the traditional Confucian ethics, which taught that women should obey men if they wanted to achieve ideal love and marriage.

In the second phase, which partly coincided with the first, in the 1970s and 1980s, a revolution of the manga heroine took place: the working heroine appeared without, however, destroying the housewife as such, since both types of women appeared in the same manga text. This is a fictional representation of the reality in which Japanese women experienced the two different roles for the first time among themselves.

In the late 1980s a manga heroine with a strong subjectivity and activity appeared at a time when a law was introduced advocating equal opportunity employment between the sexes, encouraging women to pursue their own careers. That does not mean, however, that audiences in the late 1980s and early 1990s did not feel comfortable with the good-wife-and-wise-mother type of woman. The globalized independent woman had not completely captured Japan.

However, the fourth phase, at the beginning of the twenty-first century, shows the appearance of more liberated women both in manga and in TV dramas. In reality as well as in fiction Japanese women started to seek not financial but mental support from their partners. It is a common notion that the characteristics of the ideal husband, for women, have changed from the 'three highs' (high education, high income and height) to the 'three C's' (comfortable, cooperative and compatible) in the mid-1990s. Saeki concludes by saying that, though there are still many problems to be solved in Japan, it is a fact that stereotypical heroines and heroes are no longer current either in reality or in fiction.

A major challenging factor and catalyst for change within the domain of social structure is the well-known and much-debated fact that Japan's demographic composition is rapidly changing from one in which a young labour force comprised the overwhelming majority of the population to one in which the aged dominate (Sugimoto 2003: 18–19):

The rising share of the elderly in the population will have the broadest impact. Indeed, it is the imperative underlining many current reforms. With one third of the Japanese expected to be over 65 years of age in 2040, double the 1995 level, and with the population peaking around 2010, Japan must prepare for a potentially serious labor shortage, declining savings and investment, and heavy pressure on health and welfare facilities. Companies are already preparing for the opportunities, targeting the 'silver market' with a range of new goods and services. The need to bolster national savings to fund future retirees is also influencing macroeconomic policy.

(Department of Foreign Affairs and Trade 1997: 2)

Japan will become the nation with the highest ratio of people older than 65 years in its population in the early part of this century. That requires, however, fundamental changes in such areas as employment, the pension system, medical services and business products.

National identity

This section of the book seems to deal with the manufacturing shop of a New Japan. National identity is a category that, on the one side, stimulates many changes and catalysts for change and, on the other prevents necessary changes from taking place. National identity is the specific way in which the mental programming of citizens of a particular nation is structured. A careful description of it allows us to predict what course a particular nation will take in the (near) future. The three chapters in this section stipulate the fact that Japan is in search of a new identity and is, as a matter of fact, busy in constructing one.

Tetsuo Yamaori, in his chapter 'Japanese religion adrift', points out the roots of an important problem in the construction of the contemporary national identity of Japan: the feelings of insecurity and estrangement amid all the changes. Yamaori discusses one of the most important changes in twentieth century Japanese cultural identity, of which the implications can be still felt up to the present day. It concerns the decision, under the pressure of the American occupying, forces to dissolve the State Shinto system after the Second World War and to announce that the Japanese Emperor is a human being and not a God. Yamaori ventures the hypothesis that this important and revolutionary decision led to a double void for the Japanese people: the state itself was spiritually and also politically deprived of its soul: Shinto. This empty centre around which the state had been revolving for a long time was now 'filled up' by just another void, a *symbolic* emperor with no political power whatsoever. That means that the void state was supplemented with a void emperor: the situation of the 'double void'.

According to Yamaori, this implies that the contemporary Japanese social system is not anchored, but seems to be drifting away. He concludes his chapter with the following question: 'Fellow Japanese, bereft of that precious anchor, exactly where are you wandering off to?' With the severe changes occurring at this time, this question becomes even more important.

In the second chapter of this section Yo Hamada takes up exactly this question, asking himself and his readers what should be done by the Japanese system to construct a new identity at this particular moment. He analyses the specificity of the relationship between religion and the Japanese state. He calls Japan's post-Second World War nationalism *Mu-Shukyo* (no religion) nationalism, indicating that Japanese society can never be identified by only one specific religion, but is based on the existence of equally important religions. It is a relationship between one state and a number of religions. In this sense, Japanese nationalism resists globalized (i.e. Western) secular nationalism, favouring in most cases just one privileged religion. This secular nationalism was considered by the West to be a universal value in the modernization of the world. Secular nationalism was propagated all over the world in Western colonies in Asia, Africa and Latin America. In the liberation process of the former Western colonies the concept of secular nationalism gave ideological legitimacy to their new indigenous leaders, thereby by-passing the traditional religious leaders of those new countries.

The perception of people in non-Western countries vis-à-vis Western secular nationalism is that it comes with diseases such as political scandals, a high divorce rate, racial discrimination, drug addiction and a devastated social order. The implication of Hamada's chapter is that Japan, which resisted the complete introduction of globalized Western secular nationalism, should be able to transform its *Mu-Shukyo* nationalism, based on a number of indigenous Japanese religions, to 'open nationalism'. The latter form of nationalism is characterized by an increase in Japanese soft power, tolerance and creative thinking. The *Tenno* as a symbol should be preserved and the void created by the abolishment of Shinto as a state religion should be 'filled up', replaced, by the creative diversity of Japan's cultures and religions, leading to an effective international cultural exchange where Japan functions as a centre as opposed to being a periphery of American globalization.

That this may be not as easy as it may look, is the message of Hisashi Owada in Chapter 14. In his analysis of the 'national psyche' of Japan he starts out from the globalization–localization dichotomy, asking himself and his readers where Japan stands amid the rapidly evolving changes in the world. In order to be able to answer this question, he analyses three different dimensions that are responsible for the construction of the post-war Japanese identity. First of all, it concerns the defeat of Japan in the Second World War, which created an unprecedented situation in Japan's history, with a psychic trauma and a total collapse of Japan's polity. The second dimension is based on the San Francisco Peace Treaty of 1951, resulting in a state of confusion and the division of the country into mutually hostile camps. The third dimension represents the 'virtual reality' created in Japan during the years of the Cold War. With 'virtual reality' Owada refers to a world of seclusion from the rest of the world, a 'psychological cocoon' made by Japanese for Japanese, a situation well known to the Japanese before the Meiji era.

After the Cold War the process of globalization started to intensify rapidly. This resulted in significant changes in the three dimensions mentioned above that were instrumental in constructing Japan's post-war identity. Since the 1990s, however, two new tendencies became visible, contributing to a significant change in Japan's national identity. The rise of neo-nationalism is such a tendency, which is to be understood as an emotional reaction to the tendentious approach to Japanese history consisting of an almost total repudiation of the past achievements of Japan in its process of modernization. The second tendency implies the impact of globalization upon the country. The fundamental problem regarding the construction of a new national identity is the question as to how Japan should adjust its

30   *Rien T. Segers*

society to the new, globalized world while reconciling itself with the country's own strong political, economic and social systems.

Hisashi Owada is convinced of the fact that Japan is no longer able to maintain even the remnants of a closed system: globalization is too strong a force, both inside as well as outside Japan. The deconstruction of these remnants of traditional conventions is an extremely difficult task and not just an economic problem, as Japanese governments do want to believe. It concerns first of all a reprogramming of the Japanese mindset in general and that of the 'hopelessly outdated' political culture of the country in particular. Owada is cautiously optimistic about possible fundamental changes in this respect, but he connects this optimism with an important question. The critical question in this context is whether the necessary change of the mental programming can compete with the speed of the change that is taking place so rapidly in the world outside Japan.

Towards a New Japan?

This book suggests that Western interpretations of Japan should be redirected along the localization–globalization line. The interpretive question to be asked in this respect is how precisely the localization–globalization struggle, which affects every country (western or eastern, northern or southern), is being waged in Japan. In this country the struggle implies a bewildering number of changes and catalysts for change, as well as severe problems to be solved, as the previous pages have shown.

The previous pages have also made it clear that there are two recurrent themes in all the current changes and problems. On the local, Japanese side it concerns the new question of how to respond to the often unexpected requirements of globalizing trends entering the country. In short, it involves the question of what the Japanese response to globalization should be. On the globalization level there are many aspects that are of great importance for a renewal of Japanese global strategy, but the major new items here for Japan are the rise of China and the growing tendency towards East Asian regionalization. How should Japan respond to those two crucial regional–globalizing developments?

For Japan, its government and its people the crucial question is obvious: will the changes put into motion result in their intended aims; do they have the right direction and sufficient power to make Japan more competitive by adequately responding to the challenges of globalization? Will they really result in a New Japan? Can they bring an end to the prevailing pessimism in contemporary Japan? But before we can deal with these questions in concluding Chapter 15, we have to review on a detailed basis what major changes have been taken place in four important areas in Japan over the last ten years: business and technology; politics, governance and foreign policy; a number of important social issues; and finally the problem of national identity. These areas are this book's main framework, on the basis of which the changes, catalysts for change and problems of contemporary Japan are reviewed in the next thirteen chapters.

Notes

1 *The Economist*, 14 September 2002.
2 Ibid., italics mine.
3 'Roads to Ruin', *The Economist*, 7 September 2002.
4 Ibid., 13 July 2002.
5 Respectively, Vogel 1979 and Woronoff 1990.
6 McCargo 2000, pp. 1ff.
7 Curtis 1971 and 1988, Reischauer 1977 and Vogel 1979.
8 Johnson 1982, MacCormack and Sugimoto 1986, Prestowicz 1988, Fallows 1989, Van Wolferen 1989, MacCormack 1996.
9 Nakane 1970, Doi 1971, Tsunoda 1985.
10 Adapted from Hijiya-Kirschnereit 1988, p. 203.
11 Department of Foreign Services and Trade 1997, p. 15.
12 OECD 1989, p. 16.
13 See Wikipedia under 'governance'; www.en.wikipedia.org/wiki/Governance (accessed 2 February 2007).
14 *The Nikkei Weekly*, 6 October 2003.
15 Fujiwara and Sakurai 2006 and Fujiwara 2004.
16 For a more extensive description of the 'Big Bang' see Goodman 2005, which served as a basis for this paragraph; see also the contributions in Eades, Goodman and Hada 2005.
17 Porter *et al*. 2000, p. 147.
18 *The Economist*, 1 June 1996, p. 91.

References

Aoki, Tamotsu (1996), *Der Japandiskurs im historischen Wandel. Zur Kultur und Identität einer Nation* (trans. Stephan Biedermann *et al*.). Munich: iudicium.

Befu, Harumi (1997), 'Geopolitics, Geoeconomics, and the Japanese Identity', in Peter Nosco (ed.), *Japanese Identity. Cultural Analyses*. Denver, CO: Center for Japanese Studies, Teikyo Loretto Heights University.

Curtis, Gerald (1971), *Election Campaigning Japanese Style*. New York: Columbia University Press.

—— (1988), *The Japanese Way of Politics*. New York: Columbia University Press.

Dale, Peter (1986), *The Myth of Japanese Uniqueness*. London: Croon Helm.

Department of Foreign Affairs and Trade (1997), *A New Japan? Change in Asia's Megamarket*. Barton, Australia: East Asia Analytical Unit, Department of Foreign Affairs and Trade/BHP.

Doi, Takeo (1971), *The Anatomy of Dependence* (trans. John Bester). Tokyo, New York: Kodansha International.

Eades, J. S., Roger Goodman and Yumiko Hada (2005), *The 'Big Bang' in Japanese Higher Education. The 2004 Reforms and the Dynamics of Change*. Melbourne: Trans Pacific Press.

Fallows, James (1989), 'Containing Japan', *The Atlantic Monthly* 5, pp. 40–54, www.theantlantic.com/issues/89may/fallows.htm, accessed 3 September 2006.

Fujiwara, Masahiko (2004), 'Back to Basics in Elementary Schooling', *Japan Echo* 31 (2), p. 52–55.

—— and Yoshiko Sakurai (2006), 'The Sorry State of Japanese Education', *Japan Echo* 33 (4), pp. 37–40.

Goodman, Roger (2005), 'W(h)ither the Japanese University? An Introduction to the 2004 Higher Education Reforms in Japan', in J. S. Eades, Roger Goodman and Yumiko Hada, *The 'Big Bang' in Japanese Higher Education. The 2004 Reforms and the Dynamics of Change*. Melbourne: Trans Pacific Press, pp. 1–31.

Hijiya-Kirschnereit, Irmela (1988), *Das Ende der Exotik. Zur japanischen Kultur und Gesellschaft der Gegenwart.* Frankfurt/Main: Suhrkamp.

Japan Almanac 2003 (2002), *Japan Almanac.* Tokyo: Asahi Shinbun.

Johnson, Chalmers (1982), *MITI and the Japanese Miracle. The Growth of Industrial Policy.* Stanford: Stanford University Press.

McCargo, Duncan (2000), *Contemporary Japan.* Houndsmill, NY: Macmillan.

MacCormack, Gavan (1996), *The Emptiness of Japanese Affluence.* Armonk, NY: Sharpe.

—— and Yoshio Sugimoto (eds) (1986), *Democracy in Contemporary Japan.* New York: Sharpe.

Nakane, Chie (1970), *Japanese Society.* Berkeley, CA: University of California Press.

OECD (1989), *One School, Many Cultures.* Paris: Organisation for Economic Co-operation and Development, Center for Educational Research and Innovation.

Plessner, Helmuth (1982), *Mit anderen Augen. Aspekte einer philosophischen Anthropologie.* Stuttgart: Reclam.

Porter, Michael, Hirotaka Takeuchi and Mariko Sakakibara (2000), *Can Japan Compete?* Houndsmill, NY: Macmillan.

Prestowitz, Clyde (1988), *Trading Places. How America Allowed Japan to Take the Lead.* Tokyo: Tuttle.

Reischauer, Edwin O. (1977), *The Japanese.* Cambridge, MA: Harvard University Press.

Rose, Caroline (2005), *Sino-Japanese Relations. Facing the Past. Looking to the Future?* London and New York: Routledge Curzon.

Ryan, Marleigh G. (1976), 'Modern Japanese Fiction: "Accommodated Truth"', *Journal of Japanese Studies* 2, pp. 249–54.

Satō, Manabu (2005), 'Japan's School Crisis: A Trail of Misguided Reform', *Japan Echo* 32 (4), pp. 30–9.

Segers, R. T., G. A. Bekker and H. Zhang (2007), *Energy in China. An Introduction to China and Its Contemporary Energy Situation.* Groningen: Energy Delta Institute/Cast International Publishers.

Sonoda, Hidehiro (2000), 'The Theory of Japanese Culture and the Theory of Reverse Absence', *Japan Review* 12, pp. 93–104.

Starrs, Roy (ed.) (2001), *Asian Nationalism in an Age of Globalization.* Richmond, Surrey: Japan Library/Curzon Press.

Sugimoto, Yoshi (2003), *An Introduction to Japanese Society* (2nd printing, originally published 1997), Cambridge: Cambridge University Press.

Tsunoda, Tadanobu (1985), *The Japanese Brain. Uniqueness and Universality* (trans. Oiwa Yoshinori). Tokyo: Taishukan Publishing Company.

Vogel, Ezra F. (1979), *Japan as Number One.* Cambridge, MA: Harvard University Press.

Van Wolferen, Karel (1989), *The Enigma of Japanese Power. People and Politics in a Stateless Nation.* London: Macmillan.

Woronoff, Jon (1996), *Japan – as Anything but – Number One* (2nd printing, originally published 1990). Houndsmill, NY: Macmillan.

Part II
Business and technology

2 Japanese banks

The lost decade and new challenges

Nobuyoshi Yamori and Narunto Nishigaki

Introduction

During the so-called bubble economy of the late 1980s, Japanese banks commanded high respect throughout the world. One reason for this was that, even if they had small nominal equity capital, their stock holdings were evaluated at book value, such that they held massive hidden reserves that approached 200 trillion yen. At the same time, major banks had developed close relationships with major corporations, so they had little concern that their customers would be enticed away by other financial institutions. Moreover, real estate was often used as collateral for loans. In addition to the low rate of corporate bankruptcies and irrecoverable loans, continual rises in land prices provided ample leeway for debt collection by disposal of collateral. Thus, the prospect of bad debts becoming a problem for Japanese banks was not a common concept. Furthermore, the majority of household financial assets were held as savings deposits in institutions such as banks, making the leading banks in Japan prominent globally for their asset holdings.

The ratings of the banks are evidence for the high reputation they held. As shown in Table 2.1, Japanese major banks were ranked as leaders among world banks in the late 1980s, achieving at least Aa3 in 1988. The rankings fell abruptly, however, after the bubble burst, and even Mitsubishi Bank, which had achieved the top rating among Japanese banks in 1993, dropped to the fourth-rating Aa3, while the highest rating held by a major bank in 1998 was A1. Even after that, financial conditions continued to worsen, propelling a further drop in many banks' ratings, with some not able to achieve even an investment grade rating of BBB-.

With the recent economic recovery, a rise in ratings can be seen. However, the current situation is hardly an improvement over the worst conditions of the post-bubble economy, and Japanese banks have not yet recovered the financial strength they once held. Pressed by the negative financial legacy of the bad debt issue of the 1990s, Japanese banks are no longer major players in the international financial market because a large gap has formed between them and other major banks in the world, in terms of both financial soundness and advances in financial technology.

Table 2.1 Shifts in ratings for major banks (Moody's Credit Rating)

	1988	1993	1998	2006 (end November)
Aaa	Dai-Ichi Kangyo, Sumitomo, Fuji, Mitsubishi, IBJ, Norin-chukin			Shoko Chukin
Aa1	Sanwa, Mitsubishi Trust, Sumitomo Trust			
Aa2	Tokai, Tokyo, LTCB, MitsuiTrust			
Aa3	Yasuda Trust, Toyo Trust, Yokohama, Shizuoka	Mitsubishi, Sanwa, Tokyo, IBJ, Shoko Chukin, Shizuoka	Shizuoka, Shoko Chukin	
A1		Dai-Ichi Kangyo, Sumitomo, Fuji, Norinchukin	Sanwa, Tokyo Mitsubishi, Norinchukin	Norinchukin, Mitsubishi Tokyo UFJ, Mitsui Sumitomo, Shizuoka, Mizuho Corporate, Chuo Trust
A2		Sakura, Tokai, Asahi	Sumitomo, Nippon Trust	Higo, Sumitomo Trust
A3		Daiwa, LTCB, Yokohama	Dai-Ichi Kangyo, IBJ, Yokohama	Shinsei, Resona, Chuo Mitsui Trust, Mitsui Asset Trust, Yokohama
Baa1		Mitsubishi Trust, Sumitomo Trust, Toyo Trust	Sakura, Fuji, Toyo Trust, Sumitomo Trust, Asahi, Tokai	Aozora, Suruga, Hiroshima, San-In Godo
Baa2		Hokkaido Takushoku (Takugin), Nippon Credit, Mitsui Trust, Yasuda Trust, Chuo Trust, Nippon Trust	Mitsui Credit	Nishi-Nippon City, Ogaki Kyoritsu, Kiyo, Hokuriku, Hokkaido, North Pacific
Baa3			Nippon Credit, Hokkaido Takushoku, Chuo Trust, Yasuda Trust, Daiwa, LTCB	Ashikaga

It should be noted, though, that while the bad debt issue is a direct cause of the stagnation of Japanese banks, a return of the 1980s heyday is implausible, even after disposal of bad debt comes to an end. The fundamental reason why the bad debt issue arose was that financial institutions were unable to respond adequately to the major change in the flow of funds in Japan that was involved in the bubble collapse. For Japan's financial institutions to recover soundness in the true meaning of the word and to become international players, an innovative business model must be constructed to handle the new flow of funds.

In this chapter, we describe the major changes that have taken place in the financial system over the past ten years, concentrating on the Japanese banking system and the impacts of those changes on the banks, and we discuss the new challenges for Japanese banks.[1]

In the following sections we survey the business conditions of Japanese banks. For the period from the time of the bubble collapse until 2007, we first discuss the change in the flow of funds and the weakening of the corporate governance function of banks; we then discuss what sort of changes occurred in respect of financial regulation and financial governance, and follow this with discussion of the changes in the competitive environment, such as the entry of new competitors and changes in the structure of stock cross-holding. We then discuss the impact of these changes and, specifically, we consider items such as the bad debt issue, bank management failure, and the injection of public money. Finally, we discuss new challenges for banks that have emerged recently, as a forward-looking aspect of the impact of the changes.

Major change in flow of funds and weakening bank governance capacity

Major change in flow of funds

According to Allen and Gale (2000), the essence of a bank-centric financial system lies in the fact that the bank comprehensively bears the risk for economic activities and functions to regulate corporate activities. To the extent that they bear risk, banks supervise companies intensely, and companies that find themselves in a chronic state of capital shortfall – as during a high growth period – cannot oppose such supervision. Corporate finance in Japan until the mid-1970s was undeveloped in respect of direct financing, and it was the banks that fulfilled most of the demand for strong capital investment. This resulted in an increase in the regulatory capacity of the principal trading partner bank of the corporation – what is referred to as the 'main bank'.

When high growth dropped to low growth in the latter half of the 1970s, however, capital investment dropped and the corporate sector underwent a change from a capital shortfall to a surplus; beginning in the 1980s, the means for companies to procure funds diversified because of the effects of financial liberalization, and bank loans suffered. In the mean time, because household financial assets were still concentrated in savings deposits (Figure 2.1), banks fell into a state

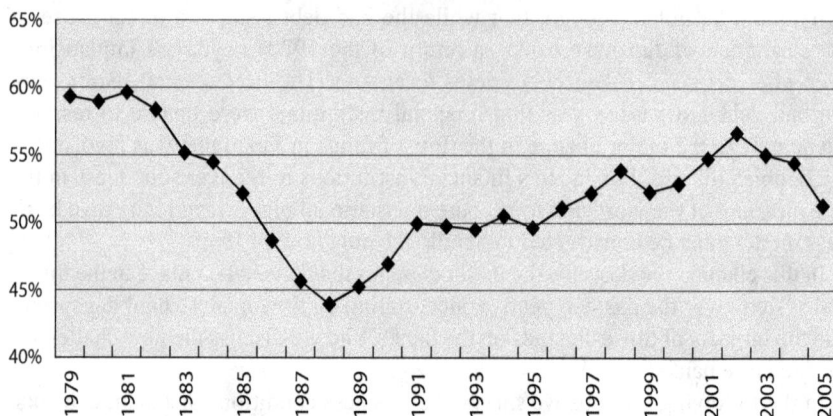

Figure 2.1 Ratio of deposits in household financial assets.

Note: Based on the Bank of Japan's *Shikin Junkan Kanjo*. Deposits include cash.

where they had to manage a large volume of incoming assets while the demand for loans was declining.

In the so-called bubble economy period of 1987 to 1991, however, banks thought they had found salvation. At the time, corporate loans were on the increase. Note that these loans were not for traditional capital investment assets, but for start-up companies engaging in speculative investment (*zaiteku* in Japanese) and the real estate industry, where borrowed money was used to purchase property. It is clear that the unreasonable and reckless lending posture of this period increased the gravity of the bad debt issue in the 1990s.

As shown in Table 2.2, corporate funding demand rapidly decreased at the start of the 1990s, and from 1997 to 2001 all investment capital was covered by internal reserves and depreciation. After 2002, this tendency grew further. But then the inclination of households toward bank savings still increased and the banks' problem since the 1980s, when cash was abundant but there were no borrowers, remained unresolved.

Table 2.2 Corporate capital procurement (trillion yen)

	1987–91	*1992–6*	*1997–2001*	*2002–5*
Capital procurement	570	278	198	186
Capital increase	32	11	11	−45
Bonds	25	−1	−3	−4
Long-term loans	129	22	−14	−26
Short-term loans	80	16	−11	−32
Reserve profits	146	29	10	126
Depreciation	158	201	205	168

Note
The above table was calculated by the authors for all industries, based on corporate statistics from the Ministry of Finance.

Weakening of corporate governance function of banks

With such a capital surplus, not only were companies able to wean themselves from their dependency on banks, but banks competed among themselves for borrowers, resulting in a decrease in their capacity to regulate companies.[2] One such example follows. Currently, Daiei, a major hypermarket, is saddled with excessive debt and is carrying out a reconstruction plan. Daiei is reported to have eluded administrative interference from the banks by pitting major banks against each other. Specifically, Daiei borrowed a total of 508.3 billion yen in March 1996, of which five loans to the amount of 30.85 billion remain at each of the Sakura, Sumitomo, Fuji, Sanwa and Tokai Banks (Toyo Keizai, 1998). Each of these five banks had the same shareholding ratio of 2.46 per cent. Consequently, none of the banks had officers assigned to Daiei and Daiei was not subject to strict supervision by any particular bank. Thus, each bank considered that if it had pointed out that Daiei's obligations were excessive, the only result would have been termination of its account by Daiei. Naturally the banks did not wish to lose a major borrower; thus through their inaction they lost their ability to participate in the business administration of Daiei. That is to say, the lack of regulation by banks became one of the reasons for the postponement of the issue of Daiei's excessive obligations.

The traditional system whereby banks regulated while bearing risk functioned during the high growth period, but deteriorated during the bubble-economy era of the late 1980s. The fact that the regulatory function of financial and asset markets, such as the stock market, was not reinforced to compensate for the falling-off in the regulatory function of banks during this period may be seen as a main reason for the expanding vacuum in corporate governance. As a result, banks faced the collapse of the bubble without changing their risk-taking behaviour, and did not have sufficient capacity to control destructive corporate behaviour. In a system where only the banks bear economic risk, without the assumption of financial risk by households, the capacity to bear economic risk greatly decreased nationwide when the capacity of banks to bear risk declined, as in the 1990s.

Changes in financial regulation and financial governance

Financial 'big bang': change in the bank regulatory environment

Japan's regulatory system in the high-growth period appears to have played a large part in stabilizing the financial order, particularly with regard to indirect finance. In the latter half of the 1970s, however, the high-growth period transitioned to a low-growth period and regulatory relaxation advanced steadily. At first, the issuance of deficit government bonds in large quantity promoted the initial liberalization of interest rates in the secondary market for government bonds. This wave of liberalization spread to short-term financing, bank deposits and the loan market up to the first half of the 1990s, when regulations for both deposit interest and loan interest were repealed. With the international trade liberalization of 1971 and the switch to a free-floating exchange rate in 1973, international capital transactions became active, leading to the reform of the Foreign Exchange and Foreign Trade Control Law (the FECL), which, in principle, liberated capital transactions, although the pre-clearance and designated financial agency systems were left intact at that stage. With regard to business regulations, the separation between the banking and securities industries began to erode when banks were allowed to resell under-written government bonds in 1977 and banks gradually expanded their securities services. In 1993, it became possible for banks, securities firms and trust banks to enter other markets through the establishment of subsidiary companies with 100 per cent equity investment.

The financial liberalization in Japan, up to the mid-1990s, maintained the tradition of incrementalism (resistance to sudden change). The financial 'big bang' of the late 1990s can be seen as a major policy change. This change was inevitable, due to the necessity of responding to the needs of a significantly ageing society and of preventing the Japanese financial system from rapidly weakening and the financial/capital market from hollowing out. What was regarded as the centre-piece of a series of financial big bang reforms during that period was the 1997 enactment of the FECL reform, which took effect the following year. This in effect abolished the system of market segmentation into domestic and international parts. Specifically, repeals included the licensing system for foreign exchange banks and exchangers, the pre-certification system for international foreign exchange trans-actions, and the designated securities company system; that is, complete liberali-zation of foreign exchange services, liberalization of overseas deposits and wires, and liberalization of overseas securities investments.[3]

The 1998 lifting of the ban on financial holding companies was also important from the perspective of promoting the subsequent reorganization of the banking industry. A financial holding company is a financial institution that focuses on holding the stock of subsidiaries such as banks, insurance companies, securities companies and other finance-related companies, and on managing these subsidi-aries. The advantages of a financial holding company include the ability to flex-ibly handle acquisitions and mergers, enjoying synergistic effects and providing comprehensive financial services. It was the liberalizing measure that made today's megabanks possible.

Further, the types of business that banks are allowed to conduct have been widely expanded, beginning in 1997. Entry into new types of business, including sales for investment trusts and insurance, has proceeded apace. Beginning in 1998, reforms that would stimulate the capital market included liberalization of stock commis-sion fees and lifting of the bans on individual stock options, over-the-counter stock derivatives and discretionary investment services. Other financial service regulations that have been relaxed since the big bang are shown in Table 2.3.

A global trend is under way of abolishing regulations that restrict competition and transitioning to a policy of autonomous administrative health in financial institutions through advance prudential regulations, focused on the BIS (Bank for International Settlements) capital adequacy requirements. Such liberalization intensifies competition among banks as well as among businesses in different

Table 2.3 Recent regulation relaxation in the financial sector

Date	Regulation
September 1998	The ban on special purpose companies (SPCs) for asset liquidation and securitization is lifted.
December 1998	The ban on bank sales for investment trusts is lifted.
April 2000	Privately placed bonds are guaranteed by Credit Guarantee Corporations.
November 2000	Floating capital treated by SPCs is expanded from real estate to property rights in general. The procedures for establishing an SPC are simplified.
April 2001	The ban on banks selling insurance products is lifted. Major products include long-term fire insurance for housing loans and overseas travel casualty insurance.
April 2002	The ban on banks selling exchange traded funds (ETFs) is lifted. The standards for issuing bonds are relaxed under the special corporate bond guarantee system.
October 2002	The number of insurance products that banks can sell is expanded. Important additions: individual annuity insurance, asset formation insurance, and long-term individual disability insurance.
December 2004	Ban on securities brokerage services by banks is lifted.
December 2005	The number of insurance products that can be sold by banks is expanded. Important additions: lump sum endowment insurance and lump sum ordinary life insurance.
April 2006	The requirements for opening a bank agency are lowered, allowing a wide range of entrepreneurs to enter the market.

fields and countries, while greatly expanding the opportunities for banks to profit.[4] Of course, unless banks establish a new business model (or are just fortunate), their profits will decrease. This is even truer when the macro-economic conditions are as harsh as those of the 1990s. For many banks in Japan, the effects of the big bang have not all been positive, so far.

Changes in the regulatory authorities

The financial big bang refers mainly to the relaxation and abolition of regulations aimed at private sector financial institutions, but financial system reform in Japan in the 1990s also encompassed changes to the regulatory and supervisory authorities.

Formerly, the Ministry of Finance (MoF) handled Japan's financial governance, along with fiscal policy. In the middle of the 1990s, however, criticism of the MoF's financial system policy grew. The first criticism was that financial system policy was being shaped in order to simplify fiscal management. For example, the MoF wanted to lower the regulated interest rate for government bonds, in spite of the fact that this policy impeded the effective functioning of financial markets. The second criticism was that collusion occurred with the financial institutions that were supposed to be under strict supervision, and necessary bank closures were postponed at the Ministry's discretion. The financial system policy function

Table 2.4 Major early corrective measures

Bank	Date of action	Most recent capital ratio	Subsequent development
Kofuku Bank	May 14, 1999	0.50%	Bankruptcy (May 22, 1999)
Hokkaido Bank	May 21, 1999	3.03%	Capital increase and public capital injection
Tokyo Sowa Bank	May 31, 1999	2.42%	Bankruptcy (June 11, 1999)
Niigata Chuo Bank	June 11, 1999	2.01%	Bankruptcy (October 1, 1999)
Namihaya Bank	June 28, 1999	−1.51%	Bankruptcy (August 6, 1999)
Chiba Kogyo Bank	April 29, 2000	0.45%	Capital increase and public capital injection
Senshu Bank	September 28, 2000	1.32%	Became subsidiary of the Sanwa Bank
Fukushima Bank	December 25, 2001	1.71%	Capital increase
Howa Bank	April 28, 2006	2.2%	Capital increase

Source: Compiled from Financial Services Agency materials (www.fsa.go.jp/kenzenka/index.html)

was therefore gradually severed from the Ministry of Finance, and the Financial Services Agency came into being in July 2000, having initially existed as the Financial Supervisory Agency from July 1998 to June 2000.

The Financial Services Agency comes under the Cabinet Office and handles general financial system policy, including proposing plans related to the banking system as well as inspecting and supervising various financial agencies. Responding to criticism that the Ministry of Finance had postponed dealing with problems, the Financial Services Agency adopted a rule-based policy so as to eliminate discretion. For example, an early corrective measure was employed, namely the issuance of business improvement and suspension orders to banks whose capital ratio was below a set standard. Since the founding of the Financial Supervisory Agency, there have been many cases of unhealthy banks that have received such orders before reaching the point of collapse (refer to Table 2.4).

Another financial regulatory and supervisory authority, the Bank of Japan, has undergone reform to enhance its capacity for autonomous policy execution. The 1997 reform to the Bank of Japan Law went into effect in April 1998. This eliminated the minister of finance's time-honoured 'right to dictate affairs' and 'the right of dismissal' of the governor of the Bank of Japan, thereby guaranteeing the independence of the administration of operations at the Bank of Japan. It also removed two government representatives from the Bank of Japan's Policy Committee and bolstered the Policy Committee's authority in decision making with respect to monetary policy. Further, it enhanced the public disclosure of information as a measure of accountability to the public.

Emphasizing user protection

Since the financial big bang, the degree of freedom in service provision in the financial industries has increased markedly. Nevertheless, the ability of consumers of financial services to select products has not readily increased. This may be because consumers are generally in the position of having inferior information as compared to the providers of financial services and products. From such a perspective, financial regulations in advanced countries have a tendency to place more emphasis on consumer protection during periods of liberalization.

Concrete examples follow. The Financial Products Sales Law obliges financial institutions to explain important matters relating to financial products. Similarly, the Consumer Contract Law provides consumers with the right to rescind agreements when a business has misled or confused them during the agreement process, with the right to claim an agreement null when the content is unilaterally disadvantageous.

During liberalization periods, financial institutions may fail, and consumers should be properly protected from those failures. In the insurance field, a protection fund for policy holders was established to transfer contracts with bankrupt insurance companies to relief insurance companies or a protection corporation. An investors' protection fund was also established as a means of guaranteeing up to 10 million yen in the case of a securities company bankruptcy.

In the banking industry, it is the deposit insurance system that bears responsibility for protecting the consumer. Since the 1990s, a large number of financial institutions have collapsed, causing the total negative liability to balloon, but the government has provided protection for all types of deposit, including interest. The Deposit Insurance Corporation of Japan (DIC) not only vicariously pays for deposits for collapsed banks, but has provided capital assistance for financial institutions taking over the business of a bankrupt financial institution or merging with it. While the depositor has therefore gone unscathed, the burden on the DIC has become extensive. As a consequence of the DIC developing financial difficulties, the policy of complete protection for deposits has been (partially) abandoned through a partial lifting of the ban on pay-offs in April 2002. Today, although settlement deposits are fully guaranteed, as well as other deposits, and deposit interest up to a principle of 10 million yen, banks now face an era of depositor selectivity.[5]

New entrants into the banking industry and changes in cross-holding structure

Changes in competition due to new entrants

The relaxation of regulations on entering the banking industry has brought about changes in operation and competition. Specifically, a new style of bank based on internet transactions and ATMs rather than brick-and-mortar locations has emerged. What is particularly noteworthy is the fact that many of these new entrants are from non-finance industries. Although the Japan Net Bank, established with funding principally from financial institutions, is an exception, Sony Bank is an entrant from the manufacturing industry, Seven Bank is from the distribution industry, and e-Bank is a completely new business. Because exclusively internet-based banks use their low overhead to provide low fees and high interest rates (on savings), they have a competitive advantage over ordinary banks. Though they do not offer corporate finance, they provide strong competition to existing banks, with some providing low-interest home loans. Some existing banks have begun to respond with measures such as improved internet banking.

Yucho Bank, a result of privatization and a split in the Japan Postal Service Public Corporation in fiscal year 2007, will have a stronger potential to compete with traditional banks as a newcomer in the market if it enters the corporate financing field. While no bank has been newly founded with a conventional business model, the environment has indeed become more competitive, with the new entrants offering specific services.

Cross-holding structure changes and increased foreign shareholders

Conventionally, financial institutions in Japan have used cross-holdings with transaction partners to effectively block any influence on bank administration on the part of shareholders. As a result, it has always been unusual for bank stocks to fluctuate greatly. In the latter half of the 1990s, however, the structure of cross-holdings underwent a great change. City banks greatly decreased their shareholdings, and the partner companies sold their bank holdings in response. With the overabundance of bank stocks on the market, foreign and individual investors bought in.

Looking at the shareholder structure for all listed companies (Figure 2.2), the ratio of city and regional banks dropped, beginning in the late 1990s. Conversely, foreigners markedly increased their presence. With regard to individual shareholders, the number of holding stocks has rapidly expanded, though in terms of value, movement is horizontal because the price of the issues purchased was

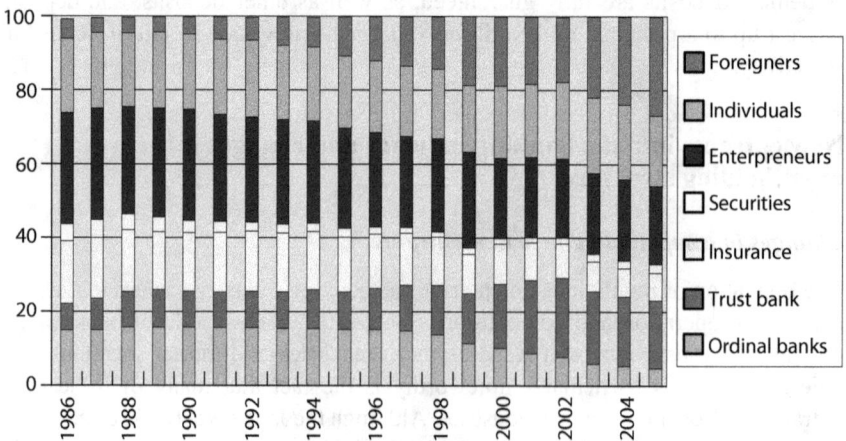

Figure 2.2 Shareholder structure for nationally listed companies (according to market price).

Note: Based on the Zenkoku Shoken Torihikisho 2005.

generally low. At the end of fiscal year 2005 (March 2006), foreigners held 26.7 per cent and individuals 19.1 per cent.

In the banking industry, the foreigner holding ratio was 26.3 per cent and individual 12.2 per cent at the end of fiscal year 2005.[6] Starting at a mere 5.9 per cent at the end of fiscal year 2002, the foreigner ratio increased dramatically, to 17.8 per cent at the end of 2003 and 19.5 per cent at the end of 2004. The foreigner holding ratio has thus risen rapidly in recent years. This trend is particularly marked with large banks. For example, the foreigner holding ratio of Mitsubishi UFJ Financial Group (holding company for the Bank of Tokyo-Mitsubishi UFJ) reached 31.3 per cent as of the end September 2006. Because the shareholder structure is the most important variable affecting corporate governance, such a change is likely to modify the behaviour of financial institutions. In general, the main object of foreign investors is to earn returns by investing in Japan's financial institutions. Administrators at large banks now list ROE (return on equity) as an administrative target (17 per cent for the Mitsubishi UFJ Financial Group, for example). It seems to be the result of the weighty influence of such investors' demands.

Bankruptcy, bad debts, and capital injection

Financial institution bankruptcy

No financial institutions had experienced bankruptcy in the post-Second World War period until the bubble collapsed. In the year 1995, a series of large-scale bankruptcies started, beginning with Hyogo Bank. Then the collapse of the regional banks and credit cooperatives followed. In November 1997, the Hokkaido Takushoku Bank, one of the city banks, collapsed, causing extreme distrust among

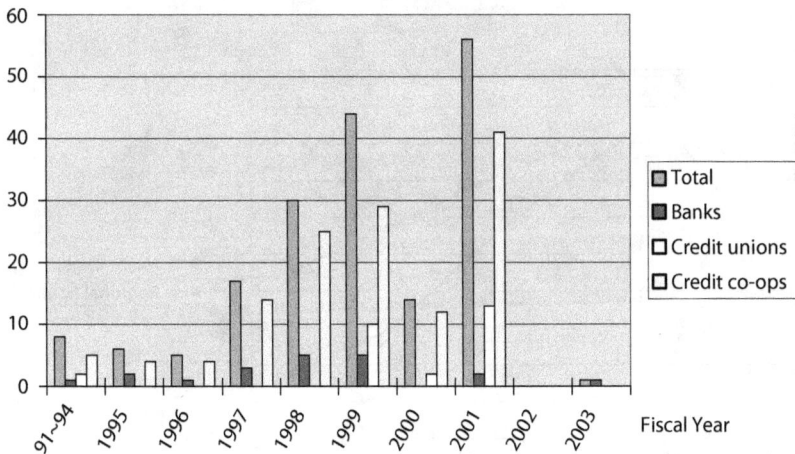

Figure 2.3 Number of financial institution collapses.

Note: Based on Deposit Insurance Organization of Japan 2005.

depositors in the management of financial institutions. Despite the promise of the government to protect all bank deposits at the time, there was a run on some major banks. In 1998, bankruptcies occurred in two major banks: the LTCB and Nippon Credit Bank failed and action was taken for special public management (temporary nationalization), demonstrating that financial institution collapse had become less uncommon (Figure 2.3).[7]

Has the bad debt issue been resolved?

The concept commonly characterized as 'bad loans' in fact has three levels: 'bankruptcy rehabilitation debts' where the debtors have already failed; 'risk debts' where the debtors are not yet in a state of corporate failure, but there is a high possibility that the principal and interest will not be recovered as agreed upon; and 'substandard assets' comprising debts at least three months in arrears and loans whose repayment conditions have been relaxed.

In the approximately ten years from fiscal year 1992 to the first half of 2001, when the monetary value of bad debts peaked after the bubble collapse, financial institutions in Japan were disposing of a massive amount of bad debts, totalling 75 trillion yen. Fiscal years 1997 and 1998 saw particularly large bad debt disposition, with injection of public funding mainly for large banks. With such an enormous amount of bad debt disposition, it would ordinarily seem that the level of bad debt would have decreased. In fact, while the amount did drop briefly in fiscal year 1996, there was no decrease over the subsequent five years.

After a peak at the end of fiscal year 2001, this trend has fortunately taken a downward turn (Figure 2.4). The Bank of Japan (2006) has briefly assessed the financial system of Japan, saying that 'the problem of bad debt, which has been the largest problem since the 1990s, has been brought under control for the most part and stability of the system has been recovered substantially'. Bankruptcy rehabilitation debt, risk debt and

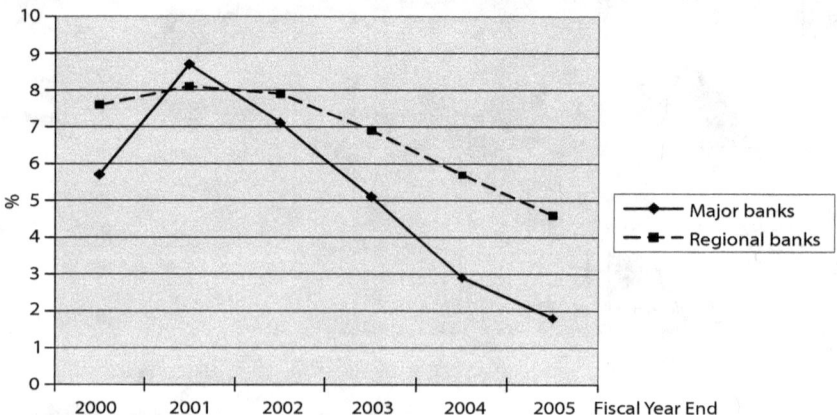

Figure 2.4 Trends in bad debt ratio.

Source: Bank of Japan 2006.

substandard assets combined (total bad debt) have dropped among the 12 major banks from 28 trillion yen at the peak of the problem (8.7 per cent bad debt ratio) to less than 5 trillion at the end of fiscal year 2005 (4.6 per cent bad debt ratio), while among regional banks the figures are 15 trillion (8.1 per cent) at the time of peak and 8 trillion (4.6 per cent) at the end of fiscal year 2005. It is still premature, however, to declare that stability is assured for Japan's financial system, based on the numbers provided here.

Impact of bank collapses

The succession of bank collapses is thought to have had a major negative impact on Japan's economy.

First is the effect on borrowers. Because soft information about companies is accumulated by banks, the collapse of a main bank causes borrowing conditions to be tightened up for companies. Yamori and Murakami (1999) analyse the collapse of the Hokkaido Takushoku Bank, finding that the value of companies that had used Hokkaido Takushoku Bank as their main bank dropped as a result of its collapse.

Next is the effect on other banks. Because of inadequate disclosure of bank management information, banks showing a high capital ratio right up to their collapse appeared to bankrupt 'abruptly'. It was therefore natural that depositors' distrust of publicly disclosed figures should have grown. Accordingly, when a bank collapse occurred, people thought that banks similar to the collapsed one were in a state worse than actually claimed. Yamori (1999a, 1999b) found that when a bank collapsed, the stock price of similar banks showed a large decrease.

Thus, while the collapse of a rival bank might very well be favourable for surviving banks, it turned out in reality to be a disadvantage. Surviving banks therefore faced further risks of having a run, causing them to be more conservative in loan determinations. This resulted in restricted lending. As a result, the argument for the need to protect borrowers as well as depositors received majority support, thereby expanding not only loans by government-affiliated financial institutions, but the credit guarantee programme as well.

Table 2.5 Bank collapses and disposition costs

Date of collapse	Collapsed institution	Money provided by deposit insurance (¥ 100,000,000)	Date of collapse	Collapsed institution	Money provided by deposit insurance (¥ 100,000,000)
8/30/95	Hyogo Bank	4,730	4/12/99	Kokumin Bank	1,837
4/1/96	Taiheiyo Bank	1,170	5/24/99	Kofuku Bank	4,941
11/21/96	Hanwa Bank w	806	6/14/99	Tokyo Sowa Bank	7,626
10/14/97	Kyoto Kyoei Bank	438	8/9/99	Namihaya Bank	6,526
11/17/97	Hokkaido Takushoku Bank	17,732	10/4/99	Niigata Chuo Bank	3,817
11/25/97	Tokuyo Bank	1,238	12/28/01	Ishikawa Bank	1,809
5/15/98	Midori Bank	7,711	3/8/02	Chubu Bank	944
10/23/98	LTCB	32,350	11/29/03	Ashikaga Bank	—
12/14/98	Nippon Credit Bank	31,414			

A great deal of public funding has been invested to handle the collapses (Table 2.5). Though it cannot be disputed that these measures were borne by taxpayers, it is not possible to assess whether the emergency measures to prevent chaos in the financial system contributed to an increase in the competitiveness of Japan's financial institutions.

New challenges

Challenges for major banks: conglomeration and new management strategies

The 'lost decade' has been reviewed in the preceding sections, a period when the competitive environment for banks underwent a major upheaval. With regulations being relaxed and troubles such as increasing bad debts, the first specific response that city banks made was to raise the average amount of capital per bank through mergers, with the object of stabilizing management. Mergers and consolidations among such city banks and among trust banks and other large banks proceeded after the ban on financial holding companies was lifted, leaving five financial groups:

- Mizuho Financial Group, a joint holding company comprising the Industrial Bank of Japan, the Dai-Ichi Kangyo Bank and the Fuji Bank;
- Mitsubishi Tokyo Financial Group (MTFG), established by the Bank of Tokyo-Mitsubishi and Mitsubishi Trust and Banking;
- UFJ Holdings, established by the Sanwa Bank and the Tokai Bank;
- Sumitomo Mitsui Banking Corporation, a merger of the Sumitomo Bank and the Sakura Bank; and
- Resona Holdings, established by the Daiwa Bank and the Asahi Bank.

Furthermore, in the spring of 2004, the UFJ Group decided to further combine management with MTFG, giving rise to Mitsubishi UFJ Financial Group (MUFG) in October 2005.

Japan's banks, which often postponed dealing with problems such as the elimination of bad loans, now have new challenges to face. The characteristics of megabanks are the massive amount of assets, tens or hundreds of locations in Japan and abroad, and a large customer base. Recently, megabanks have been trying to use such business resources to adopt business strategies not possible for regional financial institutions.

Investment bank and fee-based business services

The investment bank services cover a variety of business matters, the main items of which are structured finance (arrangement services such as for asset liquidation); real estate finance; MBO (management buyout), LBO (leveraged buyout) and other buyout financing; and financing for aircraft, ships, manufacturing equipment, construction equipment and the like. The common factor in all these services is that the source of income for banks is fees. The reason why megabanks decided to shift their focus to investment bank services is that, while there was no prospect of increasing revenue with conventional financial services, corporate finance could not be actively increased for maintaining the capital ratio at a minimum set level. Fees for money exchange, ATMs and opening accounts were traditional for fee-based services, but notice was taken of new fields related to investment banking, such as syndicated loans, debt liquidation and commitment lines.

A syndicated loan is one where multiple finance agencies form a syndicate group to collaboratively provide a large amount of funding. The arranger, or representing financial institution in the group, collects a fee from the borrowing companies. Although the profit per participating financial institution is not large, such collaborative financing has the advantage that the funding agreement is simplified and the risk is diversified.

Capital liquidation or securitization are financial techniques where new securities (asset-backed securities) are issued with a primary liability (such as a loan debt) owned by a bank as collateral, and the securities are sold on the market to investors. This is a method originally used to quickly convert loan debt with low liquidity to cash and has become popular in Japan in recent years because of its debt off-balance faculty that would raise the capital ratio of financial institutions.

SPCs (special-purpose companies) are one type of financial institution that issues asset-back securities, while in many cases banks as original creditors collect principal and interest from original debtors. This sort of collection is known as servicer work. Banks make money by charging SPCs a fee for this servicer work. For megabanks, it is possible to establish an SPC as a group company.

Trillion yen

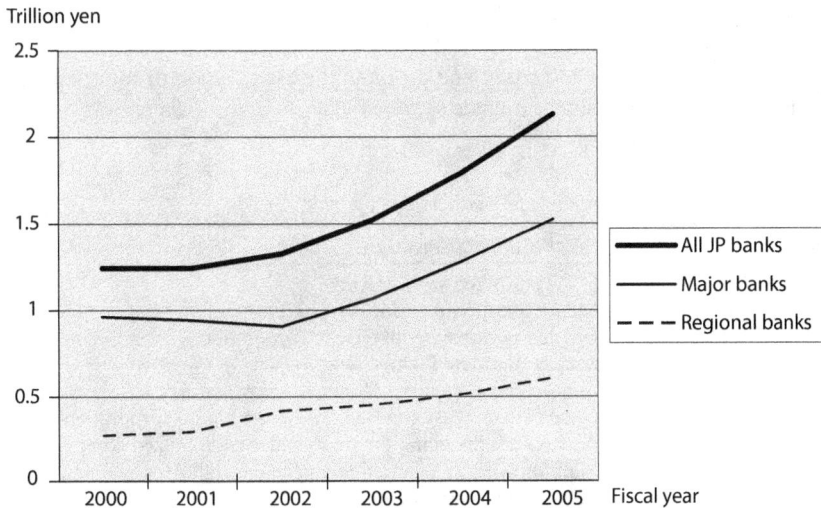

Figure 2.5 Increases of service revenues

Source: http://www.zenginkyo.or.jp/stat/index.html.

A commitment line is an agreement where a customer and a bank commit to the bank providing finance at the customer's request within a predetermined period and a limit to loan, and a set fee is charged when the commitment line agreement is signed.

Other fees that have been steadily growing are those for bond underwriting and registration, made possible by the relaxation of bank regulations. Although not an investment bank service, fee revenues for sales of investment trusts and insurance products have been rising rapidly. As a result, service revenues are steadily expanding (Figure 2.5).

Consumer finance services

With corporate financing sluggish, the area that city banks have come to focus on is personal financing channels. An example we look at is that of MUFG.

Before merging with UFJ to become MUFG, MTFG formed a strategic business and capital alliance with ACOM, one of the major non-bank companies, in March 2004. What was specifically laid out was an alliance between Bank of Tokyo-Mitsubishi (BTM) and ACOM with the following five points:

1   BTM would consign debt guarantee business to ACOM, to markedly strengthen BTM's consumer finance services;
2   BTM would consign debt guarantee business relating to small business settlement funds to ACOM;
3   ACOM and BTM would cooperate to expand business alliances with partner financial institutions and other corporations concerning ACOM's guarantee and servicer business;
4   ACOM and BTM would study and promote the effective use of their mutual network infrastructures; and
5   ACOM and BTM would study and promote the cooperation of international development of consumer finance services, mainly in the Asia region.

Table 2.6 Non-bank acquisitions and partnerships by major banks

Date		Acquisition / partnership
2004	March	BTM partnered with ACOM
	June	Mitsui Sumitomo partnered with Promise
	July	Mizuho partnered with Orient Corporation
	August	Mizuho partnered with Credit Saison
	September	Shinsei Bank acquired Showa Leasing and APLUS
	October	Chuo Mitsui Trust and Banking set up a joint corporation with Nissin with financing for small and medium-sized companies
	December	Sumitomo Trust acquired management rights for (then-named) Matsushita Lease Credit
2005	October	Sumitomo Trust acquired First Credit

Source: *Nihon Keizai Shinbun*, October 15, 2005.

Following BTM and ACOM, other major city banks have advanced their efforts towards partnerships with and acquisitions of non-banks, with the object of focusing on consumer finance (Table 2.6).

Additionally, the Bank of Tokyo-Mitsubishi UFJ has put effort into the individual annuity business by partnering with an overseas life insurance company (Canada's Manulife) to develop insurance such as for investment annuities and fixed annuities, and into wealthy consumer business by partnering with Merrill Lynch for private banking.

Internationalization: re-entry into Asia

Although Japanese banks are said to be planning a (re-)entry overseas, particularly Asia, what is actually going on?[8] We look again at MUFG as an example. Although MUFG has under its umbrella the Bank of Tokyo-Mitsubishi UFJ, the most popular of Japanese banks for international services, its overseas ratio to total assets is extremely low. For example, of consolidated total assets of 187 trillion yen at the end of fiscal year 2005, they had 166 trillion in Japan, 18 trillion in North America, 4 trillion in Central/South America, 10 trillion in Europe/the Middle East, and 8 trillion in Asia/Oceania.[9] In general, Japanese banks are said to pursue an international strategy focusing on Asian markets, but the scale of assets in Asia, including Oceania, is a mere few per cent of the total. Considering the ordinary profit base, the consolidated amount was 1.780 trillion yen for fiscal year 2005, and while the ordinary profit for Japan reached 934.7 billion yen, it was 122.9 billion in North America, 3.8 billion in Central/South America, 7.4 billion in Europe/the Middle East, and 45.5 billion in Asia. Thus, even MUFG, with the Bank of Tokyo-Mitsubishi UFJ under its umbrella, and which offers the most powerful international services among Japanese banks, gains nearly all of its profit from domestic services.

Given the setback due to the 'lost decade', competing with Euro-American banks at the current time in their home markets seems difficult. In contrast, the relatively high frequency of usage of the yen in the Asian market and strong personal and economic ties with Japan are positive factors for Japanese banks to expand their activities in Asia in the future. In fact, the return on assets (ROA) in the Asian market was stable compared to other regions with 0.63 per cent in 2001, 0.94 per cent in 2002, 0.62 per cent in 2003, 0.56 per cent in 2004, and 0.55 per cent in 2005.

Particularly, strategic development in the Chinese market, given its membership in the WTO and opening up to foreign financial institutions, would be a good testing ground for Japanese banks in the Asian market.

Challenge of regional bank strategy: relationship banking

Although the ratio of loans to total assets for city banks exceeded 65 per cent in the first half of the 1990s, this has recently dropped to a level undercutting 50 per cent, and the ratio of valuable securities has instead rapidly expanded. Compared with city banks, definite decreases in the loan ratio have not occurred with regional banks and the second-tier regional banks. Currently, two-thirds of their total amounts of capital are used for loans. Diversification in income opportunities has not arisen for regional banks as it has for city banks, and the role of regional banks as financial intermediaries for the regional economy may be said to continue.

Relationship banking is a business model that is gaining attention as a means for regional financial institutions – regional banks, the second-tier regional banks and credit unions – to continue. Relationship banking is a business method to solve the asymmetric information problem with client corporations and to simplify financing through long-term ongoing relationships with client companies.

Even though large-scale companies no longer need to borrow from banks, loans for small and medium-sized businesses in particular may be difficult to replace with the securities market because of the relatively large problem of asymmetrical information. In March 2003 the government therefore proposed a new business model for regional banks that improves the relationship banking function, in order to solve the financing problem for small and medium-sized companies.

We described above the dissolution of cross-shareholding in the banking industry and the rise in the bank shareholding ratio by foreign investors. Caution is needed here, however, in that any rise in the foreign investor ratio is only for megabanks or particular metropolitan-type regional banks such as the Bank of Yokohama, the Bank of Fukuoka or the Chiba Bank. For most regional banks today, the foreigner ratio is no larger than 5 per cent. That may be interpreted to mean that the business model in which stable profits are gained over the long term by a regional financial institution (relationship banking) does not necessarily coincide with the investment techniques of foreign investors.

To conjecture from the differences in these governance structures, then, while large banks strongly affected by foreign investors and other regional banks may compete in the individual and small/medium company financial markets, there will be large differences in business technique to adopt between these two types of financial institutions. If foreign investors deepen their understanding of Japan's financial system, they may increase their ratio in some regional banks that are located in a large metropolitan area and would be able to adopt a city-bank type management technique. For most regional financial institutions seeking a relationship banking model, it will be a critical challenge for their management to find a group of shareholders who support their business model and emphasize the steady growth of regional economies.

Conclusion

In this chapter, the conditions experienced by Japan's banks during the 'lost decade' following the bubble collapse have been described. Fortunately, the economy has undergone a recent recovery, providing temporary relief from the adverse circumstances for Japan's banks. The recovery of the economy, however, does not mean that the problems intrinsic to the financial system are solved.

The fundamental problems have not been plunging asset prices or increasing bad debts due to a depression. Instead, it is responding in a proper manner to the major changes in the flow of funds causing these problems that is the essential issue for Japan's banks. However, to respond to such changes in the 1980s, the banks expanded real estate financing, which promoted the expansion of the bubble economy. Now we can conclude that the deepening of the bad debt problem of the 1990s must have been a consequence of failure to respond properly to the changes.

Many banks are aware that the business model of increasing deposits for loans is no longer adequate, despite its effectiveness when the economy had a shortage of capital. Many banks are instead putting efforts into fee-based business such as investment trust sales and into risk diversification through techniques such as forming syndicated loans, in response to the new circumstances. The management teams at each bank are overcoming the difficult conditions of the finance industry with a sense of concern over a possible crisis, working to develop a unique approach. While the precipitous road to complete revival of Japan's banks will likely continue, we hope that all Japanese banks will continue to challenge new circumstances.

Notes

1 Hoshi and Kashyap (2004) describe the transition in Japan's financial system beginning with the Meiji Restoration in detail, and demonstrate that the problem with Japan's banking system in the 1990s was inevitable. We take the same view in this chapter.
2 However, Spiegel and Yamori (2003) make it clear that the role of the main bank was enhanced during times of financial system crisis, particularly for financially frail companies.
3 Regulations such as economic sanctions, however, were provided for easy implementation at the government's discretion in times of emergency.
4 While Yamori and Baba (2000) find that the liberalization and globalization of the trust business had a positive effect on existing trust banks, Yamori and Kobayashi (2004) find that the liberalization had a negative effect on non-life insurance companies.
5 Note that even after the ban on pay-offs was lifted, deposits made in financial agencies with unprofitable operations continue to be substantially protected. For example, some 2 trillion yen in public funding was infused into Resona Bank to avoid collapse. This infusion is analysed in Yamori and Kobayashi (2007).
6 Banks include bank holding companies.
7 Spiegel and Yamori (2004) analyse which bank types were covered with TBTF, and explain that the forecasted range of the market gradually narrowed.
8 Yamori (1997, 1998) analyses the overseas developments of Japanese banks.
9 While the sum of these is 206 trillion yen, some of the assets are offset when consolidated, resulting in a total of 187 trillion.

References

Allen, Franklin and Douglas Gale (2000), *Comparing Financial Systems*. Cambridge, MA: MIT Press.
Bank of Japan (2006), *Financial System Report 2006*, July.

Deposit Insurance Organization of Japan (2005), *2004 Annual Report*, July.

Hoshi, Takeo and Anil Kashyap (2004), *Corporate Financing and Governance in Japan: The Road to the Future*. Cambridge, MA: MIT Press.

Spiegel, Mark M. and Nobuyoshi Yamori (2003), 'Financial Turbulence and the Japanese Main Bank', *Journal of Financial Services Research* 23 (3), pp. 205–23.

—— (2004), 'The Evolution of Bank Resolution Policy in Japan: Evidence from Market Equity Values', *Journal of Financial Research* XXVII (1), pp. 115–32.

Toyo Keizai, Inc. (1997), *Kigyo Keiretsu Soran 1998*.

Yamori, Nobuyoshi (1997), 'Do Japanese Banks Lead or Follow International Business? An Empirical Investigation', *Journal of International Financial Markets, Institutions and Money* 7 (4), pp. 369–82.

—— (1998), 'A Note on the Location Choice of Multinational Banks: The Case of Japanese Financial Institutions', *Journal of Banking and Finance* 22, pp. 109–20.

—— (1999a), 'Stock Market Reaction to the Bank Liquidation in Japan: A Case for the Informational Effect Hypothesis', *Journal of Financial Services Research* 15 (1), pp. 57–68.

—— (1999b), 'Contagion Effects of the Bank Liquidation in Japan', *Applied Economics Letters* 6 (11), pp. 703–5.

—— and Taiji Baba (2000), 'Wealth Effects of the Financial Internationalization: A Case of the Yen–Dollar Agreement between the United States and Japan', *Applied Financial Economics* 10, pp. 193–8.

—— and Ayami Kobayashi (2007) 'Wealth Effect of Public Funds Injections to Ailing Banks; Do Deferred Tax Assets and Auditing Firms Matter?' *Japanese Economic Review.* 58 (4), pp. 466–83.

—— and Takeshi Kobayashi (2004), 'Does Regulation Benefit Incumbent Firm? An Investigation of Japanese Insurance Market Deregulation', *Journal of Insurance Regulation* 22 (4), pp. 35–48.

—— and Akinobu Murakami (1999), 'Does Bank Relationship Have an Economic Value? The Effect of Main Bank Failure on Client Firms', *Economic Letters* 65, pp. 115–20.

Zenkoku Shoken Torihikisho (2005), *Heisei 17 Nendo Kabushiki Bunpu Jokyo Chosa* [2005 Stock Distribution Survey]. Available at the Tokyo Stock Exchange website, www.tse.or.jp/market/data/examination/distribute/index.html.

3 Japan's current and future technological agendas

Taizo Yakushiji

Introduction

Given the fact that Japan will face an ageing society and labour shortages in the near future, argumentation about its future agenda is basically confined to the so-called 'cyclists', that is, believers in the cyclical rise and fall of a nation. It is in this connection that technology becomes an important issue in Japan's future agenda setting. Technology raises a nation but, paradoxically, it also ruins a nation. Technology increases the wealth of a nation through economic realization. Technology thus plays a part in the rise of a nation. This is nothing more than conventional wisdom. Unconventional, however, is the fact that it often triggers the decline of a nation. The reason is fourfold.

First, there emerge the strong contenders such as China. Latent competitors eventually catch up when they are successful in technological 'emulation'.[1] Strong contenders will sooner or later corrode the economy of a front-runner country through the superb fits and finishes but low prices of emulated technological products.

Second, 'techno-parochialism' occurs within a nation that took a lead in the technological race, such as Japan today, or the United States in the mid-1980s. Parochial pride leads to technological arrogance. This arrogance blinds people to the very secret of pre-eminence, that is, 'emulous power'. Without avaricious emulation, namely copying and drastic improvement of advanced technologies both abroad and at home, the hitherto technological leads are quickly eroded.[2]

Third, there exists vulnerability of international technological cooperation. Conventional wisdom says that technology is a means for international cooperation because of its value-free and universal nature. This is a naive view and the real situation is different. High technology is a two-edged sword, cooperative–uncooperative. The recent alliance of Japanese semiconductor manufacturers against South Korean Samsung is an example in point. Technological cooperation leaks important high-tech know-how. Thus, strong protectionist views will cut off existing cooperation. This is the uncooperative nature of high-technology cooperation. How to overcome such a negative aspect of technological cooperation is an important agenda Japan should take into account.

Fourth, the overriding supremacy of economic rationality prevails. Successful gains in national wealth invite a blind belief in economic efficiency. This efficiency, when it goes too far, depresses an attempt to develop technology and is often time wasting and money guzzling. For example, economically efficient mass production with a standardized technology is believed to add wealth to a nation, so that it often rejects new technological endeavours that would shut down the current profitable production lines. A famous example of this is General Electric's rejection of transistors in the 1950s.

These four agendas are interrelated. If a country succeeds in technological emulation, it becomes a strong technological country. Then, naturally, it cultivates nationalistic pride and parochialism, thereby forgetting past emulous efforts. To make matters worse, its technological cooperation helps a peripheral country to emerge as a strong contender. Then, it wants to harvest economic returns as soon as possible. This in turn requires a technological norm of mass production, because mass production guarantees a strong economy.

Arguably, the international system consists of all sovereign states. Therefore, if either a decline or a rise of one of these states occurs, the international system is perturbed. In the mean time, as seen above, technology both raises and ruins a nation. Thus, syllogistically, technology will inevitably disturb the international system in the end. What, then, do Japan's techno-agendas really mean? The agendas should be something to bridge technology and the international system whereby Japan could play a decisive role. If a state mishandles technology, it loses the basis of development. It is, then, of prime importance to manage policy for technology wisely. This paper examines in detail each of the above four agendas and, in conclusion, we propose policy options for Japan to take in future.

The first agenda (enhancement of technological 'emulation')

Twenty years ago, the United States bashed Japan for the reason that Japan copied American technology and attacked the American market with better products. American people took American technological pre-eminence for granted. But the reality was different. America also copied technologies from outside, as Japan did. Americans learned French military technology and British civilian technology, in particular textile technology. No country could become a technological superstate from scratch.

Since most Americans lived in the period of American technological hegemony, they developed a strong belief that its technological pre-eminence would be self-evident and unquestionable. This strong nationalistic sentiment invited a strong action to bash others, particularly Japan, in the mid-1980s.

This nationalistic sentiment appeared as political 'revisionism', namely revising the American relationship with its ally, that is, Japan. This revisionism was transformed into 'technological revisionism', addressing a shift in American foreign policy by incorporating technological concerns. If such technological revisionism goes to extremes, it will arrive at the 'technological containment' policy; namely, preventing a country's technological attempts to extend into an international market, by way of harsh litigation in intellectual property disputes.

Why does technological revisionism end up with a technological containment policy? It is because high technology has two peculiar properties, namely, a) the so-called 'minority regime thesis', and b) the so-called 'hybridism thesis'. The former implies that a minor actor (such as a peripheral country or firm) topples a major actor upon successful exploitation of a new technology. The latter means a marriage between traditional technology and new, thereby introducing a new hybrid product, such as a digital watch for example.

No one can exactly forecast when the hybrid mingling of different technologies will occur, or when high technology will be realized by a minor actor. However, ironically, once high technology comes to the fore, it increasingly becomes predatory and thus shatters the existing harmony of the international system, so that it seems almost hopeless for nations to be patched together and regain mutual binding.

Is there no way out of this frustrating dilemma? Perhaps there is one solution. It may be found if we look at the problem from a Copernican paradoxical perspective. The keyword here is 'creative emulation', namely, competitive copying and improving among tightly bound private firms.

Usually, because all countries either seek equal benefits from high technology or fear being left behind, international alliances are designed before the high technology is realized, and this is why problems occur. Why should we not twist this logic, and decide that international technological relations should be formed after the high technology comes into being?

Firms competitively seek ways in which they can survive. So, if some high technology is realized by one firm, other firms must competitively imitate it in the first place. Of course, imitation is not easy unless firms have technical capabilities and, moreover, high-tech is highly protected by patent barriers to secure that, for the time being, the company that attained the realization of the new technology can monopolize profits.

However, as time passes it is almost inevitable that the inventor/innovator's monopoly will eventually be broken: a newly realized technology will be competitively imitated and improved by competitors. When imitation moves to the stage of emulation by adding on something new, the inventor/innovator's monopoly quickly becomes indefensible.

Firms are doubtless the main actors in developing and commercializing high technology. Because of the predatory nature of high technology, they tend to engage in comprehensive R&D in a wide range of product lines, which obviously requires huge investment. Most firms cannot afford such huge investments, and therefore their only solution is to construct a 'strategic alliance'. This enables firms to purchase OEM (original equipment manufacturer) products, for example, from competitors and sell them under their own brand names until they are able to manufacture them by themselves. A good example is the contractual deal to manufacture mini-cars (SMART cars) between Germany's Daimler and Japan's Mitsubishi.

Interestingly enough, the underlying logic of high technology is paradoxical. That is, the unfriendly nature of predation in high technology induces an opposite end, namely corporate alliances. This contradiction is a clue to the solution to political revisionism or containment policies triggered by techno-nationalistic sentiment in a super-state. Direct investments have long been seen as a symbol of economic interdependence among nations. However, technologically, direct investments in a decaying country would help little. Rather, they should be seen as an economic contribution per se, rather than as technological help.

That is, we believe that technological revival is only possible with a strong will on the part of a declining country to *emulate* advanced technologies. Note that we are not talking merely about technology transfer from an advanced country to a less developed country. Rather, we are dealing with the transfer of technology between advanced countries. So that if direct investments take the form of building a manufacturing factory in an advanced country but operating it from a donor country, such an attempt at direct investment would not stimulate technological copying and improvement, that is, emulation.

The second agenda (pitfalls of technological 'parochialism')

Recently, a new symptom has emerged in Japan. It is 'techno-parochialism'. This techno-parochialism sees China and South Korea as adversaries making frontal attacks on an international market of high technology where Japan, the United States and Europe once dominated.

As noted above in the first agenda, twenty years ago, the United States developed a similar 'techno-revisionism' against Japan. Interestingly enough, this time it is Japan that is trying to revise relations with China and South Korea. Japan thinks that those countries are attacking international markets that Japan once occupied. Japan went to China to manufacture products for low wages. Japan helped China and South Korea build steel mills. Japan sold the lithography devices for making semiconductors to South Korea. It is now a good lesson for Japan to review the past case of American 'techno-parochialism'.

American techno-parochialism also argued that US foreign policy should rethink diplomatic ties with Japan. It delineated how glorious American inventions and subsequent market dominance were exploited by superior Japanese products. Then, it alerted US foreign policy makers that commercial technologies are all related like a 'food chain', in which one technology eats away at the next technology; this second technology washes out the third technology, and so on. In the end, the decisive technology controls all related technologies. The implication of the 'techno-food chain' thesis is obvious: a division of labour in technology that leads to international cooperation would jeopardize the hitherto technological strength of the United States.

Charles H. Ferguson's article was regarded in the 1990s[3] as typical of the techno-revisionist policy. He assumed that nearly all industrial products were being digitalized and that the American market of the digital information systems industry was on the verge of crisis because of the predatory behaviour of Japanese companies. He saw Japanese companies blocking foreign applications for Japanese patents and denying foreign competitors access to technologies and markets over which Japanese industries kept control.

Ferguson proposed to encircle Japan. When contained, its natural reaction would be either to build a similar counter-blockade with the help of Allies, or to nullify containment by suggesting a friendly, interdependent alliance. Ferguson, feeling that the US information systems industry was blocked by Japanese companies, proposed the first option. On the contrary, since Japan feared being contained, it had no choice but the second option, namely, technological cooperation with the United States. However, there remains the danger that interdependent cooperation in the area of technology can spark a collective 'witch-hunt' to encircle a target country. We will discuss this point as a separate agenda below.

The third agenda (vulnerability of technological cooperation)

There is no definitive definition of high technology. The expression 'high technology' has received popular attention, but debates on it are often shallow because of the absence of a clear definition of what it actually means. For example, economists are prone to seeing high technology in terms of their favourite variable, money. They define high technology as something that swallows a large chunk of R&D expenditures. Along these lines, international cooperation receives legitimacy because sharing a financial burden is imperative to solving the cost-overrun problems of most high-technology projects. Political scientists, on the other hand, view high technology as something related to military capabilities, and hence to national power. This view also has validity in the civilian sphere because monopoly over a given dual-use technology that can be used for military purposes gives a country a free hand to steer the international system. Because of this fear, the United States once urged Japan to participate in the MD (missile defence) project.

These two characterizations of high technology are rather peripheral or macroscopic without touching on the internal properties of high technology. As we have argued above on emulation, one micro definition of high technology states that it introduces a new product through hybrid blending of two or more radically different technologies. We called this aspect of high technology 'hybridism' in the first agenda. Such hybrid mingling of different technologies often happens between a traditional technology and a frontier one.

Another micro definition regards high technology as a radically new technology that will change the power balance of an industry. When first introduced, high technology contains much uncertainty in assessing market potentials, so that it is usually rejected by established sectors of industry. A good example is the introduction of transistors. When transistors were invented, opinions about their market potential differed between vacuum tube manufacturers, such as GE and Westinghouse, and electronic instrument companies. The former group rejected transistors, and the latter accepted them, which resulted in a shift of power in the electronic industry, namely, the principal makers of transistors turned out to be lesser-known companies such as Texas Instruments and Motorola.

As mentioned in the first agenda, this peculiar characteristic of high technology is termed the 'minority regime' character: a minor player in an industry will suddenly overthrow the major players, literally overnight, and thus create a new power regime in an industry. The third micro feature of high technology is perhaps best called the 'fuzzy boundary property'. In high technology, the boundary between science and technology increasingly becomes blurred, as can be seen in the cases of biotechnology and superconductivity. This property is a ground for the economic definition of high technology, since a large amount of R&D investment is necessary.

Given the diverse characteristics of high technology, one may draw political implications. If we admit the economists' view of high technology as 'fuzzy boundary' that needs a huge R&D investment, we will eventually be compelled to hold the view that high technology will facilitate interdependent relations among nations. This argument is the prevalent logic that is commonly taken by the G-8 countries, which usually support international scientific and technological joint projects as symbols of international cooperation.

However, since high technology also has a hybrid nature, the hows and whys of hybrid mingling among different technologies remain uncertain until a new breakthrough occurs abruptly. International agreements for budget appropriation thus cannot be justified for such uncertain projects. So a country within an economic alliance should develop independently. This independent and self-financed effort naturally works as counter-inertia to destroy existing international cooperation.

At the level of private companies, technological cooperation takes the form of joint ventures, cross-licensing or even corporate alliances. Technological alliance among companies involves functional reciprocity. If two or more parties are more or less equal or homogeneous in the size of sales, technological strength, management skills, marketing capabilities, R&D activities etc., a cooperative relationship is easily formed, on the assumption that they will gain additional pay-offs from a plus-sum game. Here, interdependence is truly a relationship among equals. Then, if two or more parties clearly articulate where they are weak and where strong, cooperation among equals is a realistic solution.

However, if the conceivable pay-off matrix becomes of a zero-sum type when a new breakthrough is made by a company outside the corporate alliance, cooperation then leads to a clash. When this happens, companies have a choice: either to acquire a breakthrough patent by trading their own patents, or to absorb a breakthrough company through merger and acquisition with an overriding financial power. At the level of government, however, these choices cannot be taken. The reason is that a breakthrough is often civilian in nature and made by private enterprise. Therefore, government cannot control it. Rather, government moves to support it because it envisions that a new breakthrough will help the economy. Other governments regard such a move as a selfish counter-initiative to break the existing international harmony. Then, bashing of a targeted country starts again. For this reason, nation-to-nation cooperation becomes rather vulnerable.

The fourth agenda (paradox of mass production)

Technological declines are often pre-programmed and further exacerbated when a full market share is sought blindly. Technology is essentially predatory, so that without an appropriate policy, strong technology will sweep all market niches. When this happens, there quickly emerge two rigidities. One is the loss of motivation to search for new technology, and the other is the arrogance to believe that no contender could threaten in the near future. But technology is a highly uncertain entity, and no one can accurately forecast what will come next. This implies that techno-hegemony is always challenged and undermined. Japanese technologies once enjoyed pre-eminence in a wider range of civilian commodities which, in turn, overrode military technologies through a 'spin-on' process. Thus, if we follow the above logic, it is possible to suspect that Japan is on the verge of a declining path, even if the end of the path is not clearly discerned now. We have to avoid this possible doomsday.

The only solution is to put Japan in the midst of the fluidity of technological emulation. This avoids the excessive market share that would lead to technological stalemate and parochialism. We list two pillars of the solution. The first is to accelerate the so-called 'confrontational alliance', by which we mean an alliance among emerging technological 'enemies', such as South Korea, China and others. Technology moves ahead through a dead-heat competition. A dead-heat race presupposes enemies. Without enemies, no technological competition is possible. For this reason, it is a good policy not to let potential enemies fade out.

Industrial decline is partly caused by what we call the 'paradox of mass production'. It means that rational decisions often discourage technological endeavours. The extreme of rational decision in the area of productive technology is, of course, mass production. The following argument owes much to Michael Piore and Charles Sable, Robert Hayes and the late William Abernathy, and M. Dertouzos and others.[4]

Mass production gives a gross sum of profits if a product hits a market. Then, corporate management mobilizes all resources to perfect mass production. However, when a new product is introduced, a firm that depends too much on mass production starts declining. Burton Klein and others have pointed out such contradictory characteristics inherent in the corporate ideology of mass production.[5]

Another negative consequence of mass production is the development of sclerotic management ideology, what Robert Hayes and William Abernathy called the management orthodoxy. Managers tend to rely on analytical techniques rather than hands-on, real-time experience, and devote their efforts to short-time cost reductions and portfolio financial controls. Through these rational choices, they are increasingly alienated from the production lines and become myopic about technological trends. In short, mass production helped create modern executives who are coagulated with management orthodoxy. Because of management orthodoxy, it is hard to apply new technology in a firm where economic rationality prevails.

Conclusion

The technological position of today's Japan is unique in that its strength rests not in hard power but rather in soft power, with a strong emphasis on civilian sectors. Since the outset of modernization, Japan has regarded science and technology (in particular technology, rather than science) as an engine for national development. Today, the boundary between science and technology is becoming blurred, so that national investment in science and technology is investment for the future. Japan's national investment in science and technology is 3.5 per cent of GDP, the top ranking of all G-8 countries. Of those investments, 80 per cent are made by the private sector, and only the remaining 20 per cent is paid for by government. China is increasing its science and technology budget by 19 per cent annually, and the United States by 11 per cent. But Japan's annual increase is less than its economic growth, around 2.2 per cent to 2.7 per cent today.

Most advanced countries spend a good deal of their science and technology budgets on military R&D. According to the OECD's statistics for 2002, the United States spends half its national R&D for military purposes, whereas Germany spends 10 per cent, France 20 per cent and the UK 40 per cent. Japan is unique in that its science and technology budget is solely civilian. Japan spends 50 per cent of its science and technology budget on pure research. Of that, 20 per cent goes on energy-related R&D, of which half is nuclear energy R&D. Note that Japan's energy self-sufficiency is only 16 per cent and that nuclear energy accounts for 87 per cent of energy use.

Currently, Japan has neither an internationally acknowledged ideology nor a world-penetrating culture. However, the situation is not all bad, because Japan is a technological state with strength in both manufacturing technology and environmental technology. As to manufacturing technology, Japanese firms are becoming more globalized and manufacture in global markets. In doing so, Japanese firms have gradually acquired important know-how to handle the third agenda of vulnerability of international operation in high technology. They know that the only solution is to continue to take the lead while providing opportunities for technological donor countries to emulate Japanese manufacturing know-how. Toyota's hybrid engines and Honda's fuel-cell engines, involving joint projects with battery manufacturers, are good examples in point. With respect to environmental technology, Japan is a leading country and it is now learning know-how to avoid the pitfalls of the third agenda. We shall discuss this below.

Today's environmental issues are global in scope. Japan and the United Kingdom both strongly emphasize the importance of scientific and technological research on measuring data or monitoring global environmental changes. Third-world countries such as China and India oppose the handling of environmental issues only by industrially advanced countries. The United States did not join the Kyoto protocol. They all fear that an international agreement will slow down their economic growth. The ambiguity of cognitive legitimacy of environmental policy shapes global environmental issues to be a geopolitical agenda.[6]

Japan may be able to raise its political leverage if it is actively engaged in international politics for the global environment, departing from hitherto passive attitudes in following the conservative course taken by the United States, the United Kingdom and other industrialized countries. It is quite noteworthy that Germany has recently been showing a more radical stance with regard to the global environment. Germany has many socio-economic incentives for non-nuclear energies such as wind power, biodiesel, solar cells, etc. If Japan plays a major role in single-handedly passing on its superior environmental technology to countries that are seriously suffering from both the security and economic threats of deforestation, desertification and acid rain caused by CO_2 emissions, it will be able to increase its 'soft power'.[7]

As the recent International Energy Agency Energy Outlook of 2006 shows, there are three imperatives for the world's energy-saving and environmental concerns: a) diversifying fuel sources for transportation, b) increasing the use of nuclear energy, and c) reducing the energy consumption of household appliances, including air conditioning, heat insulation, personal computers, etc. In 2006, Japan announced the Third Basic Science and Technology Plan, where the above three points about energy as well as environmental conservation are clearly addressed. In the aftermath of the energy crises of 1974 and 1979, Japan developed fuel-saving and emission-control technologies for automobiles and manufacturing industries. It is forecast that for the next couple of decades China's automobile ownership will increase to a quarter of the world's total. Therefore, Japanese energy-saving and emission-control technologies could make a great contribution to helping China reduce current and future energy consumption. However, as we have discussed for the third agenda, technological cooperation needs careful management. Thus, we strongly advise Japan and China to come to an intellectual property agreement before the transfer of high technologies in the environmental sector.

Today, Japan's unique position of concentrating on civilian technology and global manufacturing and the soft-power enhancement of energy-saving and environmental technologies highlights how Japan overcomes the four agendas we have discussed. First, global challenges in both manufacturing and environmental technologies need endless emulous activities (the first agenda) because Japan should always go one step ahead while allowing the follower countries to emulate Japanese technologies. Second, offshore manufacturing and implanting of environmental technologies could avoid the inward looking of technological parochialism (the second agenda) and the vulnerability of technological cooperation (the third agenda). Third, since the paradox of mass production is based on a strong mind-set concerning national development only, without broader perspectives on technological survival in the world, the operation of global manufacturing and cooperation in environmental technologies could solve the fourth agenda.

To sum up, all technological agendas are interrelated, and the most important of all for Japan is not to stop emulous activities. Emulation is really of the essence for Japan to be a viable and dynamic country in the decades ahead.

Notes

1 'Emulation' implies technological 'copying' plus a drastic 'improvement'. See: Yakushiji 1985.
2 On techno-parochialism, a similar argument is found in Dertouzos, *et al.* (eds) 1990, Chapter 3.
3 See *Harvard Business Review*, July/August 1990.
4 See Piore and Sables 1984; Dertouzos *et al.* 1989; Yakushiji 1990.
5 See Klein1977.
6 See MacNeill, Winsemius and Yakushiji 1991.
7 See Nye 1990.

References

Dertouzos, Michael L. *et al.* (eds) (1990), *Made In America.* Cambridge: MA, MIT Press.
Klein, Burton H. (1977), *Dynamic Economics.* Cambridge, MA: Harvard University Press.
MacNeill, Jim, Pieter Winsemius and Taizo Yakushiji (1991), *Beyond Interdependence.* Oxford: Oxford University Press.
Nye, Joseph S. Jr. (1990), 'Soft Power', *Foreign Policy* 80, pp. 153–71
Piore, Michael and Charles Sables (1984), *The Second Industrial Divide.* New York: Basic Books.
Yakushiji, Taizo (1985), *The Dynamics of Techno-Emulation.* BRIE Working Paper No.15. Berkeley, CA: The Centre for International Studies, The University of California.
—— (1990), 'Policy, Corporate Ideology, and the Auto Industry', in John C. Campbell (ed.), *Entrepreneurship in a 'Mature Industry'*. Ann Arbor: The Centre for Japanese Study Publications, The University of Michigan.

4 Japanese contemporary politics

Towards a new interpretation

Takashi Inoguchi

Introduction

Speaking of 'the common sense of ordinary folk' on the fiftieth anniversary of the major governing party, the Liberal Democratic Party of Japan, Hidenao Nakagawa (2006), Secretary General of the party, had this to say. The three priorities those ordinary folk have in their daily lives are (1) sustenance of a community, (2) richness of hearts and minds, and (3) responsive and responsible politics on the basis of party manifestos and public opinion. By community he had in mind the traditional virtues of family, neighbourhood community, workplace community and national community. By richness of hearts and minds he had in mind the traditional virtues of tolerance, generosity, thoughtfulness and mindfulness. By responsible politics he had in mind the constructive interactions between ordinary folk and the party of government with regard to the party manifestos promulgated each year and at every election campaign.

In an interview with the *Yomiuri shimbun* he traced the origins and key threads of the Liberal Democratic Party at its fiftieth anniversary (Nakagawa 2006). Nakagawa says that the origins of the LDP are in anti-militarism. Ichiro Hatoyama, a veteran politician from the prewar period and head of the Democratic Party, fought against the military because the latter was not able to wave the banner of the glory of the nation effectively. Shigeru Yoshida, a veteran diplomat–bureaucrat and the head of the Liberal Party, fought against the military because the latter did not bring the nation to peace with the Allied Powers. Both parties represented the common sense of ordinary folk. These two parties got together in 1956 to establish the Liberal Democratic Party and thwart the Japan Socialist Party, which had united the left-wing and right-wing socialist parties to capture power in 1955. The Liberal wing of the party stressed economic reconstruction and development. The Democratic wing of the party stressed the glory of the nation. The half-century period of economic reconstruction and development was dominated by the Liberal wing of the Party in terms of policy priorities on economic and social policy. Its politics was carried out largely by the bureaucracy. Nakagawa underlined that now is not the time for bureaucrats but that people's deputies, i.e., politicians, must carry out the three wishes of ordinary folk. As people's deputies, politicians must be responsive to public opinion and responsible for policy performance.

Whether Nakagawa's succinct recapitulation of the history of the Liberal Democratic Party and his analysis of Japanese democratic politics is agreeable or not is left for my readers to decide. In this chapter I provide my version of LDP-led Japanese politics, and delineate key features of three distinctive phases.

Japanese political development since 1945 is best understood in terms of three periods:[1]

1   The period of military occupation and reconstruction (1945–60),
2   The period of high economic growth (1960–85), and
3   The period of accelerating globalization (1985–2006).

Each period is characterized by particular political institutions and key players. In order to locate the current period in context, it is necessary to recapitulate the earlier periods, even if only in outline. More than any other political party, the Liberal Democratic Party (LDP) dominates the political system in contemporary Japan. The LDP-dominated political system has two broad, salient characteristics: flexibility and adaptability. The LDP has created a framework that has adapted itself through two significant periods in Japan's history, the post-war reconstruction and the subsequent years of strong economic growth. Now, at the beginning of the twenty-first century, the party is striving to create a framework that is capable of adapting itself to the serious work of globalization. In this chapter, I discuss the characteristics of the LDP-dominated political system throughout these three periods, describing the LDP support base, priority policies, and the predominant government ministries, delineating public mood and concerns and comparing the LDP support base with that of the opposition parties.

Features of the LDP-dominated political system through history

Having been soundly defeated in the Second World War, Japan was occupied by Allied forces for seven years. The United States (specifically General Douglas MacArthur) led the Allies, occupying and reforming Japan by indirect, rather than direct, rule. This choice was based on a strong impression that the forces were dealing not with the Japanese, who had intrepidly resisted throughout a war they had almost no hope of winning, but with a Japanese people who welcomed the occupation forces warmly. Moreover, since the US government's top priority was the global confrontation with Communism, it was deemed preferable that as much of the actual governing as possible be turned over to the people of the occupied nation themselves. Few doubt that the foundation of Japan's contemporary political system was rebuilt during the period of occupation.[2] First, the groups in power that had led Japan into war were dissolved and purged. Second, most of the key bureaucrats and personnel, with the exception of war leaders and prominent bureaucrats who conspired with them, were retained. Third, restructuring of the political parties was undertaken mostly by younger bureaucrats who rose to the top during the occupation: middle-aged politicians who had been purged as war leaders or conspirators during the war and occupation, and younger politicians who emerged on the scene after the war. This restructuring paved the way for the LDP as a center-right party by 1955. Fourth, freedom of expression, labour unions, and a general election system emerged as part of the new framework put forth under occupation reforms, and the left wing was able to significantly expand its power as well. Fifth, Japanese citizens gradually adapted to the new framework, and the general election system in particular came to function as a means of conveying public opinion to politicians.

LDP adapts through the three periods

The following paragraphs discuss the items tabulated in Table 4.1, and show how the LDP adapted itself during the three periods.

The political priorities during the first period,, the period of occupation and reconstruction, formed the cornerstone of the political focus that later came to be called the Yoshida doctrine.[3] Based on pacifism, this doctrine renounced Japanese participation in war. The Japan–US Security Treaty was designed to continue the military aspects of occupation by Allied forces, leaving Japan markedly dependent

Table 4.1 Features of the LDP-dominated political system in the three historical periods

Military occupation and recon-struction	
LDP (predecessor) support base	Self-employed farmers, self-employed businessmen
Priority policies	Employment, energy, financing, obtaining foreign currency, industrial infrastructure
Predominant government ministry	Economic Planning Agency
Public sentiment and concerns	Survival
Reasons for supporting opposition parties	Platform for elimination of poverty, removal of military bases
Strong economic growth	
LDP support base	New middle-class masses
Priority policies	Macroeconomic policies, social policies
Predominant government ministries	Ministry of International Trade and Industry, Ministry of Finance, Ministry of Health and Welfare
Public sentiment and concerns	Desire for economic rebuilding
Reason for supporting opposition parties	Platform for peace and equality
Globalization	
LDP support base	Voters who appreciate optimism in the face of stresses from globalization
Priority policies	Value of currency, science and technology, gender, population
Predominant government ministries	Prime Minister and his Cabinet
Public sentiment and concerns	Desire for risk-sharing and optimistic approach to future
Reason for supporting opposition parties	Platform for community-based system with a more human touch

on the United States for security. Also devoted to economic growth, the Yoshida doctrine focused on reconstruction to boost Japan to a respected position within the international community. Initially, however, there was very strong domestic opposition to this doctrine during the occupation, and it took a great deal of work to merely incorporate it into the Japanese political structure.

This was a period of intense political conflict in Japan. Immediately after the war, extreme poverty drove a large portion of the population to oppose the government. As recovery and reconstruction began to gradually take hold, the center-right gained power, with strong support from the self-employed. This was in 1955. The transition to power was instrumental in the founding of the Liberal Democratic Party of Japan in 1955. A large class of landowning farmers was created by the farmland reforms instituted under the occupation, and support for the LDP increased even in outlying rural areas that had been at the heart of the massive prewar farmers' movement. The increasing support from self-employed businessmen in response to government subsidies and other frameworks fell under this umbrella, as well. Although it is true that the LDP was at times referred to as 'the provincial party', the vast majority of Japan was in fact provincial during the occupation. During this period, policy priorities revolved primarily around economic management policy, to ensure economic recovery and reconstruction through government regulation and administrative guidance designed to address various issues: guaranteeing the food supply; guaranteeing energy supplies (coal for thermal power, dams for hydroelectric power, etc.); the processes for obtaining corporate capital from banks and other institutions; and obtaining the foreign currency required to achieve this.

If one must point to a predominant ministry during this period, it would be the Economic Planning Agency (known at the time as the Headquarters for Economic Stability). The driving force behind this agency was the bureaucrats who had graduated from engineering departments and had experienced an economy mobilized for war during the 1930s. Methods of economic management did not change considerably between the war years and the period of occupation, and the social engineering concepts behind them were adapted from engineering studies. Okita Saburo is a perfect example of this. He believed that, whatever else the public might be concerned about, people's greatest need is for survival, and ensuring food supplies should be given highest priority. Those with vested interests lost everything in the war, and their assets changed hands overnight to become public property through occupation reform. In 1945, Japan had the lowest national income per capita of any country in East or Southeast Asia. The low standard of income and high unemployment rate drove popular opposition to the government. Rising from the ashes was a matter of survival for both the nation and the individual. Based on this popular sentiment against the government, opposition parties enjoyed strong support at this time. Occupation reforms served to strengthen corporate and governmental labour unions, and opposition parties used this energy to their advantage.

Whether in elections or routine Diet debate, political conflict was extremely contentious. There was already strong opposition in Japan to the country's military relationship with the United States. At the time, factions that felt that welcoming US military bases would involve Japan in war, or serve to invite war against Japan, held greater sway than those that felt it would discourage or prevent Japanese involvement in war. The party that would later become the LDP took the latter stance, while the Japan Socialist Party and the Japanese Communist Party took the former. Another aspect of political contention was the issue of whether building fundamental economic strength to promote national recovery and recon-struction should be given high priority or whether greater concern should be given to improving the household finances of Japanese families and individuals. The former was put forth by the group that would later become the LDP, and the Socialist Party and the Communist Party took the latter as their platform.

During the second period, the years of strong economic growth, Japan followed a path of bureaucracy-driven development. Under this model of development, bureaucrats took the lead in directing the strong momentum behind economic development to most effectively manage the national economy. Specifically, bureaucrats in government agencies administered research and development subsidies to promote technological innovation; took the lead in directing fiscal and financial policy; arranged corporate finance; administered subsidies for less competitive industrial sectors; and ensured a continuous government budget for building industrial infrastructure. Despite the term 'bureaucracy-driven', devel-opment was in fact led by a tripartite structure formed by government agencies, business, and the governing parties (the LDP in this case).

Under this structure, the relative positioning of policy was a routine matter and not terribly complicated, determined primarily through discussions and meetings. This was facilitated by similar opinions held by those in government agencies, business, and the governing parties on a host of questions: how to ensure that Japan not participate in war; how to maintain alliances with other nations; how to supply the Japanese people with food; whether or not it was possible to maintain supplies of energy; how to develop Japanese industrial products so that they were the most competitive on the global market; how to raise household incomes so that families could afford to own homes; how to ensure that all Japanese children were able to receive higher education; and how to ensure that the elderly were cared for in their twilight years.

It was also normal procedure for government agencies to present the general principles of policy drafted by themselves to governing parties and the business community. The fact that government agencies have at times been teased with the adage 'government overrules politics' illustrates just how strongly Japanese development was ultimately driven by the bureaucrats in government. Moreover, this bureaucracy-driven political structure did not appear suddenly: its roots lie in pre-modern history, modern history, and the Tokugawa period (1603–1867). It was at the end of the Tokugawa period that the *samurai* were disarmed and became bureaucrats living in castle towns. In contrast to the Chosun dynasty, which reigned in Korea, where men of letters and scholars became bureaucrats, in Tokugawa period Japan it was the warrior class who came to make up the bureaucracy.

Although the governing unit shifted from the feudal clan to the nation with the Meiji Restoration, the bureaucracy-driven political system itself remained intact.[4] A parliamentary democracy was introduced in stages after the Meiji Restoration, and politicians came to occupy the political landscape in addition to bureaucrats. Japanese politicians were not necessarily part of the bureaucracy, but had a difficult time taking action without the bureaucrats on their side – as illustrated by the fact that politicians originally emerged as a force in opposition to government, whereas bureaucrats represented the powers that be in the government. Although the Japanese constitution would seem to indicate that politicians hold a higher position than bureaucrats, this was not necessarily the case.

It was for this reason that, among LDP Diet members, there were politicians extolled as 'special interest/issue-specific legislators' who wielded considerable influence over policy, due to their career histories and experience in specialized areas of subcommittee work in party and Diet committees. Though farmers and self-employed businessmen formed the base of support for the LDP during this period, a new body of support for the party came from the new middle-class and 'new middle-class masses' that emerged as strong economic growth and the accompanying benefits spread throughout the country (Murakami, 1984). In the process, the relative importance of farmers and self-employed businessmen among LDP supporters steadily diminished. This serious issue, however, did not necessarily pose a critical problem for the LDP, since the majority of the Japanese people considered themselves among the new middle-class masses. The gradual change in the number of Diet seats the party secured in elections was based on the slight drop in the rate of LDP support.

The party's high-priority policies during this period were securing Japan's place among the advanced nations, as well as achieving the stable and competitive economic management that would make it possible to maintain this position. Specifically, macroeconomic management and social policy were the top priorities. While the priority of the former needs no further explanation, the LDP became more keenly aware of the need to bolster its social policies if it was to keep the new middle-class masses among its support base. This decision was based on the stagnation and downward shift in support for the LDP.

The predominant government ministries during this period were the Ministry of International Trade and Industry, the Ministry of Finance, and the Ministry of Health and Welfare. In relation to the composition of the population, the budget allocation for the Ministry of Health and Welfare was not overly sizable during this period, and initially one might not consider this ministry as especially dominant within the government. However, awareness of the importance of social policy was already rising sharply. As income levels rose, the majority of the population came to identify themselves as part of the new middle-class masses, and the elderly as yet accounted for a mere 30 per cent of the population. For these reasons, the importance of this ministry had not yet been recognized.

With regard to the support base for opposition parties, one would assume that the rise in income level, coupled with decline in the ratio of workers organized under labour unions, would lower the rate of support for opposition parties; but, with extreme fluctuation at intervals in the level of support for the governing parties, support for opposition parties rose considerably more than a few times during this period. The extreme fluctuation in the level of support can be attributed to the fact that the opposition parties were able at times to attract a significant portion of the massive block of new middle-class masses to their side. While the opposition parties moved closer to the political trajectory of the governing parties, it is also true that too much similarity between multiple parties can cause conflicts. It is equally true that the constant appeal by opposition parties for greater emphasis on social policies prompted the governing parties to prioritize social policies, and the opposition parties' advocacy of pacifism caused the governing parties to give greater weight to their policy of strengthening alliances with other nations. Though the support base for the opposition parties came from the social strata among the new middle-class masses that valued pacifism and equality, this support faded in more than a few mass-production/mass-consumption industries that acquired foreign currency as market liberalization steadily advanced. Pacifism can lead to protectionism, and this tendency diluted the influence of this variety of principled stance. However, it is in the nature of politics that governing parties at times lose to opposition parties. There is no shortage of scandals involving bribes, corruption, and slips of the tongue in the normal course of things. It is these mis-steps that allow for significant progress by the opposition parties.

The third period to be examined is that of globalization, which spans from 1985 to the present. It was in 1985 that the Plaza Accord was signed by the G7 nations. The Plaza Accord was a revolutionary agreement that normalized purchases of one currency in another currency. Before this, goods and service trading had been the norm, with very little currency trading taking place. In the single year from 1985 to 1986, however, currency trading was 50 to 100 times higher than goods and service trading, and has remained at this level ever since. Dramatically promoting financial integration on a global scale, the Plaza Accord symbolizes globalization.[5]

Globalization ignores national borders; it divides national economies; and it facilitates the merger of the highly competitive. The less competitive gradually slide to lower and lower income levels. This increasing intensity of division and reintegration is what defines the period of globalization. In its broadest sense, globalization is constantly occurring. With revolutionary progress in computer technology, and goods transported daily by air, the momentum behind this phenomenon gained further strength at the end of the twentieth century.

Against this backdrop, where do governing parties find their support base? If the parties that seek to govern continued to stage a frontal attack on, or obvious opposition to, globalization, they would place themselves in a tenuous position. Moreover, globalization will move into every aspect of policy. The governing parties cannot merely accept this inevitability; they must also continuously strive to innovate technology, improve efficiency, and increase competitiveness. The primary concern with regard to the LDP support base must be the companies that continue to compete internationally and an organizational structure that will support these companies.

Accelerating globalization

In the light of recent events, France provides an enlightening comparison with Japan. Both countries are described as having a strong tradition of state-run leadership. In Japan, the Postal Privatization Bill passed the Diet. Though this achievement took longer than many expected, Japan Post, the corporation that runs the world's largest postal savings system, had taken the first step toward privatization. The bill prompted strong opposition even from within the LDP itself and, in a memorable election campaign, Prime Minister Junichiro Koizumi dissolved the Lower House for an election that he called a referendum on the issue of postal privatization, purging the group within the LDP that opposed privatization, and culminating in an overwhelming victory for the LDP (Inoguchi 2007). Globalization demands deregulation and smaller government, but Japan's long tradition of bureaucracy-driven development has slowed progress in both of these areas. For competitive Japanese companies that have already shifted their energy and resources to international development, the country's deregulation is lagging considerably behind, and what progress has been made is limited in scope. Though the US government is also aware of its own problems in adapting to globalization, the United States seems to find it preferable to demand that other countries loosen regulations and/or deregulate rather than demand much of its own uncompetitive domestic companies. The US government hoped that the Japanese government would deregulate more quickly. Sensing that the time was right, Prime Minister Koizumi took a major gamble on this issue. In order to bring public opinion around to favoring globalization, the issue was skilfully framed as a question of confidence in the Prime Minister, which led to election victory. In France, Prime Minister Dominique de Villepin, who had fought to enact a law allowing for the hiring of young people for an initial probationary period, was ultimately forced to withdraw the law due to a massive and sustained campaign of street protests. An attempt to lower the high unemployment rate among young people in France, the law was a compromise proposal designed to promote employment of young people by mitigating French labour laws, which make it difficult to fire an employee once he or she has been hired. However, embracing their social democratic ideals and customs, most of the country's citizens, not just the young people, demanded that the law be withdrawn. The country's prevalent social democratic customs, as well as its strong government regulation of corporations, are an impediment to a nimble response to the challenges globalization poses. We are beginning to see French capital leaving the country. Although the law described above was intended both to prevent this capital flight and to promote the employment of young people, Prime Minister de Villepin's penchant for secretive and independent action ultimately prompted fierce opposition.

Electoral support bases of the LDP

In a period of globalization, where does the LDP find its base of support? The Japanese citizens who supported the LDP during this period were those who sympathized with the resolve of the leaders to take an optimistic and aggressive approach to blazing new trails in the face of future uncertainties presented by globalization.[6] They were won over by the enthusiasm and courage in these leaders' willingness to take risks. The majority of the population has a vague sense that, despite the fact that government deregulation and market liberalization, symbolized by postal privatization, may seriously impact their own employment and lives, Japan will face a difficult future without these changes. This public sentiment has been based on Prime Minister Koizumi's unparalleled enthusiasm and courage in taking on these risks himself. This sentiment was further reinforced by the Prime Minister's style of strategically and skilfully expressing carefully thought-out ideas in a few words during the election campaign. In this sense, the body of support for the LDP comes more from those individuals with a strong belief that Japan should now venture optimistically into the vast uncertainty of the future, rather than from a group of people characterized by similar sociological attributes.

High-priority policies have shifted from macroeconomic management to those designed to alter economic standards and regulations as Japan faces the challenges presented by the irreversible advance of globalization. Equally important are policies that address financial relief for the less competitive in society who are left behind in the rough seas of globalization, as well as programs to help these people maintain their standard of living without losing hope for the future. In many respects, Japan has yet to establish a safety net, and even in some areas where there would appear to be such a safety net, we are beginning to see signs of stress. The social policies (the pension system, social welfare, nursing care, health care, etc.) put in place during the years of strong economic growth, when young people made up a significant proportion of the country's population, are posing an economic strain due to the considerable change in the demographics of the population and the waning of economic growth. The lack of gender equality is striking, and any change must defy social mores and prejudices. It is clear that, first and foremost, revolutionary change in corporate culture is necessary.

Resolving these issues depends on a solid approach to reversing the decline in Japan's population, a trend that had already manifested itself in 2005. The notably high trend of childless couples is closely related to each of these other issues. Employment, education, facilities, family, neighbourhoods, and other issues cannot be resolved simply by adjusting the amount of money the government allocates to addressing them. Among advanced democratic nations, it is a matter of routine to allocate significant funds to policies on which leaders have agreed a basic course of action. Globalization, however, has brought to the fore a number of issues that had not previously posed significant problems, and competing in an environment of globalization without addressing these issues is becoming increasingly difficult. For this reason, with the exception of deregulation and cutting national government expenditure, we are seeing less policy emphasis on the Ministry of Land, Infrastructure and Transport, the Ministry of Health, Labour and Welfare, the Ministry of Education, Culture, Sports, Science and Technology, the Ministry of Internal Affairs and Communications and other ministries that have traditionally been allocated large portions of the national budget. Naturally, issues taken up by individual extraordinary ministers within the cabinet may at times bring certain policies to the fore. This has been the case with the move to postal privatization endorsed by the Minister of State for Economic and Fiscal Policy and with the prominence of the position of Minister of State for Gender Equity and Social Affairs. Only ministers of state can make a certain ministry or agency predominate. At the larger ministries and agencies, bureaucrats offer strong resistance to political maneuvering, and government agency culture is not conducive to immediate decision making or swift action. With policy allocation a matter of long-established routine, it is difficult to marshal the will at agencies to redesign policy. This is another reason why the prime minister and cabinet positions are assuming increasingly prominent roles in driving government policy. On an increasing number of matters, the cabinet and the prime minister's office are now more directly in charge than bureaucrats.

As this indicates, the cabinet and the prime minister have been the dominant government agencies during the globalization period. Although there are significant systemic differences between presidential and prime ministerial systems, globalization serves to position prime ministers as presidents in countries that have no such elected official. In countries with presidents that play a merely symbolic role, the prime minister acts as president. With prime ministers who play no more than a symbolic role, ministerial secretaries, campaign strategists, or political consultants work behind the scenes on issues related to globalization. Against a backdrop of critical public opinion, the slightest statement by a politician is carefully weighed and measured against anticipated negative public reaction. Even the specialists who carefully craft these political statements are not necessarily guaranteed success: even in these circumstances, their chance is most often no greater than fifty-fifty. However, in the 23 April 2006 Seventh District by-election in Chiba prefecture for a vacant seat in the Lower House, it was clear that Prime Minister Koizumi, despite his boldness and skilful campaigning, had lost his edge to the careful calculations of Ichiro Ozawa, the new face of the Democratic Party of Japan, who put greater emphasis on mobilizing voters and giving a human touch to his campaign.

During this period of globalization, where do the opposition parties find their support base? The transition in the Lower House electoral system from mid-sized to smaller electoral districts was significant, creating serious structural change under which both the governing and opposition parties vie for a single seat in a single electoral district. No less significant, with government spending strained to the limit, the status quo of granting large-scale public works expenditures and subsidies in the form of local grants from central government to local government, or budgetary subsidies to implement large-scale social policy as an agent of the central government, is no longer viable. In order to obtain public works expenditures or subsidies, in matching funds form, local government must secure budgets equal to or greater than the expenditure disbursed by central government. Pork-barrel spending and other funding schemes will no longer come from the central government, at least not on a regular basis. Voters are no longer enticed by the promises of Diet members to bring money back from central government. In fact, these promises are more often met by troubled expressions from voters in the home district.[7]

What is it, then, that wins voters' support for a politician? The political message now serves to organize a body of support behind a party, and is what determines which demographic will be mobilized. Ozawa Ichiro's slogan in the Chiba by-election, for example, was 'From the line of vision of the people'. To illustrate: on the campaign trail he spoke standing on a pile of crates, and he rode his bicycle around his district to speak directly with the people. He did not emulate Koizumi's respected boldness, skilful rhetoric, or method of giving speeches to large groups of onlookers from the top of a campaign truck. Ozawa had a great sense of competition with Koizumi. He pursued a campaign strategy of asking for voter support at face-to-face meetings with each of the organizations in the district. This style is referred to as street-side campaigning. Not so long ago, street-side campaigning was the forte of the LDP, while exaggerated rhetoric was what the opposition parties were known for. Despite explicit confrontation on political issues, with little chance of opposition parties taking the actual reins of government, these parties were content to stay with grandeur and overstatement, resigning themselves to a permanent position out of power. Today, however, the situation has changed. The primary support for the sweeping LDP policy vision comes from critical voters and those who are anxious about an uncertain future, and the party appeals to these groups with its rhetoric and an image of courage and energy. The reason for choosing this strategy over detailed explanations of policy on the campaign trail is that the public finds it difficult to comprehend concrete policies in the face of inevitable cutbacks in government spending, increasingly strong signs that the tax rate will rise, and intensifying international competition. By contrast, opposition parties have forgone the strategic exaggeration conventionally adopted by parties resigned to being permanently in opposition. Taking advantage of the fact that they themselves are not in charge of government policy today, they have adopted a strategy of setting themselves slightly apart from the realm of day-to-day policy, emphasizing instead the human touch: shaking hands and speaking with as many voters as possible throughout their districts, listening to their troubles, providing a sympathetic ear, and creating the impression that they are the ones who really represent the people.

LDP strategies under globalization and their limitations

The increasing intensity of globalization has created a distinction between political and election campaign strategies, effectively narrowing the range of political options that politicians are able to choose from. Globalization emphasizes the economic unit, which exists in an environment of cutthroat competition. One of the only political strategies available is to take an optimistic approach and face globalization head on. Human activity, which for more than a century has been organized in units representing sovereign nations, is being reorganized at a dramatic speed into units at the global level.[8] Resisting this reorganization is an exercise in futility; it is not something that can be done, given the pace of progress in human technology.

What is possible is to determine the speed at which the market will globalize and which specific sectors will be primary focal points of globalization. Political strategies will not stem the tide of globalization, and fragmented policy will only succeed in giving one's own side avenues for retreat. This type of policy most often serves only to slow down or delay striking back. Retreat tactics are, however, extremely important politically. They also represent an emotional 'social safety net'. Even without any obvious major economic significance, retreat tactics are a social and political necessity in an era of globalization. Without these strategies, public support tends quickly to hollow out. LDP support could conceivably implode. It is for precisely this reason that election campaign strategies must embrace the public, speaking decisively to people's worries, troubles, dreams, sentiments, dissatisfaction, complaints, and the animosities of the moment. These strategies must be crafted to soothe the concerns of the public. At the same time, politicians must constantly take action in pursuit of the efficiency, profitability, harmony, and transparency that globalization demands so relentlessly. Without this strategic combination, we cannot expect timely progress on any number of battlefronts. Accordingly, politicians on the campaign trail must not only soothe concerns, but also at times must inspire the public as well.

Globalization may bring with it hardship and challenges; nevertheless, attempting to evade this phenomenon is not an option. Workers' skill sets (technical and organizational) are important tools for increasing efficiency, and corporate entities and other organizations must provide employees with career training. Technological innovation is a significant factor in creating profitability, and more money must be spent on science and technology, in the area of research and development. The greater the uncertainty, the more capital must be invested for the future. Rules and regulations, and the ability to properly enforce them, are a large part of achieving harmony. Harmony is not always created on a whim or through empathy; ensuring harmony within the wider society by establishing rules and principles is also important. As corporations need a social identity, so do political parties. Self-regulation is an important aspect of transparency. Organizations must make it possible for those outside the group to gain a clear understanding of the organizations' activities and objectives, as well as the scope and method of their activities. This is equally true for companies, for governments, and for political parties.

How successful is the LDP likely to be in implementing these strategies under globalization? The party may be limited by three notable factors. First is the significant lack of the required type of leadership. Few people at the grassroots level of the LDP are able to take on the risks involved while at the same time displaying an understanding of public sentiment, attracting voters, and soothing people's concerns. LDP politicians are more often capable of only one half of the equation. There is a strong tendency to seek consensus and to profess satisfaction when setbacks are encountered before the desired results are achieved. This outcome is explained away as the unfortunate result of group decision making. Globalization generates societies based on expertise. The primary goal of every globalization strategy must therefore be to beat out the competition through new expertise and, to do this, leaders must be capable of executing the assessment–decision–implementation cycle practically and effectively.

During the period of strong economic growth (and, naturally, during the occupation/reconstruction period as well), the LDP was able relatively easily to adopt a mode of consensus under a style of leadership that invoked trust in the idea that there was no need for fear so long as the entire country worked together. The LDP General Affairs Council operated on consensus-driven decision making, requiring continuous discussions until the last lone member opposed to any proposal had been brought round to agreement with the rest of the group. This was not a majority vote system. Globalization, however, requires speed, and it is indicative of this that the LDP General Affairs Council abandoned the consensus method on the issue of postal privatization in 2005. This shift in style was made possible by Prime Minister Junichiro Koizumi's leadership. Koizumi, an atypical member of the LDP, is no ordinary leader. He exhibits the bold attitude needed to accept risk and shoulder responsibility, and has the courage and energy required to achieve his goals. The LDP must focus on nurturing among its ranks more politicians capable of this type of leadership.

The second limitation is the matter of competence. The Republicans in the United States are often said to lack competence, while the Democrats are said to lack a coherent stance. Despite the Republicans being the party currently in power, the US public look at the appointments made to high government office and are often left wondering why there are not more people in the Republican Party committed to serving more responsibly. The Democratic Party, by contrast, is often likened to an assortment of non-governmental organizations. While the Democrats are adept at making acute arguments on the environment, energy, civil rights, gender, terrorism, corporate donations, tax cuts, and a variety of other issues, many question their coherence as a party unit. To a certain extent, this same comparison holds true between the LDP and the Democratic Party of Japan (DPJ). In the face of globalization, the LDP must work to further boost the competence of its members. It is obviously unreasonable to expect every one of the hundreds of Diet members to reach this level. As representatives of the people, Diet members serve a diverse array of people, which itself is not problematic. The fact is that, of the hundreds of representatives, a mere 10 per cent leave the impression of being well-rounded politicians, effective both politically and in terms of policy making, with a good sense of style, and capable of effectively executing measures that address globalization-related issues. We have reached the end of an age in which simply intermediating, handing out subsidies, and delegating real responsibility to civil servants was sufficient, as it was during the period of strong economic growth. The age of globalization has rapidly reduced the significance of all three of these previously sacred characteristics.[9] A public opinion survey taken in 1986 in Mito City, Ibaraki prefecture notably found a high rate of approval for the provision of services (acquisition of subsidies and individual favors) to home districts. In the survey, 14.7 per cent of respondents indicated that they had benefited from the former, while 3.8 per cent had benefited from the latter. By contrast, the Diet survey conducted prior to the 2003 Upper House election clearly indicated that almost no services were being provided to home districts. In this survey, only 0.09 per cent of respondents reported receiving the former and only 0.03 per cent reported receiving the latter.[10]

The third limitation of the LDP, the elimination of giving real responsibility to civil servants, overlaps somewhat with the second, described above. The LDP has achieved immense success by depending wholeheartedly on the class of bureaucrats who, basically, derived from the *samurai*. During the period of strong economic growth, the bureaucrats facilitated a structure that provided major support for the activities of politicians. As a group, the bureaucrats have compensated for the many elements that politicians have lacked – playing the role of the brains behind the curtain, which is why Kasumigaseki (the place where many ministry buildings are located) is considered to be the LDP brains trust. A government cannot, however, afford this type of structure in a globalized world. Bureaucrats tend to prefer middle-of-the-road, common-sense solutions. While they demonstrate technocratic competence, novel and imaginative ideas come few and far between. Bureaucrats tend to strive for simple honesty within a group-oriented, lasting legal and regulatory framework, attributes that derive from the *samurai* traditions of the Tokugawa period. The bureaucracy-driven political system is a Japanese tradition dating from this period of history. The question now becomes how successful will politicians be in extracting themselves from this tradition. The extreme unpredictability of globalization renders this system rather ineffective. In a period of globalization, understanding and embracing human emotion and public sentiment becomes of primary importance, and the *samurai* system does not translate well under these conditions. The time is ripe for politicians to take the reins. The majority of LDP politicians, however, have in the past depended excessively on civil servants, and they must cease to do so if they are to continue to be successful. Breaking the dependence on bureaucrats in the area of legislation requires a break from conventional wisdom on the part of politicians. They must become more technocratically competent than the bureaucrats themselves. Conceptual breakthroughs come in flashes of insight into how to appease the forces of globalization, use them to advantage, and rebuild the system. These insights must be integrated into a package of political measures that are then presented to bureaucrats, offered for public discussion, and passed into legislation. This is the role politicians have historically played, and it will become increasingly important in the period of globalization.

The LDP in the context of political opposition

How will the LDP position itself during this period of globalization? Three factors will have a definitive effect on determining where the LDP will stand during this period. First, globalization tends to pull both governing and opposition parties to the centre, which requires tactical retreat on a variety of issues and destabilizes the ruling party's position. The debate between liberalism and conservatism is a major factor in election campaigns. In the 2005 Lower House election, the LDP argued the liberal position on the issue of postal privatization, while the DPJ took a clear conservative stance on the issue. As far back as the 1910s (and, of course, during the period of strong economic growth), conservatism long argued the line that people must pull themselves up by their bootstraps. This principle will not be easily abandoned, no matter what the dictates of globalization. Conservatism is used as a political platform on the issue of the income gap. Japan's economic recession brought the income gap into the spotlight, with a distinction between regular and temporary employees tolerated at Japanese companies struggling with bad debt and financial bottom lines. The obvious disparity created when some temporary workers bore a heavier workload than their tenured counterparts, and at less than half the wages, fuelled dissatisfaction. The fact that companies saddled with an extremely high number of older, highly paid employees were able to hire only a very small number of young workers as regular employees further exacerbated the issue of the income gap. This phenomenon is at times referred to as the emergence of a new class society. Japan, however, does not have to deal with extremely high unemployment rates as some developed countries do. This will allow Japan to regain its footing and resolve the income gap, promote consumption among senior citizens with large savings, and restore employment among young adults, once rapid economy recovery takes hold. The fact that fixed assets taxes and inheritance taxes remain extremely high keeps the income gap from becoming too extreme in Japan.

Second, the series of reforms passed in the 1990s included the Public Offices Election Law and established a basic framework under which only one candidate is selected from each voting district. These reforms created a situation under which one party could obtain significantly more Diet seats even without winning significantly more votes overall. In the 2005 Lower House election, the LDP and DPJ secured very different numbers of Diet seats, although the margin between the numbers of votes for the parties was not substantial. Since then, both the LDP and the DPJ have moved further toward the centre as they have negotiated legislation. In the big picture, there has not been a significant change in the center-right position of the LDP and the center-left position of the DPJ. However, the faction further to the right within the DPJ has in the recent past taken positions even further to the right than the LDP. So long as this remains the case and Ichiro Ozawa continues to represent the DPJ, LDP leaders must be careful not to swing from the right.

This is well illustrated by the public battle spearheaded by Jean-Marie Le Pen, the French politician on the far right in that country's center-right coalition. The governing parties are struggling to find solutions as they realize that high rates of unemployment among young adults, strained government social spending with no room for additional cutbacks, and the flight of corporations out of France are structural issues with no ready political answers. Dominique de Villepin suffered a setback in 2005 in the face of explosive protests when he attempted to enact a law which would enable employees to hire part time and thus less than fully paid workers. In contrast to then Interior Minister Nicolas Sarkozy's aggressive attacks on and scornful attitude toward the groups of young people and immigrants taking direct political action in the streets, the far right Le Pen has appealed strongly to those on the center-right who vigorously oppose direct political action. It is, however, up to the ruling party itself to appeal to this massive group of protestors. It is not surprising that the center-right ruling party would not want to shift from the right and leave itself open to attack from both the left and the right. This hesitation also holds true for the LDP. The memory of Ichiro Ozawa as leader of the New Conservative Party scuttling a coalition with the LDP, which contributed directly to Prime Minister Keizo Obuchi's death, comes quickly to mind. Prime Minister Yoshiro Mori, who succeeded Obuchi, being forced to resign following his declaration that 'Japan is God's country', is another recent memory, as is Prime Minister Junichiro Koizumi's promise immediately after taking office to make a yearly visit to Yasukuni Shrine. Since leaving the New Conservative Party and becoming the representative of the DPJ in the spring of 2006, Ichiro Ozawa has been complicating matters for the right-wing faction of the LDP by taking positions further to the right than the LDP on the income gap and the subject of reform of the Fundamental Law of Education.

The third factor determining the LDP stand during globalization is related to international security. With the end of the Cold War, the United States has become the world's lone superpower and, as Japan's neighbours have asserted themselves more vigorously, the difference between the positions of the LDP and the DPJ on the Japan–US Security Treaty are seemingly less significant than the differences between factions within each of these parties. There is, in fact, considerable overlap between the LDP and DPJ on this issue. Pacifism governs much of the LDP stance. The constitutional reform proposed by the LDP does not alter that document's original spirit of pacifism, nor does it suggest any change to Paragraph 1 of Article 9. The reform proposes to change the wording of Article 9, Paragraph 2 from 'war potential will not be maintained' to '[Japan] will maintain Self-Defense Forces'. Since the country already maintains this type of force, the proposed reform does nothing more than affirm the status quo, and notably remains true to the basic tenets of pacifism. Nationalism governs much of the stance not only of the LDP, but also of the DPJ. The reform to the Fundamental Law of Education proposed by the governing LDP–Komeito coalition has put pressure on the DPJ from the right. Highlighting the issue of patriotic spirit and approving the introduction of public authority into the private realm through education, this reform has served to push Japanese politics in the direction generally preferred by the extreme right wing. The strength of public opinion on these two issues, however, differs slightly. Some 80 per cent of the public supporting the left strongly favor pacifism, while 60 per cent of supporters of the right say they strongly favor a nationalistic stance. The issues involved with US military realignment in Japan, as well as those involved with participation in international missions (peace-keeping missions, foreign aid, etc.) are closely associated with the advocacy of pacifism. This is the reason behind relocating US military bases currently situated amid towns in Okinawa to offshore locations along the Okinawa coast. Offshore locations are intended to minimize the amount of land to be requisitioned for base construction, as well as to minimize the opposition to base realignment. This tactic is different from that taken by the South Korean government, which relocated the US military bases in Seoul to suburbs outside of the city, a move that invited fierce protest from the owners of the land requisitioned for base use. The issues of Yasukuni Shrine, Takeshima Island and the four northern islands are also closely associated with the advocacy of patriotism. The Yasukuni Shrine visits by the Prime Minister appear designed to satisfy supporters on the right. Japan's resolute cooperation as a US ally with the military realignment triggered by the major shift in US military strategy was motivated by a desire to avoid provoking Japanese nationalism-driven anti-American sentiment. What was meant to appease the Japanese right, however, has sharply angered the country's neighbours. Fierce opposition to these moves raged in South Korea and China, making even top-level government meetings between the countries impossible for a time. Although this is in the realm of conjecture, LDP policy, so sharply focused on the United States, is thought to have created blind spots in other areas, as the party has moved to establish a US-led security structure that integrates the three branches of the Japanese Self-Defense Forces and develops a capacity for joint US–Japan military missions. The persistent anti-Japanese sentiment among people in neighbouring countries undoubtedly took the Koizumi administration by surprise.

The Iraq War is another example of blind spots created by excessive focus in one particular area. Until just before Iraq was invaded by the United States, Iraqi President Saddam Hussein apparently believed the possibility of a war waged by Iran in reprisal for the ten-year war of the 1980s to be a more likely threat, and waged a war of rhetoric, insisting up until the Iraq War began that the Iraqi military would destroy Iran even if the US military intervened. (It turns out that this bluster came from Saddam Hussein's refusal to show weakness vis-à-vis Iran precisely because Iraq was not in a position of strength at the time.) This and the statements made by Saddam Hussein as he faced trial, are evidently quite credible. By contrast, the US government had apparently decided to use possession of weapons of mass destruction (WMD) as the reason for military intervention from the outset. The UN weapons inspectors had to leave Iraq without finding WMD, and still the United States was unable to bear in mind the bluster of Saddam Hussein displayed against Iran. Needless to say, only more expansive rounds of research would have brought these issues to light. This illustrates the lesson that concentrating too extensively on one notion when determining actions with regard to other countries creates fertile ground for stunning miscalculations that do not look beyond the assumptions made.

In light of the circumstances described above, the question remains of the form these factors will take. One extremely interesting piece of data that sheds light on this question is the AsiaBarometer. The AsiaBarometer is a project coordinated by the author that examines public opinion in the Asia region, shedding light on the day-to-day life of ordinary people in these countries. A survey conducted in the summer of 2004 in Association of Southeast Asian Nations (ASEAN) countries, as well as Japan, South Korea, and China, posed the following question: 'Do you think the US has a positive effect or a negative effect on your country?' Thirty per cent of Japanese respondents cited a positive affect, with 32.2 per cent citing a negative affect; while 42.4 per cent of South Koreans surveyed responded positively, with 30.7 per cent citing a negative effect. It is commonly said that Japan toes the pro-US line, while there is a high degree of anti-American sentiment in South Korea. This data, however, suggests a difference between the views at the grassroots level and at the governmental level. The reasons behind the perception among many Japanese that the US has a negative impact on Japan are multiple. In addition to the traditional anti-American sentiment that arises from the security pact between the two countries, others see a negative effect in the mergers in all sectors that stem so readily from global integration in the financial market during globalization, as well as the strong influence of globalization on the global governance sector. All of this indicates that the anti-American sentiment among Japanese does not fall along a left-wing/right-wing paradigm, but instead lies with a fairly widespread perception of the negative effect of the US on Japanese autonomy.[11] Not only does this type of strong anti-American sentiment undermine the LDP's consistently cautious support for US military realignment and the dispatch of SDF forces to Iraq; it has also underscored nationalistic sentiment to effectively stem an increase in the perception of the US as parent to Japan regarding issues such as market liberalization and government deregulation.

The emphasis on a patriotic spirit in Japan, however, has also fuelled an intense backlash from South Korea and China, which has in turn served to further harden sentiment on the part of Japanese nationalists. Nationalists who believe that Japan should refuse to agree with anything neighbouring countries say also strongly reject any coalition with ASEAN countries, South Korea, and China that can be seen as requiring concessions to China, viewing this as the revival of the traditional China-centric structure under which that country required tribute to be paid by other countries.[12]

Why does a coalition of this sort bring to the Japanese mind this traditional hierarchical relationship among the countries of the region? Whenever bilateral free trade agreements with East Asia and Southeast Asia are forged, China is seen as benefiting from the terms to be met by developing countries with regard to world trade mechanisms; as such, China has not been required to submit detailed implementation plans for the liberalization of trade at the time the agreements have been signed. Japan, on the other hand, as a developed nation, has been obliged to submit these detailed plans. This disparity has caused long delays in negotiations on bilateral free trade agreements. This occurred at a time when Japan had yet to fully recover from recession, leaving a strong impression that China had clearly been more successful in quickly establishing active commercial relationships with the ASEAN-plus-South Korea bloc. The agreements signed gave rise to the perception that these countries were submitting to China, which had its counterparts doing its bidding. In *Suishu* ('History of Sui'), it is recorded that, at the beginning of the seventh century, Japanese Prince Shotoku sent Sui dynasty Emperor Yangdi a letter declaring Japan an equal to the Sui Dynasty, and that the Emperor Yangdi did not take kindly to this at all. Later, at the beginning of the nineteenth century, the Ching dynasty *Jia ging Huidian* listed Vietnam, Korea, and England as countries paying tribute to China, while France, the Netherlands, and Japan were listed as commercial partners. This distance continued between the fourteenth and nineteenth centuries, during which time Japan maintained no bilateral relations with neighbouring countries – the only notable relationships at all being commercial ties. This stance did not necessarily prevent friendly relations, but the lack of modern means for crossing the seas naturally kept Japan at a significant distance from the mainland.

Notes

1 Inoguchi 2006a.
2 Inoguchi 2005a.
3 Inoguchi 2005b.
4 Inoguchi 2005a.
5 O'Brien 1992.
6 Acemoglu and Robinson 2006; Inoguchi 2004.
7 Inoguchi 2007.
8 Inoguchi 2004.
9 Inoguchi and Iwai 1987.
10 Mainichi Shimbun/Tokyo University, *Joint Survey Results*, July 2003 (unpublished).
11 Sekioka, 2004; Mikuni, 2006.
12 Nakanishi, 2005.

References

Acemoglu, Daron and James Robinson (2006), *Economic Origins of Dictatorship and Democracy*. Cambridge: Cambridge University Press.

Inoguchi, Takashi (2005a), *Japanese Politics: An Introduction*. Melbourne: Trans Pacific Press.

—— (2005b), *Kokusai Seiji no Mikata* (Perspectives on International Politics). Tokyo: Chikuma Shobo.

—— (2006a), 'Social Capital in East Asia', paper prepared for the AsiaBarometer Workshop and Symposium.

—— (2007) 'Federalism and Quasi-Federal Tradition in Japan', in Baogang He, Brian Gallighan and Takashi Inoguchi (eds), *Federalism in Asia*. London: Edward Elgar pp. 266–89.

—— and Tomoaki Iwai, 1987. *Zoku giinno Kenkyuu (A Study of Legislative Tribes)*, Tokyo: Nihionkeizaishinbunsha.

Mikuni, Akio (2006), *Kuroji tengoku* (The Trade Surplus Heaven). Tokyo: Bungeishunjusha.

Murakami, Yasusuke (1984), *Shin Chakan Taishu no Jidai* (The Age of New Middle-Class Masses: An Anatomy of Post-war Japan). Tokyo: Chuokoronsha.

Nakagawa, Hidenao (2006), 'Hoshushugi interview (Interviewing on Conservatism)', *Yomiuri shimbun*, 1 December, p. 4.

Nakanishi, Terumasa (2005), *Teikoku to shiteno Chugoku* (China as Empire). Tokyo: Kodansha.

O'Brien, Richard (1992), *Global Financial Integration: The End of Geography*. London: Pinter.

Sekioka, Hideyuki (2004), *Kyohi dekinai Nihon* (Japan that Cannot Decline). Tokyo: Bunshun Shinsho.

5   Japan as a changing civil society

Public philosophy and the three-sector model

Toshihisa Nagasaka

Introduction

One of the most significant changes in the last ten years in Japan is the increase in the registration of non-profit organization (NPO) corporations as legal entities. With enforcement of the Nonprofit Activities Promotion Law in December 1998, the number of NPO registrations had reached more than 30,000 by the beginning of 2007. Since 2003 more than 5,000 civil society organizations have been registered as NPOs annually.

The civil society (NPO) sector[1] has established recognition as having a new and important role in the contemporary economic social system. Historically, it has played an important role in the formation of nation-states, democracy and the constitution of the welfare state. The worldwide network of NPOs (NGOs) has influenced the existing world system and at present is coming to play a new part in it.

This chapter examines the current implications of the new NPO sector and reports its state in Japan. The formation of the NPO sector essentially transforms Japan's structural economic social system and indicates the possibility of opening it up.

The chapter first describes the growth in the last ten years and the state of management of Japan's NPO sector. Next follow discussions on the new 'public philosophy' in Japanese academia with respect to the expansion of the NPO sector. This is followed by an examination of the implications of the NPO sector from the international point of view in terms of the issues of contemporary democracy and the international NPO network since the 1990s. Finally, the chapter views the implications of Japan's social transformation and its prospects through formation of the NPO sector.

Development of Japan's NPO sector

Increasing Japan's NPO corporations

The value of the Japanese NPO sector became obvious following the Kobe Earthquake (Hanshin-Awaji Great Earthquake) in 1995. A lot of volunteers helped the disaster victims. However, as often pointed out before, the lack of a support system for volunteers and civil society activities became a problem. In Japan, as discussed later, citizens forming groups for public interest and conducting social activities did not have any possibility of registering themselves as corporations unless there was substantial achievement. However, a law, called the Nonprofit Activities Promotion Law (Law to Promote Specified Nonprofit Activities), came into force in December 1998 to register such civic activity organizations as corporations.

Since then, the number of NPO corporations registered and certified by the law has consistently increased (Figure 5.1). The number of certifications totalled 31,855 by the end of June 2007. At the beginning of 2007 the number has reached to more than 30,000. Figure 5.1 also shows the year-by-year acceleration in the number of registrations.

However, by the end of June 2007, the number of NPO corporations that had dissolved was 1,400 and cancelled certifications accounted for another 145. Adding these two figures gives 1,545. Therefore, the current number of NPO corporations is $31,855 - 1,545 = 30,310$.

At the end of September 2006, Japan's NPO sector was defined by 17 categories of activity as specified by the NPO Law. These categories are shown in Table 5.1. The most popular is 'activities promotion health, medical, welfare (Category 1)' holding the majority at 57.8 per cent. 'Educational activities (Category 2)' come next at 46.5 per cent, followed by 'community building activities (Category 3)' at 40.4 per cent. Other popular items include 'activities nurturing healthy children (Category 11)' at 39.8 per cent, 'academics, culture, arts and sports (Category 4)' at 32.3 per cent, 'environment conservation activities (Category 5)' at 28.4 per cent and 'international cooperation activities (Category 9)' at 20.4 per cent. Furthermore,

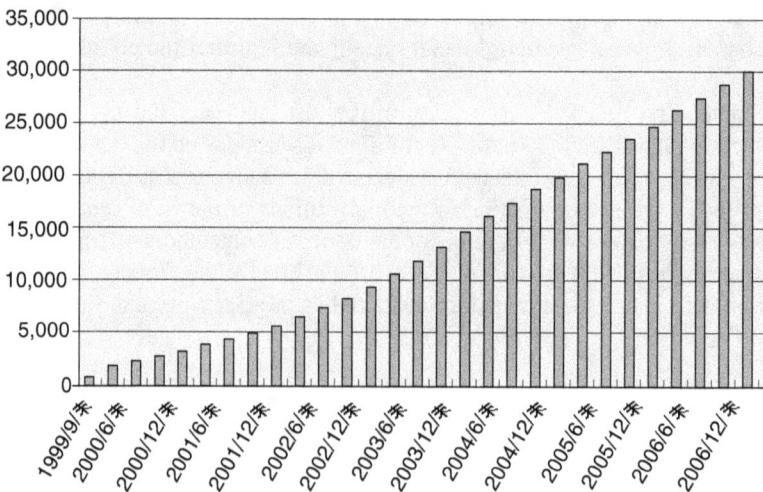

Figure 5.1 Trends in the number of non-profit organizations in Japan.

Source: Cabinet Office.

Table 5.1 Activities categorized by the specified Nonprofit Organization Law

Category	Activities	Number of NPOs	%
1	Activities promoting health, medical facilities and welfare	17,366	58.0
2	Activities promoting social education	13,873	46.3
3	Activities promoting community building	12,064	40.3
4	Activities promoting academics, culture, arts or sports	9,590	32.0
5	Activities conserving environment	8,482	28.3
6	Disaster relief activities	1,978	6.6
7	Community safety activities	2,881	9.6
8	Activities for protection of human rights or promotion of peace	4,606	15.4
9	Activities for international co-operation	6,060	20.2
10	Activities to promote gender-equal society	2,581	8.6
11	Activities to promote sound development of children	11,924	39.8
12	Activities to develop information society	2,393	8.0
13	Activities to promote scientific technology	1,226	4.1
14	Activities to activate economic activities	3,356	11.2
15	Activities to support developing vocational capability or expanding of equal opportunity	4,575	15.3
16	Activities to promote protection of consumers	1,485	5.0
17	Activities to manage or to communicate, advise or support the efforts of the organizations that conduct above activities	13,486	45.1

Source: Cabinet Office.

Notes
1 Sum of percentage column is not 100 per cent as some organizations conduct multiple activities.
2 Categories 12 through 16 cover applications made and certified after the day of enforcement of the revised specified Nonprofit Organization Law (May 1, 2003).

'activities in communication, advising and supporting NPO actions (Category 17)' is high at 44.9 per cent. This reflects the great number of organizations involved in these activities.

Definition of Japan's NPO sector

NPO refers to activities by citizens working in groups for the public interest. The John Hopkins Comparative Non Profit Sector Project defines an NPO as (a) organized, (b) private, (c) not distributing profit, (d) self-administered and self-directed, (e) voluntary and (f) for public welfare. This NPO definition is conceptually oriented.[2]

The legal definition of an NPO is given below. Japan's civil law stipulates organizational rules in the following three articles:

1 Civil law article 33 (principle of formation of corporations) – Rule that civil law and other laws can establish corporations.

2   Civil law article 34 (establishment of public interest corporations) – Rule related to organizations of public interest in the areas of religion, charity, academics and others. This article also rules about establishing non-profit associations and foundations by approval of government offices.

3   Civil law article 35 (profit corporations) – Rule about establishing corporations for profit via business and the limited liability corporate laws.

In Western civil codes in general, civil activity organizations (incorporating NPOs) are automatically registered as corporations if the application content is valid. However, in Japan, public interest corporations have been established on the basis of government policy and, therefore, the establishment of civil activity organizations has been strictly regulated by the government. This was the case from the Meiji era until the issue of the NPO law at the end of 1998. NPO incorporation on the basis of article 34 of the civil law was almost impossible in practice because of the government's extremely strict internal regulations.

Civil society sector organizations entitled 'NPO', 'NGO', 'voluntary organization', 'charity organization', etc. have different definitions depending on a particular country's laws. The following is the definition in Japan.

In Japan civil activity organizations are divided into two categories. This is the 'narrow' definition of NPO in Figure 5.2. One category is a civil activity organization (NPO corporation) registered as a corporation under the NPO Law ("narrowest" definition). The other is a civil activity organization (voluntary organization) not registered under the law.

If one expands the definition, then foundations, social welfare corporations, educational corporations, religious corporations and medical corporations established in accordance with article 34 of the civil law come under the 'broad' definition of NPOs. Mutual organizations such as labour organizations, economic organizations and cooperative unions (including common-benefit organizations) are included at times as NPOs under the 'broadest' definition, even though they pursue profit for their members and for the organization's benefit.

Article 71 of the United Nations Charter, Economic and Social Council, defines NGO using the 'broadest' definition in Figure 5.2.

In Japan, NPOs of 'broad' definition account for 312,000, including approximately 26,000 public interest organizations (associations and foundations), 34,000 medical corporations (in reality mainly individuals, and 10,000 corporations), 226,000 religious corporations, 17,700 social welfare corporations, 7,750 educational corporations, 163 rehabilitation corporations and 100 intermediary corporations.

Furthermore, as mentioned earlier, the number of 'narrowest' NPO corporations is more than 30,000. There are a lot of voluntary organizations even though the exact figure is not known. Prior to the enforcement of the NPO law, the number of civil activity organizations known to prefectural and municipal governments amounted to 87,928, according to basic research on civil activity organizations conducted by the Cabinet Office in fiscal year 1998. Many voluntary organizations are believed to have become NPO corporations since 1999. Therefore, the

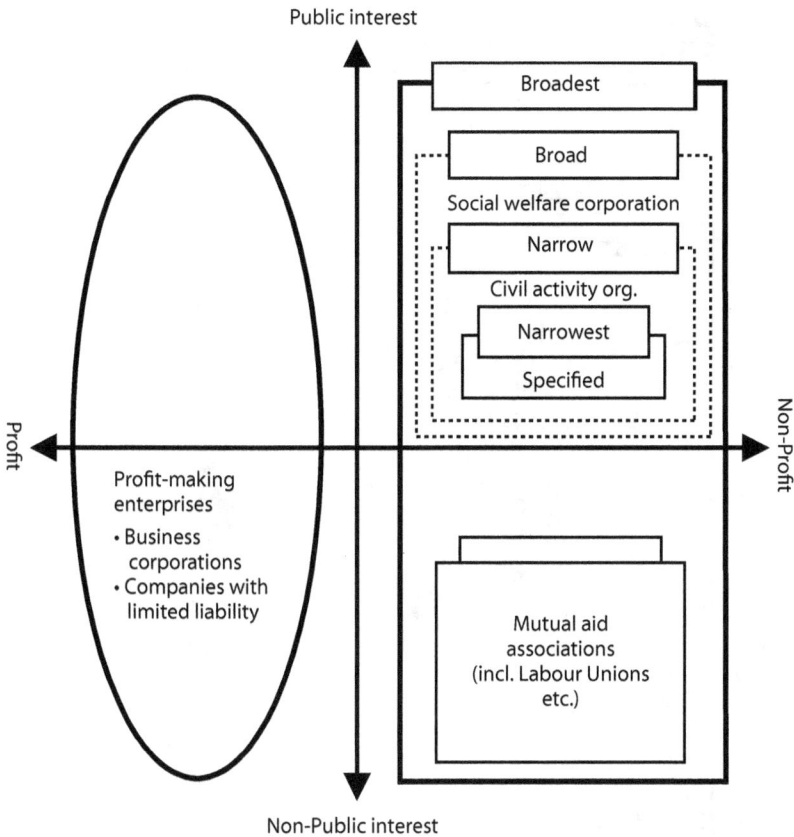

Public interest

Broadest

Broad

Social welfare corporation

Narrow

Civil activity org.

Narrowest

Specified

Profit

Non-Profit

Profit-making
enterprises

• Business
  corporations
• Companies with
  limited liability

Mutual aid
associations
(incl. Labour Unions
etc.)

Non-Public interest

Figure 5.2 Definition of Non-Profit Organization

Source: Cabinet Office, Basic *Research on Civil Activity Organizations,* FY 2000.

total number of NPO and voluntary corporations would be around 100,000. The number of NPOs of 'broadest' definition (public interest and non-profit organizations) is estimated to be about 410,000.

International comparison of Japan's NPO sector

Japan's NPO sector is still in an extremely immature stage compared to those of other countries. The size of Japan's NPO sector in terms of employment is 4.2 per cent, which is the second smallest (after Italy) among 17 developed nations, whose average is 7.4 per cent (Figure 5.3).

Comparing Japan's figures with the Netherlands – which has the most advanced NPO sector among developed countries – dramatizes how underdeveloped Japan's NPO sector is. This is illustrated in Figures 5.4 and 5.5. ('Employment rate' refers to the full-time paid employee base.)

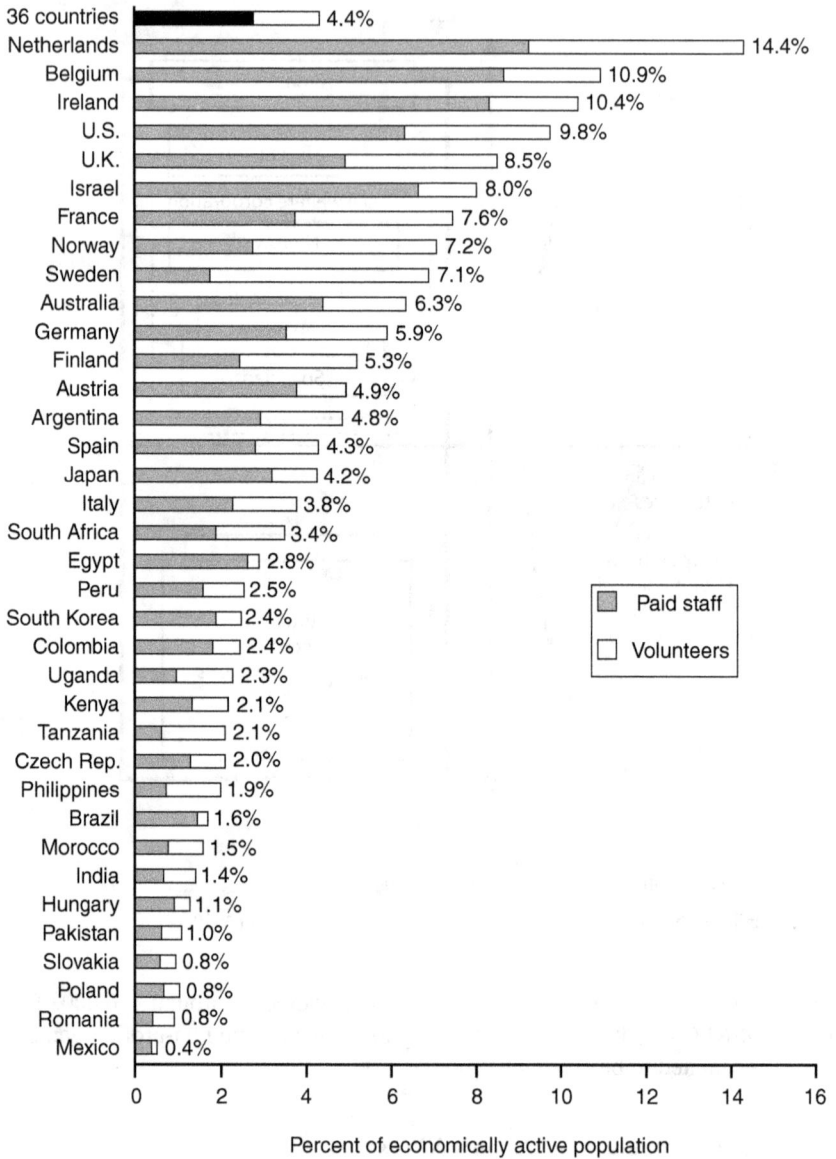

Figure 5.3 Civil society organization workforces as share of the economically active population, by country

Source: John Hopkins Comparative Non-profit Sector Project

According to the Cabinet Office's research in 2005,[3] citizens who 'have actually participated in NPO activities' amounted to fewer than 10 per cent. Those who 'wish to take part in NPO activities in the future' come to 49 per cent. However, at the same time, the proportion of citizens who 'do not wish to participate in NPO

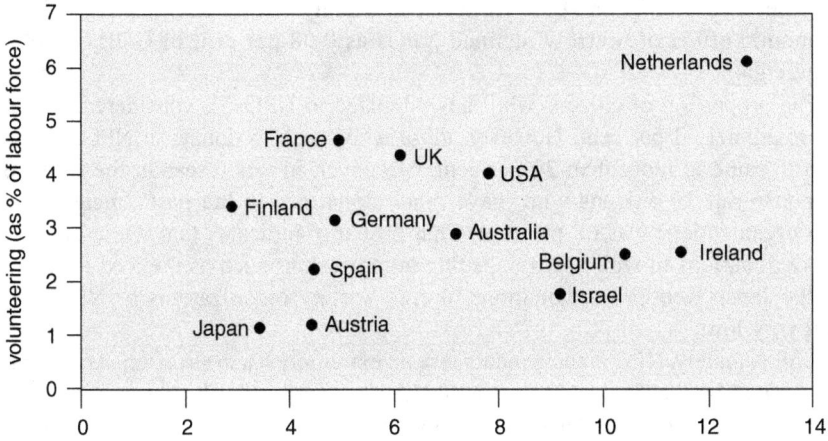

Figure 5.4 Rate of volunteer participation (vertical) and employees (horizontal) in the NPO sector

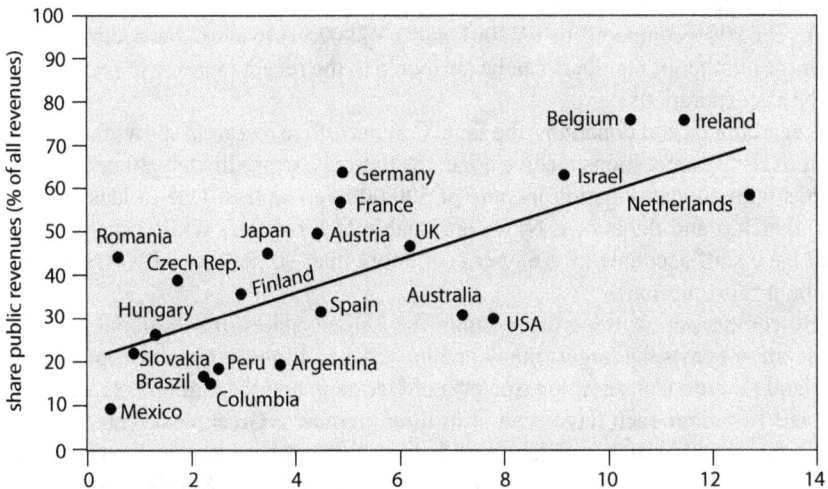

Figure 5.5 Rate of public finance (vertical) and employees (horizontal) in the NPO sector

Source: John Hopkins Comparative Non-Profit Sector Project

activities in the future' was also as high as 49 per cent. In Japan, willingness to participate in civil society activities is surprisingly low compared to the West.

One cannot simply compare the figures, as the statistical bases are different. However, as a reference, more than half the adults in the Netherlands and the United States engage routinely in volunteer activities. In the United States, more than half the adult population engage in more than 4 hours a week. In the Netherlands, the total expenditure (or the scale of activities) of NPOs was

15.5 per cent of GDP in 1995, while Japan's analysis of industries showed the economic effect of 'narrow' defined NPOs as 0.08 per cent of GDP in 1998, a huge gap.

The proportion of citizens who 'have donated to NPOs' is considered low, at approximately 3 per cent. However, those who 'wish to donate in NPOs in the future' came to more than 20 per cent. Moreover, in this research, the positive response rate of citizens who 'have made donations in the past' (meaning to any organization) was 68 per cent. That probably indicates that while citizens make donations to well-known specific organizations such as the Red Feathers or the Japan Red Cross, donations to civil society organizations or NPOs are still very low.

Unfortunately, NPO managements face an extremely harsh situation. According to research by the Cabinet Office in 2005,[4] 50 per cent of NPO corporations had an annual income of less than 5 million yen; 60 per cent had less than 10 million yen. A large number of Japanese NPOs are small in terms of income and face financial vulnerability. The reasons for this include the small size of memberships and lack of donations. Corporate donations are usually limited to larger NPOs. Regarding membership, NPO corporations having fewer than 30 members are almost 50 per cent of the total.[5] The average NPO membership declined in financial year 2005 compared to FY2001 and FY2002.[6] However, the decline in the average number of members can be attributed to the recent increase in registration of NPO corporations.

Regarding lack of donations, the same Cabinet Office research[7] shows that 43 per cent of NPO corporations receive none; the figure is approximately 80 per cent for NPOs with annual donation income of 500,000 yen or less. Due to lack of both membership and donations, NPOs are unable to hire staff. While organizations that have staff accounted for 68 per cent, more than 30 per cent of NPOs are run without full-time staff.

By comparison, as regards NPOs in the United States, the National Wildlife Federation boasts the largest membership, at 4.5 million. Naturschutzbund Deutschland (Nature Conservation Society) of Germany and the National Trust of the United Kingdom each have several million members. Greenpeace International has a membership of 2.5 million worldwide. On the other hand, in Japan, among the NGO/NPOs in the area of the natural environment, the Wild Bird Society of Japan holds the largest membership at approximately 50,000, followed by the World Wildlife Fund of Japan with 45,000 and the Nature Conservation Society of Japan with 15,000. Greenpeace Japan has a much smaller membership than the international norm, with fewer than 5,500.

The top three organizations, the Wild Bird Society of Japan, the Nature Conservation Society of Japan and World Wildlife Fund Japan, have histories of 50, 30 and 30 years respectively. Even so, membership is very small. Greenpeace Japan with its 5,500 members is rather large compared to other Japanese NPOs. It has an annual income of about 100 million yen and an expenditure of close to 200 million yen. Greenpeace International subsidizes the difference. NPOs in Japan are still underdeveloped.

The problems are not just small memberships and difficulties in management. Lack of NPO/NGOs that influence the world and operate worldwide with their visions and ideas is another issue. Advocacy-oriented NGOs that are superior internationally are extremely rare or weak in Japan. The world's expectations are higher for a wealthy country such as Japan. However, the reality is that Japan has not responded to the world's expectations. Dialogue and collaboration between NPOs and the government or businesses have increasingly progressed. However, they have not proved to be influential.

Furthermore, it must be noted that the Japanese government hardly supports the NPO sector in comparison with those of the West. For example, Western countries allocate certain portions of official development assistance (ODA) to their NPOs, generally more than 10 per cent. The Japanese government provides about 2 per cent to 3 per cent, making Japan exceptionally low among the ODA donors.[8] The Ministry of Foreign Affairs seems to have the intention of increasing the ODA ratio for NGOs. However, the ministry has not yet successfully convinced Diet members to concur.

Local governments have introduced a nationwide management commission system and have been promoting the outsourcing of work to private businesses and NPOs. This is a way for local governments to improve chronic deficits by consigning volunteers to accomplish the deficit-laden work. At the same time, partnership/collaboration between local governments and NPOs tends to be unbalanced, due to the typical Japanese attitude of dependency on the government.

Public philosophy and NPOs

Discussions of 'public philosophy' in Japan

Japan's academia has been presented with the issue of the 'public sphere' regarding the development and recognition of NPO activities worldwide and the formation of the NPO sector in Japan. In the latter half of the 1990s 'public philosophy' was actively discussed. The results of such discussions were compiled in a series of publications and have attracted attention.[9]

The creation of the public sphere by 'intermediate associations', including labour unions, cooperatives and NPOs is not a new topic for discussion. Japan's academia has arrived at a basic common concept of 'public philosophy' for the twenty-first century. This concept is called 'trilistic theory' and is discussed below.

Modernization began during the Meiji era. Japan settled into the 'dualistic theory' of 「公」 (kou) 'official' and 「私」 (shi) 'private'. Now the idea of a 公共 (koukyou) 'public sphere' coming between official and private has come to be known as the trilistic theory.

'Official' refers to government; 'private' refers to individuals, people, citizens, families and economic activity. The 'public sphere' mediates the two segments.

The 'private' sphere is expected to follow the public rules or laws stipulated by the state. Note that, historically, this idea and the expression 「滅私奉公」 (messhihoukou) 'annihilation of the private for the sake of the official' were forced on the people by the government. Being 'public spirited' meant suppressing the 'private' and elevating the 'official'.

Public philosophy should find a way in which happiness both for oneself and for others may be sought in a dynamic 'public sphere', without the 'official' swallowing up the 'private', or the 'private' expanding to the extent of excessive individualism or egotism.

With the perception of the 'new public sphere', many discussions are taking place. The following three examples give a flavour of the debate.

First, there are differences in approach to, or explanation of, the 'public sphere' in trilistic theory. The theories of such thinkers as de Tocqueville, Habermas and Kuyper may be invoked, or the many practical achievements of NPOs may be described. Explanations vary greatly in detail, depending on whom one consults. The position of 'public sphere' differs from one person to another.

Second, there are differences in the understanding of the relationship between the 'three spheres'. Some do not take 'official' and 'private' to be confrontational, but instead think of the public sphere in terms of balance. Some take the 'public sphere' as a civil society activity that emphasizes the 'public sphere from below', taking its leadership from citizens. This contrasts with the state, which used to be considered the leading player in the public sphere.

Third, are the differences in approach to consensus building in the 'public sphere'. The 'public sphere' is not merely a group concept. It is the sphere where the mediation of the private dynamically evolves into the official. People with various beliefs can coexist through personal exchanges in what is explained as the 'open public sphere'. 'Tolerance' is the basic assumption of this public sphere and its public philosophy. It is the idea that 'others' of various cultures and traditions are the subject not for 'assimilation' but 'coexistence'.

That idea is based on the premise that one forms order in cooperation with others. The principle of the public sphere is consensus building through the exchange and clash of different opinions. One can get polished, and shine, by communicating with others. By relating with the public sphere, one develops a sense of responsibility as a citizen. This idea comes from a forerunner of the modern public philosopher, Jürgen Habermas.[10]

From the beginnings of public philosophy to 'sphere sovereignty'

In connection with NPO theory, the concept of 'sphere sovereignty' has been introduced. This is the idea that citizens have sovereignty in the NPO sphere. The following historical sketch is based on the work of Hisakazu Inagaki, who introduced Kuyper's notion of 'sphere sovereignty' into Japan.[11]

The concept of 'sovereignty' appeared in the sixteenth century in Western theories of the state. Jean Bodin (1529–96) first put forward the national sovereignty theory. His argument was that the state holds absolute and permanent power, that is, 'absolute state sovereignty'. On the other hand, Johannes Althusius (1557–1638) believed that the state is created by the will of its people, the idea of 'popular sovereignty'.

In the Holy Roman Empire, those who supported the emperor used Bodin's theory to assert his sovereignty while those who were against the emperor quoted Althusius to claim various rights within their vassalage. In subsequent eras, Bodin's concept of the sovereign state was favoured.

Jean-Jacques Rousseau (1712–78) argued for 'popular sovereignty' in his 'The Social Contract, or Principles of Political Right' (1762). When people become law-making entities by the 'general will' (community will pursuing only public benefit), they become citizens. When they follow the law made by the general will as non-ego, they become subjects.

Rousseau's ideas were used by the French revolution in 1789 as the government's political philosophy. But by emphasizing purity of patriotism as part of the 'general will', a narrow-minded nationalism was created that, as a result, reinforced the absoluteness of state sovereignty. Moreover, on the basis of Rousseau's thought, the revolutionary government decided that the social contract was between the individual and the central state, explicitly denying any intermediate association between the two. As a result, up until the present day in France, there has hardly been any idea of creating a partnership between the government and NPOs, including labour unions.

John Locke (1632–1704) advocated civil government on the basis of private property and Immanuel Kant (1724–1804) advocated 'world citizenship', extending the 'general will' to the whole world, in other words, general principles of human rights. Thus public philosophy made progress little by little. However, it largely disappeared in the nineteenth-century era of imperialism.

However, the French Alexis de Toqueville (1805–59) pointed out the importance of intermediate associations through his observations of the United States. Émile Durkheim (1858–1917) asserted that intermediate associations can resolve social malaise and, by doing so, revive people's morals while at the same time paying respect to individual desires and freedoms.

In his *Wealth of Nations*, Adam Smith (1723–90) argued that egoistic economic activities must be subject to public accountability and established economics as moral philosophy. However, the current international mainstream of neoclassical economics has lost almost all the moral philosophy that Smith created. In neoclassical economics, only the government and the market appear as players. The government is official and the market is private, while 'public' is used as a synonym for 'governmental' and lacks the point of the 'civil public sphere'.

In the nineteenth century, Abraham Kuyper (1837–1920) rediscovered the philosophy of Althusius. Kuyper was a Dutch theologian, politician and journalist who established the Free University in Amsterdam and was prime minister of the Netherlands between 1901 and 1905. His reading of Althusius led Kuyper to formulate 'sphere sovereignty'. According to Inagaki, this is sovereignty decentralized to various systems of the civil society.

God (the church) not only delegates sovereignty to the state (state sovereignty) or to citizens (popular sovereignty) but also to civil society organizations. The state is merely one sphere among others. Sphere sovereignty is given by God and may not be interfered with by the state. Kuyper argued that sovereignty is given where needed for 'living' or for the 'world of life'. Government plays the role of protector of the various sovereign spheres.

From the NPO theory standpoint, NPOs hold the same sovereignty as the state (government) within the limits of their commissions. Kuyper asserts that where life and livelihood needs are present, interest organizations are formed from the bottom (bottom to top) and official organizations (government) are there to complement them. Inagaki surmises that the EU's 'subsidiarity principle' derives from Kuyper's philosophy.

Moreover, Kuyper's sphere sovereignty theory holds that the freedoms and rights of voluntary 'consociations' created by individuals have two aspects: one is sovereignty given by God and the other is a rousing of will from within that is unique to humankind.

Kuyper's philosophy clearly originates from the 'pillar society' structure unique to the Netherlands. Arendt Lijphart has developed the theory of 'consociational democracy' from similar grounds.[12]

Habermas's public sphere theory

In Europe, against the backdrop of active NPO development, the 1990s was when discussions on the civil public sphere were reactivated. Representative of the time was Jürgen Habermas (1929–).[13] Current discussions on 'the public sphere' in academia tend to originate from Habermas.

Habermas took the concept of 'civil public sphere' formed in Europe, especially the United Kingdom, during the seventeenth and eighteenth centuries as a model and applied it to the present to point out issues. He deplored the fact that the eighteenth-century 'civil public sphere' was suffocated by the state and the capitalist monetary economy, speaking of the 'colonization of the world of life by the government'.

Habermas explained that, in order to revive the civil public sphere, a process of consensus-building discussion and communication must take place to recreate it from the bottom up. In the eighteenth century, public discussion spaces, namely the coffee houses, were available. Great and lively discussions took place there and public opinions were formed in a concrete manner. Habermas went on to say that activities of the state were regulated by the public opinions thus formed. However, at present public policies are left to the government and the 'people' are merely recipients. This is a grave problem.

Habermas explained that rationality is born from discussion and dialogue and that dialogue must be oriented toward the understanding of others. He said that the essence of the public sphere is in the process of consensus building through communication. Consensus used to mean coming together in one opinion; however, currently it means 'respecting various opinions', a 'consensus of diversification'.

Hannah Arendt (1906–75) advocated in her work *The Human Condition* (1958) the idea that the public sphere is an organization of diverse people and formed through communication between the self (us) and others (them). Arendt and

Habermas introduced the 'diversity concept' into the public sphere, which greatly influenced perception. 'Trilistic theory', as mentioned before, is naturally based on these points.

Formation of a new economic social model: the three-sector model

In this chapter, a 'three-sector model' is discussed, together with its implications for NPOs now and in the future.

Welfare state and democracy supported by civil society

The importance of the civil society (NPO) sector is often discussed in the areas of the welfare state and democracy.

Welfare states gradually formed throughout the twentieth century in advanced countries. Their development was rapid after the Second World War. The United Kingdom was once the mother country of the welfare state. What the United Kingdom did during the Second World War was to conduct nationwide research on voluntary activities by citizens in the area of welfare, to select what should be done by the government and to present them as the government's social welfare system. This is how the welfare state was born in the voluntary activities of its citizens. Based on a report (1942) by William H. Beveridge (1879–1963), the Labour Party administration after the war introduced a national medical system and a national pension system. Furthermore, housing and education were improved and policies to achieve 'full employment' were developed by responding to unemployment problems and creating job opportunities. The main issues for the welfare state were unemployment problems and job creation.

In responding to the issues of 'the public sphere', the welfare state formed by stabilizing the top-down approach by state power and the government's direct influence over people's lives. As a result, the welfare state reinforced the government's power, bloating it and making it the owner of the 'public sphere'.

Later, welfare states suffered from fiscal deficits, and in the United Kingdom under Thatcherism (neoclassical economics) in the 1980s the unemployment problem was abandoned to the 'market' while the government prioritized the revitalization of the economy. As a result, the 'public sphere' was taken over by the market or corporations. As noted before, the current market has totally lost its ethic based on the moral philosophy advocated by Adam Smith and is a dog-eat-dog world. Economic globalization has further speeded up the process. The 'small government' advocated by Thatcherism developed into welfare managed by privatization – market welfare – and by civil society (NPOs) on behalf of the state.

Resisting the 'public sphere' being taken over by business corporations, civil society has stood up by forming the international network of NPOs (NGOs). Civil society is trying to take back the 'public sphere'. This trend started in the 1990s and is even more apparent in the twenty-first century.

Democracy is often perceived as citizens aggressively taking part in the formation of society. In his work 'Democracy in America' (1835–40), Alexis de Tocqueville noted that voluntary associations had supported the development of America from its founding, and that what associations could not handle was covered by the state. The associations mediating between individuals and the nation deterred the power of the nation and protected the freedom of individuals. The United States was founded based on this philosophy.

The end of the 1980s saw the collapse of many socialist nations. Issues related to the democratization of developing countries, such as the relationship between democracy and civil society (NPOs), were discussed more strongly. Western NPOs saw the need for NPO activities to be entrenched to help bring about full-scale democratization and liberalization of the USSR and Eastern Europe, and movements toward further democratization in the Philippines, Korea, China, etc.

Currently, NPOs in many countries, including the United States, provide social services. The international NPO research project led by Lester M. Salamon of John Hopkins University has found that NPOs are not unique to the Untied States and has 'discovered' that they have great presence in every developed country. At present, in developing countries and socialist countries such as China, NPOs maintain a large presence and are expected to assume greatly increased roles. Salamon states, as a result of research covering the major countries, that 'now a Global Associational Revolution is taking place worldwide'.[14]

Accumulated 'deficit of democracy'

In the twentieth century, world citizens from the United States and elsewhere sought democracy. It was their belief that once nations became democratic, war would become extinct, and people would be happy and wealthy. However, by the end of the twentieth century, people realized that democracy does not function that way and that many problems still remained. This was the realization of the 'deficit of democracy'.

'Deficit of democracy' is a term often used in the European Union. There it is mainly used in discussions about whether the institutions of the Union are properly accountable to its citizens. In this chapter the meaning of 'deficit' is extended as follows. The introduction of a democratic system does not necessarily guarantee its smooth functioning. The secret ballot system may not provide people with a 'correct' selection and those democratically elected do not necessarily act 'correctly'. Corruption and exercise of prerogatives, prioritization of private interests or one's own sect happen all the time.

Democracy has failed once in the process of modern history. It became a system controlled by an elite who were chosen by election. Though based in a nation-state, democracy ended up playing a role in justifying oppression and discrimination in colonial expansion. Nationalism was fostered to demonize the people of other countries.

After the Second World War, democracy was launched into a new era, but fifty years later, at the end of the twentieth century, a 'deficit of democracy' had accumulated. Now democracy faces another failure. The majority vote is a contradiction of democracy. In pursuit of it, minorities are cut off. Democracy treads a fine line between ignoring a minority and totalitarianism. The first failure of democracy in the first half of the twentieth century occurred due to this.

Intensity of preference is the second issue. In majority voting, the ranking of preferences counts, while the intensity of preference does not. Those who do not have a strong feeling about their choice may end up in the majority. Those who do have a strong preference may still be in the minority and have their views ignored.

The third issue is the emergence of a new flaw, as diversification of values has increased. People who agree with the majority have diverse arguments on the basis of which they agree. However, once ruled by majority vote, individual thoughts are ignored as non-existent and buried in a majority lowest common denominator. In reality, the majority is not one unified body of thought but consists of many different ideas with different intensities of feeling.

The fourth flaw is that a representative democratic system is an expression of the will of the majority concerning policy makers, and not policies. In representative democracy, the policy makers decide what legislation to enact. The individual is not given a role in the decision-making process. This has promoted political indifference in electorates.

The fifth fatal flaw is that the elected policy makers do not necessarily control governmental processes. These are generally the domain of career bureaucrats who consult the corporate sector in drafting legislation. The day-to-day running of a modern democracy is greatly influenced by the corporate sector. Individuals can only express themselves via elections held once every several years.

The weakness of the two-sector model (excluding NPOs) is partly shown by the 'market failure' induced by rapid globalization. Democracy is now faced with another failure.

However, there is no other administrative system better than democracy. To improve its functioning, what subsystems should be introduced to complement it? Democracy is a system based on the initiative and participation of the people as citizens. At the same time, it is a system that involves executive power from the top with reinforcement from the corporate sector. To adjust it, it is important for the bottom (the citizens) to use initiative not only to check the government sector but also to establish a system that influences the government sector, just as the corporate sector does. That is the three-sector model (including NPOs) that is in the topic of the following discussion.

Toward the three-sector model

The two-sector model of 'government + corporate' turned the twentieth century into a time of war, owing to economic struggles for supremacy. However, in the second half of the century, economic development brought some developing countries out of poverty. Nonetheless, after the 1980s, the corporate sector appeared to swallow the government sector. This is exemplified by all manner of collusion between government and corporations. By-passing the government sector, the corporate sector independently developed drastic economic globalization.

This corporate competition has created a dog-eat-dog world. The strong countries and corporations are richer, the poor countries and people are poorer, increasing disparity around the world. Social services, including education, medicine, water and electricity supplies, of the weaker countries have worsened. Global environmental problems have increased. To turn around the 'deficit of democracy', the basic revolutionary model of three-sector consensus building, 'government + NPO + corporate', is urgently needed. The three sectors of government (administration), corporations (industries) and NPOs (civil society organizations) establish an economic social system based on equal partnership operated by consensus through dialogue.

The three-sector model is illustrated in Figure 5.6. It is related to public philosophy (trilistic theory), as follows.[15]

One person, as an atom of humankind, creates an 'intimate sphere' with family and friends. Then, through communication with the others, citizens create a 'public sphere' through the formation of various 'spheres'. The three sectors – government, corporations and NPOs – reflect the main entities involved in the public sphere.

The inner triangle in Figure 5.6 represents the public economic social needs of people. Needs include various aspects – wanting to be prosperous, to have human rights and to live safely, for instance.

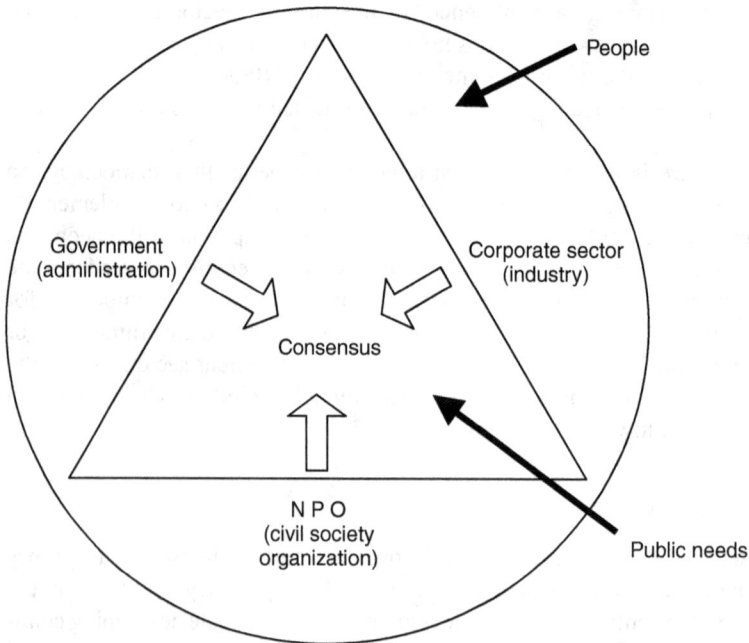

Figure 5.6 Three-sector model – three-party consensus building model

The trilistic theory of public philosophy discussed in the preceding section connects to the three-sector model via 'public needs'. The functional approach of the trilistic theory becomes the three-sector model.

The three sectors exist to respond to 'public needs'. The corporate (business) sector responds to people's living needs and wanting to be prosperous through the economy. The government sector responds to people's safety needs. The government sector provides an effective system to allocate the resources of the community (state, region) to fulfil needs effectively and to protect as well as to nurture the corporate and NPO sectors. The NPO sector works on the remaining needs that government or corporations cannot or do not want to fulfil. NPOs work on the front line of the needs of a constantly changing social structure.

'People' surround the three sectors. The government sector calls them 'people of the nation-state', the corporate sector calls them 'consumers' or 'stakeholders' and the NPO sector calls them 'citizens'.

When a sector fails in some way, a 'judgement' system comes into play. In the current judgement system, when the government fails, an election provides judgement. Judgement may also be rendered in forms such as petitions and demonstrations. When a corporation fails in some respect, citizens who are consumers or investors sell the stock or boycott the products as a means of judgement. In the case of an NPO failing, its membership and donations reduce as a form of judgement. Naturally, the judgement system only functions well if an information discovery and disclosure system is available.

International NPO network and the three-sector model

Construction of the three-sector consensus-building model is gradually under way. First, a strong NPO sector must be constructed. The three parties must build up new cooperative relationships and trust.

Of the three possible relationships, that between government and corporation has had a long history and experience, amounting at times to collusion. Breaking away from this to establish a new partnership through information disclosure is an issue. A government–NPO partnership has worked in many developed countries through the formation of a welfare state. However, the relationship has never been equal. Corporation and NPO partnerships have just begun.

In the 1990s, with the rapid progress of economic globalization, many new problems became apparent globally and internationally. In response to these, there have been not just efforts by governments and corporations, but new partnerships between governments and NPOs, and between corporations and NPOs (Figure 5.7) have been experimented with and found successful. Government and NPO partnerships especially have made evolutionary progress in the 'global public sphere'. This was made possible through the global network of NPO/NGOs.

The civil society formed by a global network is called the 'Global Civil Society (GCS)',[16] or 'Transnational Civil Society (TCS)'.[17] Below are some examples of new, pioneering international partnerships between governments and NPOs.[18] There has indeed been a 'process revolution' in the world system.

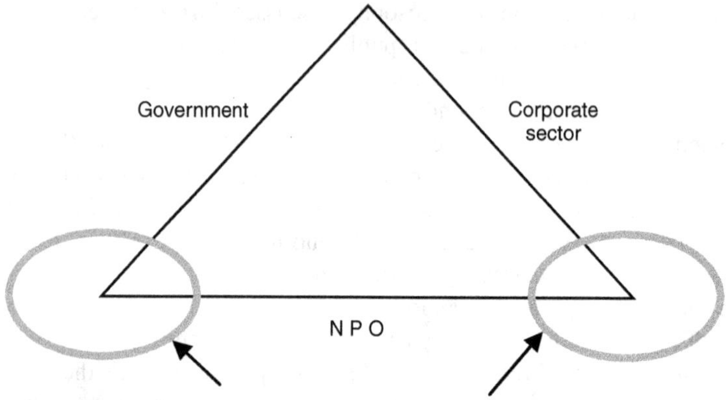

Figure 5.7 New partnerships in the three-sector model

1   The Climate Action Network (CAN), an international NGO (NPO) network working on global environmental issues together with nations supportive of their point of view, had a strong influence on the Framework Convention on Climate Change (signed in 1992) for the Kyoto Protocol (1997). The group of nations that worked with CAN included the Alliance of Small Island States (AOSIS), that suffer from rising sea levels due to global warming. Another was the 'Green Group', which was organized mainly among non-oil-producing countries in Europe, India and China. This partnership provided the momentum to introduce numerical targets into the Kyoto Protocol.

2   The International Campaign to Ban Landmines (ICBL) is an international NGO network that advocates an anti-personnel landmines ban promptly, totally and without exception. Those countries that support their assertion, called the Core Countries, worked with ICBL. They succeeded after one and a half years in enacting the Convention on the Prohibition of Anti-personnel Mines (signed in 1997 and brought into force in 1999). This was called the 'Ottawa Process' and is reputed to be the first successful case of forming an international convention outside the framework of international organizations, with an NGO involved in the security and military domain. It was a representative case that created a multilateral treaty through a 'process revolution'. As a result of its success, ICBL was awarded the Nobel Peace Prize.

3   The Coalition for the International Criminal Court (CICC), a federation of NGOs seeking an international criminal court, worked together with the nations that support the CICC's position to adopt the international criminal court establishment regulation (effective in 2002). The group of the nations is called the 'Like Minded Countries' (LMC). The negotiation process took place diplomatically at the United Nations. It evolved into an NGO participation process in United Nations diplomacy.

4   A certain level of success was achieved by the JUBILEE 2000 campaign, an NGO network that sought debt write-offs by 2000, and targeted the G8 countries, with the cooperation of the country hosting their summit.

5   Progress was made in the revision of the WTO code concerning the procurement of essential drugs for HIV/AIDS, malaria, tuberculosis and other diseases, specifically, revision of the Agreement on Trade-Related Aspects of Intellectual Property Rights (TRIPS), or the issue of so-called 'generic drugs'. This was thanks to a partnership with newly industrializing economies, including India, Brazil and South Africa.

Partnerships between corporations and NPOs have also made great progress, with concrete results. Such partnerships gave rise to a new 'corporate system theory' called 'Corporate Social Responsibility (CSR)'. In recent years, the Japanese media often report on CSR. Many corporations compile CSR reports (or sustainability reports). Currently, the European Union (EU) and the International Organization for Standardization (ISO) are standardizing 'social responsibility', including that of corporations. CSR was concretized by partnership between a corporation and an NPO through the dispute between Royal Dutch Shell and Greenpeace, an international NGO (the Brent Spar campaign). In constructing a new corporate ethic John Elkington of SustainAbility joined Shell as a consultant. His experience with Shell brought about the concept of 'triple bottom line' which puts the three aspects 'economics (earnings)', 'environment' and 'society' at the core of corporate management. From this beginning, CSR was quickly generalized into multi-stakeholder and supply chain management. The GRI (Global Reporting Initiative) was established by NGOs consisting of experts on CSR. Many of these people joined CSR evaluation organizations such as Social Responsibility Investment (SRI), which helps to promote CSR.

So-called 'corporate social contribution' in the past focused on how corporations should share their profits with society (redistribution of profits). However, corporate social responsibility theory is a new management model advocating the incorporation of 'economy (earnings)', 'environment' and 'society'. This is a structural change in corporate social contribution.

Since the Japanese NPO sector is small, pressure from NPOs on corporations is extremely weak. Corporations would not recognize CSR as a matter of partnership with NPOs; it is simply something Western and a new management cost. This is a danger for Japan's CSR management.

The Sydney Olympic Games in 2000, the so-called 'Green Games', was another pioneering case of partnership between NPOs and corporations, as well as government. NGOs (NPOs) such as Greenpeace Australia were involved from the time of the initial bid to host the games in 1993 in writing an environmental plan (environmental guidelines). As a result, the Sydney Olympics succeeded in the use of sustainable energy generated by photovoltaics (solar energy), reduction in PVC usage, use of recyclable wood (FSC), use of rainwater and vehicle emission reductions among other things.

International Olympics Committee decided in 1999 that this 'Green Games' approach would be one of the conditions for hosting future games. Beijing was appointed to host the 2008 Olympics. The Beijing government succeeded in its bid by applying the 'Green Game' approach in which 'NGOs participated from the beginning' to cope with environment issues. That is why the Beijing Olympics were called the 'Green Olympics'. Many NGOs already exist in China. Beijing's success is evidence of their influence.

Issues for and future of Japan's NPO sector

Loss of the 'public sphere' in Japan

As mentioned above, Japan's NPO sector is growing rapidly, though it is one of the smallest in any developed country. This is because of the nation-building concept during the modernization after the Meiji restoration (1868).

In its modernization, the Meiji government appears to have intentionally mistranslated or misused the meaning of 'public'. The Japanese translation of 'public' is ' 「公共」 koukyou', which literally means 'together (共) with the government (公)'.

It is my own opinion that 'public' means 'everyone's', just as in English. In the *Random House English Japanese Dictionary* and the *Longman Advanced American Dictionary*, four definitions are provided:

1   For anyone, for all the people
2   Ordinary people, people in general
3   Government (or state)
4   Not hidden from, open to all the people.

In imagining the origin of the word, meanings (2), (3) and (4) seem to derive from (1). The consistent theme is 'everyone's'. However, the Japanese translation implies that the government does everything. People do not need to be active participants in social affairs. That is the basis of the Japanese societal system in which the constitution and civil code were established and ethics stipulated.

The modern state of Japan was designed and operated by an extreme system of government initiative. Sometimes, state officials thought that they needed to be related to 'the public', and created exceptional regulations in Article 34 of the civil code for foundations and associations . However, as mentioned above, applications by people were never approved and the government established such organizations as part of government measures. This resulted in foundations and associations providing executive posts to retired government officials (golden parachuting).

Since the Meiji era, Japanese people have been brought up in a system in which the people have nothing to do with 'public'.

As mentioned briefly above, Japan's ethical base involves a typical dualistic theory of 'official' (公, kou) and 'private' (私, shi). The 'public sphere' (公共, koukyou) is integrated with the government sphere. Moreover, in order to incorporate the 'private' into the 'official', the formation of ideas and education were controlled in great detail, as shown below. The Meiji restoration (1868) made the Imperial Court (emperor) 'official'. The Charter Oath of Five Articles issued by the emperor at the Meiji restoration stated that 'meetings are rigorously encouraged and decisions should be made by discussion' and that the 'justification of public power' is to be placed in the 'civil public sphere'. However, the Promulgation of the Meiji Constitution and the introduction of the Imperial Prescript on Education (1880) made the people of the nation subjects of the emperor. In time of war, annihilation of the private for the sake of the official (滅私奉公, messhihoukou) became an official ethic – one should not mind dying for the emperor, who is the official – 「公」. During the Taisho era (1912–26), there was a 'Taisho democracy movement', but during the 'wealthy nation and strong army' Japan, the 'official–private dualistic theory' was re-established. The country went into the Second World War with this dualistic theory strongly established.

As briefly mentioned before, the government crafted some words and systems in order to incorporate the 'private' into the 'official'.

1 滅私奉公(messhihoukou), annihilation of the private for the sake of the official, meant giving up the 'private' to repay moral indebtedness and dedicating oneself to the 'official'. It is a moral virtue to be prepared to die for the 'official'. In modern Japan from the Meiji era until the end of the Second World War, only national interests existed. 'Official' meant the emperor's will and intention as executed by government. With this, the 'private' was swallowed by the 'official'.
2 官尊民卑(kansonminpi), 'government precious people lowly'. Government officials are always right and therefore precious. The government leads the people of the state in the right way and improves their lives.

The education and social systems of the prewar period, expressing moral values in these terms, lived on after the war. '滅私奉公, annihilation of the private for the sake of the official' simply replaced the emperor as 「公」 by the president of a corporation. Japanese people dedicated themselves to a corporation without thinking about themselves or their families. '官尊民卑, government precious people lowly' continued with 'government' replaced by 'bureaucracy'. After the war, Japan vigorously pushed forward in industrialization along the economic lines drafted by bureaucrats. The bureaucrat-led economy created excessive regulations and approval systems, which became the bureaucrats' power base.

More recently it has been said that '滅私奉公, messhihoukou, annihilation of the private for the sake of the official' had been reversed to become '滅公奉私, mekkouhoushi, annihilation of the official for the sake of the private'. Post-war freedoms led to what was called 'me-ism', or selfishness. Neither kind of annihilation is very desirable.

Before the war there was a national organization called 'Taisei Yokusan Kai' by which citizens of the state were directed toward a national system for all-out mobilization. An important role in this system was played by intermediate associations called 'block associations', which were in turn broken into 'community associations'. These were used for surveillance and for anonymous informing during the war.

'Community associations' remained after the war, and even at present the Red Feather Community Chest and the Japan Red Cross use them as a fund-raising system. On 1 October every year the Red Feather Community Chest conducts a campaign to sell 'red feathers'. People wear these red-coloured chicken feathers to openly express that they have made a social contribution to the poor. I cannot help thinking, at the sight of a red feather, that the Japanese national system was constructed so that people do not have to be involved with society (the public sphere). However, people do have compassion towards the poor. The government should create systems for the people to express their sense of compassion. At present, the Japanese do not know where to make donations because things in 'the public sphere' are left to the government. That is why the government takes the donations and distributes them on people's behalf. The 'Red Feather Community Chest' must have been born from such an idea. For several years after the war, the Red Feather was a national movement. With the building up of the NPO sector, over the last decade or so it has lost the momentum it used to have. It is my opinion that citizens have come to think more deeply about where to make donations.

Japan has always had a culture of helping others through communities. However, with modernization after the Meiji era, the government emphasized the national system but did not work on restructuring the civil society. Moreover, except in war time, the government appeared to function well economically until the 1960s, resulting in a delay in structuring the civil society system. The Japanese do have volunteering and charitable spirits, but they have been repressed because of the national system and education since the Meiji era.

Implications for the formation of the NPO sector in Japan

In the 1990s, as part of Japan's reforms, discussions about building up the NPO sector gradually got under way.

In financial years 1993 and 1994 the Social Policy Council discussed and reported on the issue. Against the backdrop of the volunteer movement during the Hanshin-Awaji Great Earthquake in 1995, the so-called NPO bill was passed in 1997 and took effect in December 1998.

NPO representatives requested a revision of the civil code, which was made law during the Meiji era. Bureaucrats told them that that would take 'more than 100 years', and the NPO law was introduced for the time being. That is why, legally, it was introduced as an exceptional regulation under article 34 of the civil code.

The official name of the NPO law is 'Law to Promote Specified Non-profit Activities'. 'Specified' means items specified in the exceptional regulation of article 34 of the civil code (13 in number at that time and 17 at present).[19] In the case of these items, incorporation is approved upon application.

As well as that limitation, preferential tax treatment toward Japan's NPOs is still limited. Preferential tax treatment was introduced from 2001 by the 'certified NPO corporation system'. The applicable conditions were too strict in the beginning, and even though they were relaxed somewhat later, certified NPOs are merely 70 out of 30,310 (as of June 2007).

Also, the government sector and the corporate sector have tremendous subsystems to support them. However, the NPO sector does not have much of a subsystem. For example, the corporate sector has a powerful subsystem of corporation registration, financing (the banking system), interest groups such as Nihon-Keidanren and industrial organizations, consultant companies, information organizations, research companies, corporation assessment organizations and so on. The government sector also has a large support system. However, the NPO law merely enabled civil society organizations to register themselves as corporations, so the next step is to build up a subsystem.

Currently in Japan, regional civil society movements are incredibly active after only eight and a half years, though interest in global activities is still small. Japan's rapid increase in NPO corporations definitely shows the direction of the country's substantial reform. Sometimes 1995, the year of Great Hanshin-Awaji Earthquake, is called the first year of the volunteer age. That was the year when the rapid increase in NPOs started and the NPO sector emerged. It may take nearly half a century from 1995 to really establish the NPO sector and complete Japan's reform. But the gradual increase is changing the country appropriately.

Conclusion: transformation to the trilistic theory

Japanese people still seem to be bound by the dualistic theory. That is why, as pointed out above, the transformation of ideas to the trilistic theory appears to be fresh and convincing. Kim Chechan, one of the editors of the 'Public philosophy series' (University of Tokyo Press) has come up with the term '活私開公, kasshikaikou, maximization of the self by opening up the official' as opposed to '滅私奉公, messhihoukou, annihilation of the private (the self) for the sake of the official'. By maximizing the 'private' the sphere of the 'official' opens up by the mediation of the 'public sphere'.

However, transformation to the 'trilistic theory' is not easy. The Japanese government still holds the 'dualistic theory'. However, the constitution of Japan uses the term 'public welfare' four times in articles 12, 13, 22 and 29, clearly trilistically. For instance, article 13 of the constitution states

> All of the people shall be respected as individuals. Their right to life, liberty, and the pursuit of happiness shall, to the extent that it does not interfere with the public welfare, be the supreme consideration in legislation and in other governmental affairs.

However, the government has always taken 'public' as the 'official' sphere. 'To the extent that it does not interfere with the public welfare' is interpreted as 'unless it is against the welfare of the state'. A typical example is the 'amendment' of the Fundamental Law of Education at this time. Also, the issue of Yasukuni Shrine visits by the prime minister and other ministers is based on the Meiji era idea of merging the 'private' into the 'official'.[20]

Another example involves the notion of 'private'. Former Prime Minister Koizumi advocated 'reform' and 'from official to private' was the slogan. In this case 'private' meant 'market' and was never meant to be connected to 'civil society's public sphere' or the idea of expansion of NPOs.

Also prejudice against NPOs and NGOs still persists. There is still a fixed notion of volunteering being 'clean, pure (not for money), and beautiful'. Volunteers must not be paid. NPOs cannot conduct profit-making activities. NPOs subsidized by the government are wrong. NPOs are refuges for leftists. NPOs do not pay well and have no future, so it is not recommendable for students to apply for work in them.

However, for the first time in my approximately fifty years of experience in NPO activities, attitudes toward NPOs among the Japanese are drastically changing. The government will find it more difficult to monopolize the public sphere in the future, although naturally it must play some part in it. In that sense, the 'public sphere supported by citizens' and the 'public sphere supported by government' must clearly be separated. Citizenship will be reformed through encounter with NPOs. I believe that the increase in the number of Japan's NPOs will bring this about, together with many other good effects.

Notes

1 The term 'civil society (NPO) sector' refers here to non-profit organizations (NPOs), non-government organizations (NGOs), charity/voluntary/social and economic organizations, or the third sector. The terms 'NPO sector' and 'civil society sector' are used interchangeably.
2 John Hopkins Comparative Non-profit Sector Project 2002, 2004.
3 Cabinet Office Public Relations Department 2005.
4 Cabinet Office Public Relations Department 2005.
5 Cabinet Office Social Policy Bureau 2006.
6 Research Institute of Economics, Trade and Industry 2005.
7 Cabinet Office Social Policy Bureau ???
8 Nagasaka 2007.
9 'Public Philosophy series', 20 volumes published by the University of Tokyo Press from 2001 to 2004.
10 Habermas 1990, translated into Japanese in 1994.
11 Inagaki 2004.
12 Lijphart 1968 and 1969.
13 Habermas 1990.
14 John Hopkins Comparative Non-profit Sector Project 2002, 2004
15 I have called the three-sector model the 'Dutch Model' in Nagasaka 2000.
16 John Hopkins Comparative Non-profit Sector Project 2002, 2004
17 Florini (ed.) 2000, Mekata 2002.
18 Nagasaka 2007.
19 Specified items are listed in Table 5.1.
20 Inagaki 2006.

References

Cabinet Office Public Relations Department (2005), *Public Opinion Survey on NPOs (Non-profit Organizations.)*. Tokyo: Cabinet Office

Cabinet Office Social Policy Bureau (2006), *Questionnaire Survey on Certified NPO Corporations FY2005*. Tokyo: Cabinet Office

Cabinet Office Social Policy Bureau (2006), *Basic Research Report on Civil Activities Organizations FY2005*. Tokyo: Cabinet Office

Florini, Ann (ed.) (2000), *The Third Force: The Rise of Transnational Civil Society.* Tokyo and Washington, DC: The Japan Centre for International Affairs and the Carnegie Endowment for International Peace.

Habermas, Jürgen (1990), *Strukturwandel der Öffentlichkeit.* (The Structural Transformation of the Public Sphere.) Frankfurt: Suhrkamp

Inagaki, Hisakazu (2004), *Religion and Public Philosophy.* Tokyo: University of Tokyo Press.

—— (2006), *Yasukuni and Public Philosophy.* Tokyo: Kobunsha.

John Hopkins Comparative Non-profit Sector Project (2002, 2004), *Global Civil Society – Dimension of the Non-profit Sector* (Volumes 1 and 2). Bloomfield, CT: Kumarian Press, Inc.

Lijphart, Arendt (1968), *The Politics of Accommodation: Pluralism and Democracy in the Netherlands*. Berkeley, CA: University of California Press.

Lijphart, Arendt (1969), 'Consociational Democracy', *World Politics* 2, 207–25.

Mekata, Setuko (2002), *Transnational Civil Network.* Tokyo: Toyokeizaishinpousha.

Nagasaka, Toshihisa (2000), *Dutch Model.* Tokyo: Nihonkeizai-shinbunsha.

Nagasaka, Toshihisa (2007), *60 Chapters to Get to Know the Netherlands*. Tokyo: Akashi-shoten

Nagasaka, Toshihisa (2007), From NGO's "Civil Society Power" – Towards the New World Model. Tokyo: Akashi-shoten.

Research Institute of Economics, Trade and Industry (2005), *Corporation Survey on NPO Corporations: 2005 Report on the Result of NPO Corporation Questionnaires.* Tokyo: Research Institute of Economics, Trade and Industry.

6 Major developments in Japanese foreign policy since the mid-1990s

Kazuo Ogoura

Introduction

Three major factors have exerted a particularly strong influence on Japan's foreign policy over the past decade. The first is political and economic trends in Japan, and the second is trends within other major countries and the broader international community. That these two factors should influence Japan's policy choices and strategy is a matter of course, as domestic and international trends inevitably affect the foreign policy of any nation at any time. If these two factors are taken as the givens – or the framework – of foreign policy making, then the choice of policies and strategies from among the various options that exist within that framework may be regarded as the third and final factor. Japan's foreign policy has thus been determined by (1) domestic economic and political trends, (2) conditions and changes in the international community, and (3) Japan's own choices of strategy and policy in the light of the above.

Domestic economic and political trends

I would first like to examine how the domestic political and economic currents of the past decade or so have influenced Japan's foreign policy.

From the early 1990s to around 2000, Japanese economy was characterized by stagnation, especially in comparison with the robust growth seen in China and the United States. In 1997, in the middle of this period, South Korea and a number of Southeast Asian countries were hit by what became known as the Asian financial crisis, which caused a sense of stagnation to spread not only to Japan but to the whole of Asia (with the exception of China).[1]

The prolonged economic downturn caused the Japanese public to become more inward looking, leading inevitably to a decrease in foreign investment as many banks and trading firms shut down their overseas branches and scaled back their global networks. This introspective attitude produced criticism of the country's official development assistance, with many people demanding that money be used to fuel domestic growth rather than channelled to developing countries.[2]

This period also marked a turning point for Japan's political and economic standing in the international community, which until then had regarded the country as a model of Asian economic development. While there was no qualitative change to Japan's status as the only Western-allied industrial democracy in Asia, Japan's stagnation while other Asian nations, especially China and India, were showing remarkable growth, had the effect of diminishing Japan's glow within Asia. This signalled a decline in Japan's diplomatic clout and standing, with the country no longer seen as the 'leader' but simply as a 'member' of Asia, and this has had a broad impact on Japanese foreign policy.

One manifestation of this is the strong support that Japan now expresses for regional integration in the form of an East Asian Community.[3] Until the mid-1990s, Japan was very cool to the idea of an East Asian Economic Grouping, as proposed by the then Malaysian prime minister, Mahathir Mohamad, and wary of any attempts to create an Asian community. That Japan began to warm to such a concept in the mid-1990s is clearly related to the stagnation in its domestic economy and the rapid increase in interdependence among Asian economies.

The Japanese economy's extended period of anaemic growth had far-reaching implications. Ironically, it helped alleviate what had been Japan's biggest diplomatic headache through the mid-1990s – bilateral trade friction, particularly with Western industrialized countries. To be sure, there have since been some isolated cases, such as those involving bans on beef imports following outbreaks of BSE in various countries, but overall there has been a dramatic reduction in both macro- and microeconomic disputes. Moreover, the disputes that do arise are increasingly settled in multilateral, rather than bilateral, forums. Globalization may have been the primary factor behind this shift, but Japan's economic stagnation was undoubtedly another key element.

Turning to domestic political trends, the Japanese government has been led by the Liberal Democratic Party since the Social Democratic Party's Tomiichi Murayama stepped down in 1996 as prime minister in an SDP–LDP coalition. This has resulted in a general shift to the right in the country's foreign policy. For example, sustained LDP rule contributed in no small measure to the first-ever overseas dispatch of the Self-Defense Forces and the strengthening of the Japan–US security alliance. Increased tensions in Japan's relations with its neighbours – with South Korea since the two countries co-hosted the 2002 FIFA World Cup and with China since then President Jiang Zemin's 1998 visit to Japan – are also connected to the LDP's long-standing dominance.

The populist tendency evident in domestic politics has also had a visible impact on foreign policy.[4] For instance, the growing public outcry over the abduction of Japanese nationals by North Korean agents prompted Tokyo to take a more hard-line stance against Pyongyang and with regard to the Korean Peninsula in general. Public antipathy toward China, moreover, produced calls for the 'separation of politics and economics' in Japan's relations with that country.

Conditions and changes in the international community

The biggest change in the international community over the past decade or so has been the shift in US security policies and the strengthening of global antiterrorism measures since the 9/11 terrorist attacks. There emerged after 9/11 a strong sense that threats to the international community are posed not so much by specific countries or groups of countries, as in the past, but by shadowy terrorist groups. This resulted in the diversification of international security cooperation methods, with ad hoc 'coalitions of the willing' being formed in addition to traditional security alliances, to target specific threats.

Religious and ideological differences (such as those on which the idea of a 'clash of civilizations' is based) have cast a long shadow over the world as sources of international conflict; such differences may be seen as both the cause and effect of the 9/11 attacks. Japan's policy toward the Middle East, for example, is no longer shaped only by concerns about energy supplies or resolving conflict in the region; there is an increasing focus on promoting dialogue among civilizations and deepening understanding of the Japan–US alliance in the Middle East. This is undeniably a result of 9/11.

The second major change over the past 10 to 15 years has been the advance of globalization. Globalization became a buzzword around the world in the early 1990s, and its advantages and disadvantages in relation to political and economic issues became a focus of frequent debate. Strong appeals were made for greater international cooperation to promote its benefits (such as economic liberalization, democratization, and the protection of women's and children's rights and human rights in general) and to address its downsides (including the cross-border spread of infectious diseases and the increase in transnational crime), and both of these tasks have been reflected in Japan's foreign policy. Japan and the United States launched the Common Agenda for Cooperation in Global Perspective in 1993[5] to address global problems, for instance, and Japan has placed greater emphasis on coordinating its diplomatic initiatives with the activities of nongovernmental organizations.[6]

The third notable change in the international community is the emergence of China and India as economic and political powers. This has had broad repercussions, for their economic rise may be as historically significant as Japan's re-emergence following the Second World War. And for the international community, the task of assigning these massive economies their appropriate places in the international community and having them adhere to global rules is strikingly similar to the efforts made decades earlier to incorporate Japan into the multilateral framework.

One significant difference between then and now, though, is that while Japan's rapid growth did not raise grave concerns about the world's natural resources, the rise of China and India – owing to the massive size of their economies and populations – will have a tremendous impact on the worldwide availability of oil, food, water, and other resources. This is beginning to pose very serious problems for the international community, which must find a way to cope with these resource issues.[7]

In addition to their growing economic presence, China and India have begun to hold greater strategic sway. When Japan sought to win a permanent seat on the Security Council as part of an United Nations reform, for example, it teamed up with Brazil, Germany, and India in the 'Group of Four' to submit a joint proposal. The inclusion of India in such a grouping is indicative of the country's enhanced strategic importance.

China and India are also exerting a subtle influence on the member states of the Association of Southeast Asian Nations (ASEAN).[8] China's new clout was evident in the reaction to the above-mentioned UN reform proposal by ASEAN countries, which hesitated to support it in deference to signals from Beijing. South Korea, too, is increasingly looking to China in the cultural, educational, and economic fields, and this has undeniably had its impact on Seoul's ties with both Tokyo and Washington.

As China and India have emerged as major players in the global arena, they have also been called on to embrace greater international responsibility. India was severely criticized for conducting a nuclear test, and China has been reproached for its lack of action on environmental problems. Frequent demands have also been made for the two countries to increase transparency regarding their mounting military capacity. Japan has joined the chorus and even, on occasion, been a leading voice in such criticisms.

The fourth change in the international community that has had a major bearing on Japan is the developments on the Korean Peninsula, particularly the growing threat posed by North Korea and the tension following its test missile launch in August 1998. Such tensions have been intensifying, as seen in the suspension of the activities of the Korean Peninsula Energy Development Organization, an international cooperative framework to deal with North Korea's nuclear development program, and the widespread condemnation of Pyongyang's abductions of foreign nationals, which have come to be seen both in Japan and worldwide as a violation of human rights. These tensions have greatly affected Japan's foreign policy. In particular, in combination with the strengthening of the Japan–US alliance, they have affected Japanese policy toward Iraq and other areas of the Middle East.

The fifth change is the expansion of the North Atlantic Treaty Organization and the European Union. This trend may not appear to have had a direct impact on Japan, but it has had an indirect influence by encouraging moves toward economic integration in Asia and prompting increased dialogue between Asia and Europe through such forums as the Asia–Europe Meeting.[9] In fact, there has been a qualitative shift in Japan's foreign policy toward building stronger partnerships with Europe, as symbolized by the calls heard at one time for 'Eurasian diplomacy'.

The sixth change is the 1997 Asian economic crisis, as described above. From a long-term perspective, the crisis cast doubt on the viability of the Asian model of economic development, and one must not forget the impact this has had on Japan's diplomatic initiatives. 'Asian values' that had once been viewed as models for other developing regions were suddenly disparaged as the root causes of the crisis. A new set of values is needed to serve as a common foundation to support economic growth and fashion an Asian community in light of the growing interdependence of the regional economy.

Japan's diplomatic strategy and policies

In response to the changes detailed above in both domestic economic and political currents and the international situation, the strategy and policies of Japanese diplomacy have gradually shifted in recent years.

The first change has been the strengthening of the Japan–US alliance. The progress made over the past decade in establishing defence infrastructure in Japan – particularly the reorganization of the US military in Okinawa – as a means of bolstering the deterrent power of the Japan–US alliance is one sign of this development.

As seen in the dispatch of the Self-Defence Forces to Iraq, the Japan–US alliance is being transformed from a bilateral alliance into one with regional significance and, further, into a global partnership.[10] Japan's implementation of the Anti-Terrorism Special Measures Law, for example, symbolizes the globalization of the alliance.

The so-called two-plus-two meetings (the Japan–US Security Consultative Committee, consisting of the minister for foreign affairs and the director of the Defence Agency on the Japanese side and the secretaries of state and defence on the US side) and the integration of operations with the US military, have served to bring the two countries closer together. Such developments signify that the alliance has, in a sense, crossed the Rubicon and show that strengthening the Japan–US alliance through global-scale cooperation has become a pillar of Japanese foreign policy.

The second change (though one that has not been explicitly articulated) is that China has come to be firmly regarded in Japanese foreign policy as a rival. For example, the strengthening of both the Japan–US alliance and Japan–India relations can be seen as part of an effort to check and counter China. The task of anchoring a rising China within international rules is now being given greater priority as a long-term goal of Japanese foreign policy. Japan's active support for China's accession to the World Trade Organization can, in a sense, be seen as part of this diplomatic strategy.

During the latter half of the Koizumi administration, the phrase 'separation of politics and economics' was often heard in relation to Japan's policies toward China. It was used as a way of explaining that we must develop our economic relations with China even if we are not satisfied with the political relationship and that, even if there is some political friction, in substantive terms, Japan–China relations are going well. This term could be described as the Japanese counterpart of 'economically hot, politically cold', the phrase that the Chinese side has used to characterize Japan–China relations. Following the visit to China by Japan's prime minister, Shinzo Abe, however, Japan's approach to its giant neighbour is tending toward 'a relationship driven by both politics and economics'; one can sense a shift away from 'separation of politics and economics' in Japan's China policy.

Although there was considerable friction between Japan and China in the latter years of the Koizumi administration, it is interesting to note that this did not result in a domestic political backlash. Tension with China has traditionally had an adverse impact on the domestic fortunes of Japanese governments, but this pattern appears to have been broken for almost the first time since the Second World War. The decoupling of Japan's China policy from the domestic reaction to the bilateral relationship has been a feature of the past five or six years, particularly during the Koizumi administration. Previously, the government of the day would suffer domestically if tension arose in the Japan–China relationship. In recent years, however, a new situation has emerged in which taking a firm line in dealings with China, even if it causes some tension, does not threaten the administration's standing at home.

The third change I would like to highlight is that the problems on the Korean Peninsula have become increasingly 'internationalized', in line with the strategy pursued by Japan. Japan's consistent use of the Six-Party Talks and the UN Security Council demonstrates that the country's strategy is to resolve the problems on the Korean Peninsula within international frameworks.

In Japan's bilateral relations with North Korea, meanwhile, four issues – the abductions of Japanese nationals by North Korea, Pyongyang's nuclear development program, post-war settlement, and Korean Peninsula security in the broad sense – have become increasingly intertwined in recent years. In short, Japan has adopted a two-stage approach, based on the idea that the abduction issue must be resolved before Japan–North Korea relations can move forward because the Japanese public will not accept the resolution of the nuclear issue alone. Only once a clear path has been established for resolving these two issues will Japan fully address the questions of economic cooperation and a post-war settlement.

Next, I would like to consider the influence that globalization has had on Japanese foreign policy. One example, as mentioned above, is that the 'common agenda' of global issues has taken on a growing importance. In response to this, Japan, since 1999, has been advocating the concept of 'human security'. The redefinition of official development assistance and the reorganization of ODA policy were also part of an effort to reorient Japan's economic cooperation policies in line with globalization.

Meanwhile, as globalization has progressed, Japan has bolstered its involvement in the global regime in various ways. First, it has introduced new concepts – one example being its strong advocacy of 'human security'. Second, it has taken the initiative in the construction of a new international order. Examples of this include Japan's efforts to ban anti-personnel landmines, the passage of an UN resolution on the ultimate elimination of nuclear weapons, and the adoption of the Kyoto Protocol. Japan's efforts to address the issue of global warming by hosting the Kyoto Conference (in December 1997) and getting the Kyoto Protocol approved, constitute a classic triumph of Japanese diplomacy.[11]

The third impact has been in the area of reforms in international institutions. The advance of globalization and the mounting importance of global issues have inevitably led to an increase in the role of international institutions. The fact that

Japan has pushed strongly for UN reform is evidence of a new direction for Japanese diplomacy in the context of globalization.

The final example of Japan's involvement in the international order is its participation in peace-keeping operations. The growing role that Japanese troops have played – first in Cambodia, Mozambique, and the Golan Heights and then in other places – has been one of the major developments in Japanese foreign policy over the past ten years.

The strengthening of Japan's regional cooperation strategy is another noteworthy development. Against a backdrop of European Union enlargement, unipolar US hegemony, and the rise of China, regional cooperation has become an increasingly conspicuous pillar of Japanese foreign policy. The Asia–Pacific Economic Cooperation, the ASEAN+3 Summit (bringing together the leaders of ASEAN countries, Japan, China, and South Korea), the East Asia Summit, the East Asia Summit Foreign Ministerial Meeting, the Manila Framework in the field of finance, and the establishment of a three-stage process of confidence building, preventive diplomacy, and conflict resolution in the ASEAN Regional Forum: all of these constitute efforts – and fruits of efforts – to strengthen regional cooperation in Asia. It is no exaggeration to say that Japan's participation in these efforts has been a response to the increasing regional integration seen around the world and the expansion of unipolar US power.

A final point that should not be forgotten concerns Japan–Russia relations. The 1998 Moscow Declaration[12] on Building a Creative Partnership between Japan and the Russian Federation laid the foundations for future bilateral negotiations between the two countries. Even more important, though, was Japan's adoption of a strategy to 'Asianize' Russia. This Asianization strategy was an indirect means of furthering Japan–Russia relations by drawing Russia into Asia and giving the country appropriate status in multilateral arenas.

Japan's declaration of support for Russian participation in APEC and its ultimate cooperation in expanding the Group of Seven industrialized countries into a Group of Eight with the addition of Russia was based on the strategy of giving Russia international responsibility and drawing it into Asia and into the global management of international issues, in the hope that this would prompt Russia to also resolve bilateral issues in line with international rules.

Conclusions

Based on the above argumentation, it is possible to posit that the following will be among the principal foreign policy issues for Japan to address in the medium term (the next five to ten years).

1   To what extent can the Japan–US alliance be strengthened and further globalized under Japan's legal and political systems? Why is it important to strengthen the Japan–US alliance? It is vital for Japan to establish a solid strategy of its own for addressing these questions. The argument that we must maintain and strengthen the Japan–US alliance to counter the threat from

North Korea links the alliance with the old Cold War set-up; this makes it unconvincing in the medium term from the perspective of the global role of the Japan–US alliance.

Next, in reconciling the Japan–US alliance with Japan's legal system and politics, we must not forget to take into account the United Nations. The strengthening of the alliance must be undertaken in tandem with efforts to enhance the functions of the UN and to achieve UN reform.

2   In the medium term, the biggest challenge for Japanese foreign policy is how to deal with China. The task of positioning China as a responsible partner within the international community, encouraging it to fulfil its responsibilities as a major power, and at the same time building a partnership with China will be an important pillar of Japanese foreign policy in the coming years.

To this end, one of the key strategies for Japan is to bolster relations with countries surrounding China. Cooperation in Korean reunification, in Vietnam's economic development, and in closer integration in the Association of Southeast Asian Nations (ASEAN) should be important elements of its diplomatic strategy to deal with China.

3   To cope with these challenges, Japan must have a vision for the future of the international community and must increase its efforts to share this vision as much as possible with the United States, Europe, and its Asian neighbours. Efforts to reform the UN should also be positioned within this context.

Notes

1   For economic trends from 1990 to 2000, see Ministry of International Trade and Industry (ed.) 1991–2001.
2   As their main grounds for criticizing Japan's ODA, Toshio Watanabe and Yuji Miura cite (1) environmental problems and the issue of forced relocations, (2) the commercial nature of some aid, (3) the proportion of loans, and (4) vague provision standards. See Watanabe and Miura 2003: 95–120. For public responses to questions on the future of Japan's economic cooperation, see 'Public Opinion Survey on Diplomacy' (Public Relations Office, Minister's Secretariat, Cabinet Office) at www8.cao.go.jp/survey/h18/h18-gaiko/images/h28san.csv.
3   See Ito and Tanaka (eds) 2005, Sato 2006.
4   See Otake 2006.
5   'The Tokyo Declaration on the Japan–US Global Partnership' of January 1992 was renamed 'The Common Agenda for Cooperation in Global Perspective' at the summit meeting of Prime Minister Kiichi Miyazawa and President Bill Clinton in July 1993. To achieve the common goal of building a peaceful and prosperous world in the twenty-first century, the Japanese and US governments and private sectors are working to address the serious global challenges that future generations will face, principally (1) promoting health and human development, (2) responding to challenges to global stability, (3) protecting the global environment, and (4) advancing science and technology.
6   For example, the Task Force on Foreign Relations, established in September 2001, suggests in a report titled 'Basic Strategies for Japan's Foreign Policy in the 21st Century: New Era, New Vision, New Diplomacy' that the government should strengthen collaboration with NGOs, supporting a suggestion from the Second Consultative Committee on ODA Reform. See www.kantei.go.jp/jp/kakugikettei/2002/1128tf.html.

7 See, for example, Asian Population and Development Association 1998, Flavin and Eco Forum 21 (eds) 2006.
8 Sato 2005: 46–57.
9 A regular forum proposed by Prime Minister Goh Chok Tong of Singapore and launched in 1996. In April 2006 a Japanese–Finnish joint research report titled 'ASEM in its Tenth Year: Looking Back, Looking Forward' was produced, and the 6th ASEM Summit was held in Finland from 10 to 11 September that year.
10 See US Department of Defense 1995, Advisory Group on Defense Issues 1994, Japan Defense Agency 2005, also Ministry of Foreign Affairs home page www.mofa.go.jp/mofaj/area/usa/hosho/index.html.
11 See Grubb, Vrolijk, and Brack 1999, Oberthur and Ott 1999, Takeuchi 1998, Tanabe 1999, Takamura and Kameyama 2002.
12 'The Moscow Declaration on Building a Creative Partnership between Japan and the Russian Federation' was signed by Prime Minister Keizo Obuchi and President Boris Yeltsin during their summit meeting on 13 November 1998.

References

Advisory Group on Defense Issues (1994), *Nihon no anzen hosho to boeiryoku no arikata: 21 seiki e mukete no tenbo (The Modality of the Security and Defense Capability of Japan: The Outlook for the 21st century)*. Tokyo: Japan Defense Agency, August.

Asian Population and Development Association (1998), *Constraints on Development: Focus on China and India*. Tokyo: Asian Population and Development Association.

US Department of Defense (1995), *United States Security Strategy for the East Asia-Pacific Region*. Available at http://usembassy.state.gov/posts/ja3/wwwfsec1.pdf.

Flavin, Christopher, and Eco Forum 21 (eds) (2006), *Chikyu hakusho 2006–07*. Tokyo: Worldwatch Japan (originally published as State of the World 2006).

Grubb, Michael, Christiaan Vrolijk and Duncan Brack (1999), *The Kyoto Protocol: A Guide and Assessment*. London: Royal Institute of International Affairs.

Ito, Kenichi, and Akihiko Tanaka (eds) (2005), *Higashi Ajia kyodotai to Nihon no shinro (The East Asian Community and Japan's Path)*. Tokyo: NHK Books.

Japan Defense Agency (2005), *Nihon no boei: Boei hakusho: Heisei 17 nendo ban (Japan Defense 2005 White Paper)*. Tokyo: Gyosei.

Ministry of International Trade and Industry (ed.) (1991–2001), Tsusho hakusho (White Papers on International Economy and Trade) Tokyo: Printing Bureau, Ministry of Finance. (Note: MITI became the Ministry of Economy, Trade and Industry and Gyosei was the publisher of the White Paper in 2001).

Oberthur, Sebastian, and Hermann E. Ott (1999), *The Kyoto Protocol: International Climate Policy for the twenty-first century*. Berlin: Springer.

Otake, Hideo (2006), *Koizumi Jun'ichiro popyurizumu no kenkyu: Sono senryaku to shuho (Study on the Strategy and Method of Jun'ichiro Koizumi's Populism)*. Tokyo: Toyo Keizai Inc.

Sato, Koichi (2005), 'Chugoku to ASEAN shokoku' ('China and the Countries of ASEAN'), *Kokusai mondai*, 540, March, pp. 46–57.

—— (2006), 'Towards an East Asian Community: Prospects and the Role of Japan', *Ajia kenkyu*, 52 (3), July, pp. 1–16.

Takamura, Yukari and Yasuko Kameyama (2002), *Kyoto giteisho no kokusai seido: Chikyu ondanka kosho no toutatsu ten (The International System of the Kyoto Protocol: The Destination of Global Warming Negotiations)*. Tokyo: Shinzansha Publishers.

Takeuchi, Keiji (1998), *Chikyu ondanka no seijigaku* (The Politics of Global Warming). Tokyo: Asahi Shimbun.

Tanabe, Toshiaki (1999), *Chikyu ondanka to kankyo gaiko: Kyoto kaigi no koubou to sonogono tenkai* (*Global Warming and Environmental Diplomacy: The Negotiations at the Kyoto Conference and Subsequent Developments*). Tokyo: Jiji Press.

Watanabe, Toshio and Yuji Miura (2003), *ODA: Nihon ni nani ga dekiru ka* (*ODA: What Can Japan Do?*). Tokyo: Chuo Koron Shinsha.

Part IV

Social issues

7 Symptomatic transformations

Japan in the media and cultural globalization

Koichi Iwabuchi

Introduction

The increasing spread of its media culture in the world is perhaps one of the most significant changes occurring in the last ten years or so regarding contemporary Japan. The perception of Japan as a faceless economic power has been displaced by an image of a cultural power that produces and disseminates 'cool' and 'cute' cultures to many parts of the world such as animated movies, comics, video games, characters, fashion, food, film and so on. While this change can be seen as a corrective to the under-evaluation of cultural creativity that has long been developed in Japanese society, the pendulum seems to be swinging to the other pole of over-celebration. We have witnessed the proliferation of euphoric views, both domestically and internationally, of Japanese media culture in the world that appraise new kinds of cultural creativity that are different from their American counterparts and that argue for a significant role played by Japanese media culture in the international promotion of good images of Japan as well in its national economy.

However, such positive views should not close the eyes as to how the change has occurred in the uneven globalization process in which Japanese media culture and media industries are deeply involved. Given the intensifying of the global penetration of neo-liberal market fundamentalism and the widening gap between the haves and the have-nots, the political and economic structures that govern transnational media and cultural flows have recently begun attracting more urgent critical attention. In this context, media globalization is critically discussed in terms of the further penetration of American media cultures, but such a view would be unproductive if it disregarded the increase in non-Western exports and intraregional non-Western flows, in which Japanese media culture is a prominent exemplar. The increase in the media flows from non-Western regions during the last decade can be positively regarded as evidence of the relative demise of the Western, especially American, cultural hegemony, as well as inducing a salutary corrective to a West-centric analysis of media and cultural globalization (e.g. Erni and Chua 2004). However, it should be critically examined whether and how this development testifies to the deterioration of an uneven global media structure and power relations. In what sense is the rise of Japanese cultural power disrupting the global media and cultural unevenness, and can it be considered as an alternative move to an America-centred power structure?

By examining Japan's media and cultural exports in various locations – global, local and regional – this chapter will argue that the developments are symptomatic of the restructuring of unevenness in the transnational media and cultural connections, in which apparently opposing forces of decentralization and recentralization are working simultaneously and interactively in the contemporary world. It will briefly look into the spread of Japanese media culture in the light of three decentring trends of media globalization (Tomlinson 1997): the rise of non-Western players, the prevalence of 'glocalism', and the activation of non-Western regional connections. This chapter posits that these developments do not seriously challenge but in fact are constitutive of the restructuring process of uneven cultural globalization.

'Cool Japan' and the rise of non-Western players

In a widely cited book on the political economy of media globalization, Edward Herman and Robert McChesney (1997) state that Japan has money and technology but does not have a cultural influence on the world: 'Japan is supplying capital and markets to the global media system, but little else' (Herman and McChesney 1997: 104). However, one of the conspicuous trends in media globalization is the rise of non-Western players, of which Japan is a notable exemplar. Several commentators have attested to Japan's increasing cultural influence in the last several years: 'During the 1990s, Japan became associated with its economic stagnation. However, what many failed to realize is that Japan has transformed itself into a vibrant culture-exporting country during the 1990s' (*New York Times*, 23 November 2003). 'Japan's influence on pop culture and consumer trend runs deep.'(*Business Week*, 26 July 2004). 'Japan is reinventing itself on earth – this time as the coolest nation culture' (*Washington Post*, 27 December 2003). Indeed, Japan's media culture has become celebrated both domestically and internationally as a global cool culture and Japan as a cultural superpower.

While this seems to suggest that a dramatic change occurred vis-à-vis Japanese cultural exports in the late 1990s, the spread of Japanese media culture into the United States and Europe has been a gradual and steady phenomenon. The prevalence of Japanese popular culture throughout the world came to the fore in the 1980s. At this period the focus was on the cultural influence of made-in-Japan communication technological products such as the Sony Walkman, and subsequently on Japanese manufacturers' inroads into the content business, as exemplified by Sony and Matsushita's buyout of Hollywood studios in the late 1980s, which sought to gain access to the huge archives of Hollywood movies and other content products. This new development was interpreted through a viewpoint that resonates with Herman and McChesney's (1997), as exemplified by the lines a Japanese co-star delivers to the American protagonist, Michael Douglas, in the film *Black Rain*: 'Music and movies are all your culture is good for [...]. We [Japanese] make the machines' (quoted in Morley and Robins 1995: 159).

To adopt this perspective is to overlook the significant increase in Japanese exports of popular cultural products that was occurring during the same period. Following the success of Ōtomo Katsuhiro's hugely popular animation film *Akira* (1988), the quality and popularity of 'Japanimation' came to be recognized by the US market. In November 1995, the animated film *The Ghost in the Shell* was shown simultaneously in Japan, America and Britain. Its sales, according to *Billboard* (24 August 1996), propelled it to No. 1 in the US video charts. The export value of Japanese animation and comics to the US market amounted to $75 million in 1996 (*Sankei Shinbun*, 14 December 1996). Furthermore, the popularity of Japanese games software is demonstrated by the phenomenal success of Super Mario Brothers, Sonic and Pokémon. According to one survey, as a director of Nintendo pointed out, Mario was a better-known character among American children than Mickey Mouse (Akurosu Henshūshitsu 1995).

The popularity of TV animation series *Sailor Moon* and the huge success of Pokémon in the global market of the late 1990s warrant further research into Japanese cultural exports (Tobin 2004). Pokémon's penetration into global markets exceeds even that of Mario. As of June 2000, sales of Pokémon game software had reached about 65 million copies (22 million outside Japan); trading-cards about 4.2 billion (2.4 billion outside Japan); the animation series had been broadcast in 51 countries; the first featured film had been shown in 33 countries and its overseas box-office takings had amounted to $176 million; in addition, there had also been about 12,000 character merchandises (8,000 outside Japan) (Hatakeyama and Kubo 2000). These statistics clearly show that Pokémon has become a 'made-in-Japan' global cultural phenomenon (see Tobin 2004). Last but not least, Hayao Miyazaki's animation films are now widely respected, and *Sen to Chihiro no Kamikakushi* won the best film award at the Berlin Film Festival in 2002.

According to Sugiura (2003), industry estimates of Japanese exports of popular cultural products nearly tripled from 500 billion yen in 1992 to 1.5 trillion yen in 2002. This rise is dramatic, compared to a total export growth rate of 21 per cent for the same period. Animation consisted of 3.5 per cent of total exports from Japan to the United States in 2002 and Pokémon's film earned more than $10 billion in the United States alone, and was shown in about 70 countries. 'Hello Kitty', a cat-like character produced by the Japanese company Sanrio earned $1 billion a year outside Japan (Sugiura, 2003).

I have argued elsewhere that most Japanese cultural exports to Western markets are culturally neutral, in that the positive image and association of a Japanese culture or way of life is not generally related to the consumption of the products (see Iwabuchi 2002). Animation, computer games and characters may be recognized as originating in Japan and their consumption may well be associated with high technology or miniaturization; however, the appeal of such products is relatively independent of cultural images of the country of production. In contrast to American counterparts, these products do not attempt to sell the Japanese way of life. It is also well known that the characters of many Japanese animations or computer games tend to be consciously drawn as *mukokuseki*, which means that they are free of any association with particular national, racial or cultural characteristics.

Although the question of whether Japanese animations and characters invoke the image of Japanese culture and lifestyle is still moot, what is indisputable is that Japan has come to be regarded by a large number of young people in the United States, Europe and Asia as an artistic country that produces cool animations, games and characters. Undoubtedly this shift in the perception of Japanese 'cultural odour' has much to do with the attraction of the texts and imagery in themselves. However, it also needs to be understood in a dynamic process of cultural globalization that encourages the circulation and promotion of more non-Western media contents in the global markets – a point I shall be returning to later.

Glocalization: Japanese media and TV format business

Another conspicuous trend of media globalization is the increasing centrality of localism based on cultural adaptation. While cultural globalization is often discussed in terms of the homogenization of world culture, cultural specificity and diversity are no less articulated in the process. As demonstrated by the term *glocalization*, the strategy of tailoring cultural products to local conditions has become a marketing strategy for transnational media corporations in order to achieve global market penetration (Robertson 1995).

A prominent case in point is the rapid growth of the TV format business since the late 1990s. Thanks to the development of international television trade fairs and the maturation of television production techniques outside the United States (particularly in Europe and Asia), the practice of localizing foreign TV formats has become more institutionalized and systematically managed. In the global reach of the format business, Japan also plays an important role. Around the turn of the millennium, Japanese television networks began buying new global television formats such as *Who Wants to Be a Millionaire?*, *The Weakest Link* and *Survivor*. Yet the purchase of a few prominent European/American television formats tells only a partial story in the development of the contemporary Japanese television industry. While, on the international stage, format television products have in the past been predicated on the maxim 'Western television format goes global', the paradigm is shifting. In fact, Japanese television industries, with their relatively sophisticated skills and experience in production, export a considerable number of programmes and formats to many parts of the world, far more than they import.

The Japanese television industry started selling Japanese formats to Western markets back in the late 1980s. This was recognized as an effective way to enter lucrative Western markets, where the trading price of television programmes was at least ten times higher than in Asian markets. Initially though, Japanese programmes were not well received, apart from animation. TBS, the leading exporter of television programmes and formats in Japan, has so far sold programme formats to more than 40 countries. TBS started its format business when it sold the format of *Wakuwaku* [exciting] *Animal Land* – a quiz show dealing exclusively with animals – to the Netherlands in 1987 (still a popular show called *Waku Waku* in that country); the format has been sold to more than 20 other countries. The Japanese television industry has produced new kinds of audience participation programmes and reality television shows. It is a little known fact that the globally adapted format of *America's Funniest Home Videos* was originally produced by TBS. It was a segment of a variety show entitled *Katochan Kenchan Gokigen Terebi*, which was broadcast from 1986 to 1992. The American network ABC bought the rights to the format in 1989 and since then has exported the amateur video show format to more than 80 countries worldwide. The format of a video-game-like participation game show, *Takeshi's Castle*, which was originally broadcast during the 1980s in Japan, has also been exported to several Western countries including the United States, Germany and Spain.

Fuji TV's *Ryouri no Tetsujin* [Iron Chef] is an innovative cookery show in which professional chefs compete with each other. Each week two chefs, who in most cases represent different cuisines, are assigned to produce several dishes within one hour with one featured ingredient. Their struggles are dramatically reported and filmed in a live sports telecast style, with the stylishly decorated studio fitted out as the kitchen. Cooking skills, professional creativity, subtle presentation techniques, as well as the ultimate taste are all taken into consideration by four guest celebrities who adjudicate on proceedings. The programme was first exported to a US cable network but its popularity led the television producers of Paramount Network to make an American version by purchasing the format rights in 2001.

TBS has also been successful in selling reality television formats. One of the most widely distributed formats is *Shiawase Kazoku Keikaku* [Happy Family Plan]. It is a programme in which the father is assigned to master a task (such as juggling) within one week and to perform this successfully in the studio. If he succeeds, the family will receive the prize they nominated (such as an overseas trip) before the father was informed of the task. The highlight of the show is the father's final performance in the studio, but this is built up to by the dedication with which he has tried to master the task with the encouragement of other family members. Documentary-style home-videoing of the father's exertions, frustrations, the pressures induced by repetitive failures, the subsequent strengthening of family ties, and the re-establishment or recovery of the father's authority in the family during the course of his mastering the skill constitute the key elements. The show won the 1998 Silver Rose Award in Montreux for Best Game Show and an International Emmy Award in the same year. Its format has been sold to more than 30 countries all over the world.

The idea of 'glocal' is said to have its origin in Japanese corporate marketing strategy (Robertson 1995). Featherstone (1995: 9) has also argued, referring to the Japanese willingness and capacity to indigenize the foreign, that the strategy of glocalization has come to signify a new meaning of 'Japanization', which is 'a global strategy which does not seek to impose a standard product or image, but instead is tailored to the demands of the local market'. This kind of argument still tends to stress the uniqueness of Japanese cultural influence, which is assumed to show rather a different logic from its American counterpart. Yet this is untenable, not only because it attempts to mark the origin of practices that negate the idea of the origin itself. More importantly, such a view underestimates the worldwide marketing and institutionalization of glocalism by media and cultural industries, in which Japanese media and cultural industries are actively and collaboratively working as one player among many in the marketing of local specificity through common cultural formats.

Japanese media culture in East Asian media markets

Undoubtedly, it is East Asian countries that have provided Japanese media culture with its largest export market and most avid audience. The extensive reach of manga and animé is illustrated by the fact that an English version of the best-selling weekly manga magazine *Shonen Jump* is published in the United States. Yet the popularity of this cultural form is far more firmly entrenched in East Asia, where translated versions of Japanese weekly comics are available just a few days after publication of the originals, and the number and variety of animé series broadcast by television stations is much greater than in the West. Television drama series with 11 or 12 episodes – a staple format of TV schedules in Japan – are fast becoming a genre in their own right. CDs by Japanese pop stars are released almost simultaneously in Japan and other East Asian countries. In Taiwan the many young people who love Japanese pop culture and follow it keenly have been named the *harizu* (Japan tribe), which became something of a social phenomenon in the 1990s. A 2001 survey conducted by a Japanese advertising agency found that Japanese consumer culture and products were far more likely than their American equivalents to be considered 'cool' by young people in the cities of East Asia. While the boom in popularity of Japanese media culture has now stabilized, the penetration of Japanese media cultures into East Asian markets is still much more far-reaching, compared to their spread in the Euro-American markets.

Many observers refer to the cultural proximity of Japan and other Asian countries to explain the reception Japanese pop culture enjoys in East Asia. In short, they argue that viewers and listeners in the region perceive Japanese cultural products as familiar because Japan is felt to be culturally close to them. When I conducted a survey in Taipei in the late 1990s, I often heard the view expressed that Japanese TV series appeared culturally closer, more familiar, more realistic, and therefore easier to empathize with than American series. One respondent said, 'Japanese series reflect the reality of our lives. American series portray neither our real experiences nor our yearnings.' Another commented, 'I had never seen programmes that express what we feel as accurately as Japanese dramas do. Lifestyles and culture in the West are so different from ours that it's hard to get emotionally involved in American TV series.' For these men and women, American shows may be unmatched in their production quality, but it is Japanese TV dramas they turn to for stories that they can relate to, and that they want to discuss with their friends.

Japanese TV dramas, then, with their cultural proximity, appear to be depicting the 'here and now' of East Asia in a way that US programmes fail to do. However, this development may also be subject to the process of cultural globalization, and thus the perception of cultural proximity should not be considered as something given, static or natural. The comfortable sense of familiarity that Taiwanese and Hong Kong audiences feel when watching Japanese TV series is based on a sense of coevality (Fabian 1983) or contemporaneity stemming from shared socio-economic conditions. Experiences common to inhabitants of capitalist urban spaces – such as the simultaneous distribution of information and products and the spread of consumerist culture and lifestyles, the development of the media industry and market, the emergence of young middle-class people with considerable spending power, and the transformation of women's status and attitudes – have all given rise to a sense of contemporaneity in terms of socio-cultural life (which includes sexual relationships, friendship and working conditions). It is this that underpins the favourable reception of Japanese popular culture in the Asian region. In this sense, the experience of perceived cultural proximity must be viewed as something dynamic that describes what people, society and culture are *becoming*, not what they are. It is not so much a matter of being proximate as one of *becoming* proximate, and this means we must consider not only the space axis but also the time axis. The East Asian modernity that Japanese TV dramas represent has been articulated in the interaction between the global, the regional and the local (for a detailed discussion, see Iwabuchi 2002).

Globalization has been experienced unequally around the world in the context of a modern history dominated by the West. The West's indisputable cultural, political, economic and military hegemony has forged what may be termed the modern 'world system', and the influence of the modernity configured in Western capitalist societies (especially the United States) pervades the world. But the modern experiences forced upon non-Western countries have at the same time produced disparate forms of indigenous modernity and have highlighted the fallacy of discussing modernity exclusively from the standpoint of Western experiences. As a corollary of ongoing asymmetrical cultural encounters in the course of the spread of Western modernity, people discovered that many of the world's cultures were becoming simultaneously (and paradoxically) similar to and different from their own (Ang and Stratton 1996). 'Familiar differences' and 'bizarre similarities' interconnect on multiple levels within the dynamics of unequal global cultural encounters and are engendering a complex perception of cultural distance.

If Japanese popular culture is enjoyed in Asia with the same relish as local delicacies such as *dim sum* or *kimchi* (*Newsweek*, Asian edition, 8 November 1999), this is because it represents, in an East Asian context, the cultural configuration, blending difference and similarity, that globalization encourages. In East Asia there are many young viewers who genuinely relate to the everyday (and more unusual) happenings in the lives of the young Tokyoites portrayed in Japanese TV dramas and who identify with the their dreams and aspirations. This shows, I would suggest, that Japanese media culture's being/becoming proximate also reflects the comfortable difference that Taiwanese and Hong Kong audiences feel towards Japan. Asian viewers empathize with Japanese characters because Japan is perceived as similar but different, different but common. The sense of realism in which sameness and difference, closeness and distance, and reality and dreams delicately mix elicits sympathy from viewers – a kind of sympathy that perhaps cannot be gained from American media cultures.

Intensifying media flows in East Asia

The further penetration of Japanese media culture in East Asia is closely related to the activation of regional media flows, which is the third decentring trend that has been facilitated by the cultural globalization process. In the 1990s, East Asian media markets rapidly expanded and close partnerships were formed in the media industry as companies pursued marketing strategies and joint production ventures spanning several different markets. Popular culture from places such as Japan, Hong Kong, Taiwan and Korea is finding a broader transnational acceptance in the region, leading to the formation of new links among people in Asia, especially the youth. This trend has shown no sign of letting up. Asian markets have become even more synchronized, joint East Asian projects in film and music have become more common, and singers and actors from around the region are engaged in activities that transcend national borders.

In this context, Japanese popular culture is not the only form that represents Asia's here and now through the intermingling of similarities and differences among multiple modernities. Many other East Asian regions are also creating their own cultural forms within the social and cultural contexts specific to their countries, and media flows are becoming more and more multilateral. While it can be argued that the production of TV dramas in East Asia has been, to some extent, stimulated by Japanese series aimed at young audiences, the resulting series dexterously blend a variety of local elements, and are far more than mere imitations of Japanese shows. An especially interesting case is the Taiwanese drama *Meteor Garden*, which is based on a Japanese manga about the lives of high-school students entitled *Hana yori dango* [Boys before Flowers]. This series skilfully transplants the comic's narrative to a Taiwanese context while retaining the original characters and their Japanese names. According to the *Asahi Shinbun* (12 July 2002), although this series is subject to a broadcast ban in China because of fears that the love affairs and violence depicted in the drama series may exert a bad influence on students, the series has become very popular among young Chinese thanks to the circulation of pirated videos. This is a case in which a hybridization of Japanese and Taiwanese cultural imagination has created new East Asian cultural links that have circumvented political restrictions.[1]

The most conspicuous trend at the beginning of twenty-first century is the rise of Korean 'Wave' or '*Hallyu*' (see also Chapter 8 of this volume). It is often argued that Korean television drama production has been influenced by Japanese dramas in no small way (Lee 2004). Ever since a South Korean series bearing many similarities to *Tokyo Love Story* was made in 1993, Japanese television series have given Korean drama production fresh direction. But rather than merely copying Japanese shows, the Koreans have produced drama series portraying Asia's here and now with their own appeal, which are being circulated in Asian markets. Korean television series and pop music are now receiving an even warmer welcome than their Japanese equivalents in places such as Taiwan, Hong Kong and China.

One of the main reasons for the success of Korean television dramas is their depiction of family matters, which enables them to appeal to a wider range of viewers than do Japanese programmes. Many young viewers also prefer South Korean dramas to Japanese ones in terms of realism and their ability to relate to the characters and story lines. According to interviews I conducted with Taiwanese university students in 2001, Japanese series tend to focus solely on young people's loves and jobs, and this restricts the scope of their stories. Korean dramas, on the other hand, while featuring young people's romances as a central theme, also portray the problems and bonds of parents and children, grandparents and other relatives. This resonates more deeply with the real-life experiences of young people in Taiwan. The restricted relationships and daily lives of young people featured in the world of Japanese TV dramas, which Ito (2004) describes as a 'microcosm', have attracted many followers in the Asian region, but Korean dramas have achieved a new level of realism by portraying a slightly different East Asian here and now.

Japan, too, is embracing the Korean Wave. Most notably, the Korean TV drama series *Winter Sonata* proved a phenomenal success in 2003, so much so that many viewers (mostly middle-aged women) started to learn Korean, visit Korea and study the history of Japanese colonialism. In this process a significant audience came to the realization that they harboured a prejudice against Korea as a backward country (see Mori 2004). Belief in Japan's superiority over the rest of Asia – that it is separate from the rest, though belonging geographically and culturally to Asia – remains firmly rooted, but such attitudes are being shaken as countries in Asia become more and more interconnected through media flows. This may make Japanese people realize that they now inhabit the same temporality and spatiality as people in other Asian regions and that the peoples of Asia, while being subjected to common waves of modernization, urbanization and globalization, have experienced these phenomena in similar yet different ways in their own particular contexts. This may also prove to be an opportune moment for Japanese people to critically review the state of their own modernity by engaging with other East Asian media cultures.

Decentring and recentring

It can be argued that the cases discussed so far testify to the decentring trends against US-dominated media and cultural flows. However, is the development of Japanese media exports and regional flows in East Asia really implicated in uneven globalization processes? I would argue that this is not necessarily the case. The increase in Japanese cultural exports can be viewed as a sign that some changes are occurring in the structuring forces of cross-border cultural flows and connections. Japan's cultural exports have boomed over the past decade, at a time when, paradoxically, it has become less relevant to assume absolute cultural and symbolic hegemony in specific countries or cultures. This has been a period when the globalization of culture has accelerated through astonishing advances in communications technology, enabling people in all corners of the globe to link up instantaneously, through the integration of markets and capital by giant multinational corporations, and through the dynamics of local cultural indigenization that downplay the direct cultural power of any single country of origin. The interaction of these factors has made transnational flows of culture more complex and multi-directional, yet not in such a way as to radically transform the unevenness underlying the flows.

One way to comprehend this complexity is to re-examine the cases discussed above and to analyse how contradictory vectors are operating simultaneously and interactively. First is the pair of decentring and recentring. The decentralization of power configurations, as discussed earlier, can be seen in the emergence of (transnational) media corporations based in Japan and other non-Western countries as global players. While it is no longer convincing to automatically equate globalization with Americanization, there is no denying the enormity of the American global cultural influence and a new centre has not emerged to take the place of the United States. The point is that it is no longer possible or indeed desirable to view the uneven structure of global cultural connections as bipartite, with one-way transfers of culture from the centre to the periphery. Cultural power still does matter, but it is being dispersed through the web of corporate alliances occurring in various parts of the world. Power structure is being decentred at the same time as it is being recentred in this process.

Cross-border partnerships and cooperation among multinational corporations and capital involving Japan and other non-Western regions are being driven forward, with America as a pivotal presence. While the inroads Japanese companies have made into Hollywood and the global diffusion of animé and video games may look like signs that America is, comparatively speaking, losing its global cultural hegemony, in reality these phenomena simply illustrate that the pattern of global dominance by transnational media conglomerates centred on America and other developed countries is becoming more firmly entrenched. Sony Corporation's 1989 purchase of a major Hollywood studio was a dramatic demonstration of the breakthrough of Japanese corporations into the global entertainment software business, but this was always a matter of Japanese firms integrating themselves into American cultural power and distribution networks.

The spread of Japanese animé and video games throughout the world has also been underpinned by the stepping-up of mergers, partnerships and other forms of cooperation among multinational media corporations based in developed countries, principally the United States. It is American distribution networks that help Pokémon (distributed by Warner Brothers) and the animé films of Hayao Miyazaki (distributed by Disney) to be released worldwide. What is more, the Pokémon animé series and movies seen by audiences around the world – with the exception of those seen in some parts of Asia – have been 'Americanized' by Nintendo of America, a process that involves removing some of their Japaneseness to make them more acceptable to American and European audiences (Iwabuchi 2004). In turn, Hollywood is becoming more inclined to internationally oriented film production as it realizes the profitability of non-Western markets and the usefulness of collaborating with non-Western films, as shown by its remakes of Japanese and Korean films and by its employment of more directors and actors from Hong Kong and Taiwan. Transnational media flows are being reorganized in a highly dispersed and ubiquitous power structure through the intensifying collaboration of (multinational) media corporations and media creators based in various developed nations.

Regional flows are not free from this force either. As exemplified by STAR TV, owned by NEWS Corporation and MTV ASIA, global media giants are penetrating regional media flows by deploying localization strategies. It should also be noted that the activation of regional media flows is based on the rise of regional hubs such as Japan, Korea, Hong Kong and Taiwan and their corporate alliances. Major media corporations are forging transnational partnerships and facilitating mutual promotion of media culture. Co-production and remakes of films are becoming more common, with the aim of targeting multiple markets in the region, which can be seen as the emergence of 'Asiawood' (*Newsweek Asia*, 21 May 2001). These decentring trends in the region indicate the activation of multi-directional flows. However, in reality, the mode of media production is being recentred through the alliance of major media corporations in East Asian countries. This development engenders a new international hierarchy in terms of production capacity, with Japan, Korea, Hong Kong and Taiwan in the top tier.

Another key issue concerns the interplay of homogenization and heterogenization: globalization does not mean simply the standardization of the world through the spread of the same products, values and images transmitted from the United States and other developed Western countries. Globalization is, in fact, constantly giving rise to new differences. Globally disseminated cultural products and images are consumed and received differently within the specific cultural framework formed by the political, economic and social contexts of each locality and by people of differing statuses, depending on their gender, ethnicity, class, age and other factors. At the same time, in each locality these products and images are reconfigured through a process of hybridization. American popular culture is exported to countries throughout the world, but the cultural products that perform best are those that mix in local elements while absorbing American cultural influences. Meanings are negotiated locally, resulting in the creation of new products that are more than mere copies.

Here again, this increase in cultural diversity is being governed by the logic of capital and organized within the context of globalization (Hannerz 1996). As demonstrated by the prevalence of the television format business, globalization does not destroy cultural differences but rather brings about a 'peculiar form of homogenization' while fostering them (Hall 1991). The global spread of American consumer culture has led to the creation of a series of cultural formats through which various differences can be adjusted. These formats could be described as the axis of the global cultural system. In this sense, one could say that 'America' has become a base format that regulates the process by which modern culture is configured around the world. As multinational media corporations press ahead with global tie-ups and partnerships, they are also trying to raise their profits by tailoring this axis to every corner of the world while promoting cultural diversity in every market. The world is becoming more diverse through standardization and more standardized through diversification. Symbolic power in the age of globalization is not concentrated in the place where the culture originated; it is exercised through the processes of active cultural negotiation that take place in each locality. In fact, it is now almost impossible to imagine local cultural creativity outside the context of globalization and the profits cannot be sufficiently produced without 'respecting' local specificity that is mostly equated with the national market in an essentialist manner. These moves are first and foremost organized and promoted by transnational corporations based in the developed countries, while cultural formats that are shared in many parts of the world originate almost exclusively from a handful of such countries.

Brand nationalism

The other key interplay of contradictory vectors is that of nationalism and transnationalism. It is argued that the efficacy of the nation-state's boundary policing in the modern constitution of politics, economy and culture is deeply problematized in the globalization process and that the term 'transnational' more productively directs our attention to a new perspective of the flows, disregarding the boundaries set up and controlled by the nation-states. The most important of these flows are those of capital, people and media/images (Hannerz 1996).

Nonetheless, transnational connections do not fully displace national boundaries, thoughts and feelings. Unlike the term 'global', the term 'transnational' tends to 'draw attention to what it negates' (Hannerz 1996: 6). As Michael Peter Smith (2001: 3) argues, while problematizing the assumed efficacy of the nation-state's boundary policing in the modern constitution of politics, economy and culture, the transnational perspective explicates 'the continuing significance of borders, state policies, and national identities even as these are often transgressed by transnational communication circuits and social practices'. Transnational media flows highlight the fact that it is no longer tenable for any country to contain its cultural orientation and agendas within clearly demarcated national boundaries. In spite of, or perhaps because of, the impossibility of controlling the globalization process within a national framework, the transgressive tendency of popular culture and its boundary-violating impulse of cultural hybridization are never free from the nationalizing force desperately seeking to re-demarcate and control cultural boundaries. As Roger Rouse (1995) argues, '[t]he transnational has not so much displaced the national as resituated it and thus reworked its meanings'.

This point has become salient as states become more interested in the creation and promotion of 'cool' national brands. In the 1980s and 1990s, 'culture' extended its role to other spheres and became a useful vehicle for various social actors, including marginalized people and NGOs, to pursue their own political and economic interests (Yúdice 2003). Today, though, it is the alliance of national governments and private (transnational) corporations that most powerfully use 'culture' in the establishment and export of national brand cultures such as media, tourism, fashion, foods and so forth. For states to maximize national interests and beat international competition, culture has come to be regarded as politically important to enhance 'soft power', and as economically important for attracting multinational capital and developing new industries in which creative industries play a significant role.

Perhaps 'Cool Britannia' might be the most famous state policy for this, but many national governments in East Asia are also eager to pursue this kind of policy. It is well known that the Korean government engaged with it in the 1990s, and that this contributed to the Korean Wave. Following the Korean success, the Japanese government has also actively sought to develop cultural policy. 'Cool Japan' is expected to become another Japanese core export commodity and the Japanese government has organized several committees to discuss what policies need to be implemented. Many Japanese universities have also established programmes to train professional creators by inviting the participation of prominent film directors and animation producers, including the internationally renowned film directors Takeshi Kitano and Kiyoshi Kurosawa.

Politically, it is anticipated that media culture will improve the image of Japan in East Asia to such an extent that the historical memory of Japanese colonialism will be eradicated in the region. The need to export Japanese media culture is being even more eagerly discussed with the recent rise of anti-Japanese feeling in China and Korea vis-à-vis historical and territorial issues. Following a recent survey that revealed that Korean youth who consume Japanese popular culture tend to feel more empathy with Japan (*Asahi Shinbun*, 27 April 2005), the imperative to step up the export of media culture to Asian markets has become ever more pressing. This strategy is viewed as strengthening Japan's cultural diplomacy as it presents, from a Japanese perspective, an opportunity to enhance Asia's understanding of a post-war 'liberated' and 'humane' Japan.

While the nationalistic objectives of Japan's cultural policy may seem self-evident, discussion of Japanese cultural exports tends to be confined to a narrow context at the expense of wider public interests. Media culture's potential to stimulate transnational dialogue should certainly not be dismissed out of hand; it has promoted new kinds of mutual understanding and connections in East Asia. However, even though mediated cultural exchange may improve the image of the nation and enhance a sense of empathy and belonging in its audiences, the history and memory of colonialism cannot be easily erased. Historical issues necessitate sincere dialogue with the broad involvement of all citizens, which cultural policy should try to promote.

A preoccupation with market-oriented and international policy concerns will fail to give due attention to marginalized cultures and to the issues (re)generated by transnational cultural flows. There is an urgent need to discuss and develop policy agendas on various issues, such as the high concentration of media ownership in the hands of a few global companies; intellectual property rights; and the transnational, international and intranational division of cultural labour (Miller and Leger 2001). It is also worth remembering that the new connections being forged through media culture are reinforcing practices of inclusion and exclusion of certain groups in society. In East Asia, the transnational links have been developed between the dominant media industries and between the dominant media cultures of metropolises. They tend to exclude a tremendous number of people and their 'unprofitable' cultural expressions and concerns in terms of gender, sexuality, race, ethnicity, class, age, region, etc. East Asian connections forged through media culture are underpinned by the logic of capital and market, which benefit a fortunate few, while acting freely beyond the confines of national frameworks in accordance with the fundamental tenets of consumerism. These uneven transnational flows and connectivities are not only disregarded but furthered by the collaboration between nation-states and the private media sector in the branding of the nation.

Conclusion

There is an optimistic view that the media are stimulating cosmopolitan awareness among the inhabitants of the 'global village'. However, a series of events at the beginning of the twenty-first century has forced us to realize that, with the borders dividing countries and cultures becoming porous and blurred, and the power structure fragmenting and dispersed, exclusion and imbalance are being violently institutionalized on a number of levels.

In this context, any attempt to interpret the increase in Japanese popular cultural exports needs to attend to the shifting nature of transnational cultural power. The decentring process of globalization makes it impossible to single out the absolute symbolic centre that belongs to a particular country or region. However, this does not mean that global cultural power has disappeared: it has been dispersed, but at the same time made even more solid. The view that equates globalization with Americanization is no longer convincing when analysing the cultural context. Crucially, the unevenness in transnational cultural flows is intensified by the various kinds of alliances among transnational media industries in the developed countries that include non-Western regions. As states of the developed countries strengthen their alliance with (multinational) corporations to enhance national interests, the (re)production of cultural asymmetry and unevenness has become further institutionalized in the inter-national arena.

Certainly the spread of Japanese media cultures in the world has corrected the hitherto dominant view of Japan as a faceless economic power. However, an emerging view of Japan as a cultural superpower shows another diagnostic gap between how the global spread of Japanese media culture is euphorically perceived both domestically and internationally and what it actually attests to in the era of uneven globalization. The significance of any changes in contemporary Japan regarding media culture cannot be well understood without a symptomatic reading of it in the wider context of the intricate process of decentring and recentring of transnational power relations.

Acknowledgements

An earlier version of this chapter appeared in Daya Thussu (ed.) 2006, *Media on the Move: Global Flow and Contra-flow* (London and New York: Routledge)

Notes

1 Japanese TV stations also produced their own version of the drama series based on the comic in the autumn of 2005. This was clearly influenced by the popularity of the Taiwan drama series and in this sense it is an example of contra-flow within East Asia.

References

Akurosu Henshūshitsu (ed.) (1995), *Sekai shōhin no tsukurikata: Nihon media ga sekai wo seishita hi (The Making of Global Commodities: The Day when Japanese Media Conquered the World)*. Tokyo: Parco Shuppan.

Ang, Ien and Jon Stratton (1996), 'Asianizing Australia: Notes Toward a Critical Transnationalism in Cultural Studies', *Cultural Studies* 10 (1), pp. 16–36.

Erni, John Nguyet and Siew Keng Chua (eds) (2004), *Asian Media Studies: Politics of Subjectivities*. Malden, MA: Blackwell.

Fabian, Johannes (1983), *Time and the Other: How Anthropology Makes its Object*. New York: Columbia University Press.

Featherstone, Mike (1995), *Undoing Culture: Globalization, Postmodernism and Identity*. London: Sage.

Hall, Stuart (1991), 'The Local and the Global: Globalization and Ethnicity', in A. King (ed.), *Culture, Globalization, and the World-System*. London: Macmillan, pp. 19–39.

Hannerz, Ulf (1996), *Transnational Connections: Culture, People, Places*. London: Routledge.

Hatakeyama, Kenji and Masakazu Kubo (2000), *Pokemon Story*. Tokyo: Nikkei BP.

Herman, Edward and Robert McChesney (1997), *The Global Media: The New Missionaries of Corporate Capitalism*. London: Cassell.

Ito, Mamoru (2004), 'The Representation of Femininity in Japanese Television Drama of the 1990s', in Koichi Iwabuchi (ed.), *Feeling Asian Modernities: Transnational Consumption of Japanese TV Drama*. Hong Kong: University of Hong Kong Press, pp. 25–42.

Iwabuchi, Koichi (2002), *Recentering Globalization: Popular Culture and Japanese Transnationalism*. Durham, NC: Duke University Press.

—— (2004), 'How 'Japanese' is Pokemon?' in Joseph Tobin (ed.), *Pikachu's Global Adventure: The Rise and Fall of Pokémon*. Durham, NC: Duke University Press, pp. 53–79.

Lee, Dong-Hoo (2004), 'Cultural Contact with Japanese TV Dramas: Modes of Reception and Narrative Transparency', in Koichi Iwabuchi (ed.), *Feeling Asian Modernities: Transnational Consumption of Japanese TV Drama*. Hong Kong: University of Hong Kong Press, pp. 251–74.

Miller, Toby and Marie Claire Leger (2001), 'Runaway Production, Runaway Consumption, Runaway Citizenship: The New International Division of Cultural Labour', *Emergences* 11 (1), pp. 89–115.

Mori, Yoshitaka (ed.) (2004), *Nisshiki Kantyu (Japanese Style, Korean Wave)*. Tokyo: Serika Shobo.

Morley, David and Kevin Robins (1995), *Spaces of Identities: Global Media, Electronic Landscapes and Cultural Boundaries*. London: Routledge.

Robertson, Roland (1995), 'Glocalization: time–space and homogeneity–heterogeneity', in Mike Featherstone *et al.* (eds), *Global Modernities*. London: Sage, pp. 25–44.

Rouse, Roger (1995), 'Thinking Through Transnationalism: Notes on the Cultural Politics of Class Relations in the Contemporary United States', *Public Culture* 7, pp. 353–402.

Smith, Michael Peter (2001), *Transnational Urbanism: Locating Globalization*. Malden, MA: Blackwell.

Sugiura, Tsutomu (2003), 'Hi wa mata noboru: Pokemon kōkokuron' ('On Pokémon benefiting the nation'), *Bungei Shunju*, October, pp. 186–93.

Tobin, Joseph (ed.) (2004), *Pikachu's Global Adventure: The Rise and Fall of Pokémon*. Durham, NC: Duke University Press.

Tomlinson, John (1997), 'Cultural Globalization and Cultural Imperialism', in A. Mohammadi (ed.), *International Communication and Globalization: A Critical Introduction*. London: Sage, pp. 170–90.

Yúdice, George (2003) *The Expedience of Culture: Uses of Culture in the Global Era*. Durham, NC: Duke University Press.

8 Reidentified Japan

Cultural turns in television commercials after the 1980s

Shoji Yamada

Introduction

It is a common saying that the television commercial[1] is a mirror that reflects society. We can remember the good old days by watching commercials from that time. Looking back at images reflected in the mirror, we can identify the characteristics of the period. That means commercials could be a useful resource for cultural studies. The history of the Japanese commercial started in 1953 with the opening of the first commercial broadcasting station (NTV). It is estimated that over 500,000 commercial clips were created in more than 50 years. The history of commercials in Japan is certainly lengthy enough to be taken as a topic for academic discussion.

Among the various transitions of Japanese commercials, we should pay particular attention to a 'shift' which took place during the 1980s. The 'shift' can be described in a single phrase as 'the end of culturally occupied Japan' or 'the Japanization of Japan'. This shift reflects the process of reidentification of Japan that was going on at the time. We can also find other minor 'shifts' in Japanese commercials: 'Bondage to the West' in the 1990s, and 'Japanese go to Korea' after 2004. Each of these represents the emergence of new types of commercials that we could hardly find before the 1990s.

Some scholars are beginning to focus on the 1980s as the key moment in the history of contemporary Japanese culture. Hiroyuki Hara (原宏之), for example, identifies the 1980s as the period of 'bubble culture'; it was the 'end of post-war' and the 'beginning of post-post-war'.[2] Kōji Murata (村田晃嗣) argues that Japan caught up with the West in the 1980s; it was politically conservative, economically flourishing, socially flippant, and yet all Japanese were full of vigour.[3] As Eiji Ōtsuka (大塚英志) points out, *manga* and *anime*, which have been receiving political attention in recent years as Japanese 'Soft Power', also originated in the 1980s. That decade saw the birth of *otaku* (geek, or nerd) culture.[4]

In this chapter, I will discuss these 'shifts' by focusing on commercials after the 1980s. The aim of the discussion is to clarify how commercials in Japan reflect the country's socio-economic status as well as its view of the rest of the world.

How can we use commercials for cultural studies?

First of all, let us examine how commercials could be useful material for cultural studies. It is always pointed out that 'we can see what commercial producers created; however, we cannot see how the commercials were accepted in society; it is even more doubtful to think that they reflect "real" society'.

Certainly, one cannot tell whether or not commercials reflect 'real' society. Similarly, it is difficult to know how the commercials were accepted in the past. One reason is that we have limited means of approaching the audiences of the past; we depend on documentary records or the uncertain memories of living witnesses.

However, it is not an exaggeration to say that high-profile or award-winning commercials reflect the social situation of their time, because producers of commercials put enormous effort into creating a clip acceptable to the audience. High-profile commercials can be considered to carry within them what the producers felt to be the case at the time.

The merit of using commercials as a resource for research is the ease with which they allow us to gain an intuitive grasp on the past social situation; in that sense, they are suitable for the purpose of studying public consciousness. However, I should also point out a vital defect in using commercials for academic study: most of the commercials that were broadcast have already been disposed of without leaving any records. Therefore, it is impossible to conduct a complete enumeration of past instances. What we see today is only a limited selection preserved according to various criteria. It is important to know what kind of commercials were selected and archived; in other words, researchers should also be aware of the possible quality and quantity of commercials that have not been preserved.

It is said that 300,000 to 400,000 commercial clips were produced before 1985. Only 100,000 clips have been kept in the form of original negatives, and most of these seem to have been burned in 2005 for various reasons.[5] I assume that some of them survive in digital format, but no one knows exactly.

In this article I mainly use the television commercial database (CMDB) built up at the International Research Centre for Japanese Studies (Nichibunken). The CMDB contains all the ACC (All Japan Radio and Television Commercial Confederation, 全日本シーエム放送連盟) award-winning commercials from 1961 to 1997 (4,412 clips). From these, we should be able to understand the criteria for the ACC award.

The ACC award is considered to be the highest award for television and radio commercials in Japan. It is chosen by prominent commercial creators, with their producers' eyes. ACC juries tend to give awards to clips that show visual excellence or arouse public interest. Consequently, they are not necessarily the most frequently aired commercials on television. Even among the commercials that were awarded the first prize for the year, we can find clips that were probably aired only a few times late at night or early in the morning. That means very few people may have seen them on television, despite the grand prize. Kōji Nanba (難波功士) ironically called these 'commercials made to win prizes'.[6]

In addition, ACC award-winning commercials are not necessarily those that make hits of the advertised goods or services. A car commercial from 1984 that featured a frilled lizard is a typical case: the lizard won great popularity with its odd way of running, but not so many people bought the car.

In spite of many difficulties, ACC award-winning commercials are useful for academic study. The ACC has archives of almost all the prize-winning clips. That means we can conduct a virtually complete enumeration within the award; a great benefit to scholars who want to study Japanese commercials.

In this chapter, I focus on the commercials that seem to reflect Japanese views of the West, Asia and Japanese culture. Analysing the characteristics of the clips, Japanese attitudes towards them can be divided into two stages: (1) before the 1990s and (2) after the 1990s. By comparing the commercials at these two stages, we will examine the reidentification process of Japan and Japaneseness.

The West in Japanese commercials before the 1990s

Longing for the West before the 1980s

At the end of the 1960s, the 'Longing for the West' type of commercial appeared in ACC award-winning clips. I can point out two typical commercial series:

1 Nescafé's 'World City Series' which started in 1967 and is assumed to have continued until the mid-1970s, and
2 'JAL Pack' from 1965 to the early 1980s.

The 'Longing for the West' type of commercial may have existed before the mid 1960s; however, I cannot find any ACC award-winning clips from then. That is to say, the creators did not recognize any prominence in this type of commercial, even if it existed.

Nescafé's 'World City Series' depicted mostly Western big cities such as London, Paris and New York. The London version, for example, has the following voice-over:

伝統の街、ロンドンの男たち
彼らの毎朝は、新しい儀式ではじまる。
ネスカフェの儀式、コーヒーブレイク。
大きなカップで飲む、うまいコーヒー。
イギリスの男たちは、どこにいてもこの一杯は飲む。
好みに応じて、どんなひとでも満足する特別あつらえの味、ネスカフェ
男の街の、男のコーヒー。
世界の都市で、そして日本で選ばれた味のよさ。
コーヒー呑みのコーヒー、ネスカフェ。

(translation)

Men in London, a city of tradition, are starting their morning with a new ceremony.
The Nescafé ceremony: a coffee break.
Good coffee, in a large cup: men in Great Britain have a cup of coffee wherever they are.
Nescafé suits everybody's taste and satisfies them.
It's a man's coffee in a man's city.
Nescafé is the coffee for coffee lovers: it is chosen in many cities in the world, and in Japan.

According to the clips, all people in Western cities enjoy a cup of Nescafé at coffee break. It sent a message like: 'Nescafé is a standard coffee in the West. You Japanese must have the same coffee if you want to catch up with them.' The clip induced in the Japanese audience a longing for the West. We should bear in mind that these clips differ from 'Approval of the West' type commercials, which I shall discuss later, since Nestlé is not a Japanese but a Western company and, in that sense, its products have already been approved by the West.

JAL Pack is a package tour to overseas destinations conducted by Japan Airlines. Overseas trips had been prohibited after the Second World War; the ban was lifted in 1964. The JAL Pack campaign started after the removal of the ban. The tour price was, however, well above the average monthly wage: for example, a 12-day tour of Europe cost 305,000 yen, when the average monthly salary of a newly hired university graduate was 23,000 yen. An overseas trip to Western countries was a dream for most Japanese. In a JAL Pack commercial, *Impressed* (1972), a Japanese lady travels alone to Rome, Greece and Paris and says to herself at the Eiffel tower: 'とうとう来たんだわ (At last, I've got here!)' This commercial depicted the woman's emotional fulfilment of her dream of visiting Europe.

During the 1960s and 1970s, very few Japanese went overseas. They imagined the West through movies and high-quality imported items. The West was nothing other than a place of adoration and countries with which Japan should catch up as quickly as possible.

Approval of the West after the 1970s

In the 1970s, commercials that could be described as 'Approval of the West' emerged. This type of clip featured famous film actors of the West praising Japanese products. Numerous foreign actors appeared in Japanese commercials in the first half of the 1970s; the trend itself formed the 'Approval of the West' phenomenon.

One of the most famous and the most successful commercials of this kind must be Mandam: *The Whereabouts of Men* (1971), featuring Charles Bronson (1921–2003). In the clip, Bronson goes back to his apartment in a skyscraper, takes off his shirt and remembers his gun-fighting act from a cowboy movie while putting Mandam tonic on his body, and saying 'Mmmm, Mandam'.

This commercial sparked a boom, and sales of Mandam, a male cosmetic line, shot up and relieved the financial difficulties of the manufacturer, Tanchō (丹頂). Because the product name had won such great popularity, Tanchō altered its company name to Mandam.

In the same year, a commercial for the Honda N3 (a small car equipped with automatic transmission, 1971), featuring Keiko Kishi (岸恵子) (1932–) was aired. Kishi, who lived in Paris, was well known as an actress of international calibre. Kishi drives round Paris; policemen look at the car and say 'Honda automatic!' Kishi says in the clip: 'ホンダはとてもかわいらしいし ... パリの町を縫っていくのにすごく便利 (The Honda is lovely … it's very handy for driving round Paris).' In actuality, it was not so likely that Kishi would be driving a small Japanese car in Paris in the early 1970s.

The most direct discourse of 'Approval of the West' can be found in Toyota Mark II: *The Fox Hunting* (1972). English gentry ride through the forest on their horses, dressed for fox hunting, come across a Toyota Mark II and say, 'いいじゃないか (Oh, that's good!)' In this clip, the quality of the Mark II is approved of by English nobility. It was directed by Toshi Sugiyama (杉山登志) (1936–73), a legendary commercial director, and was actually filmed at the foot of Mount Fuji.

Orson Welles (1915–85), a great movie star, also appeared in a Japanese commercial. In Nikka Whisky: *The Third Man* (1976), Welles says the following lines to the film music of *The Third Man* (1949):

Hello, I'm Orson Welles.
I direct films and act in them.
What I aim for of course is 'Perfection'.
In a film, that's only a hope.
But with G&G, you can rely on it.
Perfection!
G&G, Nikka Whisky.

(subtitles)

私はオーソン・ウェルズ
映画づくりで
いつも目ざしているのは
「完璧」
しかしいまだに夢だ
でもコイツはいい

Contrary to his lines, it was unrealistic to think that a Nikka whisky, a developing manufacturer in Japan, was 'perfection'. Welles put on an ironic smile; it seems to me as if he wants to say 'This is a joke'. The Japanese audience, however, was affected by his remarks and thought: 'Oh, that famous Orson Welles guarantees the quality of this whisky!'

In the early 1970s, many prominent actors and performers appeared in Japanese commercials: Alain Delon (1935–), Cathérine Deneuve (1943–), Sophia Loren (1934–), Audrey Hepburn (1929–93), Steve McQueen (1930–80), Kirk Douglas (1916–), Yul Brynner (1915–85) and Ringo Starr (1940–). They all praised Japanese products and recommended buying them.

The appearance of famous foreign actors in Japanese commercials, however, rapidly declined in the second half of the 1970s. Undoubtedly, the 'Oil Shock', beginning in 1973, cast a shadow on the advertising business, too. Economic difficulties after the mid-1970s apparently related to the shift within commercials: the socio-economic status of society and the expressions in commercials are closely related.

The phenomenon mentioned above, however, emerged not only for socio-economic reasons, but also because of the ability of the prominent commercial director Nobuhiko Ōbayashi (大林宣彦) (1938–), one of the most famous film-makers of present-day Japan. Starting his career as an independent film-maker, Ōbayashi soon showed his ability. He started filming clips at an early stage in Japanese commercial film history. Among the commercials mentioned above, he directed those with Charles Bronson, Cathérine Deneuve, Sophia Loren and Kirk Douglas.

Besides commercials featuring authentic actors, Ōbayashi employed look-alikes of Marilyn Monroe (1926–62) and James Dean (1931–55), who had died years earlier. His enthusiasm for foreign actors led to a growing number of the 'Approval of the West' type of clip. At the same time, it must be said that his enthusiasm corresponded with the Japanese subconscious desire to be accepted by the West.

Production of 'Approval of the West' type commercials did not completely cease even in the 1980s or after. In an Isuzu Gemini commercial (1986), for example, a pair of Japanese cars waltz through Paris. The clip amplified the image of the car that was supposed to be favoured by Parisians. A commercial series for Suntory's canned tea 'Pekoe' (1993) depicted it being drunk by upper-class English people at tea time. In the clip, two elegant ladies dance to the following jingle:

> Peter paid the piper,
> To pick some pickled peppers.
> So, merry we will go!
> So, merry we will go!
> Pekoe!
> Shelly's selling seashells,
> She sells them by the seashore.
> So, merry we will go!
> So, merry we will go!
> Pekoe!

Such a situation is, of course, quite unrealistic. The clips of 'Pekoe' were produced by Masahiko Satō (佐藤雅彦; 1954–), a legendary commercial producer. Satō emphasized 'tone' in commercials, 'tone' being defined as something that 'depicts the circumstances in which the product should be placed'.[7] Even in the 1990s, he thought that it would produce a favourable impression if 'Pekoe' were associated with an English upper-class family. Thus, 'Approval of the West' type commercials are still to be found even now.

Quintrix: turning away from the West

As I mentioned above, the 'Approval of the West' type of commercial decreased in the second half of the 1970s. I should now refer to an epoch-making clip that is thought to have been a turning point in the history of Japanese commercials a clip for the National Colour TV 'Quintrix': *English Conversation* (1974). In the clip, a large Westerner and a short Japanese talk while sandwiching a television between them:

(*W*: Westerner, *J*: Japanese.)

W: Quintrix.
J: Kuin'torikkusū.
W: Quintrix.
J: 英語でやってごらんよ！ (Speak in English!)
W: Quintrix.
J: Kuin'torikkusu.
W: Quintrix.
J: Kuin'torikkusū.
J: 外人だろ、あんた？ (Are you really a foreigner?)

'Quintrix' was a colour television technology developed by National; they used the name of the technology as the product name. The clip depicted the 'Approval of the West' by making the Westerner say its name.

Why was this clip epoch-making? The short Japanese has little appreciation of the Westerner's approval. He insists that it is not 'Quintrix' but 'Kuin'torikkusu'. It seems to me that he is not interested in the Westerner's approval but claims 'this is our original technology, not an imitation of the Western' by insisting on *katakana* English.

In the clip, we find a Japanese being proud of Japaneseness; through economic growth the Japanese are now able to stand by themselves without the 'Approval of the West'.

Returning to Japan

'Quintrix', represented a new trend at the end of the 1960s; that is 'Returning to Japan', or an emergence of nationalistic discourse in Japanese commercials. The forerunners of this kind were home electric appliance commercials, including those for colour televisions.

National and Mitsubishi presented clips titled *Japanese Autumn* in 1968 and *Takao* (高雄) in 1969, respectively. Both of these depicted the beautiful colours of Japanese scenery and put stress on the quality of technologies that can reproduce such natural beauty.

In the case of a clip for National colour television, *Japanese Colour* (1972), many traditional Japanese colour names are introduced: *kurenai, asagi, tokusa, suō, moegi, koki-murasaki, ōni, aonibi, ki-tsurubami, kon, ruri, kara-kurenai, wakanae, ki-kuchinashi*, and *kurumi* (紅 浅葱 木賊 蘇芳 萌黄 深紫 黄丹 青鈍 黄橡 紺 瑠璃 韓紅花 若苗 梔子 黄支子 胡桃). A narrator speaks as follows:

> 日本人が生み、育んだ伝統の色。
> 紅、浅葱、木賊。
> 自然の内に潜む繊細な色を、伝統の色につくりあげた、日本人の鋭い色彩感覚。
> パナカラーが再現します。
> 日本人の豊かな色彩感覚が選んだ、ナショナルパナカラー。

(translation)

> Japanese have produced and nurtured traditional colours.
> Their sharp sensitivity created traditional colours from the fine tones found in nature.
> Panacolour reproduces them.
> Panacolour: the Japanese, who have a fine sense of colour, chose it.

As you can see in the narration, a nationalistic discourse was used to express the quality of the product.

Japanese 'traditional arts' are also used in commercials. Nescafé Gold Blend: 違いがわかる男 (*The Man Who Knows the Real Taste*) series (1969–), for example, employed actors of Japanese traditional performing arts: Kichiemon Nakamura (中村吉右衛門) (1944–) of *kabuki* (1972), Mansaku Nomura (野村万作) (1931–) of *kyōgen* (1978), and Hideo Kanze (観世栄夫) (1927–2007) of *nō* (1984).

In the *kyōgen* clip, for example, Mansaku Nomura plays the fox of *Tsuri gitsune* 釣狐 (*Fishing Fox*), the most important piece in all *kyōgen* repertoire, while contrasting it to the monkey role in *Utsubo zaru* 靫猿 (*Dancing Monkey with An Arrow Case*), an entry piece that is usually played by a boy. The narration goes:

> 狂言は、猿にはじまり狐に終わる。
> 野村万作。違いがわかる男のゴールド・ブレンド。
> ３歳にして猿を演じ、いま狐に挑む。
> 挽きたての味と香り。
> ネスカフェ・ゴールド・ブレンド。

(translation)

A *Kyōgen* actor starts his career with a monkey role and ends with a fox.
Mansaku Nomura, who knows the real taste, loves Gold Blend.
He played the monkey at the age of three; now he challenges the fox.
Nescafé Gold Blend: fresh ground taste and flavour.

Even in the 1980s, very few Japanese had the experience of seeing traditional performing arts. Many Japanese, like myself, might have seen *kabuki*, *kyōgen*, and *nō* for the first time through Nescafé's commercials. Commercials as a form of popular culture used 'traditional' culture; to put it another way, 'traditional' performing arts gained popularity through commercials. Here, popular and 'traditional' cultures mutually support each other.

The best examples of the 'Returning to Japan' type clip might be ones for the Toyota Crown. In 1969, Toyota attached the promotional phrase 'High Life' to its luxury car, the Crown. In the 1969 clip, a Crown smartly runs along a straight road past a beach. In a commercial for the same car in 1978, the theme changed to a *tsuzumi* (鼓, hand drum). A male dancer in kimono performed a traditional dance to the sound of the tsuzumi in front of a Japanese garden; a Crown ran through a bamboo forest; a beauty in *kimono* sat in front with the driver. The lead actor, however, was the same man, Sō Yamamura (山村聰) (1910–2000), in each case.

The trend at that time caused a change in the type of Western actor appearing in commercials. Arnold Schwarzenegger (1947–), a Hollywood action movie star (and the governor of California today), was cast in Japanese commercials of 1990, playing a comic role, throwing off his hard-boiled image from *Terminator* (1984) and *Commando* (1985).

In the Takeda Arinamin V health drink commercial, *Devil V* (1990), Schwarzenegger played a gold-obsessed devil and was given a silly Japanese line 'ちちんぶいぶい、だいじょうぶい (*Chichin buibui, daijyōbui*)': the original is 'Chichin puipui itaino itaino tondeke' (a 'magical' incantation to comfort infants when they have hurt themselves). Such Japanese usage made the products seem familiar to the audience. In Nisshin Cup Noodle: *Body Building* (1990), Schwarzenegger did body-building with two ridiculously huge Japanese kettles in his hands.

Schwarzenegger did not make such comical appearances in his home country, because it would have destroyed his image as a serious hero. He may have taken the job only because it was work away from home. Japan was in the middle of the bubble boom; Japanese commercial creators, who had yen to burn, hired him and asked him to do a comedy turn. His roles were in sharp contrast to the way Western actors were used in the 1970s.

Japan Railways (JR, former Japan National Railways, 国鉄) also employed the image of 'Returning to Japan'. Their rivals were airline companies such as Japan Airlines (JAL); the image of 'Returning to Japan' fitted perfectly into the JR strategy, which was to steal passengers from the airlines.

After EXPO '70, a national event that drew a total of 60 million visitors, JR wanted to keep up the number of railway travellers in Japan. Immediately after the EXPO, JR started its 'ディスカバー・ジャパン (Discover Japan)' campaign to promote its 'ミニ周遊券 (Mini Circular Ticket)'. After the 'いい日旅立ち (Good Day, Start Off)' campaign from 1978, JR started the 'エキゾチック・ジャパン (Exotic Japan)' campaign in 1984. The tie-up song, *Exotic Japan* by singer Hiromi Gō (郷ひろみ) (1955–), burst into the charts and the clip, using images of esoteric Buddhism at Kōya-san Mountain (高野山), became a hit. The promotional phrase was 'いま日本はどきどきするほど刺戟的だ (Now Japan is heart-beatingly exciting)' by Hiroyuki Itsuki (五木寛之) (1932–). The strategy of JR was clear. With the yen strengthening, the number of Japanese overseas travellers was rapidly increasing in the second half of the 1980s. The campaign sent out the message: 'Let's enjoy domestic travel by train. You can find exoticism even in Japan' (Figure 8.1).

After privatization, JR continued travel campaigns for the masses using 'Japan' images. In 1991, it started the 'Nihon o yasumō 日本を休もう (Take a Rest, Japan)' campaign. The commercial series depicted leisurely landscapes of the Japanese countryside, accompanied with slow music. The accusative particle 'o' in the phrase 'Nihon o yasumō' is apparently intentionally ungrammatical, making the meaning rather obscure. The real meaning might be 'Japanese should

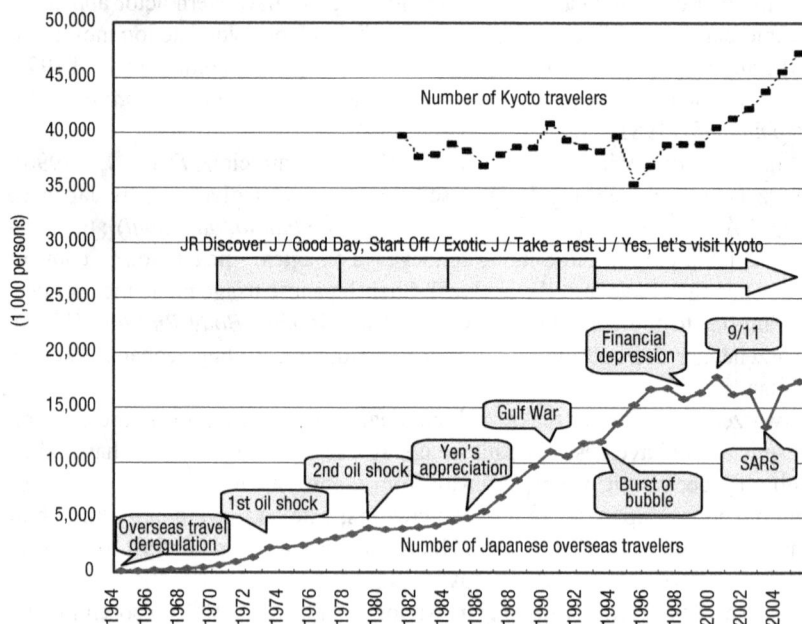

Figure 8.1 Number of Japanese overseas travellers, Kyoto travellers, and JR campaigns. (Compiled from the Tourism White Paper 観光白書 and the Kyoto City Tourism Annual Report, 京都市観光調査年報.)

take a rest in Japan, getting on a train'. JR's 'Take a Rest, Japan' campaign took advantage of the decline in overseas travel due to the Gulf War (1990), followed by the burst of the economic bubble (Figure 8.1).

In 1993, JR launched its 'そうだ京都行こう (Yes, let's visit Kyoto)' campaign, which has remained a hit commercial series right up to the time of writing (2006). The clips portray beautiful scenes in Kyoto through the four seasons to the tune of 'My Favorite Things' from *The Sound of Music* (1964). As a result of these commercials, the number of tourists to Kyoto rapidly increased, covering the decline in overseas travellers caused by the financial depression, 9/11, and SARS (Figure 8.1).

The 'Approval of the West' type of commercial, which I mentioned earlier, decreased after the mid-1970s. By contrast, the 'Returning to Japan' type of commercial has been going strong since the 1980s. One cannot deny that such a phenomenon is deeply connected to the 'Japan as No. 1' mentality, discussed in Ezra F. Vogel's book.[8] It seems that a cultural movement of 'Returning to Japan' took place during this period.

The Japanese commercial industry, in its pioneering days, had been chasing the West, especially America, in terms of expression. Such a mentality seems to have become extinct around the 1980s. This could be described as the 'End of Culturally Occupied Japan' or the 'Japanization of Japan' in commercials.

After the 1990s

Bondage to the West

As far as can be told from ACC award-winning commercials of the 1980s, the Japanese obtained a kind of self-confidence. This positive self-image, however, became uncertain again in the mid-1990s, with the burst of the bubble followed by the Heisei depression. A new image of the West emerged in commercials in the second half of the 1990s. This could be called 'Bondage to the West' or 'Japanese who want to escape from the West but cannot'. The best example of this type would be one for WOWOW (satellite pay-TV): *The Bird Man* (1998).

	(*M*: Japanese man, *F*: American girlfriend)
F:	What's the matter, honey? Is there something wrong?
M:	Let's call it off.
F:	Excuse me, why? Why so suddenly?
M:	I'm going back to Japan.
F:	What? What did you say?
M:	I must go back to Japan.
F:	You're not making any sense!
M:	I MUST go back to Japan!
F:	But, why?
M:	Don't ask me the reason 'why'.
F:	Then, why?

M:	I have to go back to Japan.
F:	For God's sake, why?
M:	I don't have time to explain. Sayonara!
F:	Why???
	(The woman stabs a table with a fork, which pierces his jacket.)
M:	Back to Japan!
F:	Why?
	(The man rides in a fighter plane in *kamikaze* fashion.)
M:	Back to Japaaan!
F:	Whyyyyy?
	(She throws her red-heeled shoe at his flying fighter plane. The shoe hits the wing.)
M:	Back to Japan … Back to Japan … Back to Japan …
	(He tries to pull the shoe off the wing.)
M:	Aaaaaah! Back to Japaaan!
	(His fighter plane falls but he is still flying by flapping his hands.)
F:	Whyyyyy?
	(Subtitle: 見たい番組がある, I want to watch a TV programme.)
Narration:	WOWOW.

The clip ends here; however, I think it is just half the story. WOWOW's flagship programmes are Hollywood movies. What the Japanese wants to see is American cultural products! That means, the poor Japanese cannot get himself out of the United States. I call such themes 'Bondage to the West'.

The situation of a 'Japanese who wants to fly away from the US' would never have been seen in the commercials of previous periods. The status of Japan in commercials had changed from that of the 1960s or the 1970s, but the United States proved to be enormously strong: the shot-down fighter plane might be taken to suggest the fate of opponents of the United States.

Let's examine other examples. TBC (a beauty salon): *Naomi* (1997) portrays a Japanese woman who successfully transforms herself into a sexy Briton (Naomi Campbell, 1970–). This clip won the 'most likable' award from CM Databank in 1997.[9]

	(*F*: father, *M*: mother, *N*: Naomi (daughter))
M:	直美、それ本当に効果あるの？ (Naomi, is it really effective?)
N:	うん。 (Mm.)
F:	何が？ (What?)
M:	TBC。エステよ。 (TBC, the beauty salon.)
F:	よしなさい！ (Don't go there!)
N:	ふん！ (Huh!)
F:	直美！ (Naomi!)
	(Naomi goes to TBC.)
N:	ただいま！ (I'm back!)
	(Naomi's appearance has changed into Naomi Campbell.)
M:	どなた？ (Who are you?)

N:	直美よ！（It's Naomi!）
F:	そんな、声まで変わって……。（Oh, my god! Your voice has changed too … ）
Narrator:	きれいになるのが——。（If you want to be beautiful, … ）
N:	TBC.

In Suntory BOSS 7: *A Dialogue* (1998), a Japanese business man is depicted who boasts of himself as 'a man who can speak out against anyone', but who actually keeps silent in front of Bill Clinton (played by a look-alike actor).

> (*J*: Japanese business man, *C*: Bill Clinton, *I*: Clinton's interpreter (female))
> (A middle-aged Japanese business man is chatting with his colleagues at a noisy Japanese-style pub.)

J:	グルーバルとか何とかいってるけどさあ、日本ってやっぱり世界でなめられてるじゃない。いっぺんガツンといってやんなきゃだめよ、あいつら。俺だったらいっちゃうよ。ガツンといっちゃうよ。俺そういうタイプだから。(They say 'global' or something, but foreigners monkey around with Japanese, don't they? We should say *gatsun* (speak straight) to those guys. I can speak out against anyone. I can say *gatsun*. I am an honest man.
C:	So …
I:	じゃあ……。
	(The scene suddenly changes. The Japanese is sitting in front of Bill Clinton in the White House with Western movie-style background music.)
C:	I'd like to hear your honest opinion.
I:	君の率直な意見を聴こうじゃないか。
C:	Tell me, *gatsun*!
I:	ガツンといってみてくれないか。
	(The Japanese is in a panic; he takes a canned coffee from his inside pocket and drinks it without saying a word.)
Narrator:	缶コーヒーのボス・セブン、新登場。(Canned coffee, BOSS 7, now on sale.)
C:	Come on!
I:	さあ！

All the Japanese portrayed in these clips are suffering from an identity crisis. While a 'new traditional Japan' was constructed in the 1980s, the 'Japan' of commercials seems to have metamorphosed yet again during the last decade.

Japanese go to Korea

Although numerous Western images were used in Japanese commercials, one can hardly find any non-Japanese Asian images in them. The only exception is

Suntory's Oolong tea commercial series, which started in the 1990s, used Chinese actresses, and went on location in China. In the series, they used nostalgic scenes from China to add a sense of authenticity to their canned Chinese tea.

With regard to Asianness in commercials, there is a remarkable example.[10] This is a clip for Ōtsuka Oronamin C drink in 2004. It is the first Japanese commercial featuring a Korean actor, Bae Yong Joon (裵勇俊) (1972–), who was the leading actor in the popular drama *Winter Sonata* (2002).

In the clip, Bae speaks the English phrase 'Of course!' after a repetition of Korean greetings and a Japanese jingle '*hatsuratsu* ハツラツ (vigorous)' in a westernized, surreal landscape assumed to be in Korea.

The second Japanese commercial featuring Bae was that for the Sony Handycam (2004). In this commercial, Bae speaks the Japanese phrase 'Boku wa Handycam 僕はハンディカム (I choose Handycam)'. After this commercial, one observes, he speaks Japanese in almost all the clips he has appeared in.

In the case of Lotte Flavono Gum (2004), Bae speaks Korean in the first version. One month after the first broadcast of the Korean edition, the clip was abruptly replaced by a Japanese version. Why did they produce these two editions? According to the testimony of the director, the Japanese clip was the official one whereas the Korean version was only temporary. The director wanted Bae to speak Japanese as fluently as possible, and he made an immense effort to do so.[11]

Until now (2006), Bae can be seen speaking Korean only in a very limited number of commercials, mainly for Lotte – a Korean company, after all. Why should he speak Japanese? This is quite a contrast to Western actors, most of whom speak their native languages in Japanese commercials.

We should recall here that under the previous Japanese colonial regime in Korea the colonizers forced their language upon the dominated people. We cannot deny that Korea was recolonized in Japanese commercials after 2004.

I also see, however, another aspect of Asianness in the commercials featuring Bae. In a clip for au (a mobile phone service) (2004), a middle-aged Japanese woman is dreaming of going on a date with Bae amid fashionable Korean landscapes.

	(*K*: Kaori, *B*: Bae, *M*: Mayumi)
	(At an au mobile phone shop.)
M:	ムービーメールが韓国から出来るんだあ。(Oh, it can send movie-mail from Korea!)
K:	韓国……。 (Korea …)
	(Bae Yong Joon appears on the mobile's screen.)
B:	こんにちは。(Hello!)
	(Suddenly, Kaori finds herself at Seoul airport. Bae arrives on a motor-bike to pick her up.)
B:	行くよ。乗って。(Come on! Get on!)
K:	は、はい。(Y ...Yes.)
	(Bae and Kaori ride double and come to a golf course.)
B:	ゴルフは？ (What about golf?)

K:	い、いえ、あの。(Oh, n … no … I mean …)
	(Kaori films Bae's swing with her mobile phone. She gazes at him with rapture.)
	(Bae and Kaori hold wine glasses at the seashore.)
B:	さあ飲んで。(Drink up!)
K:	マユミに自慢したい……。(I want to show this off to Mayumi …)
B:	しなよ。ムービーメールが送れるんだし。(Let's do that! We can send a movie-mail.)
	(Bae films Kaori and himself with the mobile phone.)
B:	恋人でーす。送信。(We are lovers! Send mail.)
	(Kaori drops on her knees.)
K:	ああ、韓国。(Oh! Korea!)
	(Kaori comes back to earth in the au shop.)
M:	カオリ？(Kaori?)
Narrator:	グローバル・パスポート。au by KDDI。(Global Passport: au by KDDI.)

Japanese women who are fans of Bae started to alter their perception of Korea from 'traditional towns' to 'Westernized fashionable cities'. It seems to me that a new Asianness (in this case, Koreanness) is being created through television dramas and commercials.

The real image of Korea is being transformed in response to the image-oriented business demand from Japan. I could observe some kind of mutual as well as global relationships in these phenomena. I think a kind of colonialism still remains in the substructure of Japanese commercials; at the same time, a new Asianness is being produced by the crossover of pop cultures between Asian countries.

Conclusion

In this chapter, I have discussed some aspects of cultural changes in regard to the Japan–Western relationship as observed in prize-winning commercial clips, mainly since the 1980s. If we focus on the clips since the mid-1990s, two characteristic patterns can be recognized; these are 'Bondage to the West' and 'Japanese go to Korea'. These did not emerge abruptly but are closely related to the contemporary international relations and socio-economic status of Japan, the developmental history of Japanese television commercials, and Japanese prewar history.

Seeing these commercials, we can observe that the Japanese were trying to reidentify themselves from the 1970s. Their hopes were temporary fulfilled by economic success in the 1980s. It was, however, only a temporary satisfaction, before the bubble burst. What kind of clips emerged in Japanese commercials after the deep recession of the mid-1990s? Nothing other than memories of previous colonial rule and defeat in the war.

I conclude that Japanese commercials are still in post-war times. The question now is how they will cease to be post-war and take a step towards a new Japan.

Notes

1 Hereinafter, I use 'commercial' within the meaning of 'television commercial'.
2 Hara 2006: 218.
3 Murata 2006: 313.
4 Ōtsuka 2004.
5 Yamada 2005.
6 Nanba 2006.
7 Satō 1996: 293.
8 Vogel 1979.
9 CM Databank is a research company of Japanese commercials. It pronounces commercials' likeability based on its original survey of consumers.
10 Hereinafter, I also refer to clips that were not awarded the ACC prize.
11 NTV 2004.

References

Hara, Hiroyuki (原宏之) (2006), *Baburu bunka-ron: <posuto sengo> to shite no 1980 nendai* (バブル文化論ー＜ポスト戦後＞としての１９８０年代). Tokyo: Keiō Gijyuku Daigaku Shuppankai.

Murata, Kōji (村田晃嗣) (2006), *Pureibakku 1980 nendai* (プレイバック１９８０年代). Tokyo: Bunshun Shinsyo.

Nanba, Kōji (難波功士) (2006), 'Shōyō shīemu to shōyō shīemu (商用ＣＭと賞用ＣＭ)' in Yamada Shōji (山田奨治) (ed.), *Bunka to shite no terebi komāsharu* (文化としてのテレビ・コマーシャル). Kyoto: Sekaishisōsha, pp. 158–9.

NTV (2004), *Dokusen!! Pe Yon'jun* (独占！！ペ・ヨンジュン) (TV program). Tokyo: NTV, 20 September.

Ōtsuka, Eiji (大塚英志) (2004), *'Otaku' no seishin-shi: 1980 nendai ron* (「おたく」の精神史ー１９８０年代論). Tokyo: Kōdansha.

Satō, Masahiko (佐藤雅彦) (1996), *Satō Masahiko zen shigoto* (佐藤雅彦全仕事). Tokyo: Madora.

Vogel, Ezra F. (1979), *Japan as Number One: Lessons for America.* Cambridge, MA: Harvard University Press.

Yamada, Shōji (山田奨治) (2005), 'CM ha dare no mono? Kako no CM ga kieteiku!' (CM は誰のもの？過去の CM が消えていく！), *Hōsō Bunka* (放送文化) Spring, pp. 76–81.

9 Current changes within the Japanese higher education system
Past and future

Yumiko Hada

Introduction

It was in the early 1960s, when the immediate postwar confusion had died away, the economy was booming and the notion of a middle class that embraced virtually the entire Japanese nation was beginning to take hold, that Japan began to think seriously about the pattern of higher education. Two reports by the Central Council for Education, one issued in 1963 and one in 1971, foreshadow, with their emphasis on the importance of graduate education and on the integrated nature of higher education, from undergraduate to doctoral level, the recommendations and the kind of institutions that have emerged over the last decade or so. And the example of the University of Tsukuba, established in 1973, offers another glimpse into the future. As the university president, Professor Iwasaki, says in his introductory message on the university's website, 'Since its founding, the University of Tsukuba has been a forerunner among Japanese universities in putting new ideas into practice.'[1] These 'new ideas' included the grouping of colleges into clusters, an emphasis on interdisciplinary studies, and active efforts to establish links with science and technology-related organizations outside the university as well as with the local community.

But for the next two and a half decades, Japanese higher education policy was shaped largely by domestic concerns and parameters. The booming economy was accompanied by rising educational expectations, and the numbers of students at four-year universities rose from 626,421 in 1960 to 1,835,312 in 1980, a staggering 192.9 per cent increase. The absolute number and the percentage of female students also increased rapidly from the mid-1960s. Policy makers and universities had their hands full, trying to cope with the implications of these rapid increases, and trying alternately to hold down and to accommodate them. In those days, on-the-job training was still the norm, and Japanese employers, who absorbed almost all the output from Japanese universities, were well acquainted with the relative merits of institutions within the system, so that by and large, Japan had no need of international measures such as globally standardized accreditation systems.

As the OECD Thematic Review of Tertiary Education[2] points out, it is only since the 1980s that Japanese society has been strongly impacted by rapid globalization. Japanese business shifted a higher percentage of its manufacturing bases overseas, and there was a significant increase in the internationalization of business in all fields. It was against this background that the National Council on Educational Reform, set up under then Prime Minister Nakasone, issued three reports from 1985 to 1987, the second of which stressed 'the importance of graduate schools as places for high-level and creative education and research' with a view to 'ensuring that Japan can make a positive contribution on an international level'.[3] The third report, issued in 1987, recommended that a separate body be set up to tackle the issue of university reform, and this led to the establishment of the University Council in the same year.

Paralleling these movements in the government administration were movements in the science and technology (S&T) sector. The accusation that Japan was 'stealing a free ride' on basic research was actively debated,[4] and companies that had until then looked down on basic R&D carried out in Japanese universities, and had bought patents from overseas while investing funds in practical and applied research in their own laboratories, focused with fresh eyes on the necessity of promoting basic research in universities. The idea of two-way collaboration between industry and academia, or three-way collaboration between industry, the public sector and academia, became a topic for open discussion. The importance of scientific research is also stressed in the 1984 report from the Science Council within MEXT (Ministry of Education, Culture, Sports, Science and Technology)[5] and the S&T White Paper of 1988, 'Aiming to Establish an Environment for Creative Research', which takes up the issue of 'Centers of Excellence' (CoEs) and gives a clear indication to the effect that graduate schools will be expected to bear the responsibility of housing CoEs. Japan, it was becoming increasingly clear, was going to be expected to pull its own weight if it wanted to continue as an international player.

So, faced with increasing pressures of the kind outlined here, what was the position of Japanese universities in the early 1990s? The answer has to be that it was not a very healthy one. From the 1980s on, in Japanese national universities in particular (which tended to be older than universities in the private sector) facilities and equipment were gradually showing signs of age, and chronic under-financing of research was an ongoing problem. The universities also faced a severe budget deficit. In the private sector too, the subsidy for management expenses allocated to them reached a peak of 29.5 per cent in fiscal year 1980, and subsequently followed a downward trend.

Things might have been allowed to carry on as they were, for a while at least, if the economy had continued to boom, but then, in 1990 the economic bubble burst and this, together with the economic recession that followed, was arguably the most important factor in bringing about a thoroughgoing reform in higher education. Even in large companies, it was no longer possible to count on lifetime employment. With growing job mobility, it became increasingly difficult for companies to invest large sums of money in training personnel without any sure knowledge of how long they would remain in the company, and this pushed increasing responsibility for pre-employment training onto the shoulders of universities. At the same time, there were rising expectations in the financial world that basic and applied university research could act as a trigger to reactivate the economy.

A further background factor is the demographic one. The 18-year-old population reached its peak in 1992, and thereafter entered a steady decline. However, even before then, the writing was on the wall, and universities knew that in the very near future they would be faced with declining student applications.

So how did policy evolve in the 1990s in the above circumstances? Mention has been made above of the recommendation in the third report issued by NCER in 1987 that a separate body be established to tackle the issue of university reform, and the first report by this new body, the University Council, was issued in 1991 with the title 'Concerning the improvement of university education'. Its targets were couched in very general terms, using such phrases as 'a rich and flexible structure and curriculum', 'provision of diverse learning opportunities', and so on, but the methods proposed as means of meeting these targets, namely 'revision of the criteria for university establishment' and 'introduction of a system of third-party evaluation' were crucial in setting a foundation for subsequent reforms. Fundamental revision of either of these areas would be a ground-breaking step. It would be several years before the implications of these suggestions would be finally realized but, with hindsight, the direction of future change is clearly visible here.

At first at least, the government's stance was not one of compulsion. For example, universities were required from 1991 onwards to make efforts towards the implementation of self-monitoring, but implementation with disclosure of the results was made a duty in 1999, and has been stipulated in the School Education Law since 2004. But this said, as the pressure for reform built up during the 1990s, reforms such as the construction of new syllabuses, the systematization of faculty development, the introduction of teacher assessment systems, the establishment of a credit assignment system for external study achievements, and the construction of a quota system for students who switch faculties were taken forward.

At this point, it is appropriate to mention a person who was to play a key role in higher education reform in Japan, Atsuko Toyama. Born in 1938, Atsuko Toyama joined the Ministry of Education in 1962, straight after graduation, and moved up through the ranks, gaining experience in a variety of different divisions. From 1985 to 1988, she was Director of the Planning Division of the Higher Education Bureau in the Ministry of Education, at a crucial time for future strategic planning of the higher education system in Japan. And in July 1992, after a period elsewhere, she returned to the Higher Education Bureau of the Ministry, this time as Director-General. She stayed in this post until July 1994, so for two years was again in a crucial position to be able to lend her weight to the impetus for reform. We shall encounter her again later in this chapter in the context of what became known as the 'Toyama Plan'.

Returning to the early 1990s, it soon became clear that, although some initiatives like voluntary self-monitoring soon got underway, the universities were not to be left in peace to carry out reform at their own pace. Mention has been made above of the S&T White Paper stressing the need to develop CoEs, and this point was reinforced by a 1992 report from the Science Council within the Ministry of Education stressing the need to 'examine specific methods of creating such institutions while making full use of existing systems'.[6] Leading on from this, it was in the mid-1990s that a clear link was established between the prioritization of graduate schools and the enhancement of Japan's capabilities in science and technology.

The Basic Science and Technology Law of 1995 put on a firm legal footing the plan unveiled in the Basic Science Technology Plan of the following year, 1996, to train and support 10,000 post-doctoral researchers. The direction of priority investment in science and technology activities was clearly set out, and there were clear expectations that science and technology would contribute to economic development in support of business and economic policies. At the same time, it was also made clear that, with regard to fostering human resources and research in the universities, priority emphasis was to be placed on applied research that would help to raise the level of international competitiveness ... rather than on basic research.[7]

Nor was reform limited to the educational field. Under the rubric of the keywords 'deregulation' and 'decentralization', a number of sweeping administrative and financial reforms, including the restructuring of a large number of government ministries, were implemented in 1999. As part of these reform measures, the Ministry of Education, Science, Sports and Culture was integrated with the Science and Technology Agency to form the Ministry of Education, Culture, Sports, Science and Technology, hereafter known as MEXT.

In the year before that formal change, however, in 1998, the University Council issued a report entitled 'An Image of 21st Century Universities and Future Reform Policies',[8] which brought together and set out systematically a number of the threads that we have been following. Two of the key pillars in the Report are, first, the call for strengthened graduate school prioritization, stressing the need for the education and training of high-level, professional specialists, and second, the call for a system of objective, third-party evaluation. It also goes without saying that the strengthening of Japan's S&T capability and its international competitiveness in an age of economic globalization remain vitally important background issues.

On the strengthening of graduate schools, the report was clear that, in order to enable postgraduate level educational research activities to take a central role, the organizational structure of graduate schools should be changed. Essentially, it was seen to be necessary to put in place at postgraduate level the same basic structure that existed at undergraduate level. It was suggested that the discretionary range of individual universities should be expanded and that organizational systems should be put in place to enable them to take advantage of this. In short, the report paved the way for universities each to develop their own personality and characteristics, including the '21st century CoE Programme',[9] and foreshadowed, as is clear with hindsight, the incorporation of universities into independent administrative institutions that was to take place in 2004.

On the issue of objective, third-party evaluation, in April 2000, as a direct result of the report, the existing organization, the National Institution for Academic Degrees, which previously had only been responsible for HE institutions other than universities (comparable to the former Council for National Academic Awards in the United Kingdom), now had its remit widened to include university evaluation, and was reorganized as a new body called the National Institution for Academic Degrees and University Evaluation. Trial university evaluation results were published over a three-year period from 2001 to 2004. At the same time, the Japan University Association, representing private universities, was also drawing up its own evaluation plans. All universities, whatever their formal status, realized that if they did not put their own house in order, the government would do it for them.

Developments in the twenty-first century

It is entirely fitting that at the beginning of the twenty-first century we should once again encounter Atsuko Toyama, who in April 2001 was appointed Minister of the enlarged Ministry of Education, Culture, Sports, Science and Technology (MEXT). She remained minister for two years, until April 2003. It will have become clear from what has been said above that Atsuko Toyama had accumulated in the course of her career a great deal of expertise in educational administration and had been intimately involved in the preparation of many of the policies that it was now her duty to implement. This state of affairs was very unusual in Japan, where a minister was traditionally expected to be nothing more than a decorative plant in the ministerial office, leaving all the planning and work to be done by subordinates. It is significant that Ms Toyama was appointed by Prime Minister Koizumi, who was himself widely known as a maverick.

The 'Toyama Plan', named after the minister, was a large-scale plan for the reorganization of universities and was announced in June 2001. Specifically, it centred on three points:

1 Drastic reorganization and consolidation of national universities, including mergers and internal regrouping measures;
2 The introduction of strategic management principles, modelled on those used in the private sector as part of the effort to transform universities into independent administrative organizations; and
3 The introduction of the concept of competition through third-party evaluations, including the creation of Centers of Excellence (CoEs) as focal points for high-level research in approximately thirty of Japan's top universities.

There was criticism in some quarters that inadequate time was allowed for preparation, but it will have become clear from the above that the central issues it embodied were ones that had recurred constantly throughout the preceding decade. Moreover, the need for radical reform was both obvious and urgent. According to the World Competitiveness Yearbook of April 2001, issued by the International Institute for Management Development, Japan ranked lowest among 49 countries surveyed with regard to 'university education meeting the needs of the economy'.[10] Minister Toyama pointed out that this dismal state of affairs could not be allowed to continue.

Specific measures were not slow in emerging. In August 2001, just two months after the 'Toyama Plan' was issued, the Subdivision on Universities, which had taken over the role of the University Council and was located within the Central Council for Education, was asked to deliberate on three points:

1   The desirable modality of the higher education system as a whole;
2   The desirable modality of establishment approvals for universities and the overall scale of higher education in future;
3   The development of new forms of graduate schools.

In response to these three requests, the following three reports were issued in August 2002:

1   'On Building a New System to Secure the Quality of Universities';
2   'On the Training of Professionals with Advanced Specialized Skills in Graduate Schools';
3   'On Standards for the Establishment of Graduate Law Schools'.

In addition, after only a very short time for consideration, preparations began to be made for the process of giving national universities the status of independent administrative organizations from the spring of 2004. The two fundamental concepts underlying this reform were those of deregulation combined with accountability. University academics were no longer to be allowed to remain in their ivory towers; if they wanted resources, they would have to argue for them and give an account of how they were used.

National universities were indeed transformed, on schedule, into independent administrative organizations in 2004, and a new era in Japanese higher education began. We will look later in this chapter at this transformation and at likely future developments, but it is time now to take a closer look at the actual numbers of students and institutions.

Educational statistics and the changes they reflect

Statistical tables

Tables 9.1 and 9.2 below set out numbers of universities and junior colleges respectively. (All the statistical tables used in this paper are taken from the *Statistical Abstract*, 2006 edition, issued by MEXT.[11] It should be noted that the tables have been substantially edited for the purpose of inclusion in this chapter.)

Changes in number of institutions

Looking at universities (Table 9.1), we see first that the number of national universities (established and heavily subsidized by central government) decreased from 99 in 2002 to 67 in 2005, as envisaged in the 'Toyama Plan', while, on the other

Table 9.1 Number of universities 1955–2005

	Total	National	Local	Private	Percentage of private
1955	228	72	34	122	53.5
1965	317	73	35	209	65.9
1975	420	81	34	305	72.6
1985	460	95	34	331	72.0
1995	565	98	52	415	73.5
2000	649	99	72	478	73.7
2001	669	99	74	496	74.1
2002	686	99	75	512	74.6
2003	702	100	76	526	74.9
2004	709	87	80	542	76.4
2005	726	87	86	553	76.2
Universities providing					
Master's courses	540	87	71	382	70.7
Doctoral courses	409	75	52	282	68.9

hand, local universities (established and heavily subsidized by large cities or prefectures) increased over the same period from 75 to 86, and private universities (established by private-sector bodies and funded overwhelmingly by student fees) increased from 512 to 553. A large percentage of all three types of university offer both master's and doctoral courses. One factor particularly relevant to the changing number of national universities is that of mergers. National (as opposed to public and private) institutions have been particularly active in this respect. Space does not permit the inclusion of a list of mergers (which would in any event be rather tedious), but in the majority of cases the underlying motivation is clearly one of rationalization coupled with the creation of new, interdisciplinary flexibility. For example, in 2002, Yamanashi University merged with Yamanashi Medical University to form the new University of Yamanashi. Following

Table 9.2 Number of junior colleges 1955–2005

	Total	National	Local	Private	Percentage of private
1955	264	17	43	204	77.3
1965	369	28	40	301	81.6
1975	513	31	48	434	84.6
1985	543	37	51	455	83.8
1995	596	36	60	500	83.9
2000	572	20	55	497	86.9
2001	559	19	51	489	87.5
2002	541	16	50	475	87.8
2003	525	13	49	463	88.2
2004	508	12	45	451	88.8
2005	488	10	42	436	89.3

the merger, the establishment was announced in 2003 of a new Interdisciplinary Graduate School of Medicine and Engineering.

Looking next at junior colleges (Table 9.2), the major point of interest is that the number of institutions fell from a peak of 596 in 1995 to 488 in 2005, a fall of 18.1 per cent. This probably reflects increasingly high educational aspirations on the part of female students, resulting in the change of many junior colleges, overwhelmingly private-sector institutions, to four-year universities. That said, it should be noted that 'with the advent of the era of an ageing society, [...] departments related to public welfare vocational skills, such as nursing, continue to be opened at junior colleges'.[12]

Numbers of students

Looking first at the number of students in universities (Table 9.3), we see a steep rise in the late 1950s and early 1960s, and then a steadier, continuing rise up to the present day. Special note should also be taken of the rise in the percentage of female students, from 12.4 per cent in 1955 to 23.9 per cent in 1985, and 39.3 per cent in 2005.

Looking next at students in junior colleges (Table 9.4), we see a rise in the numbers from 77,885 in 1955 to 353,782 in 1975, and 498,516 in 1995, and then a very steep drop of 55.9 per cent, to 219,355 in 2005. Space does not permit a detailed analysis but, in general terms, the changes in numbers reflect a shift both in the functions of junior colleges – from institutions broadly comparable to 'finishing schools', which prepared young women for marriage, to institutions that aimed to impart a specific

Table 9.3 Number of university students by course 1955–2005

	Total	Female	National	Local	Private	Percentage of Female (%)	Percentage of Private (%)
1955	523,355	65,081	186,055	24,936	312,364	12.4	59.7
1965	937,556	152,119	238,380	38,277	660,899	16.2	70.5
1975	1,734,082	368,258	357,772	50,880	1,325,430	21.2	76.4
1985	1,848,698	434,401	449,373	54,944	1,344,381	23.5	72.7
1995	2,546,649	821,893	598,723	83,812	1,864,114	32.3	73.2
2000	2,740,023	992,312	624,082	107,198	2,008,743	36.2	73.3
2001	2,765,705	1,026,398	622,679	112,523	2,030,503	37.1	73.4
2002	2,786,032	1,059,944	621,487	116,705	2,047,840	38.0	73.5
2003	2,803,980	1,087,431	622,404	120,463	2,061,113	38.8	73.5
2004	2,809,295	1,100,839	624,389	122,864	2,062,042	39.2	73.4
2005	2,865,051	1,124,900	627,850	124,910	2,112,291	39.3	73.7
Courses							
Under graduate	2,508,088	1,009,217	459,804	107,254	1,941,030	40.2	77.4
Master's	164,550	49,296	93,742	9,300	61,508	30.0	37.4
Doctoral	74,907	22,237	52,478	4,373	18,056	29.7	24.1

Table 9.4 Number of junior colleges 1955–2005

	Total	Female	National	Local	Private	Percentage of	
						Female (%)	Private (%)
1955	77,885	42,061	3,637	11,080	63,168	54.0	81.1
1965	147,563	110,388	8,060	13,603	125,900	74.8	85.3
1975	353,782	305,124	13,143	17,973	322,666	86.2	91.2
1985	371,095	333,175	17,530	20,767	332,798	89.8	89.7
1995	498,516	455,439	13,735	24,134	460,647	91.4	92.4
2000	327,680	293,690	7,772	21,061	298,847	89.6	91.2
2001	289,198	258,107	6,808	19,941	262,449	89.2	90.8
2002	250,062	220,090	4,515	17,999	227,548	88.0	91.0
2003	250,062	220,090	4,515	17,999	227,548	88.0	91.0
2004	233,754	204,463	2,975	16,510	214,269	87.5	91.7
2005	219,355	191,131	1,643	14,347	203,365	87.1	92.7

vocational skill – and in the perceptions of students, who were increasingly not content to see themselves categorized as 'marriageable products'.

Details of undergraduate students classified by field of study are not included here, but can be consulted in the relevant MEXT table of statistics.[13] Particular points of interest in the 2005 figures are the high percentage in social sciences (37.7 per cent), the low numbers in science (3.5 per cent), and the high numbers in engineering (17.3 per cent), which in Japan also includes students majoring in architecture.

Trends in the period following undergraduate study

Looking next at what happens to students after they complete their undergraduate studies, Table 9.5 (also edited for the purposes of this chapter), shows the first destination of undergraduates after graduation.

The general trend is upward in terms of both advancement to higher-level (master's) courses and entry into employment, in line with the upward trend in numbers of students as a whole. Of particular significance is the fact that percentages of advancement to higher-level courses are much higher (33.1 per cent) for national universities and local universities (15.6 per cent) than for private universities (6.8 per cent). Of particular interest also are the numbers shown for 2004 and 2005 (no figures are available for earlier years) of students going on from university under-graduate courses to specialized training colleges:[14] 12,061 in 2005. These institutions are almost all in the private sector, offer two-year courses, and are funded entirely by student fees. Their continued existence depends on the ability of their graduates to find employment. The movement shown in the table can be located within the context of a growing demand among undergraduates for marketable skills.

Our final table in this chapter, Table 9.6, shows the first destination of new graduates by field of study. What stands out immediately is the large percentage of graduates in science (41.5 per cent) and engineering (31.7 per cent) who proceed to more advanced study and the significant numbers, particularly in the social

Table 9.5 First destination of university graduates 1955–2005

	New graduates	Advancing to higher-level courses	Entering employ-ment (1)	Clinical training	Continuing to study at specialized training colleges, etc.	Advance-ment rate (4)	Employ-ment rate (5)
1955	94,735	6,520	69,841	1,611	—	6.9	73.9
1965	162,349	8,024	135,321	2,995	—	4.9	83.4
1975	313,072	15,365	232,558	2,624	—	4.9	74.3
1985	373,302	22,056	288,272	6,920	—	5.9	77.2
1995	493,277	46,329	330,998	6,732	—	9.4	67.1
2000	538,683	57,663	300,687	5,929	—	10.7	55.8
2001	545,512	58,662	312,450	6,628	—	10.8	57.3
2002	547,711	59,676	311,471	6,979	—	10.9	56.9
2003	544,894	62,251	299,925	8,184	—	11.4	55.1
2004	548,897	64,610	306,338	8,049	12,412	11.8	55.8
2005	551,016	66,108	329,045	7,903	12,061	12.0	59.7
Male	318,447	48,206	180,115	5,174	6,540	15.1	56.6
Female	232,569	17,902	148,930	2,729	5,521	7.7	64.1
National	101,248	33,484	45,792	4,063	1,295	33.1	45.2
Local	22,772	3,536	14,008	633	294	15.5	61.5
Private	426,996	29,088	269,245	3,207	10,472	6.8	63.1

sciences and to a lesser extent in engineering, who opt to go on to a specialized training college. Clinical training apart, all the other areas of study show a clear majority opting for employment immediately after graduation.

Not included in this chapter are the statistics for new entrants to master's courses.[15] These match fairly closely with the figures given in Table 9.5 for new graduates advancing to a higher level of education, but in the social sciences the figure for graduates advancing to a higher level is 7,645; but it is worth noting that if we look simply at the figure for new entrants to master's courses in the social sciences, the figure jumps to 8,747. This may be due to the influence of graduates from a number of disciplines entering a master's course to take an MBA. There is no separate category for management in the statistics.

Proceeding upwards through the education hierarchy and looking at doctoral level education,[16] what again stands out is that the figures show a fairly steady rise up to 1990, then a sudden jump between then and 1995, a further rise to a peak in 2003, and a decline for the two subsequent years. It is also clear that the bulk of doctoral study is carried on in national universities, with both local and private universities playing much smaller roles. In terms of subject specialties, medical training, grouped under 'health', has the largest figure, followed by engineering. If we look at the figures for doctoral students by field of study,[17] it is clear that the sudden jump in numbers between 1990 and 1995 is due primarily to figures for students studying engineering, possibly due to a reclassifi-

Table 9.6 First destination of new university graduates by field of study

Field of study	New graduates	Advancing to higher-level courses	Entering employment	Clinical training	Continuing to study at specialized training colleges, etc.	Advancement rate	Employment rate
Social science	215,809	7,645	141,119	—	4,798	3.5	65.4
Science	19,250	7,982	7,999	—	227	41.5	41.6
Engineering	97,931	31,071	54,496	—	1,164	31.7	55.6
Agriculture	16,015	4,119	9,057	—	274	25.7	56.6
Health	32,960	4,114	17,330	7,903	196	12.5	52.6
Mercantile marine	150	13	55	—	76	8.7	36.7
Home economics	12,438	474	9,207	—	276	3.8	74.1
Education and teacher training	31,451	2,907	18,727	—	785	9.2	59.6
Arts	15,772	1,582	6,148	—	809	10.0	39.0
Others	16,736	1,029	10,525	—	524	6.1	62.9

cation of some kind. Treating medicine as a special case, the high figures for engineering are also noteworthy.

General trends: marketization, articulation, move to a buyer's market

So, in the light of policy developments as we have traced them, focusing particularly on the period since the 1990s, and on the main statistical trends, what general tendencies are discernible in this post-incorporation era? One certainty is that, for the next eighteen years at least, the population of 18-year-olds in Japan will continue to decline. In the tables above we have looked at changes in the numbers of students registered in different types of institutions, but just as significant are the numbers of applicants. According to the Japan Brief,[18] put out by the Foreign Press Centre of Japan, the issue of 21 November 2006 of *Asahi Shinbun*, Japan's most prestigious daily newspaper, reported that the total number of applicants to national, public and private universities declined from a peak of 5.06 million in fiscal year 1992 to around 3.51 million in fiscal year 2006. These figures do not correspond to the 18-year-old population figures because of the large number of multiple applications, but the decline of over 30 per cent in the fourteen-year interval is a clear indication of the trend. Numbers of higher education institutions are already failing to meet their target quota of students and, as the OECD report points out, 'the demand for higher education in volume terms is already satisfied'.[19]

So what are the implications of this? One consequence is certainly that universities are increasingly looking for new markets and are becoming much more proactive than in the past. In his paper presented to an international symposium held in 2005 at the University of Osaka, Professor Masakazu Yano made an analysis of the different patterns of marketization adopted by representative groups of universities in Japan.[20] These range from a sharper focus on links with the local community and the local labour market to moves into new areas such as nanotechnology and robotics. Interdisciplinarity and the integration of the natural sciences and humanities are identified as common strategies on the part of many large universities. At the same symposium, Dr Naoshi Suzuki, Vice-President of Osaka University, stressed networking within the university, among different universities, between the university and industry, and between the university and civil society, and the invitation of outside specialists into the university as some of the innovative strategies being adopted by his university.[21] In other words, we can say that while competition among institutions will continue, the concept of partnership in some form or other is becoming increasingly important.

Another important point is the growth in patterns of articulation or collaboration between universities and high schools. Within the private university sector in Japan, it is relatively common to find various levels of schools attached to the parent university. But in the present climate of a steadily declining student market, universities in general, including those without any attached institutions, are engaging in a variety of activities on a range of fronts. An important stimulus for efforts of this kind was provided by the report entitled 'Concerning Improvements in Articulation between Elementary and Secondary Education and Higher Education', issued in 1999 by the Central Council for Education.[22] The report says:

> Greater effort should be put into promoting, as a pilot venture, interchange between high schools and universities, so that university teaching staff are invited into high schools to introduce their academic specialty or give a lecture, while on the other hand, school teaching staff are invited into universities to assist university staff members with teaching.

With this suggestion as a stimulus, various initiatives, originating both in universities and high schools, have been set in motion.

Underlying all these examples is one very broad and basic trend, namely a shift from a seller's market to a buyer's market in higher education. Increasingly, students will not only find it much easier to select the primary institution that they want to enter – although, as noted above, competition to enter the most prestigious institutions will persist at least for a while – but they will also be able to shape the pattern of the courses that they want to follow. Moreover, as a result of an increase in the compatibility of credits among different universities, students will no longer necessarily be restricted to one institution. And of course, now that universities, since 2004, are independent administrative organizations, they are much freer to seek their own market niche, reach out to new markets, engage with their local community and explore a variety of new initiatives. The ball is in their court.

Trends in postgraduate education

So what of trends in postgraduate education? The first point that needs to be made is that, even though undergraduate enrolments may already be declining, graduate enrolments may not necessarily follow suit immediately. First, graduates faced with an increasingly competitive job market may decide to stay on at university for graduate training in the hope that this will improve their chances. Second, there is clearly a need for more qualified personnel in professions such as law and management, and more law schools and MBA programmes are already being established to deal with this. We look in more detail below at the example of law. Third, we have noted a significant number of graduates proceeding to a course of study at a specialized training college after taking their first degree. Finally, it is also relevant to note that the level of qualifications of university teachers themselves is rising. Until the 1990s, relatively few of the older teachers in Japanese universities had doctorates. Now, many professors are acquiring them in mid-career and a completed PhD is becoming a requirement for the recruitment of new staff at the bottom of the scale.

A further trend, which seems likely to increase in the future, is a demand for higher learning through distance education. According to the OECD report, frequently cited in this paper, there are currently about 220,000 students enrolled in correspondence courses for tertiary education, and about a quarter of these are studying with the University of the Air.[23] We will look at this trend in more detail in the conclusion.

Of course, given the very radical and rapid nature of the changes outlined here, it is only natural that there are significant problems, and we look at these at the end of this chapter. But before that, we take up the case of law schools as one example of the move towards increased professionalization in higher education.

New law schools

The new law schools introduced in 2002 should be seen both within the context of higher education reform and as one aspect of 'judicial reform for the 21st century'. Sixty-eight *Hōka Daigakuin* (Law Schools, or, more properly, Graduate Schools of Law) were established in April 2004, and six more in 2005. Before the reform, anybody who was eligible could take the bar examination and about 500 passed it each year. It is intended, by means of the reform, to increase that number to 3,000 a year by 2010, with the aim of giving people more access to justice than before.

Under the new system, successful graduate students of any faculty of a university may enter the *Hōka Daigakuin* and they are required to take ninety-three units or more in three years in order to graduate. The choice of the curriculum subjects at the law schools is heavily influenced by the bar examination, although the law schools encourage their students to take a variety of related subjects. This new form of legal education is designed to train students to acquire flexibility in 'legal thinking'. On the one hand, both courts and bar associations are supporting the law schools by offering professional courses such as legal ethics, trial practice and legal clinics. On the other hand, many law schools offer courses in foreign law, comparative law, philosophy of law, sociology of law and/or international law. It should also be noted that although graduates from the law schools will be granted a degree of JD, in the American style, the Japanese name, *Hōka Daigakuin*, makes it very clear that they are academic graduate schools that teach the theory and spirit of the law.

The measures taken to ensure the quality of the education provided are particularly significant in light of the comments on evaluation earlier in this chapter. With a view to ensuring quality, all law schools are obliged to employ skilled teachers who are subject to a regular evaluation procedure by an independent body for the supervision of law schools. In fact, one law school has already been given a serious caution by MEXT because it did not satisfy its establishment criteria. Burdens of this kind make the tuition fees much higher than those of ordinary universities, but a large number of scholarships are available to students and banks are willing to extend loans to them at a very low interest rate.

At the time of going to print, it is still too early to speculate what the future of the new law schools will be. Against the background of reports that numbers of the schools are finding it difficult to meet their quota of applicants, some thinning out may be expected but, as an example of the new role being carved out by universities that meets a variety of educational, professional and vocational demands, they seem likely to become a permanent fixture, albeit with some minor modifications.

Implications arising from the prioritized emphasis on postgraduate education

One thread that has been fundamental to most of the above discussion is the increased emphasis to be put on postgraduate education, including the development of Centres of Excellence. It is therefore worth looking briefly at some of the implications of this trend.

The effects on undergraduate students

There is a danger that, as more attention is given to postgraduate education, undergraduate education will become relatively neglected, in terms both of the quality of teaching and of the competition for resources. Increases in expenditure and fees also seem inevitable. There is also a danger that, as the level of postgraduate education increases, the bachelor's degree will be devalued.

Implications for postgraduate students

There are also implications for postgraduate students. Despite recruitment efforts, a number of universities are failing to attract sufficient numbers of students for particular disciplines or programmes. In order to fill up their places, the less popular graduate schools are promoting the admission of mature students and overseas students. There is nothing intrinsically wrong with this policy, and indeed it may have many potential benefits, but special consideration must be given to these students in relation to such factors as language tuition both for Japanese students taking courses in English and for foreign students taking courses in Japanese.

The stratification of higher education institutions

The gap between universities is also continuing to grow, and competition is becoming more severe. Graduate schools in Japan are becoming indicators of the ranking of the university and the prestige of those who teach there. It is inevitable that the distribution of university resources and project funding will become increasingly unequal as government sources of research funding are increasingly divided on the basis of research output. The differences between universities, based on whether or not they have graduate programmes, will become more marked, and entry examinations will become more competitive.

Conclusion

A survey of major changes in the period 1995–2005

The major social factors that have impacted on higher education over the last decade have been the continuing decline in the 18-year-old population, following a peak reached in 1992, and the continuing economic recession. A further factor has been growing internationalization or globalization, as demonstrated by the increasing number of foreign companies in Japan and the shift of Japanese manufacturing facilities to foreign countries. Against this background, the two major pillars in higher education reform in Japan have been identified as:

- an increased emphasis on graduate education, including the promotion of world-class Centres of Excellence, and
- the establishment and dissemination of third-party, objective evaluation systems.

More specifically, key points over the last ten years can be identified as the Basic Science and Technology Law of 1995 and the Basic Science and Technology Plan of 1996, putting emphasis on a large expansion of post-doctoral training with the aim of ensuring that Japan would be able to pull its weight in the global S&T community. Next is the University Council Report of 1998, 'The Image of Japanese Universities in the 21st Century and Reform Measures', setting out the basic principles for a radical reform of higher education policies. The 'Toyama Plan' of 2002 brought together the various threads that had been maturing over the previous decade and laid the groundwork for the formal incorporation of national universities into independent administrative institutions in 2004. We have examined these developments in the foregoing text and have identified some of the implications and opportunities arising from them.

Future developments

Likely developments for the future can be grouped under three broad headings as listed below, all of which intertwine closely with such trends as mass popularization, globalization and the spread of the information-centred society.

Changes in population

As mentioned several times in the text, the dominant factor has been the decline in the 18-year-old population since 1992, resulting in the present situation in which, in purely quantitative terms, demand and supply in higher education are virtually matched. The shift to a 'buyer's market' that goes in tandem with this demographic movement seems likely to continue. A result of this is likely to be increased collaboration among higher education institutions. A further factor is the increasing prominence of women in all areas of society, and while there will still be areas of study and activity that are seen as predominantly male or female, it seems likely that there will be an increasing mix of the sexes in all fields. A further important demographic factor is the increase in elderly people. So far, apart from occasional public lectures, Japanese universities have not been particularly active in targeting this sector of the population, but there must surely be a significant number among them who would welcome the chance to participate in more advanced study courses. And, with the rapid spread and development of new forms of communication and media, it seems entirely possible that universities will consider seriously the potential for expanding into this sector.

Changes in the economy and the labour force

Japan's 'greying society' also has important implications in terms of the continuing decrease in tax revenue. This means that the government and society as a whole will have to think very hard about the amount of money invested in higher education. This also has the further implication that universities will need to be much more proactive in terms of developing links with industry and, in the context of decentralization, with the local community in which they are located. The gradual disappearance of lifetime employment and the increase in labour mobility mean that universities will have to reconsider their roles in the context of 'lifelong learning' as well as putting increased emphasis on advanced professional training for specific groups. Growing internationalization also brings with it an obligation for a rigorous and transparent third-party evaluation system. Japanese universities must be seen to be awarding degrees that have international validity.

Changes in structures and policies

Just as 'deregulation' and 'structural reform' have become key words for the reform of economic policies, these same key words have come to be used in the context of educational reform. With incorporation and the liberalization of establishment criteria, it has become not only possible for, but incumbent on, universities to develop their own individual characteristics. And, of course, as in the economic sector, increased accountability goes hand in hand with this development. One specific development is the change in faculty development which came into effect from April 2007. Job titles were changed with the aim of making them more internationally acceptable. Universities must allow young faculty members to make full use of their particular qualities and abilities. A further structural change that seems likely is the gradual disappearance of the distinction between junior colleges and specialized training institutions.

The one certainty about the future is continuing change, and it will become increasingly incumbent on universities to educate people not just at the age of eighteen, but throughout their lives, and help them to live long, healthy and productive lives.

Notes

1 Message from the President, website of the University of Tsukuba, www.tsukuba.ac.jp/eng/gaiyo_message.html (accessed February 2007).
2 Higher Education Bureau, MEXT, OECD, 'Thematic Review of Tertiary Education', March 2006. The document is available on the internet: www.oecd.org/dataoecd/25/5/37052438.pdf (accessed February 2007). It provides a wealth of basic, up-to-date information on higher education in Japan.
3 Second Report by the National Council on Educational Reform, 1986.
4 See Ikesawa 2002: 35 (in Japanese).
5 'On basic policies for the improvement of the science and technology research system', Report by the Science Council, MEXT, 1984.
6 Science Council Report, 'On Comprehensive Methods of Promoting Scientific Research in the Perspective of the 21st Century', 1992.
7 See Ehara 2004.
8 This is the English title used in the OECD report mentioned in note 2 above. An alternative title also seen in some sources is: 'A Vision for Universities in the 21st Century and Reform Measures'.
9 See OECD report, p. 18.
10 See contribution by S. Yuasa in *The Bulletin of the Japan Scientists Association*, 82, March 2002. Accessible on the internet at: http://members.jcom.home.ne.jp/jsa-bull/82.html (accessed February 2007).
11 *Statistical Abstract*, 2006 edition, MEXT (Ministry of Education, Culture, Sports, Science and Technology). As stated in the main text, the tables have been substantially edited so as to make their size more manageable and to enable particular points to be emphasized more easily. While every effort has been made not to distort the statistical information, any errors arising from the editing process are the sole responsibility of the author of this paper. Readers wishing to obtain more detailed information are encouraged to consult the original tables, which are available at: www.mext.go.jp/english/statist/ (accessed February 2007).
12 See OECD report, p. 11.

13 This table is available at: www.mext.go.jp/english/statist/06060808/xls/082.xls (accessed February 2007).
14 In the OECD report referred to in note 2, these institutions are called 'professional training colleges', but in this chapter we have adopted the MEXT nomenclature.
15 This table is available at: www.mext.go.jp/english/statist/06060808/xls/096.xls (accessed February 2007).
16 This table is available at: www.mext.go.jp/english/statist/06060808/xls/097.xls (accessed February 2007).
17 Available at: www.mext.go.jp/english/statist/06060808/xls/085.xls (accessed February 2007).
18 Foreign Press Center of Japan, 'Japan Brief: Merger of Keio University and Kyoritsu University of Pharmacy', undated but probably late November 2006. Available at: www.fpcj.jp/e/mres/japanbrief/jb_687.html?PHPSESSID=f059a550b212d6d8011050 8cada02cb0 (accessed February 2007).
19 OECD report, p. 10.
20 Yano 2005.
21 Suzuki 2005.
22 Quoted by Kazuyoshi Narita, NIER, in his paper 'Technical and vocational education in Japan; its present state and current issues still to be resolved', presented at a seminar on the theme 'From School to Work. Contemporary TVET Regional Experiences' organized by the National Institute for Educational Policy Research of Japan', January 2007.
23 See OECD report, p. 13.

References

Amano, I. (1986), *Koutoukyouiku no Nihontekikouzou*. Tokyo: Tamagawa University Press.
—— (2001), *Daigakukaikaku no Yukue*. Tokyo: Tamagawa University Press.
—— (2004), *Daigakukaikaku – Chitsujyo no Houkai to Saihen*. Tokyo: Tokyo University Press.
Arimoto, A. and S. Yamamoto (2003), *Daigakukaikaku no Genzai*. Tokyo: Toshindo Publishing Co.
Ehara, T. and T. Umakoshi (2004), *Daigakuin no Kaikaku*. Tokyo: Toshindo Publishing Co.
Ichikawa, S. (ed.) (1995), *Daigaku Taishuka no Kozo*. Tokyo: Tamagawa University Press.
—— (2001), *Miraikei no Daigaku*. Tokyo: Tamagawa University Press.
Ikesawa, Naoki (2002), 'Hi-tech Competitiveness and Nano-Technology', *Creating Intellectual Resources*, December (in Japanese).
Ito, A. (1999), *Sengoki Nihon no Koutou Kyouiku*. Tokyo: Tamagawa University Press.
Kitamura, K. (1999), *Gendai no Daigaku/Koutou Kyouiku*. Tokyo: Tamagawa University Press.
—— (2001), *Gendai Daigaku no Henkaku to Seisaku*. Tokyo: Tamagawa University Press.
Kinukawa, S. and A. Tachi (eds) (2004), *Gakusi Katei no Kaikaku*. Tokyo: Toshindo Publishing Co.
Kurohane, R. (1993), *Sengo Daigaku Seisaku no Tenkai*. Tokyo: Tamagawa University Press.
—— (2001), *Daigaku Seisakukaikaku he no Kiseki*. Tokyo: Tamagawa University Press.

Oosaki, J. (1999), *Daigaku Kaikaku 1945–1999*. Kyoto: Yuhikaku Publishing Co.

Suzuki, Naoshi (2005), 'Education and Research at Osaka University', 2005 International Symposium in commemoration of the opening of the Institute for Higher Education, Research and Practice. Osaka: University of Osaka.

Ushiogi, M. (2004), *Sekai no Daigaku Kiki*. Tokyo: Chuko Shinsho Publishing Co.

Yano, Masakazu (2005), 'A reconsideration of the Role of the University and the Latest Developments in University Reform', *2005 International Symposium in Commemoration of the Opening of the Institute for Higher Education, Research and Practice*. Osaka: University of Osaka.

10 The 'class A war criminal' syndrome

Changing historical consciousness in present-day Japan

Kei Ushimura

Introduction

The year 2006 witnessed the sixtieth anniversary of the opening of the Tokyo War Crimes Trial, officially known as the International Military Tribunal for the Far East, which began on May 3, 1946. The Japanese press did not fail to grasp the opportunity to ponder the significance of this unprecedented international trial. For instance, just one day before the sixtieth anniversary, the *Asahi Shimbun*, a major national newspaper, discussed the trial in its editorial.[1] The article, entitled 'What do you know about the Tokyo Trial?' first defined it as 'a trial conducted by the Allied Powers, including the United States, in order to condemn the aggressive war waged by Japan and to seek the responsibility of politicians, generals and admirals of Japan'. The article then enumerated some problems inherent in the trial, for example the adoption of *ex post facto* laws such as 'crimes against peace' or 'crimes against humanity' and the aspect of 'victors' justice'. A calm and objective position, to be sure; but as it began to criticize some understandings of the trial prevalent in present-day Japan, the article seemed to jump to a conclusion: 'Japan re-joined international society precisely because it accepted the Tokyo Trial by concluding the San Francisco Peace Treaty. Should one insist on the view, then, that the trial was one-sided and unfair, does that mean one dares to take exception to the peace treaty altogether?' This question suggested to readers the view that those opposed to the Tokyo Trial also have a unanimous, negative outlook on the peace treaty. But this is not the case, for those attempting to relieve Japan of total responsibility for the war are only a handful, categorized as, so to speak, short-sighted ultranationalists.

Around the time that the article was printed, the *Asahi Shimbun* featured the Tribunal on several consecutive days (April 30–May 3) and reported the findings of some surveys concerning the Tokyo Trial that it had conducted a few months earlier.[2] This was indeed an intriguing project, in which one could discern willingness on the part of the national newspaper to enlighten the public. Also, the findings were extremely significant in that they revealed unmistakably the current understanding of the Tokyo Trial among the general public. The results would have been more insightful had the *Asahi* conducted a similar kind of survey ten years earlier, that is, at the time of the fiftieth anniversary. One could then have compared any change or inconsistency in the general perception of the Tokyo Trial in Japan.

Despite the significance of the newspaper's project, however, there appears to be some problem with the following editorial statement: 'the less people know about the Tokyo Trial, the more likely they seem to be to approve of the current situation of Yasukuni Shrine'.[3] This statement prejudges its readers to a degree, for it undoubtedly implies that, if one were to gain more understanding of the trial, it is not in the least likely that one would approve of the way Yakusuni enshrines class A war criminals. In other words, instead of purely enlightening the public, the statement was attempting to persuade readers to object to so-called 'class A war criminals' being enshrined at Yasukuni. The article concluded as follows:

> one cannot judge the past unless one knows history. To begin with, one should face up to the history of one's own country. We suggest that you take the opportunity of the sixtieth anniversary of the Tokyo Trial to consider the importance of facing up to history.[4]

I cannot agree more with the sincere attitude towards history underlying this article; and yet I find some statements based chiefly on prejudgment regrettable. As this *Asahi* editorial did not fail to demonstrate, the Tokyo Trial is now associated with 'class A war criminals' in the context of the Yasukuni issue. This issue comprises two parts: first, whether 'class A war criminals' should remain enshrined and second, whether the prime minister of Japan should pay a visit to the place. This chapter will attempt to delineate and discuss how the Japanese people, especially post-war journalists, have been talking about the Tokyo Trial during the last ten years, with special emphasis on their perception or interpretation of 'class A war criminals'.

Has the *Yomiuri Shimbun* changed?

On the very same day as the *Asahi* article, the *Yomiuri Shimbun*, the national newspaper with the largest readership, also discussed the trial in its editorial, beginning with the following words: 'Japan is still being shaken due to the history of more than sixty years ago. That is, how to evaluate the International Military Tribunal for the Far East, which began its proceedings on the third of May 1946.'[5] This article, with the title 'The Japanese people themselves should attempt to search for "war responsibility"', did not appear so clear-cut as that in the *Asahi Shimbun*, for between the lines one could detect the editorial board's difficulty in presenting a well-organized, consistent view of the history behind the trial. First, the *Yomiuri* article gave a brief outline of the trial and then pointed out its problems one by one, such as the fact that the Soviet Union, which had been expelled from the League of Nations as an aggressor, sat in judgment on Japan, or that Britain, France, and the Netherlands were trying to accuse Japan of invasion, while at the same time themselves invading Asia anew.

The author of the editorial seemed to attempt to draw readers' attention to some problems in the process of selecting the defendants for the trial, in particular the problem of including Mamoru Shigemitsu (ambassador to the Soviet Union and foreign minister in the Tojo cabinet) and Shigenori Togo (foreign minister in the Tojo and Suzuki cabinets) in the list of accused, referring to the former as 'one who was added at the last moment because of a strong demand by the Soviet Union' and to the latter as 'one who did his best to try to avoid hostilities against America and Britain and who, at the last stage of the war, attempted to end it as soon as possible'.

Despite this well-balanced introduction to the trial's shortcomings, the article's view on so-called 'class A war criminals' is, among other things, far from consistent and convincing if one looks at the same newspaper's major campaign, begun the previous year, entitled 'Re-examination of "War Responsibility"'.[6] In this campaign, Premier Kantaro Suzuki, who, together with foreign minister Togo, attempted to put an end to the war, was severely criticized for not taking adequate measures to achieve that end. The contention that the foreign minister was innocent seemed inconsistent, seeing that another project of the same *Yomiuri* denounced the prime minister mainly on the assumption that, when interviewed, he 'ignored' the Potsdam Declaration, thus giving the Allies a pretext for dropping their atomic bombs. Perhaps the writer of the article was implicitly asking readers to observe that his understanding of the premier's responsibility was not the same as that of the 'Re-examination of "War Responsibility"' campaign. Still, one could conclude that such a contention was rather inconsistent, for an editorial can be expected to represent the newspaper's main view of things, otherwise its readers will be confused.

Characteristic of the campaign, in this connection, was the fact that, under the name 're-examination', the *Yomiuri Shimbun* was attempting to bring some political and military figures to justice, contending, for instance, that although not brought to trial by the Allied Powers immediately after the war, this or that politician should have been held 'responsible', not to say 'guilty', for some particular stage on the road to Japan's war. This may be regarded in some quarters as a brave attempt, but the question still remains as to whether the re-examination of history can, in effect, be equivalent to investigating individual responsibility on the basis of hindsight. At least the press should tell its readership that investigating the individual responsibility of war-time leaders is something of a new concept, which emerged after the First World War, when Kaiser Wilhelm II escaped trial.

The above-mentioned editorial unmistakably takes the same view of individual responsibility:

> given the fact that due to the 'reckless' war, millions of people were killed and great damage was done to other countries, one could conclude that the responsibility of our national leaders was serious. Who was responsible, and to what extent? If Japan had brought its leaders to trial, such politicians as premier Hideki Tojo would certainly have been found guilty.[7]

In sharp contrast to the well-balanced reference to certain problems inherent in the Tokyo Trial, this statement seems not only one-sided but also stale. It is stale because it has always been extremely easy to accuse the best-known war-time leader of Japan. Would it be expecting too much of major newspapers to demand that, before condemning some war-time leaders, they should, among other things, start to 're-examine' the validity of the new idea of investigating individual responsibility?

It was once considered that the two leading newspapers in Japan, the *Asahi* and the *Yomiuri,* would provide different views of history concerning the Tokyo Trial – the *Asahi* was conservative and the *Yomiuri* revisionist. Given this under-standing, some might conclude that the *Yomiuri* had relinquished its earlier view and shown, instead, its willingness to side with a former opponent. In fact, the two editors-in-chief, Yoshifumi Wakamiya of the *Asahi* and Tsuneo Watanabe of the *Yomiuri*, held a lengthy discussion about modern Japanese history early in 2006, and reached almost identical conclusions on the Yasukuni issue: that the prime minister of Japan should not visit the shrine.[8] The *Asahi* paid special attention to its rival's 'volte-face', saying that while the *Yomiuri* had declared in an editorial three years earlier (August 15, 2003) that 'class A war criminals' had been legally rehabilitated, it was now clearly objecting to premier Koizumi's visit to Yasukuni, where 'class A war criminals' were enshrined.[9]

Actually, quite a few referred to this 'change' but, strictly speaking, the *Asahi*'s interpretation of the *Yomiuri* column is not correct. In 2003 the *Yomiuri* wrote: '*In terms of domestic law,* "class A war criminals" have been legally rehabilitated.'[10] The fact is, that the *Yomiuri Shimbun* had not asserted, either frivolously or subjectively, that 'class A war criminals' had been legally rehabilitated; rather, the article made the assertion purely within the context of domestic law. Bearing this precedent in mind, one could read between the lines of the May 2, 2006 *Yomiuri* editorial the contention (even after the Wakamiya–Watanabe dialogue) that 'class A war criminals' should be freed from legal accusation. In other words, one could detect consistency rather than a volte-face in the *Yomiuri*'s interpretation of 'class A war criminals'.

The origin of 'class A war criminals'

Since the Yasukuni issue became one of the hottest topics in twenty-first century Japan, the phrase 'class A war criminal' has come to attract almost everybody's attention. Undoubtedly, the phrase has its origin in the International Military Tribunal for the Far East. The charter of the tribunal, announced four months prior to its opening, contained an article that defined three categories of crimes for which the tribunal would indict the defendants: (a) 'crimes against peace', (b) 'conventional war crimes', and (c) 'crimes against humanity'. Twenty-odd Japa-nese war-time leaders, high-ranking generals, and admirals were prosecuted on the assumption that they had committed crimes of category (a), 'crimes against peace'. This is the origin of the term 'class A war criminal'. Initially, 'class A' did not mean 'of first rank' or 'of prime importance'. Furthermore, given the fact that no such expression was used in the court-room, the designation was not an official one.

The German defendants tried at the Nuremberg international tribunal (1945–46), in contrast, have invariably been referred to as 'major war criminals', not as 'class A German war criminals', although the charter of the Nuremberg trial included the same three categories of crime mentioned above. For instance, the voluminous proceedings, published a few years after the conclusion of the trial, were titled *Trial of the Major War Criminals before the International Military Tribunal*.

Albeit unofficial or unconventional, the phrase 'class A war criminal' initially referred to the twenty-eight Japanese defendants indicted at the Tokyo Trial. This is the original, strict use of the phrase. However, another use has emerged and has gained considerable popularity in Japan in recent years; for instance, so-and-so finance minister is a 'class A war criminal' of the Japanese economic recession in the 1990s, or 'class A war criminals' among the players are responsible for the bad performance of such-and-such baseball team. The contents pages of monthly or weekly magazines often include such titles. Needless to say, this minister or those baseball players were not convicted in the unprecedented international trial, yet those who prefer articles full of sensational expressions resort, regardless of the context of the trial, to using the conspicuous phrase 'class A war criminals'. In other words, this new usage of the phrase is employed when one wants to blame someone severely for his misdoings or to hold him responsible for some serious blunder. It could even be said that, to those unfamiliar with modern Japanese history, the phrase 'class A war criminal' is associated more with serious criminals than with the twenty-odd former Japanese leaders tried shortly after the war. One could well refer to the prevalent use of the phrase as 'class A war criminal' syndrome.

The frequent use of the phrase 'class A war criminal' outside the context of the Tokyo Trial could testify to the fact that the majority of Japanese have discerned a very negative meaning in it. That is, although the verdicts of the Tokyo Trial were strictly legal and did not denounce any of the accused on the grounds of character, post-war Japan attached moral opprobrium to those twenty-odd nationals. Consciously or unconsciously, those who appeal to the phrase almost invariably lump the Japanese defendants together, concluding that all were villains. Accordingly, categorized as 'class A war criminals', the defendants became 'faceless', so to speak. Should one learn a little more at all about the historical background of the Tokyo Trial, one would certainly find it difficult, even impossible, to label them all with the same phrase. It could therefore be said that the current usage of 'class A war criminal' is a product of intellectual laziness in post-war Japan.

Further, given the fact that the concept 'class A war criminal' was invented by the Tokyo Trial – in which Western civilization, it was said, sat in judgment on uncivilized Japan – and that the Japanese people still stick to the phrase, the syndrome reflects a typical example of the Japanese attitude to foreign ideas: that is, *haigai shiso*, or respect for foreign, in particular Western, ideas. This is an attitude dating back to the Meiji era, when Japan was enthusiastic about introducing things Western in order to strengthen itself and avoid being colonized by its very mentor, the West.

What may seem strange about the syndrome is that even those in the revisionist camp, who usually try to stress the positive side of the actions of the accused and of the legacy of the war, sometimes use the phrase outside the context of the Tokyo Trial. For instance, the late critic Hyoe Murakami was reported as saying in the *Asahi Shimbun*, when interviewed about his opinion of premier Koizumi's Yasukuni visit,

> 'Class A war criminal' is a concept invented one-sidedly by the victorious nations. The Tokyo Trial was a revenge drama, in which Japan was judged by *ex post facto* laws such as crimes against peace or crimes against humanity. I would strongly contend that those responsible for the atomic bombings of Hiroshima and Nagasaki and the large-scale air raid on Tokyo ought to be labelled 'class A war criminals,' who violated the then existing international law.[11]

'Class A war criminals' should be discussed in the context of the Tokyo Trial, and be restricted to those Japanese indicted and convicted there. This revisionist critic, however, probably unconsciously, appealed to the alternative use of the phrase when accusing those responsible for the atomic bombings and the air raid, thus demonstrating that the phrase is now deeply rooted in Japanese thinking.

No longer 'faceless': 'class A war criminals' in transition

Up to about the sixtieth anniversary of the opening of the Tokyo Trial, 'class A war criminals' were talked about and criticized from time to time, but usually lumped together, being 'faceless'. The above-mentioned article of the *Yomiuri* in 2003, for instance, referred to this general tendency – 'Currently, "class A war criminals" are usually associated with the seven executed defendants, but the reality was that twenty-five Japanese were sentenced as "class A war criminals".'[12] With the spread of the Yasukuni issue, however, this tendency has gradually been changing. Newspapers have come to name at least the seven accused who were executed, and sometimes include the list of the twenty-eight defendants when dealing with the trial. As far as the Yasukuni issue is concerned, the press is now expected to present the list of the fourteen 'class A war criminals' who were enshrined in 1978.

Beside the Yasukuni issue, another factor that contributed to the making known of the individual members of the group of 'class A war criminals' was, perhaps, *gaiatsu* or external pressure. In the spring of 2005, large-scale anti-Japanese demonstrations broke out in mainland China. Most of the participants were strongly opposed to premier Koizumi's visit to Yasukuni. While shouting in the street, many of the participants held up placards bearing the names and faces of the major 'class A war criminals' such as Hideki Tojo, Seishiro Itagaki, who played a key role in the Manchurian Incident of 1931, and Iwane Matsui, the supreme commander-in-chief at the time of the infamous Rape of Nanjing in 1937. In their eyes, 'class A war criminals' were none other than the symbol of Japan's invasion of their land.

The press in Japan, while promptly reporting what was actually happening in China, unconsciously informed its readers of the 'faces' of those 'class A war criminals'. Subsequently, the press was forced to name each of the 'class A war criminals' when discussing the Yasukuni issue. The majority of people still spoke of their former national leaders *en masse* but, after reporting on the anti-Japanese demonstrations in China, in which 'class A war criminals' were no longer treated as 'faceless', the press at least was no longer able to lump them together. Compared to the generally prevailing attitude in the press before Koizumi assumed the premiership, one could unmistakably detect the beginnings of a radical change.

Another national newspaper, the *Mainichi Shimbun*, for instance, featured the Tokyo Trial on three consecutive days, starting at the end of April 2006. What was most striking about this series was that the *Mainichi* dealt in some detail with the post-trial days of the bereaved families of the seven executed defendants. With the exception of some history books on the subject, prior to this feature article few newspapers had shed light on this aspect of the Tokyo Trial. The *Mainichi* article opened the way to enlightening the public from a fresh perspective and introduced anew the seven 'faces' of the war-time national leaders of Japan. Of all the seven condemned, probably Hideki Tojo and Koki Hirota are the best known. Being both premier and army minister at the time of Pearl Harbor, Tojo symbolized war-time Japan both at home and abroad; Hirota, foreign minister at the time of the Nanjing massacre – who was expected by many to be acquitted – remained silent throughout the proceedings, not trying to defend himself at all, and resigned himself to the death sentence.

In contrast to the usual treatment of the defendants in the press, together with Tojo and Hirota the *Mainichi* article dealt with two other, less well-known defendants, Heitaro Kimura, vice army minister to Tojo, and Akira Muto, chief of the military affairs bureau of the army ministry in the Tojo cabinet, and dedicated a considerable part of the feature to the latter. The column focused only on providing the historical background of the trial and information essential to appreciating the event, and did not aim to lead readers to some particular view of history. Being well balanced and informative, the article contributed a great deal to making the unprecedented trial known to Japan's general public. In this process, 'class A war criminals', once lumped together and 'faceless', began to a significant degree to regain their original 'faces'.[13]

Politicians' view of 'class A war criminals'

Ours is the age of the internet, or so it is said, and the internet requires us always to face it in an active manner. Only after switching on the computer and beginning to search can one acquire information. The television, by contrast, always provides information as long as it is on: one does not have to face it actively. Put another way, television supplies information to those around it whether they want it or not. The voices of narrators can reach us even when we are not prepared to listen. With this function of television in mind, one can safely conclude that it has a more powerful influence on people than does the internet. Take politicians appearing on television, for instance. Their influence can be as strong as that of a national newspaper with a circulation of millions. It would be useful, then, to consider the current opinions of politicians about the Tokyo Trial and, for that matter, 'class A war criminals', and see whether their views have changed at all.

Jun'ichiro Koizumi was prime minister for more than five years, one of the longest serving in Japan. During his time in office, the premier visited Yasukuni Shrine six times and was severely criticized on each occasion by Asian countries in which Japan had waged war in the 1930s and 1940s. These neighbouring countries were strongly opposed to the premier's shrine visits, pointing out especially that 'class A war criminals' were enshrined there. While continuing the visits, Koizumi was forced to express his views of the Tokyo Trial and of 'class A war criminals' on frequent occasions. He reiterated his view that Japan had accepted the Tokyo Trial by concluding the peace treaty, and expressed clearly his understanding of 'class A war criminals', saying: 'I consider "class A war criminals" to be war criminals'.[14] He also declared several times that the intention of his shrine visits was to pay homage to the war dead, not to show respect to 'class A war criminals' such as Hideki Tojo.

Given the fact that Yasukuni Shrine is now closely associated with 'class A war criminals', it is only natural that quite a few, whether approving of or objecting to the premier's visits, found him far from logical. If one considers 'class A war criminals' to be criminals, it follows that one would want to refrain from visiting the shrine; on the other hand, if one insists on visiting the shrine, one should refute the view that 'class A war criminals' are criminals. So goes the logic. At least Koizumi should have given a logical explanation of his actions in relation to this issue.

Besides being prime minister, Koizumi was head of the Liberal Democratic Party. Politicians of rival parties, especially those of the Democratic Party of Japan (DPJ), tried to attack Koizumi's illogical or inconsistent attitude to the Yasukuni issue. In the summer of 2005, for instance, Katsuya Okada, then head of the DPJ, expressed his understanding of this issue in the monthly magazine *Chuokoron*.[15] While showing some understanding of Koizumi, who had said that one should not be influenced by external pressure in deciding whether or not to visit Yasukuni, Okada clearly distinguished himself from Koizumi, saying that were he premier of Japan, he would not visit the place, precisely because 'class A war criminals' were enshrined there. He also criticized Koizumi for not taking adequate steps to explain to other countries why he obstinately continued to visit the shrine while expressing his view of 'class A war criminals' as criminals. The head of the DPJ thus blamed the premier for not practicing what he preached, so to speak; yet he did not present any alternative, but simply expressed his refusal to visit the shrine.

Another politician from the DPJ, Yoshihiko Noda, took up Okada's emphasis on logic and showed an elaborate alternative in the Diet in October 2005:

> those called 'class A war criminals' have already regained their character in a legal sense thanks to the conclusion of some treaties and domestic bills, such

as the San Francisco Peace Treaty. They are no longer criminals. Precisely because of that, there is a serious flaw in the development of the case against the premier's visits to Yasukuni Shrine.[16]

It could be said that the opposition party was attempting to help the premier overcome the difficult situation in which he found himself.

However, much to the regret of the DPJ and of Japan as a whole, the newly elected head of the party, Ichiro Ozawa, presented a different view of the Yasukuni issue and, as a result, destroyed the logical interpretation of the matter that his predecessors had tried to perfect. When interviewed by the *Mainichi Shimbun*, he said, '"Class A war criminals" should be held responsible for the war. Seeing that they demanded that people should die on the battlefield rather than be taken prisoner, they are not entitled to be enshrined at Yasukuni.'[17] This is a rough and incorrect statement indeed, for his view was based merely on the assumption that *all* the 'class A war criminals' attempted to evade responsibility for the war. The truth was quite different; most of the defendants in the Tokyo court-room clearly expressed their willingness to assume responsibility. Also, Ozawa's view, televised as well as printed in the newspapers, could lead the public to suppose that *all* the 'class A war criminals' pushed people, warriors and civilians alike, to die in battle. Here, the interpretation of history has certainly regressed. Lumped together once more, 'class A war criminals,' who had at last begun to regain their individual 'faces,' were again reduced to being 'faceless'.

Conclusion

The tenth article of the Potsdam Declaration states, 'Stern justice shall be meted out to all war criminals, including those who have visited cruelties upon our prisoners.' Conducted on the basis of the Declaration as a major component of the Allied Powers' occupation policies in Japan, the International Military Tribunal for the Far East, or the Tokyo War Crimes Trial, was basically a political or diplomatic event. Still, how to interpret the trial has been one of the intellectual challenges for post-war Japan. Around the time of or shortly after the trial, most Japanese were faced with the miserable situation that defeat had brought to their country. Most had to live from hand to mouth. It was inevitable, therefore, that they tried to condemn the former leaders convicted in the Allied Powers' trial without discriminating among them. The progress of historiography notwithstanding, the general understanding of the trial and of 'class A war criminals' in Japan did not improve for more than fifty years. This was the situation until around the turn of the century. In other words, for nearly six decades after the trial, the general understanding did not change. However, because the issue of the Yasukuni visit ignited the anti-Japanese movement abroad after Koizumi's assumption of the premiership, the Japanese press was forced to provide people with more detailed information on the trial and its defendants. Thus, the general perception of 'class A war criminals' is now on the road to radical change or, to be more precise, improvement.

One might wonder, then, what would be the ideal treatment of, or solution to, the issue of 'class A war criminals'. Of course, I do not intend to suggest the total innocence of our former national leaders, the 'class A war criminals'. Now that the so-called individualization of the twenty-odd defendants is underway, the next step to deepening the understanding of the international trial and, for that matter, the prewar and war-time period in Japan is, perhaps, to try to understand each of the 'class A war criminals' more. As has been discussed in this chapter, accusing them *en masse* is an unproductive approach to the issue. Likewise, it would not be appropriate to apportion responsibility anew among the defendants. We are not expected to serve as prosecutors or defence attorneys. We are expected to understand history. In thinking about history, we should always bear in mind that the former leaders were human, like us. They were tried and convicted at the international military tribunal simply because they had held high rank during the period covered by the indictment, not because – as the second implication of the phrase 'class A war criminals' suggests – they were villains. Put simply, the former leaders of Japan called 'class A war criminals' assumed their obligation.

Probably the Dutch judge of the Tokyo Trial, Bernard Röling, could provide a clue to improving the situation. In an interview conducted nearly thirty years after the ending of the trial, he clearly expressed his sincere impression of the defendants whom he had observed over two and a half years: 'they [the defendants] were mostly first-rate people. Not all of them, but the majority of them were prominent people. The navy people, and Tojo himself, were extremely clever, that's for sure.'[18] 'Cowards? Not at all. None of them, I think. They were really very dignified fellows. Having sat opposite them for more than two years – even though I could not talk to them – I could still see their movements and hear them speaking.'[19] This perceptive comment on the characters of the defendants notwithstanding, Röling did not assert the total innocence of the accused. Instead, in his separate opinion he 'sentenced' nine of them, including Tojo, and Shimada and Oka, both of them high-ranking admirals, to the death penalty, although he insisted that five defendants be acquitted. One need not to take sides with the Dutch judge's view of the accused as prominent people; nonetheless, his contention that one should make a distinction between the characters of the accused and the seriousness of their responsibility for the warfare is worthy of attention.

The year 2008 will be the sixtieth anniversary of the conclusion of the international trial. Probably some symposia will be held both in Japan and abroad. The press will seize the opportunity to discuss the historical event in a more profound manner than before. Also, certainly, more politicians than before will express their views on the trial and on 'class A war criminals'. It should be remembered, however, that those who express their view of the phrase, be they politicians or not, will also undoubtedly reveal the level of their historical consciousness.

Even now, in discussing the trial, the concept of 'class A war criminal,' a product of the trial, provides a significant angle for deepening the understanding of the unprecedented event. Being an intellectual historian myself, I cannot but hope that a more radical change will take place in the general understanding of the trial and 'class A war criminals'. The change is to learn to treat each of the 'class A war criminals' from a multi-faceted perspective, that is, to distinguish between their characters and their responsibility for the warfare. To cure a nation of the 'class A war criminal' syndrome, one should take appropriate measures.

Notes

1 *Asahi Shimbun*, May 2, 2006.
2 *Asahi Shimbun*, May 2, 2006.
3 *Asahi Shimbun*, May 2, 2006.
4 *Asahi Shimbun*, May 2, 2006.
5 The *Yomiuri Shimbun*, May 2, 2006.
6 This project was completed in August, 2006. In addition to the two-volume book published in the summer, an English edition was also published – Yomiuri Shimbun (ed) 2006.
7 *Yomiuri Shimbun*, May 2, 2006.
8 Watanabe and Wakamiya 2006. This dialogue appeared in the monthly magazine *Ronza*, published by the *Asahi Shimbun*.
9 *Asahi Shimbun*, May 1, 2006.
10 *Yomiuri Shimbun*, August 15, 2003; my italics.
11 *Asahi Shimbun*, June 27, 2001.
12 *Yomiuri Shimbun*, August 15, 2003.
13 *Mainichi Shimbun*, May 1, 2006.
14 Statement made in the Standing Committee on the Budget in the Diet, June 2, 2005.
15 Okada 2005:118
16 Statement made at the Standing Committee on the Budget in the Diet, October 17, 2005.
17 *Mainichi Shimbun*, April 10, 2006.
18 Röling 1993: 32.
19 Röling 1993: 38.

References

Okada, Katsuya (2005), 'Watashinara Yasukuni wa Sampaishinai [Were I premier, I would not visit the Shrine]', *Chuokoron*, July, pp. 118–27

Röling, Bernard V. A. (1993) *The Tokyo Trial and Beyond–Reflections of a Peacemonger* (edited and with introduction by Antonio Cassese). Cambridge: Cambridge University Press.

Ushimura, Kei (2001), 'Eikyu Senpan o Ranyo Surunakare [Do not Abuse the Phrase 'Class A War Criminal']', *Shokun*, September, pp. 70–9

Watanabe, Tsuneo and Yoshifumi Wakamiya (2006), 'Yasukuni o kataru, Gaiko o kataru [Talking about Yasukuni, Talking about Diplomacy],' *Ronza*, February, pp. 26–39.

Yomiuri Shimbun (ed.) (2006), *Who was Responsible? From Marco Polo Bridge to Pearl Harbour.* Japan: Yomiuri Shimbun.

11 Beyond the geisha stereotype

Changing images of 'new women' in Japanese popular culture

Junko Saeki

Introduction

One of the most salient changes in Japanese society over the last ten years is the position of women both in reality and in representation. The number of female workers increased from 27.01 million to 27.50 million from 1995 to 2005, and that of female employees from 20.48 million to 22.29 million.[1] In direct proportion to the increasing number of working women, female characters in Japanese popular culture such as manga or TV dramas have shifted from being obedient, weak girls to strong, working women. This change is more clearly observed in works of female authorship, for women themselves are keenly aware of the change in their position in society. In works by female authors, we can see self-images of Japanese women that male authors have never been able to express. Male points of view, as well as those of non-Japanese, often misinterpret what is really happening in women's lives. Therefore, I would like to examine various female voices in Japanese popular culture, by focusing on works of manga and TV dramas by women.

Manga are now one of the most powerful cultural products that Japan exports to other countries, but manga of male authorship sometimes restrict images of Japanese women to objects of male desire, reproducing the geisha stereotype abroad. Images of Japanese young girls depicted in manga for boys or young men, which include those of otaku-culture (nerds or geeks), usually exaggerate female sexuality, and thus can be easily misunderstood as pornography.[2] Just as Western males saw Japanese women as erotic objects in the past by labelling Japanese women as geisha, Japanese men seem to contribute to the commercialization of Japanese female sexuality abroad. Unfortunately, that type of male gaze on Japanese women both from inside and outside Japan still seems to survive nowadays, as the worldwide popularity of a novel about geisha indicates.[3]

Instead of tracing such kinds of male fantasy, which are a world away from Japanese women's real lives, I would like to show how manga by female authors express what ordinary Japanese women are thinking about and how they feel about their own lives, supplemented by a discussion of the social and cultural background, with the purpose of introducing Japanese women's own perception of themselves. This will help others to understand what is really happening in the

lives of contemporary Japanese women, and thus correct the still-surviving misin-
terpretations of Japanese women that are perpetuated by the geisha stereotype.

Love and marriage with a happy ending: the main concern of manga for girls in the 1960s and 1970s

In the genre of shojo-manga (manga for young girls), born during the early 1960s,
the main topic is the heroine's love affair and marriage. Most shojo-manga plots
focus on the heroine's relationship with her boyfriend and end with her happy
union with her lover. Not a few female manga critics who were born around 1960
confess that they to indulged in reading such comics during their girlhood and
were very much influenced by them. Rika Yokomori says that she learned what
ideal love and marriage were from manga and adds:

> Girls of our age used to think that a woman can get happiness by being loved
> by a wonderful man, and by attaining a comfortable married life. The idea of
> seeking their own careers in the public sphere was beyond the ken of girls
> who grew up in the 1970s.
>
> (Yokomori 1999)

A similar view is expressed by Yukari Fujimoto.[4]

The extremely big eyes and beautiful guises of the heroines exaggerate their
femininity, and thus show the ideal femininity of girls that can attract the male
gaze. Women should be cute (*kawaii*) and weak, never claiming equality with
men, in order to attain ideal love and marriage. This ideal of the woman's life is in
some way influenced by Western culture, such as classical Hollywood cinema or
animated Disney films such as *Snow White and the Seven Dwarfs* (first released in
Japan in 1950), *Cinderella* (1953) and *Sleeping Beauty* (1960).

These stories of girls who are found and then loved by the ideal 'prince' became
beautiful dreams of girls at that time, along with adoration of Western culture.
That is the reason why shojo-manga often depict Western towns and countries
such as Paris or New York, or sometimes Western rural scenes, as the paradise of
romantic love affairs.

The popular female authors of shojo-manga in the 1960s and 1970s, such as
Waki Yamato (1948–), Yoko Shoji (1950–) and Yumiko Igarashi (1950–) were
born around 1950 and may well have been influenced by the love stories of
Western popular culture introduced to Japan during their girlhood. Then, as adults,
they expressed their love fantasies of Western origin, adapted to the Japanese
context. Although the heroines are ordinary Japanese girls, their boyfriends look
like young Western men with curly hair and big eyes. Shoi, the hero in *Haikara-
san ga Toru* (1975–77), who was once mistaken for a Russian nobleman, is the
paradigm. Thus, in Japanese popular culture of the 1970s the image of the ideal
man was mixed with that of Western culture in female fantasy.

Ironically enough, however, the real lives of female manga authors as working
women were not considered to be ideal role models for their female readers.

Indeed, independent heroines were hardly sympathized with at all by readers at that time. Keiko Takemiya (1950–), one of the most representative Japanese female manga writers once said:

> In the beginning, I tried to depict strong heroines in my works, but they could not gain popularity among female readers. Then, I began to write stories about boys, and those kinds of works turned out to be a great success.
>
> (Takemiya 2004; my translation)

In other words, young girls themselves hardly sympathized with strong heroines; weak and obedient women were more acceptable to them. Although the manga heroines might seem strong and subversive on the surface, like Benio in *Haikara-san ga Toru*, they could not imagine their lives without the boyfriends, who were expected to support them. They knew that it was necessary to follow the traditional Confucian ethic, which taught that women should obey men if they wanted to achieve ideal love and marriage in contemporary Japanese society.

The 'revolution' in manga: the appearance of the working heroine

It was Riyoko Ikeda (1947–), another prominent Japanese female manga author, who dramatically reformed this kind of traditional manga heroine ideal. Her masterpiece, *The Roses of Versailles* (Berusaiyu no Bara, 1972–73), which depicts the French Revolution, was also revolutionary in the history of Japanese shojo-manga. In contrast to the conservative heroines of traditional shojo-manga, Oscar, the female protagonist in *The Roses of Versailles*, demonstrates strong independence and will, working as an Imperial Guard at the Palace of Versailles (Figure 11.1).

Figure 11.1 Oscar, the female protagonist in *The Roses of Versailles*.

Raised as a male to be one of the Imperial Guards, her family's hereditary occupation, she expresses herself as the public equal of male comrades. Young female readers of the early 1970s, including myself, greatly sympathized with Oscar because of her strong will and independence. Later, the work was made into a TV series and adapted for theatrical performance, gaining an even wider audience.

A similar cross-dressed heroine is depicted in Osamu Tezuka's *Knight with a Ribbon* (Ribon no Kishi, first version 1953–56, second version 1963–66). Here, however, Sapphire, the heroine, is finally engaged to Franz, the prince of the neighbouring country, and thus ends up with the same 'ordinary happiness' as the heroines of many other manga works. At the same time, Sapphire suffers confusion about her gender identity and is eager to return to the female gender, which is identical to her biological sex. By contrast, Oscar is proud of her work and prefers to accept the male gender role rather than leading the ordinary life of her female contemporaries. In contrast to Sapphire, the creation of a male author, Riyoko Ikeda's heroine has a strong identity as a working woman.

In the early 1970s, the number of working women in Japanese society was gradually increasing, with the number of female employees rising from 10.96 million in 1970 to 11.67 million in 1975, and Oscar became a charismatic ideal for ambitious young girls of that time. Interestingly enough, the traditional heroines with the goal of happy love and marriage, and the new working woman heroine like Oscar coexisted at that time. This means that some young women had already awakened to the desire to seek their own identity and express themselves in the public sphere, even as some of their friends still believed that the ultimate happiness for a woman was a happy marriage. At the same time, even girls who clung to the conservative way of thinking at least came to sympathize with the independent heroine as the embodiment of their impossible dreams.

But in the story of *The Roses of Versailles*, the heroine Oscar loses her love, a Swedish nobleman, and dies young on the battlefield during the French Revolution. Just before her death, she finds a new love in her attendant André, but her tragic death and unconsummated love suggest that a woman cannot have a life-long career, and if she wants to work in the public sphere, she must be prepared to sacrifice her private happiness. In reality, many Japanese women of the 1970s did quit their jobs on marriage, and the M-curve in the statistics of the number of working women still exists in Japan, in contrast to other industrialized countries where M-curves gradually disappeared during the 1980s (Inoue and Ehara 2005: 80).

Oscar's tragedy implies that a woman cannot have her career and love at the same time, and if she wants to pursue her career, she must sacrifice her private life. The fact that Oscar dresses as a male indicates that working in public was male gendered at that time. It was also difficult to depict an independent Japanese heroine, even for a female author; thus, Oscar is not Japanese but French.

It seems that the author herself strongly identified with Oscar as a working woman, but, as Yokomori has discussed in her work, the author also offered another heroine with whom readers who idealized the life of a housewife could easily identify. Yokomori points out that Marie Antoinette, the last queen of France, is depicted as the embodiment of the lives of Japanese housewives who usually lead their lives inside their homes. Although she does not love her husband so much, she has three children with him, and leads a harmonious family life, at least before the French Revolution. Though she also dies tragically in the end, by execution, the lives of Oscar and Marie Antoinette show the sharp contrast between the metaphor of the working woman and that of the housewife. The author skilfully depicted two different types of heroine as a reflection of the different life courses of the Japanese women who were her contemporaries. Although the story is about eighteenth-century France, its female characters tell us about the lives of Japanese women of the 1970s.

The appearance of strong-willed Japanese heroines

An active Japanese heroine with a strong will appeared in the late 1980s along with the promulgation of the law for equal opportunity employment between male and female in 1985. The law, which was reformed in 1997 and in 2007, makes it easier for women to work under equal circumstances to men and encourages women to pursue their own careers. From 1989, the number of women university students (including junior college) in Japan began to exceed that of men, and so more women achieved educational levels beyond those of men. Kimio Ito, one of the pioneers of gender studies and 'men's studies' in Japan, has pointed out that the year 1989, when Emperor Hirohito died, was an important turning point for Japanese society because from that year women potentially surpassed men in many areas such as education, careers and self expression (Ito 1993).

Rika in *Tokyo Love Story* (Fumi Saimon, 1989), one of the representative manga heroines of the 1980s, emerged against such a social and cultural background. Unlike traditional manga heroines of unrealistic appearance, Rika is more similar to ordinary Japanese women, without any stars in her eyes (Figure 11.2).

Figure 11.2 Rika and Kanji in *Tokyo Love Story*.

Rika expresses herself freely, both in public and in private, and confesses her love for her comrade, Kanji, without any hesitation. One of her lines, 'Let's make love, Kanji,' was epoch making for the heroine in manga history, confessing love from the female side. Rika usually takes the initiative in her relationship with Kanji. Heroines in manga were no longer passive or obedient, but had become active and strong, like the heroes in manga for boys. Raised abroad in her childhood, Rika speaks English well and uses her ability in her work. With Rika, a new ideal of the Japanese woman who enjoys love and her job at the same time emerged, created by a female manga author. Although the work was first published in *Big Comic Spirits*, a manga magazine for young men, it was very popular among female readers and gained even more popularity with the female audience when it was adapted as a TV drama in 1991. At the same time, the young male readers who were supposed to be the main audience for the magazine proved ready to accept a 'new woman' such as Rika. She was not rejected by male readers, but instead attracted them by her character, not just her appearance. The work also attracted many other young Asian audiences, including some in China, Taiwan and Singapore. Critical essays by Asian critics (Iwabuchi 2003) discussed how Rika was accepted as the charismatic symbol of the 'new woman' not only in Japan, but also in other Asian countries.[5] *Tokyo Love Story* still retains a great influence on the young generation both inside and outside Japan, through rebroadcasts and a DVD released in 2001.

The author herself writes that female readers greatly sympathized with Rika, whereas Satomi, a high school classmate of Kanji, was rejected (Saimon 2002). In contrast to Rika, Satomi embodies the old stereotype of the good wife and wise mother ideal in Japanese society, in that she is usually obedient to others and does not express herself as strongly as Rika does. Working as a nursery-school teacher, she is often depicted with small children, suggesting that she would be a 'good wife/wise mother'.

Her job as a teacher is only a temporary one before marriage, and such a working style is still popular among Japanese women, as the M-curve indicates. There is a sharp contrast between Rika and Satomi, one the symbol of working women and the other of housewives, just as between Oscar and Mary Antoinette. Both are a reflection of the two different types of life course for contemporary Japanese women.

Ironically enough, it is not Rika but Satomi who wins the love of Kanji. His choice suggests that the 'good wife and wise mother' stereotype was still the male ideal of women in the late 1980s to early 1990s. This ideal stems from the educational policy of the Meiji government, which defined the purpose of education for women as raising obedient wives and mothers when the law for the establishment of women's high schools was passed in 1911.[6] Seventy or eighty years later, the policy was still at work in Japanese society.

Even for the female manga author at that time, it was hard to imagine that women like Rika could lead a peaceful family life. In a 1992 survey, 55.8 per cent of Japanese women and 65.7 per cent of Japanese men thought that women should be responsible for housework (Inubushi *et al.* 2000: 42, table 2). The percentage had decreased from 83.2 (female) and 83.8 (male) in 1972 to 70.1 (female) and 75.6 (male) in 1979. But in the early 1990s, over half of Japanese women still thought that they should do housework rather than work outside the home. Given such an ideal, it was hard to allow Rika to gain love and a job at one and the same time.

In fact, Rika in the original becomes pregnant as the result of an affair with the president of her company, and determines in the end to be a single mother. Although she could not marry Kanji, she says that she is satisfied with her life with her baby. Her words imply that women can be happy outside the marital relationship. It is clear that the female author intends to show her readers many kinds of options for women to gain happiness. But the TV series, which has greatly contributed to popularizing the story, adapts the ending and Rika remains single, without children. TV drama, which tends to follow conservative moral standards, seems unwilling to challenge traditional family values. In fact, the moral codes of TV companies usually make efforts to avoid 'destroying traditional family values'.[7] The result is that the choice between job and love in the course of a woman's life persists in the TV dramas of the 1990s. Rika's loss of her love could also be interpreted as punishment for going beyond the old ideal of the passive, obedient woman. Audiences of the early 1990s still felt comfortable with women of 'good wife and wise mother' characteristics, apart from the radical heroines of manga and drama.

'New women' in twenty-first century Japanese popular culture

However, at the beginning of the twenty-first century, more liberated heroines have appeared both in manga and in TV dramas, among them Sumire in *Kimi wa Petto* (*You are my Pet*, Yayoi Ogawa, 2000). A graduate of Tokyo University, Sumire works as a journalist in a big newspaper company. She has sufficient income to afford an apartment of her own, and begins to live with a young man as her 'pet' (Figure 11.3).

She calls him Momo, the name of her dead dog. At the same time, she begins to date Hasumi, her superior in the company. Her former boyfriend blames her for keeping a young man as a pet, but she continues living with Momo and enjoying the love affair with Hasumi simultaneously. Unlike the manga writers of the 1980s and 1990s, the female manga author of the twenty-first century allows her heroine to enjoy both her job and love. Further, the author gives the heroine a human 'pet', just as men used to keep mistresses. Male characters in TV dramas of the past often kept mistresses, as in the case of Goro Zaizen, the male protagonist in *Shiroi Kyoto* (*Ivory Tower*, original novel published 1963–65, adapted as TV drama 1967, 1978–79, 1990), one of the most popular series in Japanese TV drama history. Zaizen could afford to keep his mistress, Keiko, in a small apartment, and Keiko herself gave up her medical studies. However, in the early 2000s, the female protagonist Sumire pursues her career as a journalist and earns enough to keep herself and her 'partner', just like Zaizen in the late 1970s. She has a certain economic power, a high educational background and social status, as the

Figure 11.3 Sumire and Komo in *You are My Pet*.

male protagonists in former dramas used to have, but it is not necessary for her to disguise herself as a male, in contrast to the heroines of the 1960s and 1970s. Unlike Sapphire or Oscar, who are both raised as males to work in public, Sumire can stay with her biological gender and enjoy her life as a woman. This reflects the growing power of women in Japan through the 1980s and 1990s. Although Sumire's life does not reflect Japanese women's lives in reality (keeping a young man as a 'pet' is not a popular phenomenon among contemporary Japanese women!), it effectively expresses what the 'new women' of twenty-first century Japan, especially working women, want to do and dream of.

Obtaining economic independence, Japanese women have begun to seek not financial support, but mental comfort from their partners. It is said that the characteristics of an ideal husband changed for women from the 'three highs' (high education, high income and height) to the 'three Cs' (comfortable, cooperative and compatible) in mid-1990s Japan (Inubushi *et al.* 2000). During the 1980s, when Japan's economic success was at its peak, Japanese women tended to depend on their husband's income, but after the disappearance of the bubble economy in the early 1990s, it became necessary for women to seek economic independence for themselves. Increasing job opportunities for women after the equal employment law came into force in 1986 also encouraged women's participation in the job market. Thus, working women themselves have increased both in reality and in representation, as I mentioned at the beginning of the chapter.

Sumire, one representative of these women, finally chooses Momo as her partner. The fact that she chooses him rather than Hasumi symbolizes the change in the ideal man that I mentioned before. Momo is taking lessons to be a professional dancer, and does not have any regular income when he starts to live with

Sumire, so he lives entirely on her income. But she finds herself very comfortable with him and finally finds that she loves him. Though he is smaller than her and does not earn enough to support their lives, he finally becomes her ideal partner in that he understands her and gives her mental comfort. Hasumi, who is an embodiment of the old ideal of the 'three highs husband', and who demonstrates the stereotypical masculine fascination found in traditional manga for girls, does not attract Sumire in the end.

Momo has taken the place of the traditional 'three highs' hero of manga. He is the new ideal man in twenty-first century manga for girls.

Furthermore, Sumire is not punished for her violation of the old ideal of femininity, unlike Rika, who was punished in the end due to her strong will and independence. Instead, she attains a happy union with Momo, continuing her job as a journalist at the same time. The new manga heroine does not necessarily sacrifice her job in order to attain private happiness. Adapted as a TV drama in 2003, the work has been accepted by a large female audience as the new type of female fantasy. The two producers of the drama, both of them female, say that they wanted to make a drama that could be sympathized with by a female audience. The popularity of the drama embodies the changes in Japanese women's ideal life styles and suggests a change in Japanese society itself. The Japanese government has been encouraging women's participation in public activities for the last ten years, resulting in the 1999 Basic Law for men's and women's equal participation in public life. It is making ongoing efforts to support female social activities by trying to increase the number of daycare centres and giving leave for child rearing.

Unfortunately, these efforts for supporting working women or working mothers are not so widespread in Japan as compared with European or other Asian societies, so the M-curve has not disappeared, as I mentioned earlier. In addition, the difference in wages between men and women is comparatively great in comparison with European countries, though it has been gradually decreasing over the last ten years. In 1992, the average female wage was 52.7 per cent of the male, then it increased to 63.9 per cent in 1998 and 66.0 per cent in 2000 (Inoue and Ehara 2005: 89, 132; Inubushi *et al.* 2000: 47), whereas in countries such as Sweden, Norway and Germany the equivalent figure is around 85 per cent (Inoue and Ehara 2005: 89). This makes some Japanese women think that it is not such a good choice to live on their own income, but rather preferable to live on their husband's income. The problem of incompatibility of job and marriage for women has not been completely solved in Japanese society, therefore, and it seems that contemporary female lives are divided into two types: those of working women (often without children), and housewives with children. That is one of the reasons why the number of children per woman is continually decreasing, from 1.57 in 1990 to 1.29 in 2003 (Inoue and Ehara 2005: 4), one of the most serious social problems in the country.[8]

Given such a social and economic background, manga that depict the working mother as a heroine are not so popular in contemporary Japan. But we can find a new possibility in the recent TV drama *At Home Dad* (Masaya Ozaki and Shizuka Oki, 2004), in which a working mother succeeds in achieving a harmonious family life. As the title indicates, the male protagonist, Kazuyuki, fired by his company, decides to do the housework, while his wife, Miki, goes back to her work as a part time editorial assistant.

At first, Kazuyuki is reluctant to stay at home and unwilling to take care of his daughter or do housework, but he gradually finds his new duties enjoyable and worthwhile. Miki, the housewife to start with, also faces difficulties in her new life as a working mother, but her husband's support helps her to continue her job. In reality, life as an at-home-dad is not so popular among Japanese men,[9] and 64.9 per cent of them still think that their wives should not work outside the home, according to the 1997 survey (Inubushi *et al.* 2000: 54). However, contrary to this reality, the drama attracted a large audience by showing the possibility of the exchange of stereotypical gender roles between women and men. Miki, as a working mother, is the new heroine of Japanese TV drama, challenging the old stereotype of the female role. I hope the same kind of heroine and the at-home-dad hero will appear in future manga.

Conclusion

Though there are still many problems concerning gender issues to be solved in Japan, it is true that the stereotypical ideal heroines and heroes are no longer valid either in reality or representation. As I have discussed, in the last thirty years, the position of women in Japan has changed dramatically, and in response to such changes, female creators in Japanese popular culture are continually seeking new possibilities in the lives of Japanese women, breaking the traditional ideals of the feminine.[10] They show how Japanese women perceive their own lives and experiences, and have made great changes in their representations especially in the last ten years. Their works create not only the image of 'new women' in Japan, but also new visions of Japanese society itself.

Notes

1 Statistics on Japanese workers, Japanese Ministry for General Affairs.
2 Nobuko Matsubara (1941–), the Japanese ambassador to Italy (–2005), claimed that the images of Japanese girls in an exhibition of Otaku at the Venice Biennale (September 2004), were almost pornographic (closing remarks at the Euro-Japan Forum on Gender Studies, University of Rome, La Sapienza, November 26, 2005).
3 Arthur Golden's novel about geisha (Golden 1997) became very popular around the world, along with its Hollywood adaptation *Sayuri* (2005).
4 Fujimoto 1998. Fujimoto also discusses how many Japanese girls of her age formed their identities through shojo-manga.
5 For detailed discussion about the popularity and influence of *Tokyo Love Story* around Asian countries, see Iwabuchi 2003.
6 For detailed discussion about the 'good wife and wise mother' stereotype and images of women in modern Japanese media, see Saeki 2005.
7 The code of ethics for domestic broadcasting (established in 1959, revised in 1998) of the Japan Broadcasting Corporation (NHK, Nippon Hoso Kyokai) prescribes that 'married life should be carefully represented and family life should be highly respected

in programmes' (Chapter 8: family). Also, the code of ethics of the National Association of Commercial Broadcasters in Japan (NAB, established in 1958, revised in 2004) prescribes that 'family life should be highly respected, and corruption of family life should not be positively represented in programmes' (Chapter 4.23), and that 'subversive messages against marital relationships should be avoided' (Chapter 4.24).

8   The problem seems the most serious among Asian countries (Ochiai 2007).
9   Only five men out of 3,121 employees took child-rearing leave in 1992, six months after the enforcement of the law for child-rearing leave. Even in the last three years, no men have taken child-rearing leave in about 80 per cent of Japanese companies (Sankei Shinbun website, 26 February 2007). Both facts show that the rearing of children is still considered as a female gender role.
10 Napier has also pointed out that "the stereotypical image of passive Japanese womanhood" has changed into "aggressive, violent, often quite dominating women" in the 1990s (Napier 1998:104).

References

Fujimoto, Yukari (1998), *Watashi-no Ibasho wa Dokoniaruno: Shojo manga-ga utsusu kokoro-no Katachi* (*Where is my own place? Japanese girls' mentalities represented in Shojo-manga*). Tokyo: Gakuyo-shobo.

Golden, Arthur (1997), *Memoirs of a Geisha*. London: Chatto and Windus.

Inoue, T. and Y. Ehara (eds) (2005), *Josei no Data Book* (*Women's Data Book*). 4th edn, Tokyo: Yuhi-kaku.

Inubushi, Y., M. Mukuno and A. Muraki (eds) (2000), *Josei-gaku Key Number* (*Key Numbers for Women's Studies*). Tokyo: Yuhi-kaku.

Ito, Kimio (1993), *Otoko-rashisa no Yukue* (*The Future of Japanese Masculinity*). Tokyo: Shinyo-sha.

Iwabuchi, Koichi (ed.) (2003), *Global Prism: 'Asian Dream' toshite-no Nihon no TV drama* (*Japanese TV dramas as the 'Asian Dream'*). Tokyo: Heibon-sha.

Napier, Suzan (1998), 'Vampires, Psychic Girls, Flying Women and Sailor Scouts: Four Faces of the Young Female in Japanese Popular Culture', in Martinez, Dolores (ed.), *The Worlds of Japanese Popular Culture: Gender, Shifting Boundaries and Global Cultures*. Cambridge: Cambridge University Press.

Ochiai, E. and K. Ueno (eds) (2007), *21 seiki Asia Kazoku* (*Asian Families in the 21st century*). Tokyo: Akashi-shoten.

Saeki, Junko (2005), 'Media ni-okeru josei-hyosho to sei-teki rinri (Sexual Morality in Modern Japanese Media)', *Doshisha Media Communication Kenkyu* (*Doshisha Journal of Media and Communication Research*) 2 (20 March), Kyoto: Doshisha Center for Media and Communications Research.

Saimon, Fumi (1989), *Tokyo Love Story in Big Comic Spirits*. Tokyo: Kodan-sha.

Saimon, Fumi (2002), 'About my *Tokyo Love Story*', in Fumi Saimon, *Tokyo Love Story*, vol. 1. Tokyo, Shogaku-kan.

Takemiya, Keiko (2004), 'Bishonen Dangi (A Discussion About Beautiful Boys)', with Sumie Takabatake and Junko Saeki, in *Taisho Roman* 24, August. Ehime: Takabatake Kasho Taisho Roman-kan.

Yokomori, Rika (1999), *Ren'ai wa Shojo-manga de Osowatta* (*I learned what love is through shojo-manga*). Tokyo: Shuei-sha.

Part V
National identity

12 Japanese religion adrift

A re-examination of 'religion' in post-war Japan

Tetsuo Yamaori

Introduction: Japan in the world

In the midst of the terrorist attacks of 9/11 on New York and Washington, DC I was struck by the following scene. On the night of the attacks, President Bush made a television address in which he paid tribute to the victims and, quoting Psalm 23 from the Old Testament, called on the families of the deceased to recover their perseverance and courage.

It was appropriate, I reflected. When the heart of the nation was stricken in an instant and a large number of citizens horribly killed, and when even the lives of the survivors seemed in great peril, the president, as one individual person, took refuge in the Old Testament. In that case, when the entire earth is menaced with total destruction also, surely it will be the prophets and poets of the Old Testament who will be relied upon. On the night of 9/11, however, the words of the Bible that President Bush quoted were not from the prophets and poets, but rather from King David, who established the Israeli kingdom in the nineteenth century BCE.

> Though I walk through the valley of the shadow of death,
> I shall not fear,
> for you are with me.

These words are frequently intoned at the funerals of believers and are quite familiar to the residents of New York, a large proportion of whom are Jewish. Since friction between peoples tends to highlight religious friction, such comments may be superfluous here.

I mention here the connection between President Bush and the Old Testament, however, not to comment just on Americans or the residents of New York, but to reflect on myself. It is necessary to consider the problem as a Japanese.

Let me speak frankly. Should, for example, the Japanese capital of Tokyo be subject to a similar terrorist attack, does our prime minister have recourse, like Bush's to the Old Testament, to a sacred scripture? It need not even be scripture. When the heart of Japan, and one's own life, is endangered as a terrorist target, do we possess something on which we can ultimately rely?

This is not, of course, a question solely for the prime minister, but one each of us faces. In such times, what sort of attitude will we assume? This question points up a vacuum within me.

That the Japanese do not possess the firm words that may stand up in times of crisis has already been demonstrated in the aftermath of the Hanshin earthquake. We dealt with the calamity that took so many lives almost solely as 'volunteers'. Was there a preacher who took to the site the Buddha's message that all things are impermanent? Or one who repeated Shinran's famous words, 'Hell is to be my abode'? Or were there Christians who intoned, 'Blessed are those who mourn'? At the time, even the religious went to the sites not as religious, but as individual volunteers. Though phrases might be drawn from the Buddhist scriptures or the Bible, no one believed any more that they might alleviate the grief of the people caught in suffering.

In reflecting on this, I cannot but be impressed anew by the strength of the United States. At the same time, I regret the weakness of Japan. Regarding this, I can only sigh at the depth of the gap in the memories of history underlying the difference between the two.

I will add here one further matter, which relates to the Gulf War ten year previously. In response to the invasion of Kuwait by Saddam Hussein's Iraqi army, the coalition forces from various nations gathered. At this time, each American soldier carried in an inner pocket printed words of Moses from Psalm 91 of the Old Testament:

You will tread on the lion and adder,
You trample underfoot the young lion and serpent.

In Moses's day, the lion and snake were symbols for non-believers. During the Gulf War, they clearly referred to Saddam Hussein's Islamic army. There is a prior matter that may also be mentioned. In the closing days of the Second World War, in North Africa, British troops victoriously confronted the Nazi army tanks with the same words of Moses on their lips. We see here the historical background to Bush's use of David's words from the Old Testament to overcome the pain of sorrow. It is possible to understand the conceptual apparatus operating on a deep level to soften the blow to the spirit and transcend the momentary blankness. This is a world that the Japanese have chosen not to see. The Japanese have sought only to take on the trappings of modernity while putting under seal the dark culverts of the pre-modern.

Let us turn back once again to 9/11. The American bombing of Afghanistan commenced on 7 October. Three weeks later, on 29 October, Japan established special anti-terrorism provisions and revised articles governing the self-defence forces. Under these provisions, on November 9, three naval vessels departed for the Gulf region from Sasebo in Nagasaki with the mission of gathering intelligence.

As an aside, allow me to mention that I am basically in agreement with the actions taken, somewhat hastily, by the Japanese government in response to the

9/11 attacks, in support of the US action in Afghanistan. My reasons are quite simple. For half a century after the Second World War, the peace and security of Japan has been guaranteed through the alliance with the United States. This has allowed Japan to enjoy an opportunity for a period of reconstruction and prosperity. I have sought to keep in mind the debt of gratitude owed by the Japanese people to the United States for this. This seems to me a general rule of morality, and Japan will cease to be Japan if it is forgotten.

To return to the topic of the naval support, on 9 November, vessels of the naval self-defence forces, with young officers on board, departed from Sasebo in support of American military activities in the Gulf region. The ships sailed through the Straits of Malacca into the Indian Ocean. Just beyond the Straits of Malacca lies Singapore. The image came to my mind of the young officers watching as their ship sailed beyond Singapore, and brought to mind another image that fused indelibly with it.

Singapore was a battleground where, during the war in the Pacific, the Japanese military celebrated a great victory. Then, with defeat in the war, it turned into a site of humiliation, for many B and C class war criminals were tried and punished there. This memory of humiliation is conveyed vividly in the records published in *Kike wadatsumi no koe* (Iwanami bunko). This is a writing of a BC class war criminal who was executed in prison at Singapore. He was a man named Hisao Kimura. He entered the Department of Economics of Kyoto University in April 1942. On 1 October of the same year, he was inducted. On 23 May 1946, he was executed in Singapore as a war criminal. He had been an officer in the army, and died at the age of 28.

Kimura's final testament was written on blank spaces in his copy of a work of philosophy by Hajime Tanabe, *Tetsugaku tsūron*. Kimura had been falsely convicted of maltreatment of prisoners of war, having been made to bear the crimes of his superior officers. He writes that he has done nothing to deserve the death sentence:

> I would not be able to accept death if I thought that I was being sacrificed for the Japanese army, but if I think that I receive death for the transgressions and blame of the entire Japanese people, then I feel no anger. I go to my death smiling.

The passage continues with a dialogue with death. They are heavy and painful words full of anger, anxiety and resignation. There are words of self-consolation. 'Rather than lament my misfortune, I will to go to death with gratitude for all the divine benevolence from the gods I have received in the past.' He then states that he wishes his grave, when he has become a buddha (*hotoke*), to be colourfully adorned with dahlias and tulips.

We see that he seeks to depart for the realm of the dead with faith in the gods and buddhas. I am deeply struck anew that what eases the pain and gives comfort at the end to this young student-soldier who has been burdened with an unjust fate is the benevolence and protection of the gods and the prayer for buddhahood. This is surely not the case with Hisao Kimura alone. It was a resolve engraved on the hearts of many of the young soldiers as they headed to the battlefront.

When I think of Hisao Kimura, another unforgettable image comes to mind. It concerns Mokichi Saitō, who debated his course on the home front. He was at a loss, being in a situation of having to send off young men to the battlefield. His feelings took the form of verse. In Shōwa 19, as various reports of defeat reached his ears, he wrote:

> shinbun no / shasetsu kibishiku / narimasari
> kami no ikioi / ima ugokasamu

> The editorials in the newspapers
> grow ever more
> severe.
> The force of the gods
> now will be moved.

Mokichi was restless with the news reports. This was the formidable power of the news reports that would suddenly invade the consciousness. How should one deal with this outside influence? How should one protect oneself from this violent authority? Confronting this violence, Mokichi invokes the anger of the *kami*. Kami here refers without doubt to the traditional kami from the Man'yō period on. There is perhaps an allusion even to the 'divine wind' *kamikaze* of the time of the Mongol attacks. He implores the kami to take action, praying solely for the benevolent protection of the gods. It is a simple appeal that the lives of the youth and the country itself be protected.

We have a long history throughout the post-war period of indictment of 'war verse' that supposedly glorifies war, like this cry of Mokichi and his prayer. Mokichi, however, was anguished at the development of the war. But on reflection now, has it not been ethically shallow to continue to blame Mokichi? The call for the divine wind was at the same time a call for peace.

I wish to note the symptom of silence at present. Today, as the warfare in Afghanistan continues and the naval vessel sails out beyond the Strait of Malacca into the Indian Ocean, no voice is heard calling for the divine wind to arise. Today, support behind the battlefront requires, more than material, weapons and financial aid, an expenditure of sweat and tears. Although the global situation is such, we can find no words to give moral support for effort to resolve crises. There are, for example, no words for the youth who head toward the trouble spot. Among those who send off the self-defence forces, there is no Mokichi, and among the soldiers, there is no Kimura. Above all, we lack the words of ultimate refuge that might play a role corresponding to the Old Testament words used by President Bush.

I am reminded of the first time I visited Washington, DC and saw the Arlington Cemetery, site of the tomb of the Unknown Soldier, and the Pentagon, designed like a modern-day fortress. Close by is the marble hall of the Lincoln Memorial, which honours the sixteenth president, who brought an end to slavery in the United States through the Civil War. Even in Japan, his Gettysburg Address is well known, with its closing phrases, 'of the people, by the people, and for the people'. In the post-war educational system, perhaps these words before any others were taught as the starting point of democratic education.

A statue of Lincoln that serves as a symbol of freedom and equality is enshrined in the memorial hall, which may be said to mimic the Parthenon. It is as though Lincoln is intentionally enshrined as a god for worship. The statue is of Lincoln, seated and gazing downward before him. It stands approximately six metres high. I envisioned the great Buddha of Tōdaiji superimposed upon it. Of course, the great Buddha is sixteen metres high, so comparison is impossible. Nevertheless, I sensed a common fervour of a nation in a period of reconstruction, and briefly reflected on a comparison.

The memorial is adorned with thirty-six pillars, and on the interior of the southern wall the entire Gettysburg Address is inscribed in large letters. The final phrases caught my eye. I noticed also the frequency with which the sense of self-dedication recurred throughout the brief text. In a speech of no more than ten minutes, the word 'dedicate' occurs six times and 'devotion' twice. The address opens with 'We dedicate ourselves ...' and returns to this theme repeatedly.

'Dedicate' here means to dedicate oneself to the service of the country. At times, this means a sacrifice of blood. This was certainly Lincoln's meaning. He expresses his gratitude to God, noting that it is through the repeated sacrifice of blood that the United States has been able to be established. He prays for the protection of God.

Mysteriously, the themes of the first half of the Gettysburg Address, the prayer to God and the remarks on dedication and sacrifice, were absent from my memory. It is probable that the emphasis in my education on government 'of the people, by the people, and for the people' had been so forceful, the message of prayer and sacrifice left no impression. Perhaps this was the gist of the post-war democratic education. The dream was the establishment of a democratic nation without god, a government without sacrifice.

The results of this may be seen today, fifty years later. On the occasion of sending naval vessels to a war zone for the first time since the close of the Second World War, there was no voice of prayer in the halls of the national Diet. Nor were there the natural words of encouragement to the young officers who had undertaken the dedication and sacrifice. Such words were absent not only from the halls of government, but also from the people at large, both those who opposed the deployment and those who supported it. If this is the case, does it not indicate an ethical lapse within the nation? The moral insensitivity of the Japanese has thus been manifested.

In October 1995, I visited Jerusalem. I still remember the shock of the assassination of Prime Minister Rabin three days after my return. At the heart of the city is the Jewish temple mount. In 70 CE, the temple was destroyed by Roman troops, and in ensuing battles many Jews were killed. A remaining wall is the well-known Wailing Wall. Also on the central part of the hill is an octagonal structure with a golden dome. It is adorned with Islamic decoration and, within, a rock is enshrined from which Mohammed is said to have ascended to heaven. It is a site sacred to Muslims. Looking to the north, one sees the path that Jesus took to his crucifixion, and beyond, a church that is said to be the site where the body of Jesus was laid. It is of course a supremely sacred place to the Christians of the world.

The wall of the Jews, the tomb of the Christians, and the rock of the Muslims all coexist in Jerusalem and maintain a perilous balance. The three monotheisms that have marked history with the traces of glory and suffering, through wall and tomb and rock have devised a system of partition, mutually maintaining separation.

Considered thus, it appears that this sacred city, established in the desert on what might first appear abandoned ruins, may be the last stronghold for the survival of humankind. In actuality, however, in the secular city that surrounds the sacred sites, acts of violence are a daily occurrence. And this violence has now erupted to reach the centres of the United States with suicide attacks.

After a century of ceaseless revenge and new vengeance, the sacred city of Jerusalem seemed to me to be filled with prayer. Despair and fearful prayer. There is no one, however, who seeks to give up prayer. Rather, in desperate attempts to actualize the prayers, unjust terrorist acts occur. How can this vicious circle be stopped? As long as wall and tomb and rock exist there, the sacred site will continue to disseminate the message of peace and balance. But we must ask ourselves: what can be done?

Religion within Japan: Shigeru Nambara and Douglas MacArthur; the 'void' valued by Shigeru Nambara

Shigeru Nambara played a major role in steering the course of education in post-war Japan. He was the first president of Tokyo University after the Second World War. Regarding the issues of peace with Japan, he argued for complete reconciliation, and was ridiculed by the standing prime minister, Shigeru Yoshida. This was in 1949, when Yoshida was 71 and Nambara 60. It had the feel of a wilful older brother scolding a bright, argumentative sibling.

We should note that at this time the course of education was not simply reorganized. Even religion in post-war Japan underwent radical change. Not simply change, however. Japanese religion was immobilized, bound hand and foot; it completely lost power of judgement and, as if suspended in mid air, was cast out in the cold. And the person who stood at the crossroads and directed matters was none other than Shigeru Nambara.

Nambara was born in Kagawa prefecture. In 1907 he entered the First High School, where his thinking was influenced by the principal, Inazō Nitobe. After entering Tokyo Imperial University law school, in the department of political science, he attended the Bible lectures of Kanzō Uchimura. These influences laid the foundation for his becoming a Christian of the non-church movement. In 1925, at the age of 35, he became a professor of Tokyo University. In 1942, at the age of 53, he published the book *The State and Religion: Research in European Spiritual History* (Iwanami shoten). During this time, from the war with China to the Second World War, Nambara's university weathered a stormy period and he was able to witness at close range a steady stream of tensions in the political situation. He did not, however, like Tatsukichi Minobe and Sōkichi Tsuda of Waseda University, have his publications prohibited, nor was he driven, like Yukitoki Takikawa of Kyoto University and Tadao Yanaihara, to resign. Further, he did not undergo arrest, like Hyōei Ōuchi. Tenacious in a time of harsh war, he lived cautiously, as though crossing a stone bridge. Whence this cautiousness? We must bear this aspect of his character in mind when considering his subsequent thought and actions.

Immediately following the defeat in the war, Nambara was called before the occupation forces in regard to the problem of education and religion. In December 1945, he was appointed president of Tokyo University. In March of the following year, when an American commission to investigate education in Japan arrived in the country, he was a member of the committee of Japanese educators that met with the commission and was selected chair. At the same time, he was selected as a member of the chamber of lords and participated in the review of the draft of the new Japanese constitution. In August of the same year, he became a member of the educational reform commission, as vice-chair, and from November of the following year, as chair. This reform commission later developed into the Central Education Council.

In less than a year after surrender, Nambara came to stand at the head of the project to lay down a new course for education in post-war Japan. In concrete terms, he took on the work of replacing the prewar Imperial Rescript on Education with the post-war Fundamentals of Education Act. In the cabinet, the prime minister was Shigeru Yoshida, Kōtarō Tanaka was minister of education, and the chair of the education reform commission was Yoshishige Abe, who was later replaced by Nambara.

During this period, the principle of education that Nambara proposed was coloured by a fervent effort to bring back a 'renaissance' and 'religious reformation' to the scorched earth of post-war Japan. His goal was the strengthening of a humanism aimed at the freedom and independence of the individual. It was the adoption of a European model. He asserted that, in this way, it would be possible to achieve a 'revival of humaneness' (renaissance) and a 'rediscovery of the divine' (religious reformation).[1]

This view was expressed in an address in Washington, DC at a meeting held with the cooperation of the State Department and sponsored by the American Education Council. We should note that the same views were expressed later in Japan at the research conference of Japanese Association of Educators in 1954. Nambara seriously intended to realize a renaissance and religious reformation in order to bring about the reconstruction of post-war Japan. We may add here that in his addresses he showed a strong interest in the theme of 'human evil' and an acute wariness of an 'insolent scientism' in relation to human issues and global politics. We glimpse in him a philosopher-politician.

The illustrious tradition of the Protestant revolution was reborn in Nambara's memory. The glimpse during the youthful period in which he was a disciple of

Kanzō Uchimura arose in his mind. It was as though he could still hear his teacher speak of his notion of the 'non-church' movement. Strangely, however, this logic of the equation of high renaissance and religious reformation grew clouded. With the passage of time, the youthful energy came to be blocked. He shifted from philosopher-politician to a practical politician fighting a rearguard action. What brought about this change?

An indication of the change is obliquely acknowledged in an autobiographical note. This is a piece written for the programme 'Reader in Life' broadcast on NHK national radio in 1960. This is eight years after his retirement from the post of president of Tokyo University and seven years after the conclusion of the peace treaties. In it, Nambara speaks frankly of his spiritual upbringing and rebirth. Further, he touches on the topics of knowledge and faith, religion and socialism. He presses the question, 'What is faith?' and speaks on issues of contemporary religion. This is not surprising, for in preparing for this broadcast, he used the title, 'Is Religion Unnecessary?'

Nevertheless, from the vantage point of the present, using the title 'Is Religion Unnecessary?' appears somewhat strange. Surely it indicates that at the time, in 1960, there were about him in all levels of society voices asserting that religion was indeed unnecessary. In fact, it appears that the 70-year-old Nambara, who had already withdrawn from full activity, still felt an urgency in insisting, in rebuke, that 'No, even so religion is necessary.'

But was this really the case? In Nambara's quietly confessional piece for the broadcast, one cannot help but sense a refracted force of suppression at work. Nambara begins by speaking of his birth in an impoverished village in eastern Kagawa prefecture. Shikoku Island is known as the birthplace of Kūkai and also for the pilgrimage trails to eighty-eight sacred sites, but Nambara was born into a Jōdo Shinshū family. He says it was his mother who taught him to worship the kami and buddhas. On journeying to Tokyo to study at the First High School, his rebirth began. Emerging from a 'period of anguish', he encountered Kanzō Uchimura, and his eyes were opened to the problem of 'human evil'. He was absorbed in doubts regarding the cultured person of no religion and in the confrontation with God, that which transcends the human. This was Nambara's adolescent roaming and the quickening toward rebirth.

At this point, however, he abruptly changes the topic, and suddenly raises the problem of post-war education. It may be that the confessional and interior comments on his early life were meant to lead up to the latter theme. The central topic, of course, is the new educational act that he had a hand in establishing. As is well known, in the education laws, the need for 'religious sentiment' is asserted. The problem was how to implement it in elementary and middle schools. Concerning this question, he responds as follows. In public schools, it is impossible for teachers to teach their pupils religion. Further, such teaching must be prohibited. He then argues:

> Rather, what I hope for is that teachers, though they may be atheists, do not simply reject and deny the realm of religion, but instead *carefully leave it*

blank. If this is done, then the pupils will in the future each, through their own struggles and experiences, search for it, and at that time God himself will seek them out and they will encounter the world of religion. I understand religion to be such.[2]

(Emphasis added)

Nambara states here that in the public school, religion must be left as a blank. To be sure, here he speaks of 'blankness' with deep thought as a weighty and valuable blank or void. Further, that which redeems this important blankness is, for him, the direct encounter with God – the vertical, Christian faith that binds Nambara's soul and God. Here there arises his expectation that God himself will smile upon the pupils.

At this time, however, was it not possible that Nambara sensed that, with the passage of time, the 'valuable void' might change and withdraw into a mere vacuum? Could he not foresee that the important blankness, as a simple figure of speech, would itself become vacuous? He says that he wants teachers, even if they happen to be atheists, to leave the realm of religion as an important blank. On reflection, however, the demand on the atheist is essentially to believe in what is illogical or unreasonable. Why did Nambara, even after retirement, set forth his notion of a blank, which had proved fruitless? This was surely because he had in mind as the chief audience of the radio broadcast 'Reader in Life' socialists and materialists involved in education. Whether from the tension of such concerns, or from simply a certain slackness in spirit, the text of the broadcast is altogether lacking the high ideals of renaissance and religious reformation that he expounded in earlier days. Today, his words have the feeling of an exceedingly weak entreaty to atheists.

MacArthur's lament at the spiritual vacuum

Let us change the perspective and consider the transition from the stance of the occupation forces. As mentioned above, in December of the year of defeat, Nambara took the position of president of Tokyo University. On the fifteenth of that month, the directive on Shintō (*Shintō shirei*) was issued. This was a directive to the Japanese government from the Supreme Command of the allied forces. The objective was the dismantling of state Shintō, which had been tied to nationalistic militarism, and to advance the separation of religion and state. Of course, the revision of the constitution was carried on at the same time. In the draft of the constitution that was being worked out there were already provisions for freedom of worship and separation of church and state. Perhaps for this reason it is possible to conjecture that those involved in the revision of the constitution and the directive concerning Shintō had contact with each other behind the scenes.[3]

On the one hand, the GHQ office guiding the revision of the constitution was Government section, headed by Whitney and Kades. According to Shigeru Yoshida, these were brusque New Dealers who eagerly sought to propel Japan into radical reform without paying attention to the actual conditions.[4] On the other hand, the drafting of the directive on Shintō was done in the GHQ by the Civil Information and Education section, headed by Dyke and Bass. In addition, it appears that Henderson, the first head of the religion division who was involved in the emperor's declaration of his humanity, was consulted.[5] The directive on Shintō had the objective of sweeping away militarism and extreme nationalism, and was intended to radically advance the purposes of the occupation in the religious sphere. It may also be said to reflect a New Deal policy of separation of religion and state.

Needless to say, the overall director of the GHQ was MacArthur. He played the role of a war god in taking a scalpel to Japan's 'national polity' and bringing about fundamental change. At the same time, however, while backing up the radical reform policies formulated in the Government section and Civil Information and Education section, he continued to give broad and open expression to his own Christian beliefs. While proclaiming a strict separation of religion and state (the rejection of state Shintō), he did not hesitate to proclaim forthrightly the authority of the Christianity that supported his moral and spiritual stance. This was because, for MacArthur, Christianity was the very foundation of democracy itself, and Shintō could not be placed on the same level with it as a religion.[6]

MacArthur demonstrated his support of Christianity whenever an occasion arose, and sought to make full use of Christians and American missionaries. Yoshiya Abe has stated that MacArthur was possessed of a 'messiah complex', and that he believed himself to have a role of leadership, in the Protestant world, of an importance equivalent to that of the Roman Catholic Pope.[7] Not only that. He made it clear that he desired to make the occupation of Japan a historical laboratory for the realization of Christian ideals.

In autumn of 1945, MacArthur made the following request of four Protestant ministers, the first to visit Japan after the end of the war.

> Japan is in a *spiritual vacuum*. If the country is not Christianized, there is a strong probability that it will turn Communist. In order to prevent this, I want you to send a thousand missionaries to Japan.[8]

> (Emphasis added)

It must be said that the supreme commander of the occupation forces displayed an acute awareness in characterizing the spiritual state of the Japanese as a 'vacuum'. At this time, it is likely that the policies of the dismantling of state Shintō, the declaration of humanity by the emperor, and the separation of religion and state had already taken form in his mind. It was surely an awareness that after the accomplishment of the occupation policies, the Japanese people would certainly be in a spiritual vacuum. These convictions of MacArthur were also expressed when, in May 1947, Tetsu Katayama became prime minister. MacArthur stated that Christianity was an invincible spiritual fortress against invasion by an ideology aimed at oppressive government. Further, he stated that he believed that it was of especial importance that Japan had come to be led for the first time in history by a Christian.

Such remarks, however, eventually drew strong objections from those under MacArthur who were in charge of policy regarding religion after the occupation. This is because the department of religion in the Civil Information and Education section repeatedly emphasized the principle of freedom of worship and sought to advance the policy of separation of state and religion. Needless to say, MacArthur's comments fundamentally contradicted the religious policies of the occupation forces. In his statements regarding Christianity, he included expressions of his strategy of making it a defence against Communism, and this was considered problematic.

In this way, the supreme commander's tactical retreat began. Statements emphasizing the importance of Christianity for morality gradually grew obscured, and in the New Year message for 1948, although there was mention of religion, there was no specific comment about Christianity. Thereafter, he took care to avoid public statements in support of Christianity alone.[9]

Through MacArthur's tactical retreat, the spiritual vacuum of the Japanese was preserved. In fact, on the side of the occupation forces also, the 'spiritual vacuum' gradually came to be regarded as important. This is because of growing pressures as MacArthur's great project to dismantle state Shintō advanced. Most directly, with the development of the vacuum, the Civil Information and Education section and, more basically, the Government section were able to exercise immense authority.

When we view the entire situation, we can discern the figure of Nambara standing alongside MacArthur. We are reminded of Nambara's statement that, in public education, he wished to preserve an important blankness in regard to the realm of religion. Of course, MacArthur's true meaning was that, in having to give up the idea of Christian education for the Japanese, the best that could be done was to leave the spiritual condition of the people in a vacuum. He was conscious that this was an extremely dangerous vacuum. We should note that, by contrast, Nambara felt that the vacuum should, importantly, be preserved as the final fortress of morality and experiential religion. This is the difference in context in the statements of the two figures. In spite of this, the two men were in perfect agreement that the blankness or vacuum should be filled by Christianity. Nambara had been forced into his comments about a blank by the great vigour of socialism and materialism in Japanese society at the time. In the same way, MacArthur had to withdraw to the line of the vacuum because of the strong resistance of the Government section and the Civil Information and Education section. The supreme command of the occupation forces, on the one hand, and the president of Tokyo University and later architect of the Fundamentals of Education Act, on the other hand, against their own will, prepared the ground for the religious vacuum of post-war Japan.

The creation of a symbol: Sōkichi Tsuda and Tetsurō Watsuji

Is not Nambara's term 'blank' or 'void' (*kūhaku*) utterly passive and lacking in force? It must also be said that, in thoroughly exposing the spiritual condition of the Japanese to a void, the result is not merely a dismantling of the 'national polity' but its complete collapse. Such a condition might bring about the disintegration of the nation itself.

A reaction in thought will surely arise naturally in such circumstances – an orientation toward reconstruction that takes its strength from a sense of crisis. A movement toward the recovery of authority will inevitably arise. A replacement to complement the dangerous situation of a void or vacuum was therefore newly created: the notion of the emperor as symbol. The symbol of 'emperor' was the last resort for filling in the blankness. Going back in history slightly, the same strategy was used by the Meiji government, which, when faced with the creation of a new, modern nation, filled the vessel of 'national polity' with state Shintō. However, the policy of preserving a vacuum in the second building of the modern nation required that the dismantling of state Shintō be followed by a reconstruction. For this purpose, the creation of a 'symbol' was newly undertaken. It was to be a symbol to fill the void, a symbol that gave life and movement to the vacuum. It might be said to be the political drama of symbol and blankness giving form to the image of the nation.

Sōkichi Tsuda and Tetsurō Watsuji were probably the first to notice the value of the mutuality between the vacuum and the symbol. Watsuji was the same age as Nambara. By contrast, Tsuda was sixteen years their senior. Before entering into this topic, let us turn to the political situation surrounding the revision of the constitution, which was the greatest political issue immediately following the defeat.

The most important work of the Shidehara cabinet that took office in October 1945 was the revision of the constitution. The foreign minister was Shigeru Yoshida, the minister of education was Tamon Zenda (from January 1946, Yoshishige Abe), and the secretary was Wataru Narahashi. As mentioned above, behind the scenes, the committee on educational reform was established with Abe as chair, and the following year Nambara was appointed chair. Regarding the public work of revising the constitution, the moving force was the GHQ Government section. In the actual drawing up the revised constitution, the final guideline was MacArthur's three principles: the emperor system, the renunciation of war and the abolition of feudal institutions. Regarding the first, the first article of the new constitution states: 'The Emperor shall be the symbol of the State and of the unity of the People, deriving his position from the will of the people with whom resides sovereign power.'

We should note here that in the process by which the symbolic status of the Japanese emperor was fixed, there had already been an interesting discussion on the part of the occupation forces. According to Makoto Iokibe, in the Westminster Charter of 1931, in provisions regarding the crown, the expression 'symbol of free union' is used. This English model of monarchy thus provides a precedent, and was already known to the committee reviewing articles regarding the emperor. It bespeaks the concept of a monarch without real authority who performs a ritual role. Further, the notion of establishing the Japanese emperor as symbol already appears in documents submitted to a committee of the US State Department in May 1943. Regarding this English model, however, it is said that there was strong resistance among Japanese intellectuals, who had been influenced by German law.[10]

If this is the case, it means that the occupation forces had in mind the notion of the monarch as symbol from a very early stage. We must note that the Meiji constitution, which adopted a German model, regarded the emperor as the embodiment of the concept of direct rule; hence, the English model of the monarch as symbol was specifically directed to removing the emperor from direct rule. Conservative students of German law, who adhered to the framework of the Meiji constitution, naturally opposed the English model.

In a striking coincidence, just as the occupation forces appeared ready to put forward their proposal of sovereign as symbol, the idea of emperor as symbol began to be discussed among Japanese intellectuals. One wonders whether this simultaneity was purely accidental, or whether there was some connection.

This question is taken up with acute insight by Norio Akasaka in his *Shōchō Tennō to iu Monogatari* (The Narrative of the Symbolic Emperor). He states that after the defeat the first to take up the topic were Tsuda and Watsuji.[11] Tsuda wrote an article on the state of reconstruction in January and February 1946. He illustrates the notion of the emperor not having direct rule with examples of systems of regency, and confirms its historicity. In the background of this article was the intent of freeing the emperor from responsibility for the war. Near the close of the article, he asserts the possibility of the coexistence of the emperor system and democracy:

> If the people come to preside over all matters of the state, the emperor is naturally within the citizenry and will be one with the people. Speaking concretely, the significance of the existence of the emperor will be as the centre of the unity of the people and as a *living symbol* of the spirit of the people.[12]
>
> (Emphasis added)

Tsuda's expression 'living symbol of the spirit of the people' closely resonates with the actual wording of Article I of the constitution, which speaks of the symbol of the unity of the Japanese people. This seems especially so when we reflect that Tsuda's article was written immediately after the emperor's declaration of humanity on New Year's Day, 1946. Tsuda may have deftly foreseen the movement of the times. Or, he may have come across information suggesting the movement taking shape and cast himself into the vortex of the Japanese–American information war.

Regarding Watsuji, Akasaka states that hints may be found in the volume of essays, *Kokumin Tōgō no Shōchō* (Symbol of the Unity of the People), published in 1948.[13] In the first essay in the book, 'Feudal Thought and the Teachings of Shintō' (November 1945), Watsuji writes that the feudal thought and state Shintō that supported the modern emperor system from the Meiji period on should be seen to violate the historical tradition of the emperor system, and that through doing away with the modern system it would be possible to revive the fundamental meaning of imperial rule. We must note that, on 15 December of the same year, GHQ published its directive on Shintō. Watsuji's awareness of crisis moved in early concert with the changes in the political situation. According to Akasaka, Watsuji had already at this time been in possession of the idea of the emperor as 'the expression of the will of the people'.[14] These words closely parallel Article I of the new constitution.

In the fourth essay of his book, titled 'The Expression of the Unity of the People' and written in July 1948, Watsuji writes:

> The draft of the new constitution has been made public. It opens with the words that, based on the supreme will of the Japanese people, the emperor is the symbol of the Japanese nation and the unity of the people. ... I used the words 'expression of the will of the people' but did not use the word 'symbol'. However, if the subjective matter of the will of the people is expressed in visible form, it is none other than symbol. Hence, it is correct to say that the emperor is *the symbol of the unity of the people.*[15]
>
> (Emphasis in the original.)

The intent of Watsuji's argument is almost the same as that of Tsuda. They are in agreement in putting forth arguments identifying the notion that the emperor not have direct rule and that of emperor as symbol, and seek to justify the emperor system. It is remarkable how closely in time articles by Tsuda and Watsuji treating the emperor as symbol and emphasizing the non-ruling emperor as symbol of the unity of the people appear together with the directive on Shintō and the emperor's declaration of humanity immediately after the end of the war. What must be noted here is that state Shintō, which had up until that point been regarded as the core of the Japanese nation, lost its functioning power as a religion (or meta-religion) through the directive on Shintō, and suddenly it appeared that the condition of a spiritual vacuum was about to arise. Further, the authority of the emperor, which had served as the heart of the unity of the Japanese people, began to falter, and all at once the void in religious consciousness began to emerge. It is easy to imagine that the prewar conservative liberalists such as Tsuda and Watsuji were abruptly seized by a sharp awareness of crisis. Their argument for the emperor as symbol was a theme newly constructed as an eleventh-hour alternative by which to cover over the nihilism of the blankness or vacuum. Further, according to Akasaka, in this way the emperor became a symbol that divided kami from human with a clear line. In addition, borrowing the words of Ango Sakaguchi ('Mirage of Asuka' in *Ango's New Geography of Japan*), he states that the emperor became an existence in which there drifted a strangely mystical air. Perhaps it is the symbol or strange air that transforms the vacuum or blankness into what Roland Barthes calls the empty centre (*Empire of Signs*).

Conclusion: Filling the vessel of the blankness with the empty centre

Let us take a bird's-eye view. With the defeat in 1945, the machinery of reform of the nation began to turn quietly. The cogs of pressure from the outside and introspection within meshed with startling ease, and the sound of friction strangely harmonized began to be audible. This is because Shigeru Nambara, who was advancing educational reform, raised the banners of the renaissance and religious reformation, while MacArthur, as supreme commander of the occupation forces, forcefully proclaimed the loftiness of Christian morality. Nevertheless, this noble message, after the passage of the directive on Shintō, the emperor's declaration of humanity, and the revision of the constitution, was suddenly withdrawn and vanished. The season of introspection and outside pressure had already begun. What occupied the limelight was, on the one hand, the strengthening of the socialist movements and Marxism, and, on the other hand, the furious activities of the occupation New Dealers in establishing a bridgehead in the Far East for the American frontier spirit. In this way, from Nambara's introspection came the proposal of the blankness, and from MacArthur's control came the confession of a crisis awareness of the spiritual vacuum.

It is precisely during this same period that the concept of the emperor as symbol suddenly emerged. State Shintō appeared on stage as a scapegoat in a soft treatment of royal authority. If 'hard' state Shintō was an experimental model in an artificial monotheizing of traditional Shintō, then this 'soft' symbolic emperor system was a revival of traditional Shintō in new dress, or a trial in pantheizing state Shintō. This appeared to Ango Sakaguchi as a system filled with an ambiguous and strange air. The concept of monarch as symbol had already been discussed by the occupation forces as the English model. The creation of a symbol as an empty centre to fill the vessel of a vacuum – in this, the English model of the occupation forces and the Japanese model of Tsuda and Watsuji were in close correspondence.

In this way, a minutely detailed, political and paradoxical drama progressed, filling the blankness or vacuum of the spirit with another emptiness. It might be called a kind of magic trick. Before we knew it, a political space – a doubled emptiness enclosed in a membrane – had been constructed. The religion of the Japanese began to diverge from its original path and wander off course from precisely that moment. Religion in Japan came to be repelled by the political space that was like a sealed room, and like a volatile oil or naphtha, it vapourized. The wandering religion of post-war Japan – its chilly landscape – crystallized at that point.

In September 1965, the promotional magazine of the Iwanami publishers, *Tosho*, carried a dialogue among four people, with 76-year-old Nambara at the centre. The other participants were Masao Maruyama (Faculty of Law, Tokyo University), Yōichi Maeda (Department of Liberal Education, Tokyo University) and Kiyoko Cho (International Christian University). The theme was 'Takamasa Mitani: The Person and His Thought'. Iwanami was in the process of publishing the collected works of Mitani in five volumes. The chief editor was Nambara, and the dialogue was in celebration of the publication. As the discussion developed, it turned to encounters with Kanzō Uchimura and Inazō Nitobe and the influence on Mitani in thought and religion of these two teachers.[16]

The following comment of Cho is particularly interesting: in Taishō era culture and thought there is an appreciation of what might be called a liberal arts education. Within it, there appear to be two contrasting streams. One stream is of a strong intellectual and cultural interest represented by such persons as Jirō Abe and Tetsurō Watsuji, who were influenced by Raphael Koeber and Natsume Sōseki. The second stream centred on Nitobe and received the guidance of Uchimura. It focused on character-building liberal arts education based on Christian faith. These two streams gradually came to follow opposite paths. During the Second World War, in the tense situation in Japan, the differences in thought came to be accentuated. The Christian faith stream, including Mitani (On Happiness), Yanaihara (God's Country) and Nambara (State and Religion), clarified a position from which to objectify the state. By contrast, Watsuji wrote, for example, *The Thought of Reverence for the Emperor and Its Tradition* from a standpoint of an appreciation of cultural learning that made religion an aesthetic object, and advocated 'obedience to the emperor' and 'the way of the imperial nation'. The former stream depended on a transcendent universalism and the latter, by contrast, stood on a kind of pantheism that regarded Japanese tradition as absolute.[17]

Concerning this observation by Cho, Maruyama expressed his general agreement and interest. Maruyama had been a close student of Nambara and stood by the universalism, drawing from Nitobe and Uchimura, and it was probably with this background that he reflected on Cho's comments.

We may note here that Cho (Kiyoko Takeda) later drew attention to the fact that many of the central members of the committee that established the Fundamentals of Education Act were Christians, and that the movement for this legislation was not imposed by the occupation forces, but arose from within Japan.[18] Kōtarō Tanaka, Tatsuo Morito, Nambara, Hasshaku Takagi and Yanaihara were all so. The prewar stream of character-building liberal arts education that was able to objectify the state came to set the orientation for education in post-war Japan and laid down the track. As mentioned before, the centre of the group of this character-building stream was Nambara.[19]

In surveying the events outlined thus far in relation to Cho's comments, several things come to mind. It is plausible that the liberal arts ideal that sprouted in the Taishō period developed into two streams, and that the divergence of these two streams was emphasized in the war-time period of tension. It appears hasty and unbalanced, however, to downgrade Watsuji for asserting reverence for the emperor, and to suggest that those who adhered to an ideal of Christian education and who moved to set in place the Fundamentals of Education Act were in the right. To begin, such a view ignores the fact that Nambara himself speaks of his sympathy for the emperor system and advocated the protection and preservation of the emperor system, as noted in Setsu Katō's book, *Nambara Shigeru: Modern Japan and Intellectuals*.[20] That is not all. Nambara contrasts European and American 'liberal democracy' based on individualism with a Japanese democracy.

He views the human emperor as 'the one who expresses the unified will of the Japanese state' and proposes a conception of 'communal democracy' or 'Japanese democracy' in which the emperor system is fused with democracy.[21]

Second, there is a much more significant problem. Cho's point of view almost completely neglects what has been discussed in this article: the process of the enactment of the Fundamentals of Education Act, followed by the effort to alleviate the condition of spiritual vacuum that might arise among the Japanese people through the advocacy of the emperor as symbol. Post-war Japanese society achieved a precarious stability on the balance between, on the one hand, the spiritual condition of blankness or vacuum and, on the other hand, the psychological device of the emperor as symbol. Further, the gravity of the inescapability of this condition was probably recognized by Nambara himself. This we know because, as mentioned earlier, Nambara's thinking in recognizing the emperor as 'the one who expresses the unified will of the Japanese state' is very close to that of Watsuji, who speaks of 'the expression of the will of the people' and 'the symbol of the unity of the people'. When Nambara expressed his fervent wish that 'the realm of religion' not be rejected but rather 'importantly left a blank', it is almost certain that he had in his mind the notion of the emperor as symbol.

When the Japanese placed on weighing scales of the spirit the vacuum or blankness of religion on one side, and on the other, the emptiness termed 'symbol', there was an almost miraculous balance maintained. Into an empty vessel another emptiness had been inserted. Was this not the creation of a new tradition?

In this situation, more than half a century has passed since the end of the war. We have had fifty years under the Fundamentals of Education Act, as also of the system of the symbolic emperor. When it happens to come to our notice, we find that the anchor termed 'religion' has been torn away in rough waves, and we see the ship of the nation adrift. Fellow Japanese, bereft of that precious anchor, exactly where are you wandering off to?

(Translated by Dennis Hirota)

Notes

1 *Nambara Shigeru Chosakushū*, 7: 302–3, Iwanami Shoten.
2 Ibid., 9: 256.
3 Abe 1989.
4 Iokibe 1997: 247.
5 Abe 1989: 42.
6 Ibid.: 76.
7 Ibid.: 88.
8 Ibid.: 90.
9 Ibid.: 91–2.
10 Iokibe 1997: 219–20.
11 Akasaka 1990: 46–48.
12 *Tsuda Sōkichi zenshū*, Iwanami shoten, 3: 471.
13 Akasaka 1990: 48.
14 Ibid.: 50–1.
15 *Watsuji Tetsurō zenshū*, Iwanami shoten, 14: 336. See also Akasaka 1990: 52–3.

16 Nambara Shigeru *et al.* 1966.
17 Ibid.: 225–8.
18 Takeda 1995: 25–8.
19 Nambara himself asserts repeatedly that, in the process of setting in place the Fundamentals of Education Act, pressure was not applied by the occupation forces and that, rather, the Act is based on the thinking of the Japanese themselves. *Nambara Shigeru zenshū*, 8: 194 (Minzoku no dokuritsu to kyōiku – Nikkyōso kyōken taikai ni oite); 10: 140 (Watakushi no kyōikukan); 10: 210 (Nihon kyōiku e no shōgen – hajimete hōtei shōnin ni tatte) etc.
20 Katō 1997: 140–6 (also, *Nambara Shigeru zenshū*, 7: 90–1).
21 Ibid.:140, 146–53 (also, *Nambara Shigeru zenshū*, 9: 25–8).

References

Abe, Yoshiya (1989), *Seikyō bunri – Nihon to Amerika ni miru shūkyō no seijisei.* Tokyo: Saimaru shuppankai.

Akasaka, Norio (1990), *Shōchō Tennō to iu monogatari.* Tokyo: Chikuma shobō.

Iokibe, Makoto (1997), *Senryōki – shusō-tachi no shin-Nihon.* Tokyo: Yomiuri shinbunsha.

Katō, Setsu (1997), *Nambara Shigeru – kindai Nihon to chishikijin.* Tokyo: Iwanami shoten.

Nambara, Shigeru (1942), *The State and Religion: Research in European Spiritual History.* Tokyo: Iwanami shoten.

Nambara, Shigeru *et al.* (eds) (1966), *Mitani Takamasa – hito, shisō, shinkō.* Tokyo: Iwanami shoten.

Takeda, Kiyoko (1995), *Shunretsu naru dōsatsu to kanyō – Uchimura Kanzō o megutte.* Tokyo: Kyōbunkan.

13 Japanese religiosity amid the changing chaos of several forms of nationalism

Yo Hamada

Introduction

*Mu-shukyo (*無宗教*) (non-religious or religiously neutral) nationalism in post-war Japan*

I would like to start this chapter by considering the relation between religions and the state in Japan right after the end of the Second World War. Imagine a kind of evacuated state. If we evacuate some container, it immediately comes under pressure from every direction. This analogy makes it easier for us to understand what happens when an evacuated state of mind occurs on the scale of a whole society or nation. In a moment various religions, thoughts and values would insist on their own validity and try to steal in from all sides.

Tetsuo Yamaori, in his chapter in this book, points out that in the process of dissolving the state Shinto system (国家神道体制) at the end of the war, with such measures as the Shinto Directives (神道指令) of 4 October 1945, and the announcement that *Tenno* (天皇 Emperor) Hirohito was a human being (人間宣言) on 1 January 1946, Japanese society experienced a kind of spiritually and politically 'evacuated' state. At the time Douglas MacArthur hoped to fill the void with Christianity. Sigeru Nambara (南原繁), who was president of Tokyo University and a leader of the reformation committee on education (教育刷新委員会), as a Christian, thought that 'recovery of humanness' as a renaissance and 'recovery of God' as a reformation were extremely important for a new Japan. However, because MacArthur was opposed by staff at the Government Section and the Civil Information and Education Section and because he and Nanbara were anxious about the influence of Communism on the evacuated state, they had to compromise. They became interested in the English model of monarchy, which was provided by the Statute of Westminster in 1931 and took account of the crown as a symbol denoting 'the free association of the members of the British Commonwealth of nations'. Furthermore, the Japanese conservative liberal Tetsuro Watsuji (和辻哲郎) and the famous scholar of Japanese history Sokichi Tsuda (津田左右吉) proposed similar expressions for the *Tenno*. Watsuji's 'Feudal Thoughts and a Doctrine of Shinto' in November 1945 described the *Tenno* as an 'expression of people's consensus' while Tsuda's 'Circumstances about the Founding of Our

Country' in January and February 1946 took up the expression 'a living symbol of the national spirit'. In the end, the solution proposed to satisfy all the various political and ideological groups was a symbolic emperor with no political power. That is, they filled up the void in Japanese society with another void, this symbolic *Tenno*. That is the essence of Yamaori's article.

We could say that his explanation is a hypothesis of a doubly void state. The important point is that this symbolic emperor has played a kind of negative role, and because of it no other religion or ideology could attain a central position in Japanese society. The prohibition of religious education by Article 9 of the former Fundamental Law of Education (旧教育基本法), enacted in 1947, guaranteed the negative function of this symbolic *Tenno*.

Thus we could say that the nationalism of post-war Japan is *Mu-shukyo* nationalism. The term *Mu-shukyo* consists of two elements, *mu* (無), nothingness, and *shukyo* (宗教), religion. However, the nothingness is not only negative. *Mu-shukyo* expresses the fact that Japanese society can never be identified by only one specific religion, but that it accepts the possibilities of other religions and thoughts. This is not mere secular nationalism.

Various profiles of Japanese nationality

A scholar of the sociology of religion and of religious terrorism, Mark Juergensmeyer, has tried to capture the outline of complicated nationalisms by separating them into secular nationalism and religious nationalism (Juergensmeyer 1993). Tsuyoshi Nakano, also a scholar of the sociology of religion, classified nationalisms according to two indicators: whether they are secular or religious, and whether they are political or cultural (Nakano 2002). From his point of view, secular-political nationalism is the classic case. Hindu nationalism in India is classified as religious-political nationalism, while the negative campaigns against new religions, such as the anti-cult movements in the United States, are considered to be phenomena of religious-cultural nationalism. The trend of seeking Japanese cultural identity that we typically observe in the popular discourses on Japan and the Japanese, Nihonjinron (日本人論), relates to secular-cultural nationalism.

Whether these classifications are appropriate or not, the age in which we could simply use the word 'nationalism' has passed away, and now we are in a new era, and must add some adjective (secular, religious, cultural and so on) to the word to express our meaning adequately. Present-day scholars and political leaders depict aspects of nationalism with their favourite expression. What is the most suitable epithet to express post-war Japanese nationalism? It is clear that we cannot use religious nationalism. But simple secular nationalism is also inadequate. Moreover, neither political nationalism nor cultural nationalism seems to be appropriate enough. Perhaps the term *Mu-Shukyo* nationalism is still applicable to present-day Japan. In other words, in the process of institutionally establishing the doubly void state by the symbolic *Tenno* system of Article 1 of the Constitution and prohibition of religious education by Article 9 of the former Fundamental Law of Education, we have formed a social atmosphere where neither religious values nor atheistic ones, as in Communism, can become sole supports of Japanese nationalism.

The Western model of secular nationalism is not universal

What is nationalism?

Here let us review what nationalism is according to Juergensmeyer, looking at the meanings of the terms nation, state and nation-state.

A nation is a community where people are linked by a specific political or regional culture, and it has the power of self-government. A state is a field of power and decision making in some geographical region. So a nation-state is a form of national body where the power of the state systematically involves and rules all the people of the nation. Nationalism is the concept that legitimates a nation-state from the political and moral points of view. Additionally, Anthony Giddens suggests that nationalism involves a symbolic or faith system that emphasizes the communality of members of some political order.

Nation, state and nation-state are translated as *Kokumin* (国民), *Kokka* (国家) and *Kokumin-kokka* (国民国家) in Japanese. These expressions only came into being as translations. As a result, they rehash Western concepts in a Japanese version. Therefore, the influence of the contextual meanings in the original Western language always follows when we use these translated expressions, though in terms of cultural nationalism it is demanded that Japanese cultural values should be recalled by them. Nationalism used to be considered as a universal movement offered by the West, and it was thought to have neutral values such as the system of separation of church and state. However, the ideal image of universality has been broken today. We have to say that Western nationalism cannot be considered neutral.

Western nationalism is not culturally neutral

According to Juergensmeyer, Arend Theodor van Leeuwen argued in his book *Christianity in World History* (1946) that Western secular nationalism is a mask for Christian culture in Europe. Today his statement that the secular nationalism that the modern West offered has its origin in Christian tradition has become recognized by peoples in many areas of the world who do not know his name. According to van Leeuwen, the idea of separating the things of the world and the things of God as a way to deny the divine right of kings was created at the start of ancient Israel and became a main motif in Christian history. Then, as Christianity spread throughout Europe, it conveyed the secular message of separation of the mundane and the divine. From this point of view, the relation between church and state in the Middle Ages would be explained as a defection: the Enlightenment returned a Christian mission of secularization to its rightful place.

Because many other religious traditions have their own complicated types of relationship with the state, it would be biased to assume that all types of secularism originated from Christianity. However, this peculiar form of secular society, which progressed in the modern West, did not just happen to appear at a turning point in history without any relation with the religious culture.

It was in the eighteenth century that Western nationalism appeared in the United Kingdom and the United States. Since then the nation-state has taken root to such an extent that it can claim people's ideological devotion without the help of religious or ethnic identity. The political and military device of the nation-state became powerful enough to surround a geographically large area. John Locke and Jean-Jacques Rousseau's theories of the social contract on the origin of this large area, that is, the community of citizens, hardly demanded any role for religious faith in order to become established. The new secular nationalism was the notion that individuals could take their place in the economic and political system of the homeland where their ancestors were born or that, as in the case of the United States, they chose. This notion was considered to be the expression of a citizen's intention, not God's.

As religion became less political, Western nationalism became more religious. The French Revolution, a model for the various nationalisms that developed in the nineteenth century, had as romantic and warlike an aspect as religious passion. A majority of the leaders of the War of Independence in the United States were affected by the deism of the eighteenth century, which was regarded as the religion of science and natural law. In both cases, the people concerned developed their own 'religious' characters, combining both an ideal of secular nationalism and the symbols of Christianity with a so-called civil religion.

We cannot consider Western secular nationalism to be value neutral, because the separation of the secular and the religious is a notion based on a historical development peculiar to the Christian tradition.

Popularity and decline of secular nationalism (Western nationalism) in the world

However, this secular nationalism peculiar to the West was considered a universal value as modernization spread globally. It was propagated all over the world with missionary zeal, brought to newly colonized areas of Asia, Africa and Latin America, and became an ideological ingredient in establishing nation-states. Secular nationalism in colonized countries in the nineteenth and twentieth centuries caused discord between two different ways of realizing the relation between individual and state: the way of religion and that of secular contract. Juergensmeyer continues his argument as follows.

In the mid-1950s, soon after third-world countries accomplished their political independence, nationalism was preached with almost religious passion all over the world. Fervent secular nationalists had a vision of national legitimacy rooted in the will of the people, free from any religious force. This vision of a secular country with both freedom and equality became popular not only among Western scholars but also among new ethnic leaders in former colonies.

We can find typical examples in the cases of Gamal Abdel Nasser in Egypt and Jawaharlal Nehru in India. The concept of secular nationalism offered ideological legitimacy to the new leaders, and willing electors gave them a base from which they could jump to the top position, beyond traditional ethnic and religious leaders. Many of the leaders came from highly educated urban elites. Secular nationalism was a means of promoting the separation of religion and politics and avoiding the difficulties that traditional religious devotion might make for the political goals of the state.

However, secular nationalism, though it was considered a universal value, has not yet succeeded in many areas of the world, or has, even, apparently failed. The people of former colonized countries had extremely high expectations of secular nationalism; so discouragement resulting from its failure reached severe proportions. In many areas of the world, secular governments could not achieve their pledges to accomplish economic prosperity and realize both political freedom and social justice. Many people of the middle classes, educated under the values propagated by the leaders of secular nationalism, feel that the reformation was not realized and have been returning to the traditional values preserved in their religions. In addition, the global mass media has conveyed to people in non-Western countries the message that secular nationalism in the West brings in its wake severe social diseases, such as political scandal, increasing divorce rates, racial discrimination, drug addiction and other social disorders. Doubts about secular nationalism are most entrenched in areas that have never achieved political or economic success. All this throws up the difficult question of what nationalism should be around the world, given the fact that Western nationalism has shown its historical and cultural limitations.

Culture, morality and religion amid nationalism in Japan

Which term is proper to express nationalism in Japan: cultural nationalism or moral nationalism?

Thus, people are now adjusting or recreating their own nationalism based on a criticism of the historical bias of Western nationalism. Japan is no exception. Not only in the field of politics but also in those of economy and education, problems with this nationalism have been pointed out. In other words, limitations in the double void system, unnoticed before, have gradually become obvious. There are fears that Japan may no longer be able to produce nationals with sufficient ability to lead the community, or react to effectively in the face of rapid political, economic, military, cultural and scientific changes in international affairs. Amid such fears, voices have been raised that Japan needs an education system that nurtures the patriotic mind (愛国心教育, *Aikokushin-kyoiku* in Japanese). Moreover, severe social problems, such as brutal crimes committed by youngsters, increase because the old values essential to maintain the community have weakened at the family and local levels, while alternative values, such as ecology or feminism, are not stable yet.

In order to cope with this situation, is cultural nationalism the course that Japanese society should follow? In other words, should Japan consciously appeal to its own culture and use it to strengthen nationalism, while rejecting the superficially value-neutral position of *Mu-shukyo* nationalism?

Cultural nationalism is a movement by which people aim to produce new citizens by creating and developing their cultural identity and unity. The essential point is to create cultural identity. In recent years Joseph Ney's 'Soft Power' theory has become popular. According to this theory, the soft powers of culture are more important in raising the international status of countries than the hard powers of politics, economy and military might. From this point of view, we could say that at present many countries and nations have become interested in cultural nationalism to enhance their soft power. The promotion of the arts and tourism and environmental campaigns by government leaders are examples. Japan also relates to this worldwide trend.

However, the term 'cultural nationalism' is not enough for us to express the course of Japanese nationalism. We probably have to use the term 'moral nationalism' as well. Needless to say, education plays an important role in enhancing nationalism. From the viewpoint of cultural nationalism, people pay attention not only to intellectual education but also to values education. Values education includes instruction in religion, morals, citizenship, multiculturalism, tolerance and so on. It means teaching and studying standards of decision making and acting, ideals and ways of life. At present in Japan moral education is central to values education. In April 2002, the Japanese government distributed the *Kokoro Notebook* (『心のノート』 *kokoro* meaning mind, spirit, mentality) as a moral education text to all elementary and junior high schools in Japan. In public education, where the state produces citizens, national values and ideas are thought to be best cultivated by moral, rather than cultural, education. The course of Japanese nationalism is turning in the direction of moral nationalism supporting cultural nationalism.

Is moral nationalism different from religious nationalism?

Many would agree with the analysis of Japanese nationalism in terms of cultural nationalism. Even some who do not accept the term 'moral nationalism' would not deny that, at present, moral education is expected to regenerate values that support nationalism. However, if we used the term 'religious nationalism' to describe the Japanese case, most Japanese people would be reluctant to accept it. Why is this? Why do they wish to separate morality and religion? After all, when we look back at Japanese history we notice that Shinto and Buddhism have played important cultural roles.

First, though, we have to note that the modern Japanese expressions for 'morality', *Dotoku* (道徳), and 'religion', *shukyo* (宗教), did not have the same meanings in pre-modern Japan. The elements *Do* (道), 'way' and *Toku* (徳), 'virtue, goodness', *Shu* (宗), '(Buddhist) sect, religion' and *Kyo* (教), 'faith, teaching philosophy', tended to express their separate meanings.

From the separation of *Dotoku* and *Shukyo* to their mutual approach

The separation of morals and religion in Japan

By fifteen or twenty years after the Meiji restoration rather peculiar meanings of *Dotoku* and *Shukyo* had become established. The process of realizing Japanese nationalism institutionally meant the separation of the public area, relating to national values, and the private area. The public system of values came to be indicated with the *Do* nomenclature and the private with *Kyo*. *Dotoku* became the general term for the *Do* system, and *Shukyo* for the *Kyo* system. For example, Shinto (*Shin+Do* 神道, God + way), *Kodo* (皇道、Imperial way) and so on are included under *Dotoku* and *Bukkyo* (仏教, Buddhism), *Kirisutokyo* (キリスト教, Christianity) under *Shukyo* (Isomae 2003).

We must not overlook the fact that the whole series of terms such as Shinto, *Kodo*, *Bukkyo*, and *Kirisutokyo* were established simultaneously, just as nationalism was progressing and the nation-state being formed in Japan. Shinto shrines and the imperial household were brought into the public domain, where they could be controlled by the government.

This was an effective trick to generate cultural nationalism and to restrain the cultural influences of the great Western powers with their Christian tradition. A position called *Kyodo-shoku* (教導職, a kind of national teacher of moral and religion) was set up in the Ministry of Religious Affairs (教部省, Kyobu-sho) in 1872 (Meiji 5). Both Shinto priests and Buddhist monks were appointed to the position. However, after values related to Shinto shrines were brought into the public domain, the *Kyodoshoku* position lost its reason to exist. It was abolished in 1884 (Meiji 17) and the establishment of the Constitution of the Empire of Japan in 1887 (Meiji 20) promoted the separation of morality and religion. Oddly, the enactment of freedom of religion by the constitution made it easier for the government to control the moral domain. This was due to the suppression by Shinto values of other religions. The situation is further complicated in that both suppressors and suppressed used terminology translated from Western concepts and retaining their bias.

For example, in pre-modern Japan, people used the terms *Shinkyo* and *Butsudo* as well as Shinto and *Bukkyo*. The terms must have had rather different meanings then, when the public and private domains were not separated as they were later. That is, without nationalism we would not have the modern term *Shukyo*. *Dotoku* must also have had a different nuance from what it has today. *Dotoku*, once linked to the public domain, was considered more rational and superior to *Shukyo* in its private domain.

Kanzo Uchimura (内村鑑三) was a famous thinker who clashed with the nationalism of those days, while Tetsujiro Inoue (井上哲次郎) was a scholar who went along with it. He considered Shinto not to be a religion and insisted that Shinto and religion were mutually exclusive concepts. At Tokyo Imperial University, which was independent of any religion or denomination, he lectured in comparative religions and Eastern philosophy, and became a pioneer of the study of religion in Japan. His thought was mostly based on the idea that a universal moral reality exists in the world and may be discerned in historical phenomena. Though his thought seemed to be universal, it was a typical nationalistic practice at a national university where the values of Shinto were ensured.

Dotoku *and* Shukyo *approach each other*

However, after the Meiji 30s (1897–1907), a curious situation occurred. *Dotoku* and *Shukyo* began to invade each other's domain. We can see this by taking examples of the study of Shinto and the study of religion in this era according to Junichi Isomae's discourse. They were both new fields, started by students of Tetsujiro Inoue, Yoshito Tanaka (田中義能) and Masaharu Anezaki (姉崎正治).

Yoshito Tanaka, who studied education and Shinto in the philosophy course of the Department of Literature at Tokyo Imperial University, tried to elaborate the study of Shinto as comparable with modern studies in Western countries. In this new field he not only considered Shinto and religion as mutually exclusive, but also made Shinto a superordinate concept unlimited by the concept of religion. In short, he insisted that the values of Shinto must influence the private domain. His idea in founding the study of Shinto was to revive Shrine Shinto (*Jinja* Shinto 神社神道) as a real national religion rather than merely a ritual. The reason behind this idea was that the citizens of a nation-state should not only vow faithfulness rationally in public but also have a kind of religious passion for the state in private, emerging from their inner spirit. The victory in the Russo-Japanese War in 1905 (Meiji 38) promoted such a feeling.

The Imperial University was in just the right privileged position as a centre for regenerating cultural identity based on Shinto nationalism, if we use this term to describe Tanaka's academic activity. While Shrine Shinto and Imperial Shinto (*Koshitsu* Shinto 皇室神道) were usually regulated by only morality and ritual, and Denominational Shinto (*Kyoha* Shinto 教派神道) in various forms such as *Kurozumi-kyo* (黒住教), *Taisha-kyo* (大社教), *Konko-kyo* (金光教) and *Tenri-kyo* (天理教) was counted as religion, Tanaka's study of Shinto was not limited to either morality or religion, and could deal with and idealize any forms of Shinto.

Meanwhile Masaharu Anezaki opened his lectures on the study of religion at Tokyo Imperial University in the year of the victory in the Russo-Japanese War. Anezaki's study of religion tried to provide a way to instil national identity into each individual to a deeper extent than moral education could. He regarded religion as an aspect of consciousness that is inherent in all humans. As a result, differences among denominations have no essential meaning. Such a discourse suggested to people who felt inner disorder that everyone has some common religious consciousness, whether or not he or she belongs to some specific religious group, and indicated to the government, aiming at the integration of the nation, that through religion people's minds could be controlled. In other words, Anezaki attempted to offer a discourse that could satisfy the desires both of individuals and of the government and unite them. His efforts offered religious leaders and intellectuals who were not familiar with nationalistic moralism a discourse on nationalism such that individuals could belong to the nation-state with their own inner worlds intact.

Although Anezaki's study of religion was an attempt to bridge the gap between modern individualism and national communalism, it had the weak point of lacking any critical analysis of religion or the nation-state. Today's religious studies, whose main centre has been Tokyo University since the end of the Second World War, have led to an academic tendency that imagines an ideal community as real at some stage and optimistically describes its communality. While Anezaki devoted his attention to the nation-state, his academic successor Hideo Kishimoto (岸本秀夫) took notice of village communities. Later scholars became interested in groups of new religions or smaller spiritual communities.

Both Tanaka's study of Shinto and Anezaki's study of religion saw some autonomy in the human inner mind, and by doing so they offered a system to erase the local and religious concerns of individuals and incline them to the nation-state.

The possible options for Japanese nationalism

It is necessary for us to look back at the prewar relation betwen *Dotoku* and *Shukyo* after the Meiji restoration in order to forecast the future course of Japanese nationalism. People often think that Japanese nationalism has no relation to religious nationalism. In Japan the links between nationalism and religion tend to be considered as phenomena elsewhere: political claims from Islamic countries, the growth of the new Christian right in the United States, conflicts between Israel and Palestine, Hindu nationalism and so on. Many Japanese do not see any link between their country and such cases. However, as we have observed, when the key term *Dotoku* is put together with *Shukyo* (religion), we can consider Japanese nationalism as part of the global trend.

Now that the difficulties of *Mu-shukyo* nationalism have become obvious, Japanese nationalism has been seeking values to support national identity. The reform of moral education in schools is considered necessary. However, *Dotoku* (again the Japanese translation of 'morals') is itself a concept that was hastily shaped in the process of forming Japanese nationalism after the Meiji restoration. Before the end of the Second World War, Japan went through three stages: a pre-modern state where the public and private domains were not separate, the formal separation (Meiji 20s) and mutual influence on each other (Meiji 30s). Finally the state Shinto system appeared (Murakami 1974, Chugai Nippo 1938–55). What we should pay attention to is that the third stage is currently reappearing in other contexts. For instance, we could say that a coalition government of the Liberal Democratic Party and the Clean Government Party (the Komeito) is one example of the mutual influence of public and private.

Generally speaking, the trend to expand the moral area into the private can be observed in the government's present efforts to reform education. The experiment of introducing the *Kokoro Notebook* to all public elementary and junior high schools by the Ministry of Education, Culture, Sports, Science and Technology, is a typical example of this trend.

The important thing is not the expressions *Dotoku* and *Shukyo* themselves, but their content as concepts. Although we may call Japanese nationalism moral nationalism, we can find some similarities between it and religious nationalism in many areas of the world, because *Dotoku* has invaded the domain of *Shukyo*.

However, it is curious that Japanese nationalism pretends to be unconscious of the origin of the terms *Dotoku* and *Shukyo*, while it emphasizes its own universality and separation from religion. It strengthens its identity by appealing to the original culture of the nation. However, at the very time Japan views the Western model of nationalism as universal and approaches it, the myth of value neutrality has been severely questioned both in the West and elsewhere.

It is a dangerous and extremely naive policy to produce citizens who are unconscious of this world trend, when Japanese nationalism is trying to regenerate its own values. Here, in fact, we find a weak point of both the *Kokoro Notebook* and education aimed at nurturing patriotic feelings in people's minds. In such education the importance of various social groups such as family, groups of friends, acquaintances at school or company, of other social associations and of the realities of international society is lost. Such materials and education do not offer a better way of producing citizens with enough ability to survive in the multi-valued global world.

The nation-state still plays an important role in international politics and is an essential unit in the global economic system. The nation-state has its exclusive territory, an economic system ruled by the government, a system of mass education and a system of parliamentary democracy. Nationalism plays the part of an adhesive among these elements.

As long as the nation-state exists, Japan cannot ignore the need to regenerate the values of nationalism. The Japanese also need to question the course of their nationalism in the face of changing world nationalisms. It is vital for Japan to find a new form of nationalism to replace *Mu-shukyo* and moral nationalism. Both of these naively claim their own universality by separating themselves from *Shukyo* (religion). If only Japan came to recognize the origin of the modern concepts of *Mu-shukyo*, *Dotoku* and *Shukyo*, it would find a potential common ground where the various values are not separate but can communicate. To bind the institutions of the nation-state the Japanese should attempt to produce the values necessary to make their community open, flexible and creative, instead of merely hastily or artificially recreating their traditional values in order to force them on the community. In order to undertake this and strengthen their soft power they need a programme of multi-value education at various grades, not only in public schools but also in private schools, other institutions of higher education, companies and local communities. This is open nationalism. Though it needs constant repair, this form of nationalism has a flexible durability because of its openness. Its characteristics are neither exclusive nor thought stopping, but tolerant and creative.

This proposal is no mere ideal. The superficial view that Japan can survive by entrusting its future to an ideal of universality derived from Western nationalism is just as dangerous as isolating the country from the rest of the world.

Opening up Japanese nationalism

Various issues surrounding the 'memorial day of the end of the war'

Now I would like to discuss a quite symbolic topic, *Shusen-kinembi* (終戦記念日), the 'memorial day of the end of the war', in thinking about Japanese nationalism. In order to reveal this nationalism, we have to re-examine many fields as well as that of education. So it is also important to open up internationally discussion concerning the end of the Asia–Pacific War, that tragic war that caused such damage inside and outside Japan.

The 'memorial day of the end of the war', on 15 August, has become quite vocal in Japan. The problems of *Yasukuni* and the historical perception issue are inevitably highlighted, and the echoes reverberate inside and outside Japan. With only Babel and anxiety, we cannot feel calm or happiness. This is present situation of the *Shusen-kinembi.*

However, as scholar of media history Takumi Sato and other researchers have pointed out, in reality, the war that ended on 15 August 1945 did not exist as a historical fact (Sato 2005). The date of the Imperial Rescript on the Termination of the War by the *Tenno* was 14 August, and on the same day the Japanese government gave notice of the acceptance of the Potsdam Declaration to the United States and the United Kingdom. It was on 16 August that a cease-fire order was given from the Imperial Headquarters to the army and navy. As an international standard, 2 September was V-J Day, when the instrument of surrender was signed on the battleship *Missouri* on Tokyo Bay. The date 15 August was simply the day when the radio broadcast of the *Tenno*'s reading of the Imperial Rescript on the Termination of the War (recorded on 14th) was transmitted to the people (subjects). This was the so-called *Gyokuon-hoso* (玉音放送) (Broadcast of the Emperor's voice).

The vast Asia–Pacific War was not only ended by the acceptance of the Potsdam Declaration or by the *Gyokuon-hoso.* On Okinawa, already occupied by the United States Army, the mopping-up war continued until the surrender of the Japanese army on 7 September, while Hokkaido was exposed to the attack of the Soviet army, exercising its strategy toward the Karafuto and Chishima islands. Furthermore, the countries that now assume 15 August to be the day of 'the end of the war', are only South and North Korea, where people consider 15 August as Independence Day. In Russia, China and Mongolia, V-J Day is 3 September. In each country of South-East Asia the day when the Japanese army surrendered and disarmed locally is celebrated, 3 September in the Philippines, 12 September in Singapore and Malaysia, 13 September in Thailand and Burma and 25 October in Taiwan. Furthermore, the San Francisco Peace Treaty, through which Japan was able to return to international society, was signed on 8

September 1951 and came into force on 28 April 1952 (the end of the occupation of Japan by the Allied Powers).

Listing these dates concerning the end of the war, we realize how inadequate it is to have only one memorial day. Sato proposes that the 'memorial day of the end of the war', which presently has the official meaning both of mourning for the war dead and of praying for peace, should be divided into two. Japan would then have a new Day of Praying for Peace on 2 September and a Day of Mourning for the War Dead on 15 August. In that case, the 'memorial day of the end of the war' would be 2 September, when the instrument of surrender was signed.

This is a reasonable solution. Japan cannot have a separate memorial day on every date involved in the process of ending the war, which would just be confusing. With two days, Japanese people could express the fact that the war did not end on just one day, but recall other important days as well. In addition, having two days could lead to rational discussion of the historical perception issue. The important point would be not only to recall 15 August and 2 September, but to try to understand the process of ending the war and Japanese colonialism, based on the two days.

A proposal for a 'mourning period for the war dead'

In addition, I would like to suggest an alternative idea concerning the Day of Mourning for the War Dead on 15 August. Instead of a single day of mourning, the Japanese people could establish a 'mourning period for the war dead', continuing from around 13 to 16 August. During this period, there could be several ceremonies for the *Tenno* to attend, and the various denominations of Shinto, Buddhism, Christianity, other religions and *Mu-shukyo* could hold mourning ceremonies according to their own styles. In this way, people of every kind could mourn and feel some sense of unity.

Generally speaking, the weakness of a memorial day is that the solemnities are over so quickly. The *Gion Matsuri* (祇園祭), a traditional Japanese festival, is quite different. It was originally conceived to give solace to the undesirable souls considered to cause epidemics to people around the ancient capital of Kyoto, begins on 1 July, has the evening festival of *Yoiyama* (宵山) from 14 to 16 July, the parade of colourful floats of *Yamahoko Junko* (山鉾巡行) on 17 July, and continues until 31 July, a whole month. The *Gion Matsuri* is a series of small festivals that has lasted through all vicissitudes for more than one thousand years.

Even in the case of the *Gion Matsuri* it takes one month to pray for the peace of one city. One day might never seem enough to pray for the larger areas of Japan, Asia and the world.

Another reason why I have proposed the 'mourning period for the war dead' is to reflect positively the fact that the period would be during *Obon* (お盆). *Obon* is a series of customary events in which Japanese people greet, hold memorial services for and see off the souls of the dead. Although it has preserved close relations with Buddhism, in Japan *Obon* is not limited to that religion or any modern concept of religion. It is a kind of folk religion.

The festivals of Obon *making Japanese nationalism open*

Obon was suppressed during the Asia–Pacific War. The *Chugai Nippo* (中外日報) is a non-sectarian and multi-religious newspaper that was founded in 1897 (Meiji 30) and thus has a history of more than 110 years. Its back numbers provide quite valuable material through which we can analyse religious phenomena in Japan from a broad perspective. When tracing back reports we observe how folk and local features of *Obon* were suppressed by state logic.

In a report on 14 August 1938, one year after the beginning of the Second Sino-Japanese War, there was an opinion that 'if we burn the send-off fire at the *Daimonji* mountain the enemy could make use of it as a mark for bombing the whole Kyoto-Osaka area', thus criticising the *Daimonji-no-okuribi* (大文字の送り火), a famous *Obon* event in Kyoto. From 1943 to 1945 the event was stopped because of the blackout. It is ironic that, though the number of dead increased dramatically at this time, the send-off fire, whose intent is to take the souls of the dead to the next world, could not be lit.

A comment entitled 'Associated with *Obon* events' on 17 August 1943, symbolizes the split between the way of thinking at the state level and that at the level of folk belief. It observed,

> even in this tense summer of decisive battle, *Obon* events will have been conducted in each home, yet we wonder how many people reflected on whether we should follow the ancestors who passed away easily on their *tatami* mats or the soldiers of noble soul who died splendid deaths as members of this nation?

It was claimed that people could learn much more from the *Eirei* (英霊), the souls of the soldiers who died in the war, than from their ancestors, and Buddhist monks were admonished that they, as spiritual teachers, should not lose a good chance to make use of *Obon* in order to praise the *Eirei*.

Many *Bon Odori* (盆踊り), the dancing festivals whose meaning is to greet and comfort the souls of the dead, were also prohibited during the war. Traditional *Obon* for the souls of ancestors and of *Muen-botoke* (無縁仏), deceased persons with no surviving relatives, were displaced by mourning ceremonies for the *Eirei*.

Today, at Yasukuni Shrine, there are many difficult problems to solve, such as worship by the prime minister, joint or split enshrinement of 'war criminals', and requests for erasure from the Book of Souls (*Reiji-bo* 霊璽簿) by non-Japanese bereaved families. However, I think Japan should not stick to the Yasukuni issues only. It would be better for Japanese people to turn their eyes to other communications with the souls of the dead, to consider their meanings seriously, and to reflect on how Japan could make the *Obon* festivals of *Okuribi, Bon Odori* and others much more vital and well understood by people in other countries at a time of global cultural exchange.

If the dates of the acceptance of the Potsdam Declaration and of the *Gyokuon-hoso* had not overlapped the period of *Obon*, the Japanese people would have mourned the war dead in a quite different atmosphere, without any support from their own spiritual tradition.

The *Obon* season in Japan, centred around 15 July in the old calendar and 15 August in the new, is different from the seasons of its equivalents, *Chuseok* (秋夕) in Korea (15 August in the old calendar or around the end of September in the new) and Ching Ming (清明節) in China and Taiwan (from the spring equinox for the following fifteen days in the old calendar or 5 April in the new). Though the dates are different, it is wonderful that the customs of relating to dead souls have such rich diversity as well as unity in East Asia. Each has continued down the centuries. When Japanese people greet and see off the dead souls and pray for their repose at the season of *Obon*, they pray also for the souls of *Muen-botoke* and could also pray for war victims inside and outside Japan. Some kind of intercommunicative feeling would arise, not connected only with national identity.

Mu-Shukyo people, who are religiously neutral, could reflect on peace at this time too. It would be a flexible style of mourning, not limited to one memorial day on 15 August. It would be neither exclusive nor unnaturally universal. Such a style would serve a new, tolerant plurality.

Conclusion

Japan should preserve the system of the symbolic *Tenno* of the 'small void state' and simultaneously fill up the 'large void state' of society with the creative diversity of its cultures and religions. For example, Japan cannot put Confucianism at the forefront of its cultural policy as today's China does. It is impossible for one traditional form of culture or religion to represent Japan. We need the establishment of a system with various cultural and religious channels together with the symbolic *Tenno*, and to make use of these as tools of international cultural exchange. This is the course Japan should take.

References

『中外日報』1938–1955年, 1965, 1975, 1985, 1995の8, 9月記事. (*Chugai Nippo* newspaper. Back numbers of August and September in 1938–1955, 1965, 1985 and 1995.)

磯前順一『近代日本の宗教言説とその系譜』岩波書店、2003. (Isomae, Junichi (2003), *Discourses of Religious Studies in Modern Japan and their Descent*. Tokyo: Iwanami Publisher.)

ユルゲンスマイヤー, M.『ナショナリズムの世俗性と宗教性』阿部美哉訳、玉川大学出版部, 1995 (1993). (Juergensmeyer, Mark (1993), *The New Cold War? Religious Nationalism Confronts the Secular State*. University of California Press.)

村上重良『慰霊と招魂 —靖国の思想—』岩波新書、1974. (Murakami, Shigeyoshi (1974) *Memorial Service and Call of Souls-A Thought of Yasukuni.* Tokyo: Iwanami Publisher.)

中野毅『宗教の復権』東京堂出版、2002. (Nakano, Tsuyoshi (2002), *The Revival of Religions.* Tokyo: Tokyodou Publisher.)

佐藤卓己『八月十五日の神話 終戦記念日のメディア学』ちくま新書、2005, (Sato, Takumi (2005), *The Myth of August 15th – Media Study on the 'Memorial Day of the End of the War'.* Tokyo: Chikumashinsyo Publisher.)

14 In search of a new national identity

An analysis of the national psyche of post-war Japan

Hisashi Owada

Introduction

The demise of the Cold War has brought about a sea-change in the international relations of the twenty-first century. It has changed the framework of the basic relations between states that prevailed during the Cold War days. More than that, what is significant is that the whole global environment has changed, not only for many states in the world, but also for many people in the world.

The disappearance of the bipolar division of the world has led many people, not just in the United states and Europe, which were the direct parties to the Cold War, but throughout the world, to feel that they are no longer living in the stability of a predictable world, in the global sense. This stability may have been the kind of stability that one should regard as unnatural and therefore unhealthy. Nevertheless, it was the key factor that ensured the predictability of the world. It is true that stability was secured on a very precarious basis, as illustrated, for example, in the political arena by the Mutual Assured Destruction (MAD) doctrine. It was, nonetheless, stability that came to exist because the two superpowers, which were virtually in control of the global affairs of the divided world, were conscious that they could not risk the destruction of the whole world, including themselves.

Now that this situation has disappeared, the world of the twenty-first century is faced with the paradoxical situation of moving in two opposite directions. On the one hand, there has emerged a societal transformation of the world towards the creation of one global society in the socio-economic sense, as exemplified in 'globalization'. On the other hand, the demise of the bipolar stability in the world has produced a trend towards the emergence of a fragmentation of this world in the politico-ideological sense, demonstrated by the upsurge in local, regional and inter-religious conflicts. On both accounts, the future seems to be much more opaque and unpredictable.

Where should one place Japan in this whole picture? What are the problems that she faces, especially in the context of this evolving change in the world? I wish to place the main focus of this chapter on the impact of this evolving change in the world in the aftermath of the Cold War, which, in my opinion, has plunged Japan into wholly uncharted waters, against the background of the national psyche of Japan as moulded through her post-war years.

In the wake of the ending of the Cold War in the early 1990s, Japan appeared to be moving in the direction of behaving more proactively in the global arena, so that she could be a significant partner in joint efforts for constructing a new order based on what might be described as *pax consortis*, a coalition of the major players who are willing and capable to work for the maintenance of international order in this new situation. What has happened since that period? In order to understand the present state of the national psyche of Japan, one must examine the impact of the Cold War as the factor that has moulded the basic structure of post-war Japan.

Legacy of the Cold War as a crucial framework for post-war Japan

In order to understand post-war Japan in her proper perspective in relation to her present, it is important to appreciate that the Cold War has left a unique legacy to Japan. Indeed, this legacy presents a special challenge to the Japanese even now, when Japan is faced with a situation where she is expected to play a much more proactive role in the international arena. In my view, this is a challenge unique to Japan, which no country in Europe or the United states has had to face in the wake of the end of the Cold War.

What is this unique challenge? For many countries in Europe or for the United states, the period of the Cold War was one of 'interlude' interrupting the main course of history running through the whole post-Second World War period, both before and after the Cold War. By contrast, for post-war Japan the advent of the Cold War, coming as it did immediately after the shattering defeat in the Second World War, played a decisive role in creating a special framework in which a new post-Second World War Japan was moulded. It is the legacy of what followed from this that Japan has had to grapple with since the end of the Cold War.

There are in my view three different dimensions to this legacy of the post-war period for Japan.

Defeat as a spiritual crisis for Japan

The defeat of Japan in the Second World War had an effect the impact of which on the spiritual life of the Japanese has not been fully appreciated in the outside world. The crux of the matter is that the defeat of Japan created an unprecedented situation in her history, in which the whole nation suffered a psychic trauma. It was not just that the defeat brought about a sea-change on the political scene; it created a psycho-spiritual trauma of the first degree for the great majority of the Japanese people. The reason was simple: the defeat signified a total collapse of the national polity of modern Japan, together with all the value systems that had supported this polity, in which people had placed their total faith and devotion since the tide of modernization started in the Meiji period. The defeat meant that the whole system of governance of modern Japan was, in effect, shattered. Out of the blue, the Japanese people were told that the entire value system that they had believed in as the spiritual pillar of the nation had been false and that they should now disown it.

An interesting comparison could be made in this context between the case of Japan and the fall of the Third Reich in Germany. It is conceivable that, to the German people as well, the collapse of the Third Reich was a shattering experience of equal magnitude. The illusory vision of the world into which the German people under the Nazi regime had been led – the vision that the German people were to be the superior *Volk* destined to lead the whole world – came to naught through defeat. However, my own view is that to many Germans the period of Nazi Germany, which lasted only for ten-odd years, could be regarded as an 'aberration' of horrible nightmare, in which, it is true, the German people were led to take part but from which, at least spiritually, they could quickly recover and restore their sanity.

Another interesting comparison would be the case of the collapse of the Soviet Union. Here again, the dismay of the Russian people at the loss of the great Empire and superpower status that followed the demise of the USSR must have been equally devastating. In fact, its psycho-spiritual impact – different from the case of the collapse of Nazi Germany – is easily discernible in the current upsurge of nationalistic sentiment and resurgent aspiration for great-power status in present-day Russia. However, it seems to me that the collapse of the Communist regime as a spiritual framework, distinct from the demise of the Soviet Union, has not created a spiritual crisis of the kind that the Japanese people had to go through, presumably because that regime, like Nazi Germany, had, even after an eighty-year reign of dictatorship, simply failed in transforming its Bolshevik ideology into a national faith of the people that could form the polity of the Soviet state.

By contrast, the case of Japan was qualitatively different. Rightly or wrongly, the process of modernization was made possible, and even successful from certain angles, by creating the polity of Japan as a modern state in the Western constitutional sense, grafting the ideology of the modern state in the image of nineteenth century Europe onto the socio-political culture of traditional Japan. In this historical perspective, what was created in prewar Japan could not be likened, for the purpose of our present analysis, to the work of a handful of fanatics conspiring to transform the polity of a nation by deluding the people, nor to an artifice forced upon the people at large by a group of radicals usurping power.

Of course it is an undeniable historical fact that the rise of the military in Japan in the 1930s, who exploited the prerogative of the crown as commander-in-chief by interpreting it as being a 'power beyond the reach of the constitutional government' (*tōsuiken no dokuritsu*) and vetoed policy decisions of the government that were contrary to their interests, allowed the virtual usurpation of power by the military, thus leading the whole country into the abyss of military adventurism and the fatal defeat in 1945. In spite of this apparent similarity between what emerged in Japan and what took place in Germany in the 1930s, however, the fundamental difference of Japan's case lies in the fact that essentially the whole nation – not just the military but the great majority of leaders in government, the business community and in the intellectual community – believed in the nationally identified goal of making Japan a 'modern state' in the image of the West through the imperialistic design (which was still fashionable in those days) and supported the general direction in which the country was heading.

When seen against such a background, it is not too difficult to understand that the whole generation that formed the nucleus of Japanese society in those days felt betrayed by the state in which it had placed its trust. Inevitably, a great majority became nihilist in the basic sense. They could no longer believe in any values. As a result of this nihilistic outlook, some became cynics, while others became opportunists. It was in this spiritual vacuum that the arrival of the Cold War, coinciding with this shattering experience, left its indelible imprint on the national psyche in moulding the essential outlook of post-war Japan. In my opinion, present day Japan is not yet completely free of this trauma.

'Mini-cold War' filling the spiritual vacuum of Japan

The second point is that the arrival of the Cold War on the world arena introduced into the Japan of that period – still suffering from the spiritual vacuum that has just been noted – what I would describe as a 'mini-Cold War'. The fact that the conclusion of the San Francisco Peace Treaty of 1951 coincided with the outbreak of the Cold War was decisive in this respect. The conclusion of peace in San Francisco – in itself a very wise decision, particularly in hindsight – was a very controversial decision in the then societal context of Japan. The prevailing perception was that the peace treaty had been forced on Japan by the United States as a strategic device, overriding the strong objections of the Soviet Union, and that it had the effect of incorporating Japan into the camp of the free world in the context of the deepening confrontation of the Cold War. Against the background of the prevailing spiritual vacuum described above, the conclusion of the San Francisco Peace Treaty, bringing Japan into an alliance relationship with the United States, inevitably threw the Japanese into a state of confusion, dividing the whole country into mutually hostile camps. Thus, the Cold War became 'internalized' in the form of a 'mini-Cold War' within Japan.

Here again, a comparison with the experience of post-war Germany is instructive. It is possible that a somewhat similar political confusion could also have emerged in the case of Germany. However, the division of the Reich between West Germany and East Germany at the termination of hostilities in 1945 prevented this from becoming a reality, although, in a highly paradoxical sense, the post-war division of Germany had an aspect of 'blessing in disguise', in that the Cold War in Europe had to be faced head on as an external threat to the Federal Republic of Germany (FRG). This situation saved the Federal Republic of Germany from an 'internalization of the Cold War' on the domestic scene. Thus, the ideological issue as to which side the FRG should take in this war and what kind of national policy it should pursue could never become a major issue dividing the populace.

Another decisive point distinguishing the two cases of Germany and Japan was the fundamental difference in the external regional environment of the two countries. West Germany had to be, and was in fact, integrated into the European community at an extremely early stage in the post-war European reconstruction: first through the foresight of people such as Jean Monnet and Robert Schuman in creating the European Coal and Steel Community in 1948, later through the establishment of the European Economic Community in 1957. This process of Germany's integration into the community of Europe had the effect of bringing about a historic reconciliation between Germany and its former enemies and of forging West Germany solidly into the camp of the liberal democracies of the West, in the context of the Cold War.

Japan was not so fortunate in her external environment. Apart from the construction of solid relations of alliance with the United States through the US–Japan security arrangement, the process of reconciliation between Japan and her neighbours, who had been the victims of her past aggressive policy, was made virtually impossible by the advent of the Cold War. The outbreak of the Korean War in 1950 removed the possibility of reconciliation with Japan's former colony from the picture. The emergence of the People's Republic of China to power in 1999 as a fellow traveller of the Soviet Union, united with her in ideological alliance, and the expulsion of the Nationalist Government of Chiang Kai-shek – the regime that had fought against Japan for fourteen years – signified that the possibility of seeking reconciliation between Japan and China was practically lost in the context of the deepening Cold War. The fact that the Yoshida government was forced by the United States in 1951 to choose the Nationalist Government in exile in Taipei as its counterpart for the Treaty of Peace with China, thus ostracizing the People's Republic, which had come to represent the entire mainland of China, made this schism decisive.

It was thus inevitable that the US–Japan Security Treaty, as an essential component of the whole picture, should become a highly controversial subject in the national debate. While the conclusion of the US–Japan Security Treaty at this juncture can now be appreciated as an eminently wise decision in the global context of the period, it was feared by a sizable segment of society in Japan as a dangerous ploy of the United States to force her will on an unprepared Japan. It must be accepted that the government, acting on the strength of the occupying power, did not attempt to reach any degree of consensus in the nation as a whole over the significance of the treaty. This would probably have been difficult in any case, in the highly charged political environment prevailing in Japan at the time.

Be that as it may, the absence of national consensus at the starting point of a new Japan had after-effects that were to last for many years. In order properly to understand the depth of the resulting schism, one need only recall that the occasion of the revision of the Security Treaty in 1960, which was in fact a great improvement over the original treaty, developed into a riot, resulting in the downfall of the Kishi government, which had forced its way to the ratification of the revised treaty.

This internal mini-Cold War, an ideological struggle fought, as it were, between East and West by proxy within Japan, went deep into the social fabric, far beyond the realm of foreign affairs, throughout the Cold War period. From the 1950s to the early 1990s, when the so-called '1955 Regime' finally collapsed, uncompromising confrontation in the Diet between the Liberal Democratic Party (LDP)

– which always managed to remain in power and became increasingly degenerated as a result – and the Japan Socialist Party (JSP) – which never came within reach of power and thus never grew up to be a responsible opposition – did not provide fertile ground for fostering the political maturity badly needed in the renascent nation. In this situation, there was little room for genuine policy debate. The Liberal Democrats tended to force their hand on issues they were trying to promote on the strength of their majority, combined with the support of the United States, while the Socialists constantly raised objections to everything the government proposed to do, whether political, economic or social. In fact, it was only to be expected, in the environment of a mini-Cold War on the domestic front, that political debate in the Diet and, more broadly, in society at large, including the mass media, would be polarized, leading to confrontation and to unilateral action by the majority without full substantive discussion.

It was a logical conclusion of this that, when the Cold War framework suddenly disappeared from the global political scene in the early 1990s, the domestic political framework for the mini-Cold War in Japan also had to go. Most importantly, in parallel with the development on the world scene, the whole structure of domestic politics had to undergo a radical change. That was the basis on which the 1993 political upheaval in Japan took place, when LDP rule fell from grace for the first time in post-war history. The LDP government was replaced by a new government headed by Morihiro Hosokawa, who became the first prime minister without an LDP coalition partner since 1955, thus putting an end to the '1955 Regime' of the LDP. On the face of thing, it might appear that what happened in Japan in 1993 was the reflection of a new wave, similar to that brought about in many European democracies by the demise of the Cold War. What is important to note in the case of Japan, however, is that the change in the world situation, by ending the mini-Cold War that had dominated the political scene for so long, had a direct impact on that country's basic post-war political structure. This change in the political scene not only destroyed the Socialist Party, which disintegrated in very much the same way as the Soviet Union disintegrated, but also shook the conservative LDP, which had been relying heavily on the traditional strata of society, taking for granted the political framework created by the Cold War. This meant that the political structure that had served the purpose of keeping intact many remnants of the vested interests of traditional society became exposed to scrutiny. Through the long years of continually being in power, a triangular collusion among the political circle in power, bureaucracy and big business had taken firm hold and created a hotbed for monopoly of power. All this has had to change during the process of societal transformation occuring in Japan under the impact of the end of the Cold War. This sea-change in society is precisely the background against which Junichiro Koizumi was catapulted to power, in the face of resistance from the *teikō-seiryoku* (forces of resistance) and the *shukyū-ha* (groups defending the old regime with its vested interests) of his own party – the LDP.

Virtual reality created in Japan by the Cold War

The third point is that, during the Cold War years, the Japanese became accustomed to living in a world of virtual reality. Through the combination of a number of factors, in the post-war period the Japanese had succeeded in creating for themselves what one might describe as a 'psychological cocoon', secluding themselves from the realities of the outside world. In this self-contained, smug world of their own creation, people did not have to think about the external world as posing real threats to Japan. The typical mantra went like this: we, the people of Japan, have been the victim of the horrors of war; we aspire for peace; we are resolved not to create trouble or to disturb the peace of other people; *ergo*, all is right with the world. This litany very conveniently fitted the mind-set of people affected by cynicism and opportunism born of post-war nihilism, as explained above. The simplistic cult of pacifism as spiritual relief, without serious introspection into their own past, struck a deep root in the minds of the people throughout the post-war period.

It is interesting to compare this mental attitude with what happened in post-war Germany. To a certain extent, one can discern some similarity between the national psyche of the two nations of this period. In the case of Germany, this mental attitude can be summarized in the then popular slogan among the German youth of the period: '*ohne mich*! (without me!)' Common among many in both Japan and Germany at this period was a belief that the only things they could seize on in the midst of their nihilistic outlook on the world were the material aspects of life on which they could physically lay their hands. This led to a belief in material prosperity.

It may be said that, for post-war Japan, such an orientation was only to be expected in any case, because material prosperity was essential to the new Japan that had to rise from the ashes of total destruction after the war. The first and foremost imperative for Japan at that time was to emerge from the misery of the devastated country. However, what was at issue in the minds of people was much more existential than that. For the national psyche of a whole nation affected by the disillusion of defeat, the only thing they could believe in, despite their nihilism, was material wealth, because that was something tangible: *tango ergo est* (I touch, therefore it exists).

The pursuit of material prosperity became the only clearly identifiable value for post-war Japan to pursue, on which the national consensus came to be forged. To give an example, it became a matter of course among the intellectual elite of Japan to speak of 'economic diplomacy', as if the diplomacy of Japan were to be summed up in one single goal, the pursuit of economic prosperity. It seemed there was nothing else in the minds of the elite working in the government and the political establishment except the pursuit of economic wealth, mainly through the exporting of goods.

It was also during this period that a prominent leading bureaucrat famously stated that the national model of the new Japan should be a mercantilist state – *chōnin kokka* – and was acclaimed for his wisdom. This is a metaphor directed at the feudal Japan of the Tokugawa period, the *chōnin* class (literally 'town people', mostly engaged in commercial ativities), while looked down upon as second-class citizens by the *samurai* class (literally 'attendants to the lord', engaged in the affairs of the state), nevertheless wielded influence over feudal lords through their accumulated wealth. This advocacy of the *chōnin kokka* in effect suggested that the new Japan should not aim in her international relations to be a normal state with values and principles to defend, but should try to focus on seeking material prosperity, forgetting about such values and principles.

It is interesting to note that this was the period when Japan was looked on by the outside world also as an exemplary mercantilist state, as the episode of President Charles de Gaulle of France typically demonstrated. President de Gaulle, after meeting his state guest from Japan, Prime Minister Hayato Ikeda, for the first time, reportedly spoke of him as nothing more than "the salesman of transistor radios".

Another episode that illustrates the same point relates to the occasion of the first oil crisis, which erupted after the Middle East war of 1973. A group of oil-producing Arab states, frustrated at the attitude of a number of pro-Israel Western states, decided to put an embargo on the export of crude oil to certain states. Japan was on the list. At this news the whole country fell into a panic. Prime Minister Kakuei Tanaka immediately had to take action to proclaim the government's official policy on the Middle East in the form of a 'statement by the Chief Cabinet Secretary', with a view to having Japan removed from the list of states targeted by the oil export embargo.[1] The deputy prime minister was despatched as the government's special envoy to a number of hard-line Arab states for the purpose of securing the removal of Japan from this list, inviting derisive comments from overseas observers as the 'diplomacy of oil begging'.

In the face of such a widening gap between the perception of Japan by the outside world and that of the Japanese, the latter continued to live in a virtual reality of their own creation, comfortable in their conviction that a pacifist Japan that did not harbour ill will to any of her neighbours would be a welcome presence in the world.

This psychological cocoon in which the Japan of the Cold War period smugly secluded herself from outside realities came to an abrupt end with the ending of the Cold War. When seen against the background of this history, it is not difficult to understand that the new upheaval came as a shock to the minds of many Japanese. In a sense, the Japanese were thrown into the cold water of the harsh realities of the real world, with no clear sense of orientation.

A caveat is needed that the above is a somewhat caricaturized picture of postwar Japan. The real situation was much more nuanced and complex, but one could claim that, *grosso modo*, what has been described was more or less what people felt when the Cold War came to an end. People have since then been confused as to what exactly to do.

The somewhat composed, and even ambivalent, reaction of the Japanese to the issue of the nuclearization of the Democratic People's Republic of Korea illustrates this point. When North Korea made its experimental launch of the mid-range missile Rodong I in the late 1980s in the direction of the Sea of Japan, the incident did not attract much attention in Japan. It was only when the clandestine activities of North Korea in the production of fissionable nuclear material came into the open in 1992 that public opinion in Japan was aroused. People realized for the first time that the nuclearization of a hostile neighbour such as the DPRK would pose a serious security threat. The North Korean launch in 1998 of the long-range missile

Taepodong I, which fell into the Pacific in the vicinity of Japan after overflying her airspace, finally persuaded the Japanese of the nature of the threat posed to their security.

New problems in the aftermath of the Cold War

To be precise, it is not quite accurate to say that the mental attitudes that affected the national psyche of the Japanese people continued unchanged during the Cold War years. While it is, no doubt, true that the mini-Cold War that characterized the socio-political milieu of Japan for so many years of the Cold War period moulded the unique intellectual environment of Japan, the mini-Cold War itself went through a process of gradual evolution, just as in the real world the West gradually came to overwhelm the East in the East–West confrontation. Against that background two new sets of problems appeared in the aftermath of the Cold War: a reaction to the postwar revisionist view of Japanese history and the impact of globalization on traditional Japanese society.

Reaction to the revisionist view of history

It would be fair to say that, in the immediate post-war years, there was a period when the whole country was totally polarized in a societal sense, and especially in the intellectual domain. In the field of education especially, with the arrival of the defeat, the whole educational system in Japan came to be totally dominated by the influence of the Japan Federation of Teachers' Unions (*Nikkyōso*), primarily controlled by the Communists and their affiliates. Teachers, many of whom were repatriates from the battlefields, were the direct product of the contemporary environment that was the outgrowth of the post-war nihilism mentioned earlier. So-called 'pacifist education' was practised all over the country. The thrust of this education tended towards the total repudiation of the past achievements of Japan in her process of modernization. In fact, the new ideology of total rejection of all past values came, paradoxically, to take the place of the former orthodoxy, claiming to be the only legitimate ideology for post-war Japan. In the course of this development, the revisionist approach to history prevailed to such an extent that the Marxist–Leninist doctrine of the materialistic reinterpretation of the history of Japan replaced the historiography based on the *kōkoku-shikan* (nationalist school of Japanese imperial history) of the prewar days.

In due course, however, as Japan gradually restored her self-confidence and a sense of balance, with the fading of the post-war trauma and especially with a generational change, such total repudiation of the past came to be viewed with a growing degree of suspicion. In fact, this new development in people's minds led to a counter-reaction to the revisionist approach. People began to wonder whether the teaching of history that consisted in the total repudiation of everything in the past really was the right approach. It was, in my view, this reaction to revisionist post-war education that led to the emotional outburst of the 'neo-revisionists'. This new group, some in academia and others in the mass media, began to raise their voices against the so-called 'masochistic interpretation of history' (*jigyaku shikan*). In fact, it is my submission that this *ressentiment* against the post-war revisionist current in history is a major element behind the phenomenon of what appears to outsiders to be a rising tide of neo-nationalism in Japan, such as we witness in the textbook issue.

This neo-nationalism which is rising in Japan, like the neo-conservative movement in the United States, is, thus, essentially an emotional reaction to the tendentious approach to history that had held sway throughout the post-war period. As such, it is a movement that is essentially 'defensively aggressive' in nature. It can be described also as a reflection of 'wounded nationalism', as some would put it. It is no doubt true that such 'wounded nationalism' is far from the healthy type of nationalism that one would expect in any society as a reflection of a newly found national identity based on restored national pride. In the case of Japan, it would be only natural that such national pride should stem from the achievements the country has realized in all these years. Nevertheless, it is important to understand that such 'wounded nationalism' is, in essence, nothing other than a reaction against what had been distorted in post-war Japan as a result of the revisionist approach to its past.

The textbook issue is a typical manifestation of this emotional reaction. One could easily dissociate oneself from this neo-revisionist school of history, to the extent that it tries to distort history in the other direction by engaging in overall praise of Japan's past. As a matter of principle, it must be said that such an attempt to rewrite history could fall into the same pitfalls that the post-war revisionist school fell into, to the detriment of Japan's credibility in the world. At the same time, however, it is not hard to understand why this wave of neo-revisionism in history had to emerge, and why it can evoke such a strong resonance of sympathy among a very broad section of the public in contemporary Japan, especially among the younger segment of the population. It is not that people are embracing *in toto* what some of the authors of neo-revisionist textbooks are trying to advocate. The resonance of sympathy is essentially an understandable reaction to the excessive distortion of the past that had gone into the works of the post-war revisionists in the form of a total repudiation of the actual course of history and a total rejection of everything that Japan had achieved in the process of modernization. People are justifiably questioning whether such an approach is indeed one that is faithful to history. In their search for a new national identity, many in Japan feel that certain legitimate aspects of the past have to be treated in a more balanced way.

The problem here, however, is that a very paradoxical alliance has developed as a result of this new situation – that is, an unholy alliance between those who have a legitimate claim to restoring the balance by trying to be objective without purporting to justify the old, prewar, ultra-nationalistic values, and those neo-nationalists who try to revive the old, prewar values *in toto* by rewriting history. Both of these groups have come to be identified as occupying common ground, inasmuch as they are agreed on the point that the post-war revisionists who engaged in the total repudiation of all past values were wrong. That is the background in which the textbook issue has come to be entangled with politics, in the context of a complex process of evolution in the national psyche of the people. It is this complexity that has led to the apparent formation of an unholy alliance between the two groups of such different orientation. I submit that this creates a source of confusion not only for outside observers of Japan but also for those within the country who tend to oscillate between the two camps.

If one understands all these complexities created in the aftermath of the Second World War, one can better appreciate that Japan at this time is in a very complex and confused situation so far as her national psyche is concerned. Of course, the economic difficulties that Japan has been experiencing since the beginning of the 1990s have been no help either; they are, in fact, an added aggravating factor in this confusion. If the economy were going well, people would feel a little more confident about themselves and their own identity. So long as one can be sure of one's identity and have faith in one's future, all those difficulties – societal, political and psychological – described above would be something that could be overcome, or at least kept under control. But when the economy is going down, it aggravates the unsettled psychic anxiety of the people.

The impact of globalization on traditional society

As if these complexities were not enough, there are other external factors that must be examined in order to understand accurately the state of the national psyche of Japan at this juncture in history.

Foremost in importance in explaining the malaise of the Japanese at this juncture is the impact of globalization, which has hit Japan at the same time as the ongoing process of societal transformation in the aftermath of the demise of the Cold War. In my view, the fact that the process of globalization is affecting the whole society in a fundamental way is not sufficiently appreciated even in Japan, not to mention the outside world. To my mind, the persistent trend of stagnation in the economy, which has plagued the country since the 1990s, and which it is still too early to suppose over, is also a manifestation of the impact of globalization. The present weak state of the Japanese economy is, in my view, something more than a passing phase of recession in the business cycle. With the arrival of the age of globalization, Japan was, inevitably, plunged into the whirlwind of globalization, as every other nation of the world, while struggling with her own urgent problem of how to adjust to the new, post-Cold War era by restructuring her society – which still retains traditional political, economic and social systems that have outlived their usefulness. I submit that this dilemma poses a fundamental problem for the future of Japan, because it is inseparably linked to the way in which the country has been carrying out her process of modernization in a much broader historical context. In this sense, the process of globalization now raises the fundamental question of whether the whole process of modernization, starting with the Meiji restoration and continuing since, has not been 'a miracle' only in a mundane sense. This problem also requires a fundamental soul-searching exercise on the part of the Japanese people – a transformation in their mind-set.

There is no question that the process of modernization since the Meiji period has succeeded in shaping Japan as a modern state in the Western sense of the word. All this process of modernization since the late nineteenth century, in its material aspect of 'industrialization', has been taking place in the context of a Japan expanding economically in a benign environment that made such growth possible. The only exception to this generalization was the period from the early 1930s to the 1940s, when the Great Depression plunged the growing economy into an abyss of economic havoc. It is well known that this economic disaster was at least one of the major factors for the destruction of the economic and social foundation of nascent democracy of Japan. This development in turn provided a hotbed for the rise in influence of traditional Shintoist fundamentalism, offering a fertile ground for exploitation for political purposes by the military. The rest was history for everyone to see. Japan was led into the sway of totalitarianism and eventually to the Second World War.

Except for this brief period, however, the entire process of modernization in Japan, including the process of its post-war reconstruction, has been achieved quite smoothly in the context of an uninterrupted linear growth of her economy. This, however, may have been a 'blessing in disguise' *in reverse*. It could be argued that, within this benign environment, some traditional pre-modern aspects of society that would otherwise have been swept away as standing in the way of modernization have continued to this day, without being seriously addressed. This pre-modern aspect of society in essence boils down to the fact that the traditional society of Japan has been built as basically a *closed circuit* system operating on its own.

At the time when Japan embarked on the process of building a modern state through industrialization in the image of the nineteenth-century Western powers, many intellectuals who had been brought up in the social and cultural heritage of traditional Japan had to struggle with the problem of how to reconcile the system of values inherited from the traditional social system, as well as social conventions followed through hundreds of years in an environment of relative seclusion, with the new framework of values entrenched in the civil society of modern Europe.

It is symbolic, in this respect, that a professor of civil law at the Imperial University of Tokyo in the latter part of the nineteenth century famously lamented that 'with the rise of the Civil Code, the traditional value system of loyalty to the Emperor and piety to parents is to perish'. To reconcile this dilemma of living through the two cultures, the approach advocated by the intellectuals of the day, and practised as a convenient vehicle to carry out the process of modernization, was the idea of *wakon yōsai*, the combination of 'Japanese spirit and Western learning'. This approach to the situation of conflict of cultures was received with enthusiasm by intellectuals and conceptualized as a justification for the national behaviour of Japan in subsequent years – increasingly, in later years, with more emphasis on 'Japanese spirit' than on 'Western learning'.

However, the crucial question to ask is whether such a facile combination of elements of different cultures is feasible. Western learning is nothing else than the outcome of the Western spirit as represented by rationalism, individualism, an analytical and even sometimes confrontational attitude to nature and the like; whereas the Japanese spirit, consisting in such elements as intuition, harmony, a symbiotic attitude to nature and the like, forms part and parcel of the social and cultural institutions that Japan has developed throughout history.

Thus, it seems clear to me that the concept of *wakon yōsai*, however attractive it might be as an eclectic approach to solving a dilemma, is extremely difficult, if not impossible, to realize in practice. Indeed, it could be said that the process of modernization in Japan since the Meiji period has been no more than an attempt to graft a new oak branch of modern Western technological civilization onto the traditional pine tree firmly rooted in the closed circuit of the socio-cultural system of Japan, rather than trying to replace the old pine by a new oak tree.

It is this dilemma, which the process of modernization in Japan since the Meiji restoration has not completely succeeded in solving, that present-day Japan has to face squarely, in the midst of the tide of globalization symbolized by an open global society, in which the country has to play an integral part.

The case of a well-known traditional Japanese institution called *dangō*, which used to be widely practised in the area of economic activity in traditional Japan and has even survived until today, may be cited as a symbolic example to illustrate the point. *Dangō* is a conspiracy in the anti-trust sense, where the parties involved in a competitive situation conspire with each other to work out a common under-standing in which all share some profit, to the exclusion of those who are not included in the conspiracy. This clearly goes against the basic concept of fair competition. But the conventional practice of *dangō* was widely observed in tradi-tional Japan, where society formed a closed system, on the grounds that it would create a perfect harmony in society among its participants. The problem is that it works to the exclusion of outsiders, who do not share the rules of the system – a situation that presents no problem so long as it operates in a closed system, but becomes a major problem as soon as the system is opened globally to outsiders.

Japan, as an isolated island country, for many years formed a secluded society, even before the 260-year-period of *sakoku*, when she literally closed herself to the outside world as the official policy of the Shogunate. Because of her geographical environment, Japan was for long a society leading a harmonious life of its own as a self-contained unit, more or less secluded from neighbouring societies. In that sense Japan has always tended to form a societal closed circuit. It was on this basis that Japan succeeded in creating a remarkably equitable society, placing societal priority on the maintenance of 'harmony' (*wa*) of society as a whole. In a society of this kind, it is natural for the members to live together on the basis of harmony, trying to subordinate their respective interests to the welfare of society as a whole.

The institution of *dangō* comes right into this culture. It is a device to achieve 'harmony' in the process of deciding on the question of who gets a contract among competing bidders, by making a prior informal arrangement among the participants in a tender so that they may share the profits through a mechanism of 'consultation' among all participants. To the extent that one can work out a solu-tion that satisfies everyone's desire by half, so the argument goes, it is a better system than one in which a certain member of the group gets full satisfaction while the others get nothing. So long as everyone gets a certain share on an equitable basis, everyone is happy.

This was a significant aspect of the 'harmonious society' that prevailed in Japan before modernization. The modernization process, based on the principle of rationalism, could have dealt a fatal blow to such a culture, because it went against the logic of rationality in the Western sense inasmuch as it killed the spirit of free competition, which is the basis of fairness and the driving force for progress. In Japan, through the process of modernization, however, it has not had the effect of killing the spirit of progress, mainly because the economy has been constantly growing. So long as the pie was large enough and growing bigger and bigger, there was no urge to cope with such problems. It is only now, with the arrival of globalization, that, all of a sudden, one is faced with a totally novel situation. It is the reality of globalization, in which the pie may still be growing but in which one has to compete in the open, on a level playing field, in the presence of outsiders in a global market. It is interesting to note that Americans used to criticize Japan for keeping the market closed both to them and to foreigners in general, in order to favour the Japanese. In fact, this criticism was quite wide of the mark. Japan may have been closed to those Americans who asked for equal opportunity in competition, but they were shut out not because they were Americans, not because they were foreigners, but because they were outsiders. Japanese outsiders within Japan would also be excluded under such a system. With globalization, these things cannot go on as they used to.

Conclusion

It is clear that globalization is forcing Japan to face the new situation squarely and to engage in structural transformation as society, in order to survive and prosper in this new environment. The challenge of structural reform in the economic arena, to my mind, lies precisely in this point. The conventional view held by many in Japan, that the economic reform that needs to be tackled concerns the structural reform in its formalistic and institutional aspects, including the technical questions of how to overcome the impact of the current economic recession, seems to me to be highly questionable for this very reason. If that were the case, the problem could be handled fairly easily on a technical basis, through such measures as rationalization of production lines, revision of salary scales, introduction of a lay-off system, or abolition of the lifetime employment system – although this last point might be somewhat linked to the problems that come with the fundamental issue of a closed-circuit system. All these issues clearly have to be addressed by Japanese business as short-term measures to be taken in the context of the cyclical recession that has hit Japan and they have, by now, largely been addressed. In my view, however, there are far more fundamental problems remaining. We have to face them in order to cope with globalization. What this means is that we in Japan can no longer maintain the remnants of a closed system, with all that it implies. What is involved here is the question of the spiritual outlook on life and society. Otherwise we cannot compete on the global market.

This is an extremely difficult task, and not simply an economic problem. It applies to professions such as doctors and lawyers as well as to institutions such as universities. In essence, it is a question of the mind-set of the people. One cannot expect the change to happen in a day or even in a year. It may take years, just because it involves the fundamental mind-set of people and society. One may be optimistic that eventually the Japanese will succeed in overcoming this fundamental problem as well, but it will take time. The critical question is whether they can compete with the speed of the change that is taking place in this age of globalization.

When one looks at all these things, one inevitably becomes less optimistic about the future. That, to my mind, is the real source of the present confused state in which the Japanese find themselves.

Naturally, there are certain bright areas also. The ending of the Cold War has brought about a new situation in which the Japanese have finally been exposed to the outside world in the real sense of the term. They have become keenly conscious of their problems. They are no longer secluding themselves in a psychological cocoon. With their innate ability, as has been demonstrated in the past, they will be able to adapt themselves to the new situation. The basic problem, however, is whether there is enough time for the necessary changes and whether there is the political will to realize those changes with the necessary resolve.

Let me state, by way of conclusion, that this last point is the most difficult problem that Japan faces at present. The political system or, to put it more precisely, the political culture that we have in Japan is the most problematic part of the whole picture. The mind-set of many of the people immersed in the political culture of Japan tends to be tied to the vested interests of the past, being insensitive to the new problems that globalization is posing by way of a gigantic challenge. It is this political element that forms the crucial factor on which the future of Japan will hinge.

Notes

1 The text of the 'statement by the Chief Cabinet Secretary' of 22 November 1973 is as follows:

 1 The Government of Japan has consistently hoped that a just and lasting peace in the Middle East will be achieved through the prompt and complete implementation of Security Council Resolution 242, and has continued to request the efforts of the parties and countries concerned. It has been prompt in supporting the United Nations General Assembly Resolution concerning the rights of the Palestinian people for self-determination.

 2 The Government of Japan is of the view that the following principles should be adhered to in achieving a peace settlement.

 a The inadmissibility of acquisition and occupation of any territories by use of force;
 b The withdrawal of Israeli forces from all the territories occupied in the 1967 war;
 c The respect for the integrity and security of the territories of all countries in the area and the need of guarantees to that end; and
 d The recognition of and respect for the legitimate rights of the Palestinian people

in accordance with the Charter of the United Nations in bringing about a just and lasting peace in the Middle East.

3 The Government of Japan urges that every possible effort be made to achieve a just and lasting peace in the Middle East in compliance with the above-mentioned principles. Needless to say, it is the intention of the Government of Japan to make as much contribution as possible towards that end.

4 The Government of Japan, deploring Israel's continued occupation of Arab territories, urges Israel to comply with those principles. The Government of Japan will continue to observe the situation in the Middle East with grave concern and, depending on future developments, may have to reconsider its policy toward Israel.

Part VI
Conclusions

15 Conclusions

The necessity for a reinterpretation of a changing Japan

Rien T. Segers

Looking back

Looking back at the preceding chapters there are two themes that are dealt with in almost every chapter, obviously with a varying degree of intensity. Both themes form the basis for fundamental changes to be undertaken in constructing a new Japan. They also underline the necessity of reinterpreting Japan and of bridging the perception gap concerning Japan's contemporary identity.

First is the globalization–localization debate. Even if not it is specifically mentioned in these words, all chapters are implicitly or explicitly concerned with finding an answer to the question of how Japan should respond to the new requirements of globalizing trends entering the country. In the preceding chapters the common understanding is that Japan should change fundamentally because of outmoded practices and conventions, and the general agreement is that many things have already changed. However, it is important for policy makers in the public and private sectors to consider carefully whether the proposed changes reflect and respect Japanese culture, its tradition and the mental programming of the people. This implies that globalizing (which means, in many cases, American) trends should not just be imposed on Japanese culture, but should be adapted and transformed as far as possible so that they fit neatly into the Japanese mental programming. This adaptation process should contain Japan's solution to globalization.

A second common theme consists of a mixture of two very important contemporary developments, not only for Japan as such but for the world in general. It concerns the rise of China and the growing tendency toward East Asian regionalization. What has been clear to specialists since the early 1990s became known to a global public on the basis of a publication by C. F. Bergsten (2000) in *The Economist* around the turn of the millennium. It concerns the widely shared belief that we are standing at the threshold of a new world, of a new division of hard and soft power. An old country, China, and a new region, East Asia, are finally rising to the top (again). This will have consequences for the world in general, but most severely for Japan in particular, as many chapters have shown.

These two common themes are elaborated in the second and third sections of this concluding chapter; in the fourth section the consequences of these two important factors will be outlined in relation to a reinterpretation of contemporary Japan.

The Japanese solution to globalization

In the preceding chapters of this book a clear pattern can be distinguished. In most domains of Japanese society a clash becomes visible between global conventions (which now often mean American conventions) and local, Japanese practices. This interesting process can be described on the basis of an example from the business sector.[1]

What is the current global situation in the business environment vis-à-vis Japan? Grimes and Schaede provide the following succinct survey:

> Internationally, Japan's trade prowess, increasing manufacturing presence around the world, and economic leadership in Asia have made the country an integral member of multilateral organizations such as the World Trade Organization (WTO). Japan is increasingly expected to uphold the norms of free trade and economic openness as articulated in a variety of international treaties, and to assume a geopolitical role commensurate with its global economic position.
>
> (Grimes and Schaede 2003: 243)

The global conventions in this respect are free trade and openness, which is obviously not the same as saying that every WTO member sticks to those principles 100 per cent. But what are Japanese practices at home?

> Domestically, Japan has been challenged by the need to transform an industrial structure that has proven unfit to ensure growth across most sectors in the new economy of the twenty-first century, a situation reminiscent of the early 1970's. Having built their economic success on high quality manufacturing, many Japanese manufacturing firms are still among the world leaders, whether in cars, office machinery, or consumer electronics. Yet with the decline of some of the former flagship industries, no new sectors have stepped up to allow for a transfer of employment and technical skills into industries with high growth potential. Low mobility of labour and capital have made such adjustment even more difficult. As a result, many declining industries continue to receive protection, at a time when there has been an obvious need to support growth in both currently successful industries and the emerging new economy sectors.
>
> (Grimes and Schaede 2003: 243–4)

That means that the local Japanese conventions are restricted protection based on specific economic sectors and specific economic policies. To overstate somewhat the clash between global and local conventions one could say that it concerns the struggle between openness and closedness, where openness is the dominant global convention (or at least the global discourse) to which closedness is subjected.

Obviously, in most cases the particular cultural system of a nation-state never fully adopts a global tendency. The stronger the culture, the greater the resistance. For all clashes that occur between the global and the local, the local cultural system provides a solution, consciously or not. In this case the Japanese politico-economic system opted for a solution that could be called 'permeable insulation' as opposed to the complete insulation during the two and a half centuries preceding the Meiji era. 'Insulation' implies that, in many areas, government and corporate policies continue to have at their core an attempt to shield companies from full competition and the rigour of market forces. The insulation is permeable in the sense that it is not absolute, but allows for differentiation by industry, institution or issue area. Permeable insulation means allowing entry and market competition for foreign companies in areas where that is the best approach for existing Japanese, relatively strong companies, while protection will be installed in less competitive sectors. As Grimes and Schaede mention: 'Permeable insulation is Japan's attempt to manage the process of [economic] globalization by differentiating its speed and reach by political issue-area and economic sector' (Grimes and Schaede 2003: 4).

Grimes and Schaede are right when they state that permeable insulation may well be an effective way for Japan to cope with globalization and domestic reorganization, at least in the short term. It is evident that globalization creates pressures for large-scale structural adjustment in the economy, but such adjustment is always painful, both economically and politically. Therefore, permeable insulation is Japan's particular attempt both to adapt to globalization and still to maintain some of the bases of the domestic political and social order. Managed globalization may mean that Japan's integration into the global economy will be slowed – but that may be the intended consequence of permeable insulation.

This condensed and rather superficial outlook on Japan's current economic context is meant as an example, as a case. It is one element of the contemporary cultural system that is subjected to the struggle between localization and globalization. The same adaptation process (managed globalization) can be seen in almost all major areas of Japanese society, as has been outlined in most chapters of this book. Obviously, the pace, quality and intensity of this process may be different according to the specificity of the area.

It goes without saying that this same process of managed globalization is also visible in most other cultures. But the representation of this paradox seems to be much more manifest in Japan than anywhere else in the world. Obviously, the globalization–localization paradox has not been unknown to Japan since the Meiji era. But the intensity of this paradox in the first decade of the new millennium is unprecedented. More than ever before, the concept of hybridity seems to be adequate to describe Japan's changing cultural identity. It shows that in clashes that are occurring between the global and the local, the local cultural system in many cases provides – consciously or not – an adaptation to soften the clash.

Cultural hybridity means the coexistence *and* blending of (parts of) several cultural systems, reflecting both adaptation and resistance. In Japan at this partic-ular moment it means the blending presence of mainly Japanese, Asian, American and some European cultural systems and conventions.

In most cases a unipolar interpretation of Japan cannot acknowledge this new cultural hybridity of Japan. Unipolar interpretations, by nature, flourish by concentrating on worn-out clichés and stereotypes concerning a Japan that is considered homogeneous, invariable and unchangeable. On the other hand, a multi-polar interpretation considers a country not necessarily as a unity, but consisting of different groups with their own specific agendas which may overlap but also differ. In addition, a multi-polar interpretation considers a nation-state as part of a regional and global system. Finally, a multi-polar interpretation bases itself on constructivism, implying that the cultural identity of a nation-state is not innate, but constructed, which means – among other things – that its cultural identity may vary significantly, even over a relatively short period of time, causing elaborate changes for the people and the institutions of that nation.

The development into a strongly hybrid cultural situation, whether or not appre-ciated inside Japan itself, will be a hallmark of twenty-first century Japan. This hybridity, still in the beginning phase of its development, has already changed the contemporary cultural identity of Japan to a significant extent. That fact makes clear why the localization–globalization paradox incorporates the first reason for the necessity of a reinterpretation of contemporary Japan.

Increasing East Asian regionalization

From the chapters in this book a second reason for the necessity to reinterprete Japan can be inferred, closely connected with the first reason, the localization–globalization paradox. It concerns the tendency towards increasing East Asian regionalization and the fast tempo of the rise of China.

Based on these two stunning developments, not only Japan but also the West should critically review their outlook on the world, its conventions and strate-gies and should fundamentally upgrade their knowledge concerning Asia, at the expense of becoming second class.

The corporate sector in Japan has already gained a strategic insight and trust in most 'continental' Asian countries: many partnerships with foreign Asian compa-nies have been established; the Asian market has been successfully covered; some Asian countries, notably China, serve as excellent manufacturing shops for Japanese companies. Now it is high time that the Japanese government and Japanese politics followed suit. It is a regrettable anachronism that, more than sixty years after the end of the Second World War, war issues still dominate Asian political relations. Japan, as a former aggressor and as the contemporary leading Asian nation, has a special responsibility in these issues that stretches further than the conservative limits of the major Japanese political parties. There is not much time to lose for Japanese politics in this respect.

Western clichés concerning East Asia should be replaced as soon as possible by sound knowledge of and real interest in this region. Obviously, this interest cannot be based on cuisine and temple curiosity or just on trade issues, but should be based on language and culture, facts, figures, strategies and the fast developments taking place in that part of the world. That at least is the conviction of those who believe in a paradigm shift, where the centre of gravity of world power no longer rests in the West, but is clearly situated in Asia, and – to be more precise – in East Asia. The basis for this new centre of gravity would be a stronger integration of the East Asian countries with China, Japan and South Korea, Taiwan and Singapore as the leading power houses. It would not be surprising if this shift in the global centre of gravity took place in the next fifteen to twenty years.

However, in the West there still seems to be a widespread belief that the West, and especially the United States, is still and will remain the one and only centre. But if economic performance and all activities related to this performance are taken as a basis for comparison, then things have already changed. As Sugihara mentions:

> In the fields of politics, military affairs, intellectual property and international finance, the West is still the center of the world. However, it is clear that the center of the world economy has moved from the Atlantic to the Asia-Pacific region over the last 50 years.
>
> (Sugihara 2005: 37)

If it is true that economic development and economic dominance precede developments and dominance in other fields, such as politics, military power, culture and enhancements in the energy situation, then it is likely we really are standing on the threshold of a new balance of power between the three blocs: the USA, the EU and East Asia.[2] Following this line of thinking, one could read the current situation in the world in this respect as follows: while the USA focuses on the seemingly eternal Sisyphus project that is Iraq, increasingly dividing both Iraq and the USA, and while the EU is struggling with its internal cohesion, its immigration drama and the cancellation of its bold agreement to become the world's most competitive economic region by 2010, the real game is being played in East Asia, where dragons are awakening, tigers are roaring and the sun is rising again. The Western perception comfortably leans on constructions based on the negative aspects: the unsustainability of China, the impossibility of Japan really changing and coming to terms with its war past, the violation of human rights in a number of ASEAN countries and the disparity among the systems of state governance in East Asian countries. On the basis of these and other similar constructions, many opinion leaders and decision makers in the West turn a blind eye to East Asia and continue with business as usual, focusing on the USA as the eternal centre of the world. But history and constructivism tell us that there are no fixed certainties and that change seems to be the only inherent characteristic.

It is an undeniable fact that a second wave of Asianization of unprecedented nature can be expected. The first Azianization wave dates back to the 1970s and

1980s, was Japan based and flooded the world with quality Japanese products. This wave started out very modestly with the export from Japan of small and cheap Japanese cars. They were perceived by political and business leaders in Europe and the US as unreliable, ugly and no threat to the Western automotive industry whatsoever. Those first cars were considered to be the practical joke of some far-away Eastern country producing cheap and bad products.

More than thirty years later there is a striking similarity in the European perception of the arrival of the first Chinese car, the Land Wind, in the Belgian port of Antwerp in June 2006. Reactions were similar to those expressed about the first Japanese car: too cheap to be true, ugly and unsafe – obviously the worst labels for a car. The perception that the Chinese Land Wind is unsafe was because of a crash test performed by the German Automotive Club (ADAC) immediately after its arrival in Antwerp, with devastating results. The widespread conclusion in the EU press was quickly drawn: the Chinese car is no threat whatsoever to the existing automotive industry in the EU.

Obviously, the opinion leaders who downplayed the quality and appeal of the first Japanese cars were taken by surprise at the stunning success of the first Japanese wave of Asianization. To see this shocking impact one only has to compare the poor perception, the outright arrogant laughter on the arrival of the first Japanese car around 1970 and the reviews of one of the most recent Japanese models, full of innovative technology, brand design and energy saving, the Toyota Prius, world car of the year 2004. The perception changed completely from one end of the scale to the other in just one generation!

Asianization is just as Americanization was and still is: a form of globalization where strong global flows coming from one region enter other regions and exert considerable influence, destroying parts of the original business and cultural identity of that region. An important global flow is, for instance, represented by technology, as can be seen by the enormous waves of products in the fields of IT, of the automotive and aviation industry, biomedical engineering and robotics, spreading into every corner of the world, seemingly without any great difficulty. In some cases these waves have a tsunami-like character, destroying the local production infrastructure, with the consequential loss of many local jobs.

Over the last twenty-five years East Asia has seen the rise and fall of three national models dominating the region. In the 1980s, East Asia saw the dominance of the Japanese national model, to be followed by its decline in the 1990s and its succession by the dominance of the USA; around the turn of the millennium the USA and Japanese models were severely challenged by China. But at the same time a new and different development became visible, as Katzenstein has mentioned: 'The time is ripe for a shift in perspective. East Asia is moving rapidly beyond any national model to the coexistence of several viable alternatives and the emergence of a truly hybrid form of regionalism' (Katzenstein 2006: 2).

This would imply that the several national models currently striving for dominance on the East Asian scene (the American, the Chinese and the Japanese) have been integrating to a certain degree into a new, hybrid East Asian reality. This is not the same as declaring this development to be the start of a sort of East

Asian Community, a kind of EU in the making. Obviously, this also does not imply the end of the East Asian nation-states; on the contrary, nationalism is rising very strongly in most nations of the region.[3] But attention should be drawn to the changed character of the region, where hybridity is increasingly taking over the dominant role played in earlier decades by one national model: Japan, the USA or China.

The success of the second wave of Asianization, the integration process of East Asia and the subsequent rise to power of East Asia in the global system, including easy access to the gold of the twenty-first century, energy sources, seem to be dependent on East Asia's successful avoidance of a number of potential dangers that could ruin its glooming prospects. There exist four potential threats to an Asian, especially an East Asian, dominance of the world: the North Korean issue, the status of Taiwan, the sustainability of China (especially the growing gap between the economic wealth of the Pacific region between Shanghai and Macao, and the poor status and bad outlooks for the farmers and other people in mainland China, the largest part of the population) and then, finally, the relations between China and Japan. Each threat incorporates such a dangerous dimension that a severe clash in any of them would have severe implications for the region as a whole, and probably also for the world in general.

The China–Japan relationship is of pivotal importance to the regional and global success of the second wave of Asianization. That relationship is based on an economic and on a cultural factor.

In principle, the economic side of the relationship is seen as a strong asset for sustainable cooperation between the two countries. At this moment the economic figures are such that this view seems to be justified. However, in analysing the situation, another scenario may be possible. This scenario contains a development in which the current economic cooperation is gradually undermined by a fear of domination, based on a Chinese perception that Japan is getting a much better deal from the economic ties and on that basis has become the undisputed leader in a number of fields in Asia. On the other hand, in Tokyo the perception may gradually develop that China is rather quickly turning into an economic giant and thus into the undisputed leader of Asia. These perceptions would definitely put a hold on, or at least slow down, the economic relations on the basis of interventions by either or both governments.

The second factor that determines the development of the relationship between the two countries is the cultural. In the long run this factor may turn out to be much more decisive than the economic relationship. It consists of the two grand narratives that each nation has constructed of the other (see Rose 2005: 123).

The Chinese grand narrative focuses on the 'bad Japanese'. After the war, until the 1980s the grand narrative of the Communist Party, in which the Communists were victorious in the War of Resistance against Japan, became the major legitimacy of the party, constructing the country's collective memory and thus its cultural identity. As Rose correctly mentions:

The grand narrative would (and could) not be questioned until the 1980s, when the academic environment was relaxed and more independent research could be undertaken. During this time, China's younger generation, which had no direct experience of the war came to be taught only about the 'bad Japanese' in their textbooks and media. When the Chinese leadership attempted to move away from this view, for example, in an attempt to improve relations with Japan and cast Japan in a better light, they faced a huge challenge in the form of deeply held antipathy towards the Japanese which the party had encouraged for so long, and which, of course, had been reinforced by the wartime experiences related by parents and grandparents.

(Rose 2005: 123)

Also, the Japanese from their side constructed a grand narrative concerning the Chinese. It represents the 1930s and 1940s as a 'Dark Valley' for Japan and the Japanese, an aberration for which the instigators had been punished, reparations made, justice done and many official apologies given many times. Therefore the war is a closed book and the Chinese should stop always playing the history card. This is the current political grand narrative, which is from time to time heavily challenged not only from the Chinese side but also from within Japan, by scholars, teachers, some war veterans and left-wing politicians. Many historians are asking to look at the real war statistics, research them and set them down in textbooks.

It goes without saying that the two national grand narratives represent a clash of historical war interpretations and so far hamper close cooperation between the two countries in any field apart from economic relations. Obviously, narratives don't necessarily describe a situation as it is by referring to 'objective statistics'. Narratives oversimplify and overstate their case, which is also the function of narrative discourse.

Regionalization, driven by economic and media factors, is such a strong force in East Asia that even the governments of China and Japan will not be able to stop this tendency; they may be able to obstruct and slow it down, but deconstructing it will be virtually impossible (the worst-case scenario of outright war excluded). The business sector and the citizens have become too powerful to let only the government decide what is good for them. For instance, the Japanese corporate sector will continue to expand its operations in China, irrespective what the Japanese government is saying or doing. The corporate sector has become rather independent in this respect. For instance, the Japanese business community repeatedly recommended former prime minister Koizumi to refrain from visiting Yasukuni shrine, which significantly hurts Japanese trade and manufacturing in China and other Asian countries.

It has become evident that the contemporary situation in East Asia shows a strong tendency to regionalization, whatever form this tendency may take. There is an undeniable trend to talk to each other, to collaborate and to find common solutions, preferably within a framework such as ASEAN+3, despite all historical wounds and unresolved antagonisms. Based on global strategic developments, such as the security of energy supplies for instance, East Asian countries will gradually understand that shouldering the burden together has a great number of advantages and is as a matter of fact a necessary development if the region is really striving for a leading place in the world.

However, the creation of an East Asian community is not an easy task and comparison with the creation of the European Union has only limited validity. The historical circumstances, the global context and the relations between the prospective member states show a distinctly different character. And even after crossing the first difficult hurdles in the formation of a union, new extremely difficult problems will arise, as is currently the case within the European Union.[4] But a society or a region without grand dreams and ideals is derived of its very *raison d'être*. Therefore, the attempt to establish an East Asian union is not only necessary from an economic point of view, but even more so from a socio-cultural perspective.

What are the implications of a growing regionalization for the interpretation of Japan? It implies that the interpretation can no longer be focused on Japan as such, but should take into consideration the region in which Japan is functioning. An interpretive framework based on Japan as such is passé, an operation of the past that significantly distorts the situation in which Japan finds itself at this particular moment. A new interpretation should take notice of the changing role Japan is playing in the region. This role is multi-polar and Japan's reality has become multidimensional.

Towards a new interpretation of Japan

The implication of the analyses given above concerning the globalization tendencies and the phenomenon of increasing East Asia regionalization is that Japan at this particular moment stands at the juncture of a vertical axis, characterized by developments in its domestic situation from the end of the Second World War to the present day, and a horizontal axis, marked by changes in the international environment, particularly in Asia.[5] It has been briefly explained that a so-called unipolar interpretation only focuses on a country as such and not on the regional and global context in which that nation-state functions. Unipolar interpretations of Japan easily lead to either Euro- or Japano- centrism. Such interpretations have the tendency to lead to a deformation of the contemporary complexity of any given society, and of Japanese society in particular.

Can an alternative model be developed with a multi-polar character, where an interpretation is based on the nation-state itself as well as on the context in which that country functions? Such a model should not only be able to focus on Japan's cultural specificity, but should also be able to function as a *tertium comparationis*, as a criterion on the basis of which the Japanese society can be compared with any other society in the world (and vice versa). In addition, it should contain the possibility of applying the model to the interpretation of other nations or specific groups within a nation.

In this respect the concept of cultural identity will be proposed as a tool for the new interpretive framework. This concept has a great affinity with the Japanese quest to understand itself and the other. Since the Second World War the concept of cultural identity – in many cases without having being coined as such – has been a primary focus in Japan's search to determine what kind of country it really is and in what respect and to what extent Japanese culture differs from other cultures. There are few, if any, (post)modern societies in which cultural and national identity are as compelling a subject of both scholarly and popular discussion as in Japan (Nosco 1997: 1). On the other hand, the concept of cultural identity will also be acceptable to the West, since it has made a triumphant journey through the social sciences and the humanities since the 1980s.

As opposed to the old essentialist and structuralist views concerning cultural identity, here a redefinition will be proposed along the lines of constructivism: identity as a construction. Within such a constructive framework, the cultural identity of a particular nation or of a certain ethnic group within that nation can be based on three factors: (1) the statistics, the factual data concerning that nation or group at a given time in history; (2) the self-image of the inner group concerning its own 'local' culture, which is the inner group's self-image: the mental programming upon which cultural identity can be constructed, e.g. Japanese identity as constructed and seen by the Japanese themselves; (3) the outside image of the foreign group concerning the culture of the inner group – e.g. the Chinese perception of the Japanese (Figure 15.1).

What are statistics with respect to cultural identity? They are 'facts' or 'figures', 'data', that can be found in statistical handbooks, yearbooks and reports concerning the several domains of a particular society. For instance, they consist of the total number of citizens, the size of the country, the gross national product, average income, percentage of unemployment, the number of museums, libraries, etc.

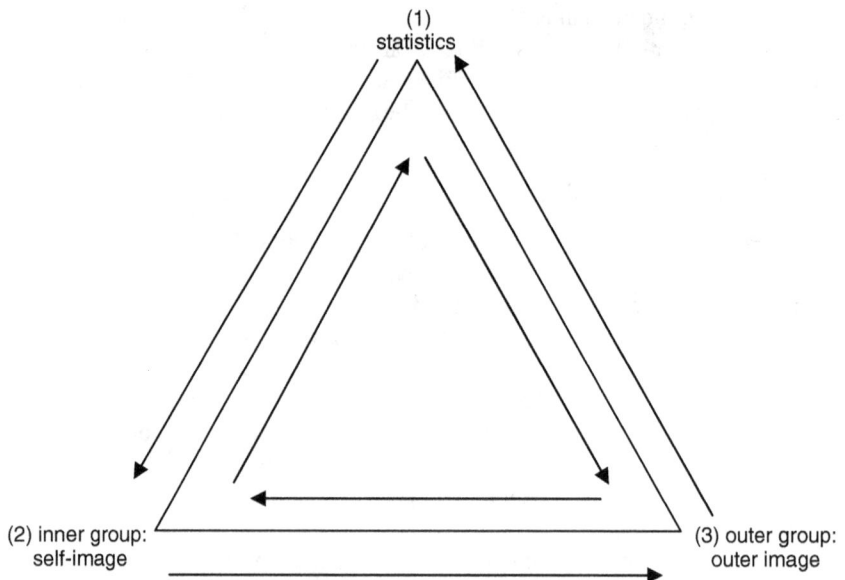

Figure 15.1 The concept of cultural identity as a construction

Those statistics determine to a certain degree the self-image and the outside image of a society. As soon as these factual data are interpreted and stimulate certain actions, the actions themselves no longer belong to the domain of statistics but to the self-image of the inner group.

The second angle, the self-image, is the way in which mental programming has shaped the construction of habits and conventions as well as the institutions of a community. It is concerned with the view people in a particular community or country construct about their own, 'local' culture and their place in a wider context (a nation, a region or even 'the world'). And with 'culture' is meant here the style of conduct and communication, and the specificity of private and public organizations and institutions. The self-image is the reflection of a people on its own style of conduct and communication. The construction of a self-image implies the rejection of some styles of conduct and the over-zealous acceptance of others. This canonization process is undertaken by opinion-constructing and opinion-leading institutions such as the government and the political system in general, the educational system (textbooks), the media and, last but not least, by the smallest but maybe the most powerful institution: the family.

As there is no direct access to how consciousness is programmed, the researcher is dependent on visible indicators. People's behaviour and communication must be observed, which may indicate their visible cultural identity. Behaviour and communication has a broad meaning here: institutions (parliament, education, public health, army, system of law, etc.) and their operation within the community are important components of it. Politicians and important voices within a community can steer, suppress or refrain from interfering with this visible cultural identity. It is impossible to speak of cultural identity without examining how politicians and other influential figures define it.

The third element of the triangle concerns the outer image, consisting of the constructions made by people from outside, again usually opinion leaders or opinion-leading institutions, regarding the style of conduct and communication and the specificity of the institutions and organizations of the inner group. In the introductory chapter of this book such an image can be found, as constructed by *The Economist*, concerning Japan. If the outside view stems from a very dominant world player (such as the USA) with a lot of hard and soft power, then that view may be accompanied by cultural influences that take on a global character. Examples in this respect are, among others: American 'fast' food, 'fast' media, 'fast' movies, 'fast' popular books, but also influences by great American institutions in domains such as higher education, medical science, technology and business and by American constructions of how to look at the world.

Here the hypothesis could be ventured that the outer image of Japan is heavily influenced by the American view of things Japanese. That implies that the perception of 'the world' concerning Japan is heavily based on American constructions. This American outside image had (and probably still has) such a dominant character that it has even had a strong impact on Japanese self-perception!

The three factors of cultural identity are strongly related. A change within any one factor has direct consequences for the composition of both other factors.

The conception of cultural identity as a construction implies that it is a mental conception that varies with person, time and place of construction. That means it is impossible to speak of 'the' cultural identity of a community. In theory there are as many cultural identities of a given community as there are places, times and people to construct those identities. This need not keep social scientists and other scholars from the important and necessary task of describing and systematizing the common characteristics of contemporary Japan, based on those several existing identities. Moreover, we are often confronted in reality by one dominant version of national or ethnic cultural identity.

All three angles have an equal function in the construction of the cultural identity, and thus in the interpretation process. Every angle in the triangle functions as a mechanism of checks and balances vis-à-vis the other two. A one-sided, disproportionate and unrealistic self-image will meet with inside as well as outside resistance and may stir up considerable and severe conflicts. If cultural identity is seen as a construction process with equal rights for every angle of the triangle, it will be of great relevance for a reinterpretation of Japan. Two points need to be clarified in this respect.

The first point concerns the radical break proposed here between identity as a constructivist versus an ontological concept. When lecturing on this subject one is invariably challenged by those who believe identity is primarily innate, so the argument for a socially based identity is often felt to be contradictory. In response, the ideas developed by Stuart Hall (1995: 181) could be applied: when cultural conventions are shared by the same population in a single, small, tightly defined area that community will become ever more closely knit. Language, religion, education and other conventions are accentuated and standardized. This also applies to kinship through 'true-bred' marriages. The culture assumes such a measure of uniformity that a street of houses can no longer be identified as lying in the north, south, east or west part of the city or even of the country. Japan can be viewed as an outstanding example of this phenomenon, for everyone and everything seems to resemble everyone and everything else for those not familiar with the country. This helps to explain why foreigners (and Japanese themselves) easily get lost in Japan's urban jungle. It also explains the ease with which many Japanese believe that cultural identity is genetic, a fact the Nihonjinron theorists have efficiently exploited.

A second remark on this conception of cultural identity needs to be made. It offers two advantages over existing, more ontological or structuralist views: the possibility of comparison and modification. An ontological opinion presumes that certain cultural conventions are genetically determined and also unique. That virtually excludes comparison and contrast with other identities, thereby deftly ensuring that there can be no discussion about identity. In an ontological–essentialist opinion, cultural identity is therefore equated with only one of the three dimensions of the triangle: the self-image of the inner group. Yet comparison and discussion, which directly stem from a constructivist view, are central elements to any analysis, particularly of one's own mental programming.

In a constructivist conception of cultural identity the identity triangle's three building blocks function as 'checks and balances'. A far too prejudicial, exaggerated and (consequently) over-sensitive view of one's own culture will simply be parried by the image thereby created in the minds of foreigners, itself an influence on the economic life of the home culture. A nation that willingly and knowingly violates human rights on a large scale can count on angry reactions abroad, often leading to various kinds of boycott.

A final question concerning the concept of identity. Is it a curse or a blessing? If cultural identity is interpreted in an essentialist sense (that is, without taking heed of one's own outer image and statistics), then such an attitude can have disastrous consequences, particularly when taken by leading politicians and governmental figures. Countless examples bear witness to the implications of a biased, over-rated cultural identity – often narrowed to a nationalist self-image – expressed as repression domestically and feelings of superiority with respect to foreigners. Mental conventions sparing no one and nothing often lead straight to dictatorship and war; brute militaristic power and economic achievement dominate (Nye 2002: 8–9). Cultural identity is employed as a weapon by way of nationalist propaganda.

It need not necessarily always work that way. If the political establishment and the government view cultural identity as a construction and strive after a balance of self-image, outer image and statistics, then cultural identity can develop into social harmony and economic prosperity. *Hard power* is exchanged for *soft power*, which consists not of militarism or economic achievement but of values believed and maintained. As Joseph Nye states:

> These values are expressed in our culture, in the policies we follow inside our country, and in the way we handle ourselves internationally [...] Like love, it is hard to measure and to handle, and does not touch everyone, but that does not diminish its importance.
>
> (Nye 2002 : 9)

A balanced proportion of self-image, outer image and statistics strongly stimulates the transition to soft power. It will become increasingly important as an instrument to influence other nations. Whereas the hard power of rigid militarism and a strong economy used to be the appropriate way to dominate others, soft power will increasingly replace it. A civil society is less prone to take up arms; ultimately it is more productive to be liked than feared.

Nye is largely on target but is perhaps a bit too convinced by the 'hard' soft power approach used by the United States, which he views as the undisputed champion of this practice. Nye underestimates the soft power of other nations, of Japan for example. He points out that Japan does possess soft power based mainly on pop culture, which attracts teenagers throughout Asia. He also notes two elements that are detrimental to Japanese soft power: Japanese culture is much more inward looking than United States culture, and Japan continues to resist acknowledging its aggressive, militarist campaigns of the 1930s and 1940s

(p. 70). Like James Fallows, Nye too eases the old American fear that Japan will soon be able to compete with the USA in this respect.[6] Fear not, he writes reassuringly, Japan won't make it. Nye fails to note one great Japanese soft-power advantage: the image of its products abroad. Japanese price-to-quality ratios remain unsurpassed in many lines of trade and products worldwide. This considerably augments Japanese soft power and cultural attractiveness.

Closing the gap between identity and image of contemporary Japan

The introductory chapter and this concluding chapter have argued for a reinterpretation of Japan based on three elements: (1) the structural inadequacy of existing interpretive models to tackle the specificity of Japan's contemporary situation, resulting in unipolarity and in Eurocentrism; (2) the intensity of the struggle between the global and the local in contemporary Japan, resulting in an unprecedented intensity of hybridity; and (3) the increasing regionalization in the world in general and in East Asia in particular, resulting in Japan's strong dependence on other regional and global players and vice versa. As has been outlined, this reinterpretation should be multi-polar; an interpretation where all three aspects of the identity triangle are accounted for: statistics, inside and outside perceptions and constructions.

The example of Japan's capitulation in 1945 could serve as an example to demonstrate what is meant by the concept of multi-polar interpretation. The focus here is on the drastic alteration of Japanese behaviour immediately following the surrender: from fanatical life-and-death struggle to the correct and friendly reception of their conquerors. This amounted to a complete turnabout in mental programming within just a few days.

The Japanese interpreted their behaviour as more or less self-evident; after all, the Emperor had spoken ... The Americans understood nothing of this and typified the Japanese as 'cowards', 'incomprehensible' and possessing 'the mental constitution of a twelve-year-old'. Two different value systems result in two different interpretations of the same statistics (so many Japanese soldiers surrendered themselves, so many American soldiers occupied the country, so many had died in the battles, etc.).

The question then arises, how *should* the capitulation be interpreted? In other words, which interpretation is correct? Rather than answering this question, it should be noted that the question is not stated properly. Almost every cultural situation supports not a single, but multiple truths. The question as to whose interpretation is correct cannot be answered if one proceeds from the principle of multi-polarity based on the equivalence of different cultural value systems. The Japanese value of 'situation-determined behaviour' is no better or worse than the comparable American value that behaviour should be consistent and not situation determined. Situation-determined behaviour results from what Henshall (1999) has called 'situational ethics', which regulate behaviour with conventions specific to each situation. Put another way, these conventions are not determined by a universal moral code. Of course Westerners prefer consistent to situational behaviour, but that is not to say that 'the' conclusion is 'therefore' that consistent behaviour is better than situational behaviour, assuming that the behaviour meets internationally accepted criteria, irrespective of a particular culture or nation-state. Such criteria can be found, for example, in the UN Charter or Universal Declaration of Human Rights. The world would not be the same if there were not a number of nations that subscribed to these minimal human rights conventions. Many member states of ASEAN believe that human rights are based on specific circumstances and experiences that differ from country to country. Human rights are dependent upon these circumstances and experiences, and therefore cannot be (by the West, as they maintain) prescribed and enforced in a partisan way (Hernandez 1998). This form of extreme cultural relativism is challenged by NGO groups from those very nations that do not endorse human rights conventions.

This concluding chapter has been dealing with a search for an alternative methodology to interpret Japan. That this is not an easy task has become clear and is caused by a lack of consistency in the interpretation industry concerning Japan:

> [D]espite Japan's enormous influence and visibility in the modern international system, it can also safely be said that there is little consensus among those who make it their business to understand or explain Japan about the fundamental principles of interpretation that might be applied to this society.
>
> (Clammer 2000: 203)

John Clammer argues for a new paradigm in which the study of Japan can be revitalized. This revitalization holds for both sides: the Western outside and the Japanese inside interpretation.

A well-known example is the Western clichéd interpretation of Japan as the 'mysterious stranger'. Of course not every Westerner subscribes to this perception (notably, the social sciences have strongly distanced themselves from it), but now and again, mainly in journalism, in politics and among business people this old stereotype crops up, is dusted off, cleaned up and paraded out. As Kenneth Henshall correctly indicates:

> We still like to think of Japan in many ways as a Topsy-Turvy Land, a Back-to-Front Land where everything is the opposite to our own cosy ways. That fictional hero of the Western world, James Bond, tells us that 'the bloody Japs do everything the wrong way around'. The word 'wrong' is particularly telling, for it confirms the rightness of our own ways. We do like to see the Other as wrong. Japan is a particularly convenient Other here, not only because so much about it is still rather unclear to us, but also because of its defeat in the war. Victory has given us a sort of license to criticize it with impunity.
>
> (Henshall 1999 : 1)

A multi-polar approach to the interpretation of Japan has the advantage of providing an answer to identity questions that are vital to the choices Japan is currently making, postponing or deciding not to make. A reinterpretation of Japan implies the analysis and description of all three angles of the cultural identity triangle. The basis of such an interpretation consists first of all of a reliable analysis and description of the self-image. We hope that the analyses in this book provide a sound basis for a reinterpretation. We hope to have shown that the often-reported perception in the foreign press during the 1990s that Japan is unable to change, that Japan is 'on the road to ruin', that it is high time for 'Japan-passing' by going directly to China are all examples of one-sided, unipolar interpretations.

The essays in this book show a Japan that is full of vitality and changing at a rapid speed, according to the requirements of a modern globalized world in which it undoubtedly will play a leading role. This is the reinterpretation of Japan that the authors of this book offer to the outside world.

Notes

1 See for this example Grimes and Schaede 2003.
2 By 'East Asia' is meant here and throughout the chapter: the member states of ASEAN (Brunei Darussalem, Cambodia, Indonesia, Laos, Malaysia, Myanmar, the Philippines, Singapore, Thailand and Vietnam) plus China, Japan, South Korea and Taiwan.
3 For a survey of the rising nationalism in the East Asian region and in some countries bordering the region see Starrs 2001.
4 For a survey of current EU problems concerning culture and identity see Segers and Viehoff (1999).
5 *Japan Times*, 21 September 2006, p. 1.
6 For an analysis of Fallows (1989) see the introductory chapter, second section.

References

Bergsten, C. F. (2000), 'East Asian Regionalism, Towards a Tripartite World', *The Economist*, 15 July, pp. 19–21.
Clammer, J. (2000), 'Received Dreams: Consumer Capitalism, Social Process, and the Management of the Emotions in Contemporary Japan', in J. S. Eades, Tom Gill and Harumi Befu (eds), *Globalization and Social Change in Contemporary Japan*. Melbourne: Trans Pacific Press.
Fallows, James (1989), 'Containing Japan', *The Atlantic Monthly* 5 (1989), pp. 40–54, www.theantlantic.com/issues/89may/fallows.htm, accessed 3 September 2006.
Grimes, William and Ulrike Schaede (eds) (2003), *Japan's Managed Globalization. Adapting to the Twenty-first Century*. Armonk, NY and London: M. E. Sharpe.
Hall, Stuart (1995), 'New Cultures for Old', in Doreen Massey and Pat Jess (eds), *A Place in the World. Places, Cultures and Globalization*. Houndsmill, NY: Oxford University Press/The Open University, pp. 175–213.
Henshall, Kenneth G. (1999), *Dimensions of Japanese Society. Gender, Margins and Mainstream*. Houndsmill, NY: Macmillan/St. Martin's.
Hernandez, Carolina (1998), 'Values and Civilizations', in Hans Maull, Gerald Segal and Jusuf Wanandi (eds), *Europe and the Asia Pacific*. London and New York: Routledge.

Katzenstein, Peter J. (2006), 'East Asia – Beyond Japan', in Peter J. Katzenstein and Takashi Shiraishi (eds), *Beyond Japan. The Dynamics of East Asian Regionalism.* Ithaca and London: Cornell University Press, 2006, pp. 1–36.

Nosco, Peter (1997), 'Introduction. Cultural Analyses of Japanese Identity', in Peter Nosco (ed.), *Japanese Identity: Cultural Analyses.* Denver, CO: Center for Japanese Studies, Teikyo Loretto Heights University, pp. 1–9.

Nye, Joseph S. (2002), *The Paradox of American Power. Why the World's only Superpower Can't Go it Alone.* Oxford: Oxford University Press.

Rose, Caroline (2005), *Sino-Japanese Relations. Facing the Past. Looking to the Future?* London and New York: RoutledgeCurzon.

Segers, Rien T. and Reinhold Viehoff (eds) (1999), *Kultur, Identität, Europa. Über die Schwierigkeiten und Möglichkeiten einer Konstruktion.* Frankfurt/Main: Suhrkamp.

Starrs, Roy (ed.) (2001), *Asian Nationalism in an Age of Globalization.* Richmond, Surrey: Japan Library/Curzon Press.

Sugihara, Kaoru (2005), 'Interview with Sugihara Kaoru', by Hisashi Kondo, *Asia Pacific Perspectives* 2 (12), pp. 36–9.

Index

Syusen-kinenbi 229–30

Taisei Yokusan Kai 107
Taisho era (1912-1926) 107, 216
Taiwan 25, 130–2, 135, 192, 257, 259
Takeda Aramin V 149
Tanabe, Hajime
    Tetsugaku tsuron 203
Tanaka, Yoshita 226
taxation 81, 108
    decrease in revenue 172
TBC 152–3
technology 17, 55
    civilian 17, 56, 59, 62, 63
    dual-use 59
    environmental 62
    exploitation 57
    exports 22
    innovation 78
    military 56, 59
    pre-eminence 56
technology and business 14
television commercials 141–56, 182
Tennō *see* Emperor
terrorism 201
Thatcherism 99
Thematic Review of Tertiary Education 157
three sector model 99, 101, 102–3
Tocqueville, Alexis de (1805-99) 97
    Democracy in America 100
Togo, Shigenori 178
Tojo, Hideki 178, 181, 183
Tokugawa period (1600-1867) 71
Tokyo University 209, 225–6
Tokyo War Crimes Trial *see* International
    Military Tribunal for the Far East in
    Tokyo (1946-48)
tolerance 96, 232
totalitarianism 101
Toyama, Atsuko 159, 161
Toyama Plan 159, 161, 162, 171
Toyota 3
trade 10, 254, 260, 266
    agreements 84
    bilateral relations 13
    currency 73
    international 258
traditional arts 148–9
traditions 13

training 78, 157, 158, 172
transformation
    social 87
    societal 244
Transnational Civil Society 103
transparency 78, 115
trends
    economic 112
    political 112
trilistic theory 95, 99, 102–3, 109–10
Tsuda, Sōkichi 212, 213, 214
    *Circumstances about the Founding of
    Our Country* 219–20
Tsunoda, Tadanobu
    *Japanese Brain, Uniqueness and
    Universality, The* 7–8
TV dramas 193, 195
    women portrayed 187

Uchimura, Kanzō 206, 208, 216, 225
unemployment rates 81
    France 81–2
United Kingdom 99
United Nations 21, 113–14
    reform 118, 119
    Security Council 117
Universal Declaration of Human Rights
    267
universities
    links with business 168
    links with community 168, 172
    local 163
    networking 168
    private 163
University Board 24
University Council 158, 159, 160, 162, 171
University of Tsukuba 157
US–Japan Security Treaty, *see*
    Japan–US Security Treaty
USA
    as a centre of gravity 257
    compared to Japan 6
    economic growth 112
    Japan–US alliance 237
    media culture 131
    media culture of Japan 126
    military relationship 71
    nationalism 84
    superpowers 82

For Product Safety Concerns and Information please contact our EU
representative GPSR@taylorandfrancis.com
Taylor & Francis Verlag GmbH, Kaufingerstraße 24, 80331 München, Germany

www.ingramcontent.com/pod-product-compliance
Lightning Source LLC
Chambersburg PA
CBHW050701280326
41926CB00088B/2416